Lecture Notes in Computer Science

Commenced Publication in 1973
Founding and Former Series Editors:
Gerhard Goos, Juris Hartmanis, and Jan van Leeuwen

David Lee   Antónia Lopes
Arnd Poetzsch-Heffter (Eds.)

Formal Techniques for Distributed Systems

Joint 11th IFIP WG 6.1 International Conference FMOODS 2009
and 29th IFIP WG 6.1 International Conference FORTE 2009
Lisboa, Portugal, June 9-12, 2009
Proceedings

 Springer

Volume Editors

David Lee
The Ohio State University, 395 Dreese Laboratories
Department of Computer Science and Engineering
2015 Neil Avenue, Columbus, OH 43210-1277, USA
E-mail: lee@cse.ohio-state.edu

Antónia Lopes
University of Lisbon, Faculty of Sciences
Department of Informatics
Campo Grande, 1749-016, Lisboa, Portugal
E-mail: mal@di.fc.ul.pt

Arnd Poetzsch-Heffter
Technische Universität Kaiserslautern
Fachbereich Informatik, Gebäude 34
Gottlieb-Daimler-Straße, 67653 Kaiserslautern, Germany
E-mail: poetzsch@informatik.uni-kl.de

Library of Congress Control Number: Applied for

CR Subject Classification (1998): D.2, D.2.4, I.2.2, D.3, F.3, F.4, I.2.3

LNCS Sublibrary: SL 2 – Programming and Software Engineering

ISSN   0302-9743

ISBN   978-3-642-02137-4 Springer Berlin Heidelberg New York

springer.com

© IFIP International Federation for Information Processing 2009

Typesetting: Camera-ready by author, data conversion by Scientific Publishing Services, Chennai, India
Printed on acid-free paper   SPIN: 12687480   06/3180   5 4 3 2 1 0

Foreword

This year's edition of the international federated conferences on Distributed Computing Techniques took place in Lisbon during June 9–11. It was hosted by the Faculty of Sciences of the University of Lisbon and formally organized by the Institute of Telecommunications, the research center I am associated with.

The DisCoTec conferences jointly cover the complete spectrum of distributed computing subjects ranging from theoretical foundations to formal specification techniques to practical considerations. The event this year comprised the 11th International Conference on Coordination Models and Languages (COORDINA-TION), the 9th IFIP International Conference on Distributed Applications and Interoperable Systems (DAIS), and the IFIP International Conference on Formal Techniques for Distributed Systems (FMOODS/FORTE). COORDINATION focused on languages, models, and architectures for concurrent and distributed software; DAIS on methods, techniques, and system infrastructures needed to design, build, operate, evaluate, and manage modern distributed applications in any kind of application environment and scenario; and FMOODS (the 11th Formal Methods for Open Object-Based Distributed Systems) jointed forces with FORTE (the 29th Formal Techniques for Networked and Distributed Systems) creating a forum for fundamental research on theory and applications of distributed systems.

In an effort for integration, each of the three days of the event started with an invited talk suggested by one of the conferences, in a plenary session, and, furthermore, one of the technical sessions was composed of a paper from each conference. The common program also included the first tutorial series on Global Computing, a joint initiative of the EU projects Mobius (Mobility, Ubiquity and Security) and Sensoria (Software Engineering for Service-Oriented Overlay Computers), which contributed to a very interesting program. I would like to thank all the invited speakers for accepting to give talks at the event, and all the authors for submitting papers.

As satellite events, there were two workshops, the Second Workshop on Context-aware Adaptation Mechanisms for Pervasive and Ubiquitous Services (CAMPUS 2009), focusing on approaches in the domain of context-aware adaptation mechanisms supporting the dynamic evolution of the execution context, and the Third Workshop on Middleware-Application Interaction (MAI 2009), focusing on middleware support for multiple cross-cutting features such as security, fault tolerance, and distributed resource management. The 10th International Conference on Feature Interactions in Telecommunications and Software Systems (ICFI) and meetings of the EU COST action on Formal Verification of Object-Oriented Software and the Sensoria project were co-located with Dis-CoTec.

I hope this rich program offered every participant interesting and stimulating events. It was only possible thanks to the dedicated work of the members

VI Foreword

of the Organizing Committee — Ana Matos, Carla Ferreira, Francisco Martins, João Seco and Maxime Gamboni — and to the sponsorship of the Center of Informatics and Information Technology (CITI), the Portuguese research foundation Fundação para a Ciência e a Tecnologia (FCT), the Instituto de Telecomunicações (IT), and the Large-Scale Informatics Systems Laboratory (LaSIGE).

April 2009   António Ravara

Preface

This volume contains the proceedings of the IFIP International Conference on Formal Techniques for Distributed Systems. The conference is organized as the joint activity of two conferences: FMOODS (Formal Methods for Open Object-Based Distributed Systems) and FORTE (Formal Techniques for Networked and Distributed Systems).

The goal of the conference on Formal Techniques for Distributed Systems – FMOODS/FORTE – is to provide a forum for fundamental research on theory and applications of distributed computing models and formal specification, testing and verification methods. The application domains for these techniques include a variety of application-level distributed systems, telecommunication services, Internet, embedded and real-time systems, as well as networking and communication security and reliability.

The proceedings contain 12 regular and 6 short papers. They were selected by the Program Committee (PC) among 42 submissions. Each paper was assigned to at least three PC members for a detailed review. Additional expert reviews were solicited if the reviews of a paper had quite diversified assessments or the reviewers indicated low confidence. The final decision of acceptance was based on an online discussion of the PC. The selected papers constitute a strong program of stimulating and timely topics in the areas of formal verification, algorithms and implementations, modeling and testing, process algebra and calculus, and analysis of distributed systems.

In addition to the selected contributions, the proceedings feature the article "The Orc Programming Language" by Jayadev Misra of the University of Texas at Austin, USA, who was the invited speaker of FMOODS/FORTE this year. He is an international expert in applying formal methods to distributed systems, in particular in the area of specifying and designing synchronous and asynchronous systems.

We are deeply indebted to the PC members and external reviewers for their hard and conscientious work in preparing 159 reviews. We thank António Ravara, the General Chair, for his support, and the Steering Committees of FMOODS and FORTE for their guidance. Our gratitude goes to the authors for their support of the conference by submitting their high-quality research works. We thank the providers of the conference tool EasyChair that was a great help in organizing the submission and reviewing process.

June 2009

David Lee
Antónia Lopes
Arnd Poetzsch-Heffter

Organization

Program Chair

David Lee   The Ohio State University (USA)
Antóni   University of Lisbon (Portugal)
Arnd Poetzsch-Heffter   University of Kaiserslautern (Germany)

Program Committee

Gregor v. Bochmann   University of Ottawa (Canada)
Paulo Borba   Federal University of Pernambuco (Brazil)
Mario Bravetti   University of Bologna (Italy)
Ana Caval   INT Evry (France)
John Derrick   University of Sheffield (UK)
Reinhard Gotzhein   University of Kaiserslautern (Germany)
Susanne Graf   University of Joseph Fourier and
                              CNRS/VERIMAG (France)
Teruo Higashino   Osaka University (Japan)
Dieter Hogrefe   University of Göttingen (Germany)
Gerard Holzmann   NASA/JPL (USA)
Claude Ja   ENS Cachan - Bretagne (France)
Einar Broch Johnsen   University of Oslo (Norway)
Ferhat Khendek   Concordia University (Canada)
Myungchul Kim   Information and Communications University
                              (South Korea)
Hartmut Koenig   Brandenburg University of Technology
                              (Germany)
Luigi Logrippo   University of Quebec - Outaouais (Canada)
Peter Mueller   ETH (Switzerland)
Elie Najm   ENST (France)
Uwe Nestmann   Technical University of Berlin (Germany)
Manuel Nunez   Complutense University of Madrid (Spain)
Olaf Owe   University of Oslo (Norway)
Alexandre Petrenko   CRIM Montreal (Canada)
Frank Piessens   Katholieke Universiteit Leuven (Belgium)
Jean-François
   Pradat-Peyre   Cedric-CNAM (France)
Wolfgang Reisig   Humboldt University of Berlin (Germany)
Arend Rensink   University of Twente (The Netherlands)
Martin Steffen   University of Oslo (Norway)

Carolyn Talcott   SRI International (USA)
Ken Turner   University of Stirling (UK)
Keiichi Yasumoto   Nara Institute of Science and Technology
                           (Japan)

Nina Yevtushenko   Tomsk State University (Russia)
Xia Yin   Tsinghua University (China)
Gianluigi Zavattaro   University of Bologna (Italy)
Heike Wehrheim   University of Paderborn (Germany)
Martin Wirsing   LMU Munich (Germany)

Additional Referees

F. Bessayah   R. Langerak
S. Blom   H. Lehner
J. Borgstrom   L. Llana
Y. Bouzida   A. Mammar
M. D'Amorim   A. Nakata
A. Darvas   A. Schaefer
L. Desmet   R. Schlatte
A. Dury   G. Schneider
S. Evangelista   J. Schfer
D. Fahland   N. Shibata
R. Gheyi   G. Shu
C. Gierds   A. Simao
M. Gromov   J. Smans
H. Hallal   S. Taheri
D. Hogrefe   K. Leai Larry Tan
I. Hwang   C. Versari
J. Iyoda   Z. Wang
A. Kamel   G. Warner
S. Kang   I. Yu
S. Klueppelholz
M. Kohnrich

Table of Contents

Short Papers

The Orc Programming Language

David Kitchin, Adrian Quark, William Cook, and Jayadev Misra

The University of Texas, Austin

Abstract. Orc was originally presented as a process calculus. It has
now evolved into a full programming language, which we describe in this
paper. The language has the structure and feel of a functional programming language, yet it handles many non-functional aspects effectively,
including spawning of concurrent threads, time-outs and mutable state.
We first describe the original concurrency combinators of the process calculus. Next we describe a small functional programming language that
forms the core language. Then we show how the concurrency combinators of the process calculus and the functional core language are integrated seamlessly. The resulting language and its supporting libraries
have proven very effective in describing typical concurrent computations;
we demonstrate how several practical concurrent programming problems
are easily solved in Orc.

1   Introduction

Concurrency has become an urgent practical problem with the advent of multi-
core and multi-CPU systems. Unfortunately, concurrency is difficult for programmers, who are expected to define and manage threads and locks explicitly.
These basic concurrency constructs do not serve well to express the high-level
structure of control flow in concurrent programs, especially when handling failure, time-outs, and process termination. It is also important to easily compose
processes at different granularities, from small processes to complete workflows,
and to seamlessly integrate asynchronous human interactions within a process.

The Orc process calculus [8] was designed to express orchestrations and wide-
area computations in a simple and structured manner. Its intent was to overcome
some of the problems listed above. It is inherently concurrent and implicitly
distributed. It has a clearly specified operational semantics. Human actors and
computational processes of varying granularity are treated uniformly.

Orc was originally conceived as a formal model rather than a concrete tool.
We have now implemented Orc as a complete programming language and be-
gun writing substantial applications in it [11]. This paper describes the language
and some of the motivating philosophy in its design. The language includes the
three original concurrency combinators of Orc and a fourth one, introduced to
detect terminations of computations. These combinators are seamlessly integrated with a core functional language. The complete language, called just Orc,
has the structure and feel of a functional programming language; yet it handles many non-functional aspects effectively, including spawning of concurrent
threads, time-outs and mutable state.

D. Lee et al. (Eds.): FMOODS/FORTE 2009, LNCS 5522, pp. 1–25, 2009.

The paper is structured as follows. In Section 2, we review the Orc concurrency calculus. In Section 3, we present the functional core of Orc. Section 4 integrates the functional core with the concurrency calculus, resulting in the full Orc programming language, which is subsequently enhanced with some helpful syntactic sugar, a library of useful services and functions, and the capability to interact with other languages such as Java. Section 5 presents a series of examples demonstrating solutions to common concurrent programming problems using the Orc language. We consider Orc's relationship to similar concurrent languages in Section 6, and conclude with some remarks on future work in Section 7.

We encourage the reader to visit our website [11] for more information. It hosts a comprehensive user guide, a community wiki, and a web-based interface for experimenting with Orc.

2   The Orc Concurrency Calculus

The Orc calculus is based on the execution of *expressions*. Expressions are built up recursively using Orc's concurrent *combinators*. When executed, an Orc expression calls services and may *publish* values. Different executions of the same expression may have completely different behaviors; they may call different services, receive different responses from the same service, and publish different values.

Orc expressions use *sites* to refer to external services. A site may be implemented on the client's machine or a remote machine. A site may provide any service; it could run sequential code, transform data, communicate with a web service, or be a proxy for interaction with a human user.

We present the calculus informally in this paper. The formal operational and denotational semantics of the calculus are given in [4].

2.1   Site Calls

The simplest Orc expression is a *site call* $M(\bar{p})$, where M is a site name and $\bar{p}$ is a list of parameters, which are values or variables. The execution of a site call invokes the service associated with M, sending it the parameters $\bar{p}$. If the site responds, the call publishes that response.

Here are some examples of site calls.

`add(3,4)`	Add the numbers 3 and 4.
`CNN(d)`	Get the CNN news headlines for date d.
`Prompt("Name:")`	Prompt the user to enter a name.
`swap(l_0,l_1)`	Swap the values stored at locations l_0 and l_1.
`Weather("Austin, TX")`	Find the current weather in Austin.
`random(10)`	Get a random integer in the range 0..9.
`invertMatrix(m)`	Find the inverse of matrix m.

A site may give at most one response to a call. A site call may explicitly report that it will never respond, in which case we say that the call has *halted*.

For example, the call might represent an invalid operation (invertMatrix on a non-invertible matrix), it may have encountered a system error (trying to swap with a protected memory location), or it may simply have no available response (calling CNN on a future date). Some site calls may neither respond nor halt. For example a call to Prompt will wait forever if the user never inputs a response.

Though the Orc calculus itself contains no sites, there are a few fundamental sites which are so essential to writing useful computations that we always assume they are available. The site let is the identity site; when passed one argument, it publishes that argument, and when passed multiple arguments it publishes them as a tuple. The site if responds with a signal (a value which carries no information) if its argument is true, and otherwise halts.

2.2   Combinators

Orc has four combinators to compose expressions: the parallel combinator |, the sequential combinator >x>, the pruning combinator[1] <x<, and the otherwise combinator[2] ;.

When composing expressions, the >x> combinator has the highest precedence, followed by |, then <x<, and finally ; with the lowest precedence.

Parallel Combinator. In $F \mid G$, expressions F and G execute independently. The sites called by F and G are the ones called by $F \mid G$ and any value published by either F or G is published by $F \mid G$. There is no direct communication or interaction between these two computations.

For example, evaluation of CNN(d) | BBC(d) initiates two independent computations; up to two values will be published depending on the number of responses received.

The parallel combinator is commutative and associative.

Sequential Combinator. In F >x> G, expression F is evaluated. Each value published by F initiates a separate execution of G wherein x is bound to that published value. Execution of F continues in parallel with these executions of G. If F publishes no values, no executions of G occur. The values published by the executions of G are the values published by F >x> G. The values published by F are consumed.

As an example, the following expression calls sites CNN and BBC in parallel to get the news for date d. Responses from either of these calls are bound to x and then site email is called to send the information to address a. Thus, email may be called 0, 1 or 2 times, depending on the number of responses received.

(CNN(d) | BBC(d)) >x> email(a, x)

---

[1] In previous publications, F <x< G was written as F **where** $x \in G$.
[2] The ; combinator is a new addition to Orc, inspired by practical experience writing Orc programs. Its formal semantics will appear in a forthcoming technical report.

The sequential combinator is left associative, i.e. F >x> G >y> H is F >x> $(G$ >y> $H)$. When x is not used in G, one may use the short-hand F >> G for F >x> G.

Pruning Combinator. In F <x< G, both F and G execute in parallel. Execution of parts of F which do not depend on x can proceed, but site calls in F for which x is a parameter are suspended until x has a value. If G publishes a value, then x is assigned that value, G's execution is terminated and the suspended parts of F can proceed. This is the only mechanism in Orc to block or terminate parts of a computation.

In contrast to sequential composition, the following expression calls email at most once.

email$(a,$ x) <x< (CNN(d) | BBC(d))

The pruning combinator is right associative, i.e. F <x< G <y< H is $(F$ <x< $G)$ <y< H. When x is not used in F, one may use the short-hand F << G for F <x< G.

Otherwise Combinator. The execution of F ; G first executes F. If F publishes no values and then *halts*, then G executes. We say that F halts if all of the following conditions hold:

1. All site calls in the execution of F have either responded or halted.
2. F will never call any more sites.
3. F will never publish any more values.

The following expression calls CNN to get the news for date d. If CNN(d) responds, email is called using that response, and the BBC is never called. However, the site CNN may halt, as described in Section 2.1, if there is no news available for date d. In this case BBC(d) is executed, and if it responds, email is called.

(CNN(d) ; BBC(d)) >x> email$(a,$ x)

The otherwise combinator is associative, i.e. $(F$; $G)$; H is the same as F ; $(G$; $H)$.

signal and stop. For convenience, we allow two additional expressions: **signal** and **stop**. The expression **signal** just publishes a signal when executed; it is equivalent to if(true). The expression **stop** halts when executed; it is equivalent to if(false).

2.3 Definitions

An Orc expression may be preceded by a sequence of definitions of the form:

def $E(\overline{x})$ = F

This defines a function named E whose formal parameter list is $\bar{x}$ and body is expression F. A call $E(\bar{p})$ is evaluated by replacing the formal parameters $\bar{x}$ by the actual parameters $\bar{p}$ in the body F. Unlike a site call, a function call does not suspend if one of its arguments is a variable with no value. A function call may publish more than one value; it publishes every value published by the execution of F. Definitions may be recursive.

2.4 Time

Orc is designed to communicate with the external world, and one of the most important characteristics of the external world is the passage of time. Orc implicitly accounts for the passage of time by interacting with external services that may take time to respond. However, Orc can also explicitly wait for a specific amount of time, using the special site Rtimer.

The call Rtimer(t), where t is an integer, responds with a signal exactly t milliseconds later[3].

The following example defines a metronome, which publishes a signal once every t milliseconds, indefinitely.

```
def metronome(t) = signal | Rtimer(t) >> metronome(t)
```

We can also use Rtimer together with the <x< combinator to enforce a time-out. For example, we can query BBC for a headline, but allow a default response if BBC does not respond within 5 seconds.

```
email(a, x) <x< (BBC(d) | Rtimer(5000) >> "BBC timed out.")
```

3 Functional Core Language

In the preceding section, we introduced an abstract language intended to highlight several issues pertaining to concurrency. However, concurrent programs contain large amounts of sequential code, with attendant data and control structures. We enhance Orc by adding a functional core language to it. In this section we describe *Cor*, the functional core. In Section 4 we will show how any Cor expression can be written as an equivalent Orc expression; this will allow us to integrate Cor into Orc.

A Cor program is an expression. Cor expressions are built up recursively from smaller expressions. Cor evaluates an expression to reduce it to some simple value which cannot be evaluated further, for example a list of numbers or a Boolean truth value. This value is called the *result* of the expression. Some expressions do not have a result, because they represent an invalid computation (such as division by zero) or an infinite computation. Such expressions are called *silent*.

Values and Operators. Cor has three types of constants: numbers (5, -1, 2.71828, $\cdots$), strings ("orc", "ceci n'est pas une |", $\cdots$), and

---

[3] An implementation can only approximate this guarantee.

booleans (`true` and `false`). It provides the usual arithmetic (`+` `-` `*` `/` `···`), logical (`&&` `||` `···`), and comparative (`=` `<` `>` `···`) operators. They are written infix with Java-like operator precedence. Parentheses can be used to override this precedence.

```
(98+2)*17          evaluates to 1700.
4 = 20 / 5         evaluates to true.
"leap" + "frog"    evaluates to "leapfrog".
```

Conditionals. Cor has conditional expressions: **if** E **then** F **else** G. If E evaluates to `true`, then F is evaluated. If E evaluates to `false`, then G is evaluated.

```
if true then 4 else 5              evaluates to 4.
if 0 < 5 then 0/5 else 5/0         evaluates to 0.
if false || false then 4+5 else 9/0   is silent.
```

Variables. We introduce and bind variables using a **val** declaration, as follows. Below, x and y are bound to 3 and 6, respectively.

```
val x = 1 + 2
val y = x + x
```

Variables cannot be reassigned because Cor is a pure functional language and has no mutable state. If the same variable is bound again, subsequent references to that variable will use the new binding, but previous references remain unchanged. Declarations obey the rules of lexical scope.

What if a variable is bound to a silent expression? Consider:

```
val x = 1/0
val y = 4+5
if false then x else y
```

Any expression that evaluates x will be silent. However, the evaluation of **val** y = 4+5 and **if** false **then** x **else** y proceeds as normal.

Data Structures. Cor supports two basic data structures: *tuples* ((3, 7), ("tag", true, false), `···`) and finite *lists* ([4,4,1], ["example"], [], `···`). A tuple or list containing expressions to be evaluated is itself an expression; each of the expressions is evaluated, and the result is a tuple or list of those results.

```
[1,2+3]                              evaluates to [1,5].
(3+4, if true then "yes" else "no")  evaluates to (7, "yes").
```

Tuples and lists can contain any value, including other tuples or lists.

The prepend (*cons*) operation on lists is written x:xs, where xs is a list and x is some element to be prepended to that list.

```
(1+3):[2+5,6]     evaluates to [4,7,6].
2:2:5:[]          evaluates to [2,2,5].


val t = [3,5]
1:t               evaluates to [1,3,5].


2:3               is silent, because 3 is not a list.
```

Patterns. We can bind parts of data structures to variables using *patterns*. We write _ for the wildcard pattern.

```
val (x,y) = (2+3,2*3)
    binds x to 5 and y to 6.
```

```
val t = ["two", "three"]
val [a,_,c] = "one":t
    binds t to ["two","three"], a to "one", and c to "three".
```

```
val ((a,b),c) = ((1, true), (2, false))
    binds a to 1, b to true, and c to (2,false).
```

Functions. Functions are defined using the keyword **def**, in the following way.

```
def add(x,y) = x+y
```

The expression to the right of the = is called the *body* of the function.

The syntax for function calls is typical for functional programming. However, the interpretation of a function call is more elaborate, in anticipation of the concurrency combinators to be added. A call, such as add(1+2,3+4) is converted to a sequence of **val** declarations, one per formal parameter, followed by a goal expression, which is just the body of the function:

```
val x = 1+2
val y = 3+4
x+y
```

Notice that the evaluation strategy of functions allows a call to proceed even if some of the actual parameters are silent expressions, so long as the values of those actual parameters are not used in the evaluation of the body.

Functions may be defined recursively, as in:

```
def sumto(n) = if n < 1 then 0 else n + sumto(n-1)
```

Mutual recursion is also supported. There is no special keyword for mutual recursion; any contiguous sequence of function definitions is allowed to be mutually recursive.

Functions are actually values, just like any other. Defining a function creates a special value called a *closure*; the name of the function is a variable and its bound value is the closure. Since a closure is a value, it can be passed as an argument to another function, thus allowing us to define a *higher-order* function. Cor functions obey *lexical closure*.

```
def onetwosum(f) = f(1) + f(2)
def triple(x) = x * 3
onetwosum(triple)
```

This is the same as `triple(1) + triple(2)`, i.e. 1 * 3 + 2 * 3.

We may create a closure without giving it a name, using the keyword **lambda**. For example, onetwosum(**lambda**(x) = x * 3)   is equivalent to onetwosum(triple) as defined above.

Functions can be defined as a series of *clauses*, each of which has a different list of patterns for its formal parameters. When such a function is called, the function body used for the call is that of the first clause whose formal parameter patterns match the actual parameters.

```
def sum([]) = 0
def sum(h:t) = h + sum(t)
```

```
def fib(0) = 0
def fib(1) = 1
def fib(n) =
  if (n < 0) then fib(0)
             else fib(n-1) + fib(n-2)
```

4   The Orc Programming Language

The full Orc programming language combines the concurrency calculus with the functional core language, and adds to it a few notational conveniences and the support of a large library of sites and predefined functions. The full language has many features which we do not discuss here due to space constraints; see the Orc User Guide [5] for details.

4.1   Translating Cor to Orc

Every Cor expression can be translated to an equivalent expression in the Orc calculus, using a small set of primitive sites to perform tasks such as arithmetic and list manipulation.

Values and Operators. The arithmetic, logical, and comparison operators translate directly to site calls; for example, 2+3 translates to add(2,3), where add is simply a site which performs addition.

If a value or variable is mentioned alone, such as 3 or x, it becomes a call to the identity site let with that argument.

Cor expressions may be recursively nested. However, site calls in the Orc calculus may only have values or variables as arguments. For example, 2+(3+4) cannot translate directly to add(2, add(3,4)), since the call add(3,4) cannot be an argument. Instead, we translate `2+(3+4)` to `add(2,z) <z< add(3,4)`, where z is a fresh variable name. This translation can be applied to any such nested expression.

Conditionals. The conditional expression **if** E **then** F **else** G translates to:

`( if(b) >> F | not(b) >c> if(c) >> G ) <b< E`

Variables. The declaration **val** `x = G`, followed by expression F, translates to:

`F <x< G`

Data Structures. Data structures are created by site calls. The site `let` creates tuples directly. The site `nil` returns the empty list when called. The site `cons` implements the cons operator and is also used to construct list expressions. For example, `[1,2]` translates to `cons(1,t) <s< cons(2,t) <t< nil()`.

Patterns. Patterns can be translated into a set of calls to pattern deconstruction sites followed by a set of variable bindings to match up each of the pieces with the appropriate variable names. For example, the site `trycons` takes one argument; if that argument is a nonempty list, then it returns a tuple of the list's head and tail, otherwise it remains silent.

Functions. Cor function definitions translate to Orc definitions, though we must extend the calculus slightly to permit such definitions to occur within the scope of normal expressions and create closures.

The expression **lambda** `( ... )` $= E$ translates to the following Orc expression, where f is a fresh variable name:

```
def f( ... ) = E
let(f)
```

4.2   Integrating Cor and Orc

As we have seen, any Cor expression can be translated into an equivalent Orc expression. This allows us to integrate the concurrency combinators with Cor.

Mingling Cor and Orc expressions. The combined language allows any Cor or Orc expression to appear as a subexpression of any other Cor or Orc expression. Sometimes, an Orc expression which publishes multiple values will appear in the context of a Cor expression which expects only one value, for example `2 + (3 | 4)`. In such a case, the Orc expression executes until it publishes a value, and then is terminated. Therefore `2 + (3 | 4)` is to be understood as `(2 + x) <x< (3 | 4)`. While this may be an unexpected behavior, it is quite useful once it becomes familiar. In fact, it is used so often in Orc programs that the pruning combinator itself is rarely written explicitly.

Patterns in Combinators. The combined language also allows patterns to replace variables in the >x> and <x< combinators. If a publication does not match the pattern of a >x> combinator, the publication is ignored, and no new instance of the right hand expression is executed. For the <x< combinator, the publication is ignored, and the right hand expression continues to run.

```
(3,4) >(x,y)> x+y              publishes 7.
x <(0,x)< ((1,0) | (0,1))  publishes 1.
```

Functions. A function call in Orc, as in Cor, binds the values of its actual parameters to its formal parameters, and then executes the function body with those bindings. Whenever the function body publishes a value, the function call publishes that value. Thus, unlike a site call, or a pure functional Cor call, an Orc function call may publish many values.

In the context of Orc, function calls are not strict. When a function call executes, it begins to execute the function body immediately, and also executes the argument expressions in parallel. When an argument expression publishes a value, it is terminated, and the corresponding formal parameter is bound to that value in the execution of the function body. Any part of the function body which uses a formal parameter that has not yet been bound suspends until that parameter is bound to a value.

An Example. We show an Orc program that does not use any of the concurrency combinators explicitly. In fact, the program is almost entirely functional, with the sole exception of the site call random(6), which returns a random integer between 0 and 5. Each nested expression will translate into a use of the pruning combinator, making this program implicitly concurrent without any programmer intervention.

This program runs a series of experiments. Each experiment consists of rolling a pair of dice. An experiment succeeds if the total shown by the two dice is c. The function exp(n,c) returns the number of successes in n experiments.

```
def throw() = random(6) + 1

def exp(0,_) = 0
def exp(n,c) =
  (if throw() + throw() = c then 1 else 0)
  + exp(n-1,c)
```

Here is the translation of this program into the Orc calculus. Site add returns the sum of its arguments, not returns the negation of its boolean argument, and equals returns true iff its two arguments are equal.

```
def throw() = add(x,1) <x< random(6)

def exp(n,c) =
   ( if(b) >> let(0)
   | not(b) >nb> if(nb) >>
     ( add(x,y)
         <x< ( ( if(bb) >> 1 | not(bb) >nbb> if(nbb) >> 0 )
                     <bb< equals(p,c)
                     <p< add(q,r)
                       <q< throw()
                       <r< throw() )
         <y< ( exp(m,c) <m< sub(n,1) ) ) )
   ) <b< equals(n,0)
```

4.3   The . Notation

We will see many sites which represent objects with multiple behaviors. It is often convenient to trcat such sites as if they had *methods*, in an object-oriented style. We access methods on sites using a special form of site call, as in c.put(4).

This call form, like every other new syntactic form introduced so far, can be encoded in the Orc calculus. The site c is sent a special value called a *message*, in this case the 'put' message. It responds to that message with another site which will execute the desired method when called. So c.put(4) translates to c('put') >x> x(4).

4.4   Site Library

The Orc programming language has access to a library of useful sites. We introduce a few essential ones here.

Channels. Orc has no communication primitives like π-calculus channels [7] or Erlang mailboxes [1]. Instead, it makes use of sites to create channels of communication.

The most frequently used of these sites is Buffer. When called, it publishes a new asynchronous FIFO channel. That channel is a site with two methods: get and put. The call c.get() takes the first value from channel c and publishes it, or blocks waiting for a value if none is available. The call c.put(v) puts v as the last item of c and publishes a signal.

A channel may be closed to indicate that it will not be sent any more values. If the channel c is closed, c.put(v) always halts (without modifying the state of the channel), and c.get() halts once c becomes empty. The channel c may be closed by calling either c.close(), which returns a signal once c becomes empty, or c.closenb(), which returns a signal immediately.

References. Unlike imperative programming languages, Orc does not have mutable variables. Mutable state is provided by sites instead. The `Ref` site is used to create new mutable references, which are used in a style similar to Standard ML's `ref` [9].

A call to `Ref` may include an argument specifying the initial contents of the reference; if none is given, then the reference's value is undefined. Given a reference `r`, `r.write(v)` overwrites the current value stored in `r`, changing it to `v`, and `r.read()` publishes the current value stored in `r`. If `r` is undefined, `r.read()` blocks until some write occurs.

Semaphores. Unlike other concurrent languages, Orc does not have any locking mechanisms built into the language. Instead, it uses the `Semaphore` site to create semaphores which enable synchronization and mutual exclusion. `Semaphore(k)` creates a semaphore with the initial value `k` (i.e. it may be acquired by up to `k` parties simultaneously). Given a semaphore `s`, `s.acquire()` attempts to acquire `s`, blocking if it cannot be acquired yet because its value is zero. The call `s.release()` releases `s`, increasing is value by one.

4.5 Function Library

The Orc programming language also includes a library of predefined functions. These are functions written in Orc, using **def**. We introduce a few important ones here.

each. One of the most common uses for a list is to send each of its elements through a sequential combinator. Since the list itself is a single value, we want to walk through the list and publish each one of its elements in parallel as a value. The library function `each` does exactly that.

Suppose we want to send the message `invite` to each email address in the list `inviteList`:

```
each(inviteList) >address> email(address, invite)
```

repeat. A site in Orc responds with at most one value. If we wish to model a service that outputs a stream of values, we can either encode the stream as a single value, or we can call the site repeatedly to receive successive values in the stream. The function `repeat` is very useful for the latter approach: `repeat(M)` calls site `M`, waits for it to respond, publishes the response, and then repeats the process, until the call to `M` halts. For example, `repeat(c.get)` will take and publish values from the channel `c` whenever they are available.

List Functions. Orc adopts many of the list idioms of functional programming. The Orc library contains definitions for most of the standard list functions, such as `map` and `fold`. Many of the list functions internally take advantage of concurrency to make use of any available parallelism; for example, the `map` function uses a fork-join to dispatch all of the mapped calls concurrently and assemble the result list from their responses.

4.6   Interacting with Other Languages

The current Orc implementation allows Java classes to be used as sites. A special declaration makes a Java class constructor available to Orc as a site with the same name. Calling that constructor site creates an instance of the Java object. That object's methods and fields can then be accessed using the dot notation described earlier. We anticipate that this mechanism may be generalized to other languages.

4.7   Complete Syntax

The complete abstract syntax of the Orc language used for the remainder of this paper is given below.

$$
\begin{array}{lll}
\text{Constant} & C ::= & \text{boolean, number, or string} \\
\text{Variable} & X ::= & \text{variable name} \\
\text{Message} & m ::= & \text{message name} \\
\text{Pattern} & P ::= & C \mid X \mid (\overline{P}) \mid [\overline{P}] \mid \_ \\
\text{Declaration} & D ::= & \textbf{val}\ P = E \\
& \mid & \textbf{def}\ X(\overline{P}) = E \\
\text{Expression} & E ::= & C \mid X \mid (\overline{E}) \mid [\overline{E}] \mid \textbf{signal} \\
& \mid & E\ op\ E \mid X(\overline{E}) \mid X.m(\overline{E}) \\
& \mid & \textbf{if}\ E\ \textbf{then}\ E\ \textbf{else}\ E \\
& \mid & \textbf{lambda}\,(\overline{P}) = E \\
& \mid & D\ E \\
& \mid & E \mid E \\
& \mid & E >P> E \\
& \mid & E <P< E \\
& \mid & E\ ;\ E \\
& \mid & \textbf{stop}
\end{array}
$$

5   Programming Idioms

In this section we give Orc implementations of some standard idioms from concurrent and functional programming. Despite the austerity of Orc's four combinators, we are able to encode a variety of idioms straightforwardly.

5.1   Fork-Join

One of the most common concurrent idioms is a *fork-join*: evaluate two expressions F and G concurrently and wait for a result from both before proceeding. This is easy to express in Orc:

$(F,\ G)$

Recall that this is equivalent to:

$(\ (x,y)\ <x<\ F\ )\ <y<\ G$

This implementation takes advantage of the fact that a tuple is constructed by a site call, which must wait for all of its arguments to become available. In fact, any operator or site call may serve to join forked expressions. For example, if F and G produce numbers and we wish to fork-join and add their results, we write simply F + G.

Example: Simple Parallel Auction. Orc programs often use fork-join with recursion to dispatch many tasks in parallel and wait for all of them to complete. Suppose we have a list of bidders in a sealed-bid, single-round auction. Calling b.ask() requests a bid from the bidder b. We want to ask for one bid from each bidder and then return the highest bid. The function auction performs this task (max finds the maximum of its arguments):

```
def auction([]) = 0
def auction(b:bs) = max(b.ask(), auction(bs))
```

Note that all bidders are called simultaneously. Also note that if some bidder fails to return a bid, then the auction will never complete. Section 5.5 presents a different solution that addresses the issue of non-termination.

Example: Barrier Synchronization. Consider an expression of the following form, where F and G are expressions and M and N are sites:

```
M() >x> F | N() >y> G
```

Suppose we would like to *synchronize* F and G, so that both start executing at the same time, after both M() and N() respond. This is easily done using the fork-join idiom. In the following, we assume that x does not occur free in G, nor y in F.

```
(M(), N()) >(x,y)> ( F | G )
```

5.2 Sequential Fork-Join

Previous sections illustrate how Orc can use the fork-join idiom to process a fixed set of expressions or a list of values. Suppose that instead we wish to process all the publications of an expression F, and once this processing is complete, execute some expression G. For example, F publishes the contents of a text file, one line at a time, and we wish to print each line to the console using the site println, then publish a signal after all lines have been printed.

Sequential composition alone is not sufficient, because we have no way to detect when all of the lines have been processed. A recursive fork-join solution would require that the lines be stored in a traversable data structure like a list, rather than streamed as publications from F. A better solution uses the ; combinator to detect when processing is complete:

```
F >x> println(x) >> stop ; signal
```

Since ; only evaluates its right side if the left side does not publish, we suppress the publications on the left side using **stop**. Here, we assume that we can detect when F halts. If, for example, F is publishing the lines of the file as it receives them over a socket, and the sending party never closes the socket, then F never halts and no signal is published.

5.3   Priority Poll

The otherwise combinator is also useful for trying alternatives in sequence. Consider an expression of the form F_0 ; F_1 ; F_2 ; $\cdots$. If F_i does not publish and halts, then F_{i+1} is executed. We can think of the F_i's as a series of alternatives that are explored until a publication occurs.

Suppose that we would like to poll a list of buffers for available data. The list of buffers is ordered by priority. The first buffer in the list has the highest priority, so it is polled first. If it has no data, then the next buffer is polled, and so on.

Here is a function which polls a prioritized list of buffers in this way. It publishes the first item that it finds, removing it from the originating buffer. If all buffers are empty, the function halts. We use the getnb ("get non-blocking") method of the buffer, which retrieves the first available item if there is one, and halts otherwise.

```
def priorityPoll([]) = stop
def priorityPoll(b:bs) = b.getnb() ; priorityPoll(bs)
```

5.4   Parallel Or

"Parallel or" is a classic idiom of parallel programming. The "parallel or" operation executes two expressions F and G in parallel, each of which may publish a single boolean, and returns the disjunction of their publications as soon as possible. If one of the expressions publishes true, then the disjunction is true, so it is not necessary to wait for the other expression to publish a value. This holds even if one of the expressions is silent.

The "parallel or" of expressions F and G may be expressed in Orc as follows:

```
let(
  val a = F
  val b = G
  (a || b) | if(a) >> true | if(b) >> true
)
```

The expression (a || b) waits for both a and b to become available and then publishes their disjunction. However if either a or b is true we can publish true immediately regardless of whether the other variable is available. Therefore we run if(a) >> true and if(b) >> true in parallel to wait for either variable to become `true` and immediately publish the result `true`. Since more than one of these expressions may publish `true`, the surrounding `let(...)` is necessary to select and publish only the first result.

5.5   Timeout

Timeout, the ability to execute an expression for at most a specified amount of time, is an essential ingredient of fault-tolerant and distributed programming. Orc accomplishes timeout using pruning and the `Rtimer` site. The following program runs F for at most one second, publishing its result if available and the value 0 otherwise.

```
let( F | Rtimer(1000) >> 0 )
```

Example: Auction with Timeout. The auction example in Section 5.1 may never finish if one of the bidders does not respond. We can add a timeout so that each bidder has at most 8 seconds to provide a bid:

```
def auction([]) = 0
def auction(b:bs) =
  val bid = b.ask() | Rtimer(8000) >> 0
  max(bid, auction(bs))
```

This version of the auction is guaranteed to complete within 8 seconds.

Detecting Timeout. Sometimes, rather than just yielding a default value, we would like to determine whether an expression has timed out, and if so, perform some other computation. To detect the timeout, we pair the result of the original expression with `true` and the result of the timer with `false`. Thus, if the expression does time out, then we can distinguish that case using the boolean value.

Here, we run expression F with a time limit t. If it publishes within the time limit, we bind its result to r and execute G. Otherwise, we execute H.

```
val (r, b) = (F, true) | (Rtimer(t), false)
if b then G else H
```

Priority. We can use a timer to give a window of priority to one computation over another. In this example, we run expressions F and G concurrently. For one second, F has priority; F's result is published immediately, but G's result is held until the time interval has elapsed. If neither F nor G publishes a result within one second, then the first result from either is published.

```
val x = F
val y = G
let( x | Rtimer(1000) >> y )
```

5.6   Metronome

A timer can be used to execute an expression repeatedly at regular intervals, for example to poll a service. Recall the definition of metronome from Section 2.4:

```
def metronome(t) = signal | Rtimer(t) >> metronome(t)
```

The following example publishes "tick" once per second and "tock" once per second after an initial half-second delay. The publications alternate: "tick tock tick tock ...". Note that this program is not defined recursively; the recursion is entirely contained within metronome.

```
  metronome(1000) >> "tick"
| Rtimer(500) >> metronome(1000) >> "tock"
```

5.7   Fold

We consider various concurrent implementations of the classic "list fold" function from functional programming:

```
def fold(_, [x])  = x
def fold(f, x:xs) = f(x, fold(xs))
```

This is a seedless fold (sometimes called fold1) which requires that the list be nonempty and uses its first element as a seed. This implementation is short-circuiting — it may finish early if the reduction operator f does not use its second argument — but it is not concurrent; no two calls to f can proceed in parallel.

Associative Fold. We first consider the case when the reduction operator is associative. We define afold(b,xs) where b is a binary associative function and xs is a non-empty list. The implementation iteratively reduces xs to a single value. Each step of the iteration applies the auxiliary function step, which halves the size of xs by reducing disjoint pairs of adjacent items. Notice that b(x,y):step(xs) is an implicit fork-join, as described in Section 5.1. Thus, the call b(x,y) executes in parallel with the recursive call step(xs), and as a result, all of the calls to b in each iteration occur in parallel.

```
def afold(b, [x]) = x
def afold(b, xs) =
  def step([]) = []
  def step([x]) = [x]
  def step(x:y:xs) = b(x,y):step(xs)
  afold(b, step(xs))
```

Associative, Commutative Fold. We can devise a better strategy when the fold operator is both associative and commutative. We define cfold(b,xs), where b is a binary associative and commutative function over two arguments and xs is a non-empty list. The implementation initially copies all list items into a buffer in arbitrary order using the auxiliary function xfer. The auxiliary function combine repeatedly pulls pairs of items from the buffer, reduces them, and places the result back in the buffer. Each pair of items is reduced in parallel as they become available. The last item in the buffer is the result of the overall fold.

```
def cfold(b, xs) =
  val c = Buffer()

  def xfer([])   = stop
  def xfer(x:xs) = c.put(x) >> stop | xfer(xs)

  def combine(1) = c.get()
  def combine(m) = c.get() >x> c.get() >y>
                     ( c.put(b(x,y)) >> stop | combine(m-1))

  xfer(xs) | combine(length(xs))
```

5.8   Routing

The Orc combinators restrict the passing of values among their component expressions. However, some programs will require greater flexibility. For example, F <x< G provides F with the first publication of G, but what if F needs the first n publications of G? In cases like this we use channels or other stateful sites to redirect or store publications. We call this technique *routing* because it involves routing values from one execution to another.

Generalizing Termination. The pruning combinator terminates an expression after it publishes its first value. We have already seen how to use pruning just for its termination capability, without binding a variable, using the let site. Now we use routing to terminate an expression under different conditions, not just when it publishes a value; it may publish many values, or none, before being terminated.

Our implementation strategy is to route the publications of the expression through a channel so that we can put the expression inside a pruning combinator and still see its publications without those publications terminating the expression.

Enhanced Timeout. As a simple demonstration of this concept, we construct a more powerful form of timeout: allow an expression to execute, publishing arbitrarily many values (not just one), until a time limit is reached.

```
val c = Buffer()
repeat(c.get) <<
    F >x> c.put(x) >> stop
  | Rtimer(1000) >> c.closenb()
```

This program allows F to execute for one second and then terminates it. Each value published by F is routed through channel c so that it does not terminate

F. After one second, Rtimer(1000) responds, triggering the call c.closenb().
The call c.closenb() closes c and publishes a signal, terminating F. The library
function repeat is used to repeatedly take and publish values from c until it is
closed.

Interrupt. We can use routing to interrupt an expression based on a signal
from elsewhere in the program. We set up the expression like a timeout, but
instead of waiting for a timer, we wait for the semaphore done to be released.
Any call to done.release will terminate the expression (because it will cause
done.acquire() to publish), but otherwise F executes as normal and may
publish any number of values.

```
val c = Buffer()
val done = Semaphore(0)
repeat(c.get) <<
    F >x> c.put(x) >> stop
  | done.acquire() >> c.closenb()
```

Publication Limit. We can use the interrupt idiom to limit an expression to
n publications, rather than just one. Here is an expression that executes F until
it publishes 5 values, and then terminates it.

```
val c = Buffer()
val done = Semaphore(0)
def allow(0) = done.release() >> stop
def allow(n) = c.get() >x> ( x | allow(n-1) )
allow(5) <<
    F >x> c.put(x) >> stop
  | done.acquire() >> c.closenb()
```

We use the auxiliary function allow to get only the first 5 publications from
the channel c. When no more publications are allowed, allow uses the interrupt
idiom to halt F and close c.

Non-Terminating Pruning. We can use routing to create a modified version
of the pruning combinator. As in F <x< G, we'll run F and G in parallel and
make the first value published by G available to F. However instead of terminating G after it publishes a value, we will continue running it, ignoring its
remaining publications.

```
val r = Ref()
(F <x< r.read()) | (G >x> r.write(x))
```

Publication-Agnostic Otherwise. We can also use routing to create a modified version of the otherwise combinator. We'll run F until it halts, and then
run G, regardless of whether F published any values or not.

```
val c = Buffer()
repeat(c.get) | (F >x> c.put(x) >> stop
                ; c.close() >> G)
```

We use `c.close()` instead of the more common `c.closenb()` to ensure that G does not execute until all the publications of F have been routed. Recall that `c.close()` does not return until c is empty.

5.9   Larger Examples

In the previous sections we demonstrated how various concurrent programming idioms are expressed simply in Orc. Now we apply these idioms to solve non-trivial problems. The following examples illustrate how the different aspects of Orc — including the functional core, concurrency, time, synchronization and mutable state — combine to produce concise and efficient programs.

Dining Philosophers. The dining philosophers problem is a well known and intensely studied problem in concurrent programming. Five philosophers sit around a circular table. Each philosopher has two forks that she shares with her neighbors (giving five forks in total). Philosophers think until they become hungry. A hungry philosopher picks up both forks, one at a time, eats, puts down both forks, and then resumes thinking. Without further refinement, this scenario allows deadlock; if all philosophers become hungry and pick up their left-hand forks simultaneously, no philosopher will be able to pick up her right-hand fork to eat. Lehmann and Rabin's solution [6], which we implement, requires that each philosopher pick up her forks in a random order. If the second fork is not immediately available, the philosopher must set down both forks and try again. While livelock is still possible if all philosophers take forks in the same order, randomization makes this possibility vanishingly unlikely.

The following program gives the Orc implementation of dining philosophers. The `phil` function simulates a single philosopher. It takes as arguments two binary semaphores representing the philosopher's forks, and calls the `thinking`, `hungry`, and `eating` functions in a continuous loop. A `thinking` philosopher waits for a random amount of time, with a 10% chance of thinking forever. A `hungry` philosopher uses the `take` function to acquire two forks. An `eating` philosopher waits for a random time interval and then uses the `drop` function to relinquish ownership of her forks.

Calling `take` attempts to acquire a pair of forks `(a,b)` in two steps: wait for fork a to become available, then immediately attempt to acquire fork b. The call `b.acquirenb()` either acquires b and responds immediately, or halts if b is not available. If b is acquired, signal success; otherwise, release a, and then try again, randomly changing the order in which the forks are acquired using the auxiliary function `shuffle`.

The function `philosophers` recursively creates a chain of n philosophers, bounded by fork a on the left and b on the right. The goal expression of the program calls `philosophers` to create a chain of five philosophers bounded on the left and right by the same fork; hence, a ring.

```
def shuffle(a,b) = if (random(2) = 1) then (a,b) else (b,a)

def take((a,b)) =
  a.acquire() >> b.acquirenb() ;
  a.release() >> take(shuffle(a,b))

def drop(a,b) = (a.release(), b.release()) >> signal

def phil(a,b) =
  def thinking() =
    if (random(10) < 9)
      then Rtimer(random(1000))
      else stop
  def hungry() = take((a,b))
  def eating() =
    Rtimer(random(1000)) >>
    drop(a,b)
  thinking() >> hungry() >> eating() >> phil(a,b)

def philosophers(1,a,b) = phil(a,b)
def philosophers(n,a,b) =
  val c = Semaphore(1)
  philosophers(n-1,a,c) | phil(c,b)

val fork = Semaphore(1)
philosophers(5,fork,fork)
```

This Orc solution has several nice properties. The overall structure of the program is functional, with each behavior encapsulated in its own function, making the program easy to understand and modify. Mutable state is isolated to the "fork" semaphores and associated take and get functions, simplifying the implementation of the philosophers. The program never manipulates threads explicitly, but instead expresses relationships between activities using Orc's combinators.

Quicksort. The original quicksort algorithm [3] was designed for efficient execution on a uniprocessor. Encoding it as a functional program typically ignores its efficient rearrangement of the elements of an array. Further, no known implementation highlights its concurrent aspects. The following program attempts to overcome these two limitations. The program is mostly functional in its structure, though it manipulates the array elements in place. We encode parts of the algorithm as concurrent activities where sequentiality is unneeded.

The following listing gives the implementation of the quicksort function which sorts the array a in place. The auxiliary function sort sorts the subarray given by indices s through r by calling part to partition the subarray and then recursively sorting the partitions.

The function part partitions the subarray given by indices s through t into two partitions, one containing values ≤ p and the other containing values > p. The last index of the lower partition is returned. The value at a(s) is assumed to be ≤ p — this is satisfied by choosing p = a(s)? initially. To create the partitions, part calls two auxiliary functions lr and rl concurrently. These functions scan from the left and right of the subarray respectively, looking for out-of-place elements. Once two such elements have been found, they are swapped using the auxiliary function swap, and then the unscanned portion of the subarray is partitioned further. Partitioning is complete when the entire subarray has been scanned.

This program uses the syntactic sugar x? for x.read() and x := y for x.write(y). Also note that the expression a(i) returns a reference to the element of array a at index i, counting from 0.

```
def quicksort(a) =

  def swap(x, y) = a(x)? >z> a(x) := a(y)? >> a(y) := z

  def part(p, s, t) =
    def lr(i) = if i < t && a(i)? <= p then lr(i+1) else i
    def rl(i) = if a(i)? > p then rl(i-1) else i

    (lr(s), rl(t)) >(s', t')>
    ( if (s' + 1 < t') >> swap(s', t') >> part(p, s'+1, t'-1)
    | if (s' + 1 = t') >> swap(s', t') >> s'
    | if (s' + 1 > t') >> t'
    )

  def sort(s, t) =
    if s >= t then signal
    else part(a(s)?, s+1, t) >m>
         swap(m, s) >>
         (sort(s, m-1), sort(m+1, t)) >>
         signal

  sort(0, a.length()-1)
```

Meeting Scheduler. Orc makes very few assumptions about the behaviors of services it uses. Therefore it is straightforward to write programs which interact with human agents and network services. This makes Orc especially suitable for encoding *workflows* [2], the coordination of multiple activities involving multiple participants. The following program illustrates a simple workflow for scheduling a business meeting. Given a list of people and a date range, the program asks each person when they are available for a meeting. It then combines all the responses, selects a meeting time which is acceptable to everyone, and notifies everyone of the selected time.

```
val during = DateTimeRange(LocalDate(2009, 9, 10),
                           LocalDate(2009, 10, 17))
val invitees = ["dkitchin@cs.utexas.edu", "quark@cs.utexas.edu"]

def invite(invitee) =
  Form() >f>
  f.addPart(DateTimeRangesField("times",
    "When are you available for a meeting?", during, 9, 17)) >>
  f.addPart(Button("submit", "Submit")) >>
  SendForm(f) >receiver>
  SendMail(invitee, "Meeting Request", receiver.getURL()) >>
  receiver.get() >response>
  response.get("times")

def notify([]) =
  each(invitees) >invitee>
  SendMail(invitee, "Meeting Request Failed",
                    "No meeting time found.")
def notify(first:_) =
  each(invitees) >invitee>
  SendMail(invitee, "Meeting Request Succeeded",
                    first.getStart())

map(invite, invitees) >responses>
afold(lambda (a,b) = a.intersect(b), responses) >times>
notify(times)
```

This program begins with declarations of during (the date range for the proposed meeting) and invitees (the list of people to invite represented by email addresses).

The invite function obtains possible meeting times from a given invitee, as follows. First it uses library sites (Form, DateTimeRangesField, Button, and SendForm) to construct a web form which may be used to submit possible meeting times. Then it emails the URL of this form to the invitee and blocks waiting for a response. When the invitee receives the email, he or she will use a web browser to visit the URL, complete the form, and submit it. The corresponding execution of invite receives the response in the variable response and extracts the chosen meeting times.

The notify function takes a list of possible meeting times, selects the first meeting time in the list, and emails everyone with this time. If the list of possible meeting times is empty, it emails everyone indicating that no meeting time was found.

The goal expression of the program uses the library function map to apply notify to each invitee and collect the responses in a list. It then uses the library function afold to intersect all of the responses. The result is a set of meeting times which are acceptable to everyone. Finally, notify is called to select one of these times and notify everyone of the result.

This program may be extended to add more sophisticated features, such as a quorum (to select a meeting as soon as some subset of invitees responds) or timeouts (to remind invitees if they don't respond in a timely manner). These modifications are local and do not affect the overall structure of the program. For complete details, see examples on our website [11].

6 Related Work

Many attempts have been made to rethink the prevailing concurrency model of threads with shared state and put forth programming languages based on novel approaches.

Erlang is perhaps the most widely adopted of these languages [1]. It is founded on an actor model of concurrency, wherein sequential processes communicate via message-passing. While the Orc language is very different in design, Erlang has often served as a basis for comparison.

Oz is another novel concurrent programming language [12]. Though it uses a more conventional thread-based approach to concurrent computation, its model of shared state is much more structured and safe than that of mainstream languages. Rather than reducing all programs to a small calculus, Oz instead starts with a kernel calculus and incrementally expands it with new concepts that provide additional expressive capability, such as ports, objects, and computation spaces. While Oz is more structured than a pure message-passing model and its unification-based assignment operation is more expressive than Orc's pattern matching, evaluation of Oz programs requires access to a global unification store, which Orc programs do not need. The site Cell in the Orc library, which creates write-once mutable cells, was inspired by Oz's single-assignment variables.

Pict is a concurrent functional language [10] which is based on the π-calculus, in much the same way that the Orc language is based on the Orc calculus. In fact, Pict was an inspiration for some of the design choices of the Orc language. The primary difference between Pict and Orc is that Pict imposes a functional, continuation-passing structure on an unstructured communication calculus, whereas the Orc calculus is already structured, so a translation into the calculus preserves much of the structure of the original program and may thereby ease formal analysis.

7 Conclusion

We have presented Orc, developed from a simple concurrency calculus into a complete programming language capable of addressing real-world problems while maintaining its original formal simplicity.

Future Work. The language continues to be actively developed; current areas of development include a static type system with partial type inference, an explicit exception handling mechanism, a module system for namespace management and separate compilation, support for atomic sections using transactions, and dynamic modification of programs.

Acknowledgements. We would like to thank Andrew Matsuoka and John Thywissen for helpful discussions about the design of the Orc language.

References

1. Armstrong, J., Virding, R., Wikström, C., Williams, M.: Concurrent programming in ERLANG, 2nd edn. Prentice Hall International (UK) Ltd., Hertfordshire (1996)
2. Cook, W.R., Patwardhan, S., Misra, J.: Workflow patterns in Orc. In: Ciancarini, P., Wiklicky, H. (eds.) COORDINATION 2006. LNCS, vol. 4038, pp. 82–96. Springer, Heidelberg (2006)
3. Hoare, C.A.R.: Partition: Algorithm 63, quicksort: Algorithm 64, and find: Algorithm 65. Communications of the ACM 4(7), 321–322 (1961)
4. Kitchin, D., Cook, W.R., Misra, J.: A language for task orchestration and its semantic properties. In: Baier, C., Hermanns, H. (eds.) CONCUR 2006. LNCS, vol. 4137, pp. 477–491. Springer, Heidelberg (2006)
5. Kitchin, D., Quark, A., Cook, W.R., Misra, J.: Orc user guide,
   http://orc.csres.utexas.edu/userguide/html/index.html
6. Lehmann, D.J., Rabin, M.O.: On the advantages of free choice: A symmetric and fully distributed solution to the dining philosophers problem. In: POPL, pp. 133–138 (1981)
7. Milner, R.: Communicating and Mobile Systems: the π-Calculus. Cambridge University Press, Cambridge (1999)
8. Misra, J.: Computation orchestration: A basis for wide-area computing. In: Broy, M. (ed.) Proc. of the NATO Advanced Study Institute, Engineering Theories of Software Intensive Systems, NATO ASI Series, Marktoberdorf, Germany (2004)
9. Paulson, L.C.: ML for the Working Programmer. Cambridge University Press, Cambridge (1991)
10. Pierce, B.C., Turner, D.N.: Pict: A programming language based on the pi-calculus. In: Plotkin, G., Stirling, C., Tofte, M. (eds.) Proof, Language and Interaction: Essays in Honour of Robin Milner, pp. 455–494. MIT Press, Cambridge (2000)
11. Quark, A., Kitchin, D., Cook, W.R., Misra, J.: Orc language project website,
    http://orc.csres.utexas.edu
12. Van Roy, P., Haridi, S.: Concepts, Techniques, and Models of Computer Programming. The MIT Press, Cambridge (2004)

Keep It Small, Keep It Real: Efficient Run-Time Verification of Web Service Compositions

Luciano Baresi[1], Domenico Bianculli[2], Sam Guinea[1], and Paola Spoletini[3]

[1] Politecnico di Milano - DEEP-SE Group - DEI, Milano, Italy
{luciano.baresi,sam.guinea}@polimi.it
[2] University of Lugano - Faculty of Informatics, Lugano, Switzerland
domenico.bianculli@lu.unisi.ch
[3] Università dell'Insubria - DSCPI, Como, Italy
paola.spoletini@uninsubria.it

Abstract. Service compositions leverage remote services to deliver added-value distributed applications. Since services are administered and run by independent parties, the governance of service compositions is intrinsically decentralized and services may evolve independently over time. In this context, pre-deployment verification can only provide limited guarantees, while continuous run-time verification is needed to probe and guarantee the correctness of compositions at run time.

This paper addresses the issue of efficiency in the run-time verification of service compositions described in BPEL. It considers an existing monitoring approach based on ALBERT, which is a temporal logic language suitable for asserting both functional and non-functional properties, and shows how to obtain the efficient run-time verification of ALBERT formulae. The paper introduces an operational semantics for ALBERT through an extension of alternating automata, and explains how to optimize it to produce smarter, and thus more efficient, encodings of defined formulae. The optimized operational semantics can then be the basis for an efficient implementation of the run-time verification framework.

1 Introduction

Services represent reusable software components that provide their functionality to many clients through a standardized network and middleware infrastructure. Clients may combine services in different ways, to create new composite applications that can be themselves published as a service. In the realm of Web services, service compositions are usually described by means of the BPEL [1] language, which supports the definition of workflow-like service compositions.

BPEL orchestrations usually involve multiple stakeholders, as service aggregators rely on parts that are owned and managed by other organizations. The overall quality of a BPEL process largely depends on the quality of the composed services. Since these services are run and administered autonomously, in a decentralized manner, providers are entitled to change them freely. For this

D. Lee et al. (Eds.): FMOODS/FORTE 2009, LNCS 5522, pp. 26–40, 2009.

reason, the actual partner services invoked by a composite service can evolve (or even change) at run time. Pre-deployment verification is of limited usefulness; run-time verification becomes mandatory to probe and check the quality and correctness of service compositions while they execute.

Run-time verification may check different properties, ranging from quality of service parameters (e.g., response time, throughput) to behavioral assertions. These properties are often expressed by means of special-purpose languages. In [2], we introduced ALBERT, an assertion language for the specification of functional and non-functional temporal properties of BPEL processes. ALBERT plays a key-role in SAVVY-WS [3], our proposal for an integrated design- and run-time verification methodology.

This paper focuses on the *efficient* verification of ALBERT formulae at run time. It starts by proposing an operational semantics for ALBERT based on the correlation between temporal logic and a class of alternating automata, called ASA (ALBERT's Semantics Automata). Since this "plain" operational model would lead to quite inefficient verifications, the paper also proposes a smart encoding of ALBERT formulae by means of an optimized semantics defined in terms of an extension of ASA, called LASA (Limited ASA). This new operational semantics is equivalent to the previous one, but fosters more efficient verifications. Experimental results corroborate this hypothesis and show how the proposed optimization limits the number of threads needed for a complete evaluation of a given formula.

The rest of the paper is organized as follows. Section 2 provides a brief introduction to ALBERT. Section 3 presents the "plain" semantics ascribed to ALBERT in terms of our extension of alternating automata. Section 4 explains how to optimize the mapping of ALBERT formulae onto the formal model, and Sect. 5 fosters this hypothesis by means of some experimental results. Finally, Sect. 6 surveys related work, and Sect. 7 concludes the paper.

2   ALBERT in a Nutshell

The aim of this section is to accustom the reader with ALBERT, focusing on the main aspects that are needed to understand the theoretical framework presented in the paper.

ALBERT [2] is a temporal assertion language for stating functional and non-functional properties of BPEL workflows. ALBERT formulae predicate over *internal* and *external* variables. The former consist of data pertaining to the internal state of the BPEL process in execution. The latter are data that are useful for the specification, but are not part of the process' business logic and must be obtained externally (e.g., the values returned by some external services).

Given a finite set of variables V and a finite set of natural constants C, an ALBERT formula ϕ is defined by the following syntax:

$$\phi ::= \chi \quad | \quad \neg\phi \quad | \quad \phi \wedge \phi \quad | \quad (\text{ op id in var } ; \ \phi) \quad |$$
$$Becomes(\chi) \quad | \quad Until(\phi,\phi) \quad | \quad Between(\phi,\phi,K) \quad |$$
$$Within(\phi,K) \quad | \quad InFuture(\phi,K)$$

$$\chi ::= \psi \text{ relop } \psi \quad | \quad \neg \chi \quad | \quad \chi \wedge \chi \quad | \quad onEvent(\mu)$$
$$\psi ::= \text{var} \quad | \quad \psi \text{ arop } \psi \quad | \quad \text{const} \quad | \quad past(\psi, onEvent(\mu), n) \quad |$$
$$count(\chi, K) \quad | \quad fun(\psi, K) \quad | \quad elapsed(onEvent(\mu))$$
$$op ::= \texttt{forall} \quad | \quad \texttt{exists}$$
$$\text{relop} ::= < \quad | \quad \leq \quad | \quad = \quad | \quad \geq \quad | \quad >$$
$$\text{arop} ::= + \quad | \quad - \quad | \quad \times \quad | \quad \div$$
$$\text{fun} ::= sum \quad | \quad avg \quad | \quad min \quad | \quad max$$

where var $\in V$, const $\in C$, $n \in \mathbb{N}$, $K \in \mathbb{R}^+$ and *onEvent* is an event predicate. *Becomes, Until, Between, Within* and *InFuture* are temporal operators. *count, elapsed, past*, and all the functions derivable from the non-terminal fun are temporal functions of the language. Parameter μ denotes an event: it may identify the *start* or the *end* of an *invoke, reply* or *receive* activity, the reception of a message by a *pick* or an *event handler*, or the execution of any other BPEL activity. The above syntax only defines the language's core constructs. The usual logical derivations are used to define other connectives and temporal operators (e.g., $\vee$, *Always, Eventually*).

The informal meaning of ALBERT formulae can be explained by referring to sequences of states of the BPEL process, each of which represents a snapshot of the variables of the process, taken at a certain time instant, when the process is executing a certain set of activities.

Sequences of process states are strictly monotonic with respect to time. Between successive states there is always at least one time-consuming interaction with the outside world or the execution of an internal BPEL activity (e.g., an *assign* activity) or the occurrence of an event.

All ALBERT formulae represent invariant assertions over a BPEL process, therefore they are understood to be in the scope of an implicit universal temporal quantification, i.e., each formula is prefixed by an *Always* temporal operator. The predicate *onEvent* can be used to express a formula that must hold when the execution reaches a given point of the workflow. In the case where the parameter μ denotes *assign, pick, event handler*, or the *end* of *invoke, reply* or *receive* activities, *onEvent* is true in a state whose label identifies the corresponding activity. In the case of the *start* of an *invoke, reply* or *receive* activity, it is true in a state if the label of the next state in the sequence identifies the corresponding activity. In the case of a *while* or a *switch* activity, it is true in the state where the condition is evaluated.

Function $past(\psi, onEvent(\mu), n)$ returns the value of ψ in the nth past state in which $onEvent(\mu)$ is true. Function $count(\chi, K)$, evaluated in a state whose time-stamp is t_j, computes the number of states in which χ is true, and whose time-stamp is greater than or equal to $t_j - K$. The non-terminal fun stands for any function (e.g., average, sum, minimum, maximum ...) that can be applied to sets of numerical values. The function, evaluated in a state whose time-stamp is t_j, is applied to all values of expression ψ in all states whose time-stamp is greater than or equal to $t_j - K$. Function $elapsed(onEvent(\mu))$, evaluated in a state whose time-stamp is t_j, returns the difference between t_j and the time-stamp of the most recent past state in which $onEvent(\mu)$ is true. Since these functions compute their value from a trace storing a past history of states, their value becomes part of the process state. Moreover, a change in the value of function *count* and of the functions derivable from non-terminal fun may lead to the generation of a new state.

Temporal predicate *Becomes* is evaluated on two adjacent elements of the sequence of states. The formula is true if its argument is true in the current state, and false in the previous. The temporal predicate $Until(\phi_1, \phi_2)$ is true in a given state if ϕ_2 is true in the current state, or eventually in a future state, and ϕ_1 holds in all the states from the current (included) until that state (excluded). The temporal predicate $Between(\phi_1, \phi_2, K)$ is true in a given state if both ϕ_1 and ϕ_2 will be eventually true, with ϕ_2 occurring exactly after K time instants from the first time in which ϕ_1 was true. The temporal predicate $Within(\phi, K)$ is true in a given state if ϕ is true at most after K time instants. Predicate $InFuture(\phi, K)$ is true in a given state if ϕ is true in exactly K time instants.

Finally, boolean, relational, and arithmetic operators have the conventional meaning; the same is true for quantifiers.

3   ALBERT's Operational Semantics

The sequence of process states is linear and analogous to the sequence of states on which the operators of Linear Time Logic (LTL) — either in its classical definition or in the one with both modalities — are evaluated. The only main difference is that ALBERT operators also contain an explicit reference to time-stamps. Therefore, ALBERT temporal predicates can be described in terms of LTL operators. Furthermore, we consider sequences of infinite length since *a priori* we suppose that Web service compositions can be involved in long-running, never-ending business transactions. Notice that this does not represent a limitation if the system is stopped: in that case, the formulae are evaluated on an infinite sequence comprised of a prefix, represented by the states collected until that moment, and of a suffix of the form $false^{\omega}$.

Let s_c be the current state in a sequence of states and s_i be a sequent state that is at most K time instants after s_c and such that the successor state s_{i+1} comes more than K time instants after s_c, i.e., with the reference to time-stamps, $t_i - t_c \leq K$ and $t_{i+1} - t_c > K$. An ALBERT temporal predicate can be evaluated in state s_c according to the following equivalences with formulae of LTL with both modalities[1]:

- $Becomes(\chi) \equiv \mathsf{Y}(\neg\chi) \wedge \chi$
- $Until(\phi_1, \phi_2) \equiv \phi_1 \mathsf{U} \phi_2$
- $InFuture(\phi, K) \equiv \mathsf{X}^i(\phi)$
- $Within(\phi, K) \equiv \phi \vee \mathsf{X}(\phi) \vee \ldots \vee \mathsf{X}^{i-1} \vee \mathsf{X}^i(\phi)$

The temporal predicate $Between(\phi_1, \phi_2, K)$ is derived and can be expressed as $(\neg\phi_1)\mathsf{U}(\phi_1 \wedge InFuture(\phi_2, K))$.

---

[1] Y stands for "Yesterday", U for "Until", X for "neXt" and X^i for X nested i times.

Since ALBERT can be described in terms of LTL operators, in which however the number of nested Xs is not known *a priori*, we can exploit the well-known correlation between temporal logic and Büchi alternating automata (BAA) [4], as presented in [5], to give ALBERT an operational semantics that could be implemented straightforwardly. BAA generalize the traditional concept of non-determinism by supporting both *existential* and *universal* non-deterministic branching.

Since ALBERT's temporal model involves both a sequence of states and operations on their time-stamps, in the rest of this section we first introduce AL-BERT's Semantics Automata (ASA), an extension of BAA that uses variables to deal with time-stamps, and then we show how the classical correlation between BAA and LTL can be reformulated for ASA and ALBERT.

3.1 ALBERT's Semantics Automata

Informally speaking, a BAA is a finite state automaton that recognizes words of infinite length and supports two branching modalities, universal and existential. These modalities are formally expressed in the model through positive Boolean combinations of formulae; given a set M of propositions, $\mathcal{B}^+(M)$ denotes the set of positive Boolean formulae over M built from elements in M using $\wedge$ and $\vee$ but not $\neg$, plus the formulae *true* and *false*. Universal branching in a BAA potentially allows for reducing the dimension of the automaton in which parallelism is not made explicit at design time.

Dealing with ALBERT formulae in a concise way requires that the BAA model be enriched with a set of bounded time counters, and with the corresponding assignment and comparison operators, to take care of the explicit temporal aspects. Formally, given a finite set $C_K = \{v_1, \ldots, v_n\}$ of time counters ranging over the non-negative rational numbers $\mathbb{Q}^+$ and bounded in value by a positive integer K, let Ψ_{C_K} be the set of counter constraints of the form $v \mathbin{\square} c$ where $v \in C_K$, $\square \in \{<, \leq, =, \neq, >, \geq\}$ and $c \in \mathbb{Q}^+$. For the same set C_K, let Υ_{C_K} be the set of assignments over C_K of the form $v \leftarrow c$, where $v \in C_K$ and $c \in \mathbb{Q}^+$ and $c \leq K$, including also the empty assignment ε_Υ. ALBERT's Semantics Automata are defined as follows.

Definition 1. *An ASA is a tuple* $(\Sigma, Q, C_K, q_0, \delta, F)$ *where* Σ *is a finite alphabet,* Q *is a set of states,* C_K *is a finite set of time counters bounded in value by a positive integer* K, $q_0 \in Q$ *is the initial state,* $\delta : Q \times \wp(\Sigma) \times \mathbb{Q}^+ \times \Psi_{C_K} \to \mathcal{B}^+(Q \times \Upsilon_{C_K})$ *is the transition function and* $F \subseteq Q$ *is a set of accepting states.*

For the sake of readability, when indicating the elements in $\mathcal{B}^+(Q \times \Upsilon_{C_K})$ we will use the symbol / to separate the component in Q from the component in Υ_{C_K}.

An ASA accepts (or rejects) timed ω-words that are defined as sequences $w = w_1 w_2 \ldots = (a_1, t_1)(a_2, t_2) \ldots$ of pairs from $\wp(\Sigma) \times \mathbb{Q}^+$. For each $i > 1$, t_i describes the amount of time passed between reading a_{i-1} and a_i and t_1 represents the amount of time passed from the initial time (0) to the instant when a_1 was read. We also define the functions $D(w_i)$ and $t(w_i)$ that project, respectively, the data and the time component of the ith symbol of a word w. Due to universal branching, BAA's (and consequently ASA's) runs are not sequences, but trees. Indeed, every time a universal branch is taken, the automaton goes in all the states expressed by the $\wedge$ combination of formulae; hence, more than one state can be reached at the same time, as in a tree structure. This can be seen as the process of creating a duplicate of the automaton, at a certain level of the tree, for each state reached when performing the universal branch. A run of an ASA is *accepting* if every path starting from the root of the tree (corresponding to the run) hits accepting states infinitely often.

3.2 From ALBERT to ASA

Our proposal is to use an ASA for the run-time verification of an ALBERT formula, by defining the semantics of ALBERT formulae in terms of the operational model represented by the class of ASA. The implementation of the run-time checker becomes straightforward, as it follows the definition of the operational model. Indeed, while the truth value of a formula depends on the word on which it is evaluated, the equivalent corresponding automaton accepts the same word if and only if the formula is true on the word. Moreover, as ALBERT formulae represent invariant assertions over a BPEL process, the automaton equivalent to the formula to be verified, is supposed to run until the BPEL process for which ALBERT formulae are defined, is executed.

The basic idea is that an ASA equivalent to an ALBERT formula can be built from the latter (in the same way as a BAA can be derived from an LTL formula) by constructing a state for each temporal sub-formula in the formula, and by defining the transition relation between pairs of states $\langle q_j, q_k \rangle$ only if the truth value of the formula represented by state q_j depends on the truth value of the formula represented by state q_k. Moreover, the boolean connectors $\wedge$ and $\vee$ are implicitly represented by means of universal and existential branching.

In the following definition of the semantics, we do not consider ALBERT functions, but we treat them as part of the process state, as described in Sect. 2.

Standard Semantics. Let ϕ be an ALBERT formula, X the finite set of atomic propositions that occur in ϕ, and $Sf(\phi)$ the set of sub-formulae of ϕ. In order to define the semantics, we introduce some further definitions. Given an ALBERT formula ϕ, $Dual(\phi)$ is a formula obtained by interchanging in ϕ *true* and *false*, $\wedge$ and $\vee$, and complementing all the sub-formulae of ϕ. Moreover, let $H_D : \mathbb{N} \rightarrow \wp(X)$ and $H_t : \mathbb{N} \rightarrow \mathbb{Q}^+$ be, respectively the data[2] and the time history functions, which return, for a given n, respectively, the subset of atomic propositions that held in, and the time-stamp of, the nth-last data collection performed by the run-time checker. The ASA for ϕ is a tuple $(\Sigma, Q, C_K, q_0, \delta, F)$ where $\Sigma = X$, C_K is a finite set of time bounded counters such that $|C_K| \leq |Sf(\phi)|$, $Q = \{\gamma \mid \gamma \in Sf(\phi) \text{ or } \neg\gamma \in Sf(\phi)\}$, K is the greatest bounded temporal distance occurring in the temporal predicates of ϕ, $q_0 = \phi$, and $F = \{\gamma \mid \gamma \in Q \text{ and } \gamma \text{ has the form } \neg Until(\phi_1, \phi_2)\}$. The transition function δ is defined as follows, where χ, ϕ_1, ϕ_2

---

[2] Notice that $\forall\sigma, D(\sigma) = H_D(0)$.

are ALBERT (sub)formulae, σ is an input symbol, which is actually a pair from $\wp(X) \times \mathbb{Q}^+$, $v_\Psi \in \Psi_{C_K}$ is a generic constraint on a counter $v \in C_K$ and $v_\Upsilon \in \Upsilon_{C_K}$ is a generic assignment to a counter $v \in C_K$:

- $\delta(\chi, \sigma, v_\Psi) = true/v \leftarrow 0$ if $\chi \neq onEvent(\mu)$ where μ is a *start* event and $\chi \in D(\sigma)$;
- $\delta(\chi, \sigma, v_\Psi) = false/v \leftarrow 0$ if $\chi \neq onEvent(\mu)$ where μ is a *start* event and $\chi \notin D(\sigma)$;
- $\delta(\phi_1 \wedge \phi_2, \sigma, v_\Psi) = \delta(\phi_1, \sigma, v_\Psi) \wedge \delta(\phi_2, \sigma, v_\Psi)$;
- $\delta(\neg\phi, \sigma, v_\Psi) = \delta(Dual(\phi), \sigma, v_\Psi)$;
- $\delta(Becomes(\chi), \sigma, v_\Psi) = true/v \leftarrow 0$ if $\chi \neq onEvent(\mu)$ where μ is a *start* event, $\chi \in D(\sigma)$, and $\chi \notin H_D(1)$;
- $\delta(Becomes(\chi), \sigma, v_\Psi) = false/v \leftarrow 0$ if $\chi \neq onEvent(\mu)$ where μ is a *start* event and $\chi \notin D(\sigma)$ or $\chi \in H_D(1)$;
- $\delta(InFuture(\phi, K), \sigma, v_{InFuture(\phi,K)} = J) = InFuture(\phi, K)/v_{InFuture(\phi,K)} \leftarrow (J + t(\sigma))$ if $J < K$;
- $\delta(InFuture(\phi, K), \sigma, v_{InFuture(\phi,K)} = J) = \phi/v_{InFuture(\phi,K)} \leftarrow 0$ if $J = K$;
- $\delta(InFuture(\phi, K), \sigma, v_{InFuture(\phi,K)} = J) = Previous(\phi, v_{InFuture(\phi,K)} = J)/v_{InFuture(\phi,K)} \leftarrow 0$ if $J > K$, where $Previous(\phi, v_\Psi)$ is equal to the Q component returned by $\delta(\phi, (H_D(1), H_t(1)), v_\Psi)$;
- $\delta(Until(\phi_1, \phi_2), \sigma, v_\Psi) = \delta(\phi_2, \sigma, v_\Psi) \vee (\delta(\phi_1, \sigma, v_\Psi) \wedge Until(\phi_1, \phi_2)/\varepsilon_\Upsilon)$;
- $\delta(Within(\phi, K), \sigma, v_{Within(\phi,K)} = J) = false/v_{Within(\phi,K)} \leftarrow 0$ if $J > K$;
- $\delta(Within(\phi, K), \sigma, v_{Within(\phi,K)} = J) = \delta(\phi, v_{Within(\phi,K)} = J) \vee Within(\phi, K)/v_{Within(\phi,K)} \leftarrow (J + t(\sigma))$ if $J \leq K$.

For the sake of conciseness, in the above definition we omitted the semantics of: (a) the temporal operator $Between(\phi_1, \phi_2, K)$, since it is equivalent to the formula $Until(\neg\phi_1, \phi_1 \wedge InFuture(\phi_2, K))$; (b) (sub)formulae of the form $\chi = onEvent(\mu)$, where μ is a *start* event, since its semantics is equivalent to the one of the formula $InFuture(\chi, 1)$.

Figure 1 illustrates the ASA for the invariant $f \equiv A \implies Between(B, C, 10)$, which is equivalent, as a result of the logic equivalences mentioned above, to the formula $\neg A \vee Until(\neg B, B \wedge InFuture(C, 10))$. This ASA can be systematically derived from the definition of the operational semantics. The number of states in the resulting ASA is equal to the number of temporal operators plus two states for representing acceptance and rejection. In this case we have five states: one for the formula itself (since it is an invariant, the formula is implicitly contained within an *Always*), two for the *Until* and *InFuture* operators, one for acceptance, and one for rejection. The transition relation of the state containing the complete formula states that the automaton must stay in an acceptance state as long as $\neg A$ is true, i.e., an A is not received. On the other hand, as soon as A is received, the automaton must both stay in the same state to continue to check for A (due to the implicit *Always*), and move to another state to check $Between(B, C, 10)$ — transformed to $Until(\neg B, B \wedge InFuture(C, 10))$ — by creating a new copy of the automaton (the conjunction of the two copies is represented by a ◆). This copy remains in that state until a B is received. When this occurs, it moves to yet another state that checks the value of C while keeping an eye on the time counter $v_{InFuture(C,10)}$.

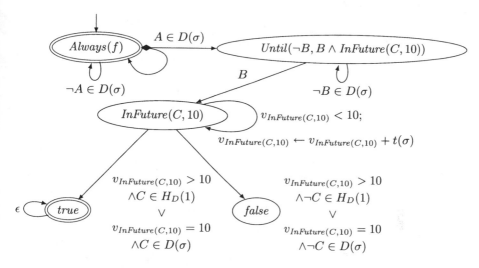

Fig. 1. ASA equivalent to the ALBERT invariant $f \equiv A \implies Between(B,C,10)$

4 Towards an Efficient Implementation

The advantage of using alternating automata is that through *universal branching* we do not need to explicitly represent parallelism. The representation is exponentially more concise than standard Büchi automata. Universal branching, however, leads to the activation of multiple copies of the automaton. A direct implementation would spawn a new thread for each duplicated copy — an obvious efficiency bottleneck of the approach. For example, the evaluation of the ALBERT formula in Fig. 1, shows that when the automaton is in the initial state, it duplicates whenever an A is received. This is a problem because, if the automaton continues to duplicate (i.e., A is true in each state) without ever receiving B, the number of copies that are created can be unbounded.

This highlights the need to optimize the approach by fine-tuning the theoretical foundation with respect to implementation needs. An unbounded number of automaton duplications is unacceptable, and even a bounded but continuous duplication can be quite inefficient. This is why we propose to limit the number of duplications, while preserving the correspondence between the automaton and the ALBERT formula.

In the following, we informally describe how our optimization works, on a per-operator case. Since our ASA run on infinite words, when we use the verb "terminate", we refer to the situation in which (a copy of) an automaton reaches the *true* state, reports that the ALBERT property has not been violated, and remains in that state. Moreover, we assume that our run-time verification framework supports two modes of operation, which differ from each other in the way the system behaves when a violation of a property is detected. In *standard* mode the system logs the violation and continues the execution of the process; in

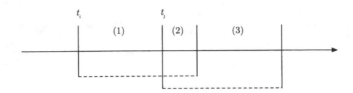

Fig. 2. Time line with overlapping regions of different activations of a *Within* operator

critical mode the framework stops the process execution, so that the cause of the violation can be dealt with immediately.

The evaluation of formulae of the form $Until(\phi_1, \phi_2)$ could lead to an unbounded number of duplications. Indeed, every time the corresponding automaton is activated, it checks if ϕ_2 holds. If it does, the automaton terminates in the *true* state. If both ϕ_1 and ϕ_2 do not hold, it terminates in the *false* state. Finally, if ϕ_2 does not hold but ϕ_1 does, it continuously checks ϕ_1, waiting to terminate when ϕ_2 becomes true or ϕ_1 becomes false. If the same formula has to be checked again, a new copy of the automaton would be required. If a preexisting copy is still active, it will be checking ϕ_1, which is the exact behavior required of the new copy. Therefore, only one copy of the automaton is needed to evaluate the formula. This avoids a potentially infinite number of duplicates, which could occur when ϕ_1 is always true and ϕ_2 never becomes true. Since the *Between* can be seen as an *Until*, it benefits from the above considerations too.

As for the evaluation of formulae of the form $Within(\phi, K)$, the duplication is bounded by the number of states that occur, in the sequence of process states, in an interval of K time instances. This is true if the run-time verification framework operates in *standard* mode. However, if the operation mode is *critical*, e.g., if the discovery of a violation leads to a complete halt in the verification activities, we can use just one duplicate. Consider, for example, the time-line sketched in Fig. 2, where two copies of the automaton corresponding to the sub-formula $Within(\phi, K)$ are activated, one at time instant t_i and the other at instant t_j, with $t_i < t_j < t_i + K$. If ϕ evaluates to true in region (1), the first duplicate terminates in the *true* state, meaning the second duplicate activated in t_j is actually the only copy running. If ϕ evaluates to true in region (2), it will make both copies terminate in the *true* state, meaning the second duplicate is actually not needed. Finally, if ϕ is true for the first time in region (3), it implicitly induces a violation of the property, which is detected by the first copy of the automaton. When the automaton notifies the violation, if the framework is operating in *critical* mode, the verification activities are stopped, meaning, once again, that the second copy of the automaton is not needed.

4.1   A Formal Model for an Efficient Implementation

We can now formalize the above intuitions by defining a variation of ASA for which an efficient implementation can be derived, and showing its equivalence to the original ASA, in terms of which the standard semantics was defined.

We first need to modify the ASA in a way that leads to a limited number of duplications. The model is abbreviated as LASA, which stands for Limited ASA.

Given a set $B = \{f_1, \ldots, f_n\}$ of boolean variables, Ψ_B^{Dup} is the set of constraints over B, of the form $f_i = 0$ or $f_i = 1$ with $f_i \in B$, including the no constraint $\varepsilon_{\Psi^{Dup}}$, and Υ_B^{As} is the set of assignments over B of the form $f_i \leftarrow 0$ or $f_i \leftarrow 1$ with $f_i \in B$.

Definition 2. *A LASA is a tuple* $(\Sigma, Q, C_K, q_0, \delta', B, F)$ *where* Σ, Q, C_K, q_0, F *are defined as in an ASA*, B *is a set of boolean variables and the transition function* δ' *is defined as* $\delta' : Q \times \wp(\Sigma) \times \mathbb{Q}^+ \times \Psi_{C_K} \times \Psi_B^{Dup} \times \Upsilon_B^{As} \to \mathcal{B}^+(Q \times \Upsilon_{C_K} \times \Upsilon_B^{As})$. *The acceptance condition of a LASA is defined similarly to the one of an ASA.*

When a LASA is used to model an ALBERT formula ϕ, $|B| \leq |Sf(\phi)|$. The variables in B allow us to keep track of duplications. Non-universal transitions are not involved in duplications and therefore are not needed. If a flag f_i is set to 0, there are currently no active duplicates for the state reached by the transition. We use assignments in Υ_B^{As} to change the values of flags when a duplicate is created, to disable the transition. The value of a flag can be changed back to 0 when the corresponding duplicate terminates. Notice that variables in B are initially set to 0 and changed according to the Υ_B^{As} component in the transition function.

Optimized Semantics 1 (*standard* mode). Let ϕ be an ALBERT formula, and let $B = \{f_1, \ldots, f_n\}$ be the set containing a boolean variable for each element in $Sf(\phi)$. The transition function δ' of the LASA for ϕ is defined as follows, by redefining[3] the original δ of an ASA, where $f_{\Upsilon} \in \Upsilon_B^{As}$ is a generic assignment on a variable $f_i \in B$:

- $\delta'(Until(\phi_1, \phi_2), \sigma, v_\Psi, f_{Until(\phi_1, \phi_2)} = 0, f_{\Upsilon}) =$
  $\delta'(\phi_2, \sigma, v_\Psi, \varepsilon_{\Psi^{Dup}}, f_{Until(\phi_1, \phi_2)} \leftarrow 0) \vee (\delta'(\phi_1, \sigma, v_\Psi, \varepsilon_{\Psi^{Dup}}, f_{\Upsilon}) \wedge Until(\phi_1, \phi_2)/$
  $\varepsilon_{\Upsilon}/f_{Until(\phi_1, \phi_2)} \leftarrow 1)$.

Informally speaking, the new transition function inhibits duplicates of the LASA every time a duplicate for that instance of the operator is already running. The automaton defined according to this semantics allows for a bounded number of duplicates, and can be proved (see below) to be equivalent to the one defined according to the standard semantics, i.e., they recognize the same language.

The optimizations included in the definition of Optimized Semantics 1 are valid under the assumption that the run-time verification framework is running in *standard* mode. A further optimization can be performed on the encoding of *Within* formulae, if the run-time verification framework operates in *critical* mode and thus the discovery of a violation of a specification leads to a complete halt in the verification activities. The following definition details these changes.

---

[3] Due to lack of space, in the following we will only describe the elements of the definition that change in the proposed semantics. All the other cases remain as in the definition of the standard semantics, with Ψ_B^{Dup} and Υ_B^{As} empty, and the occurrences of δ changed into δ'.

Table 1. Comparison of the number of duplications of an alternating automaton, for the standard operational semantics and the proposed optimized semantics

Operator	# of duplications[a]		
	Standard Semantics	Optimized Semantics 1	Optimized Semantics 2
$Until(\phi_1, \phi_2)$	potentially infinite	1	1
$Within(\phi, K)$	N_K	N_K	1

[a] N_K represents the number of states in the sequence of process states that may occur in an interval of K time instances.

Optimized Semantics 2 (*critical* mode). Let ϕ be an ALBERT formula, and let $B = \{f_1, \ldots, f_n\}$ the set containing a boolean variable for each element in $Sf(\phi)$. The transition function δ'' of the LASA for ϕ is redefined[4] as follows, where $f_{\Psi^{Dup}} \in \Psi_B^{Dup}$ is a generic constraint on a variable $f_i \in B$:

- $\delta''(Within(\phi, K), \sigma, v_{Within(\phi,K)} = J, f_{\Psi^{Dup}}, f_\Upsilon) =$
  $false / v_{Within(\phi,K)} \leftarrow 0 / f_{Within(\phi, K)} \leftarrow 0$ if $J > K$;
- $\delta''(Within(\phi, K), \sigma, v_{Within(\phi,K)} = J, f_{Within(\phi,K)} = 0, f_\Upsilon) =$
  $\delta''(\phi, \sigma, v_{Within(\phi,K)} = J, \varepsilon_{\Psi^{Dup}}, f_{Within(\phi,K)} \leftarrow 0) \vee Within(\phi, K) /$
  $v_{Within(\phi,K)} \leftarrow (J + t(\sigma)) / f_{Within(\phi, K)} \leftarrow 1$ if $J \leq K$.

Theorem 1. *Given an ALBERT formula ϕ, the ASA for ϕ obtained according to the definition of the standard semantics is always equivalent to the LASA defined according to Operational Semantics 1, and is equivalent to the LASA defined according to Optimized Semantics 2 only in* critical *mode.*

Proof. See [6].

Table 1 summarizes the gain, in terms of number of duplications, we can achieve for the *Until* and the *Within* temporal operators (and the ones derivable from them), by encoding ALBERT formulae in terms of LASA, as defined according to the two proposed optimized semantics.

5 Experimental Evaluation

We implemented the proposed encoding of ALBERT formulae within *Dynamo*, our run-time verification framework, by extending the existing component that is in charge of evaluating ALBERT formulae; more details about the architecture of the framework can be found in [2].

Our experiments were performed on a computer running Mac OS X 10.5.6 with a 2.16 GHz Intel Core 2 Duo processor and 2 GiB of memory. The current

---

[4] Due to lack of space, in the following we will only describe the elements of the definition that change in the new semantics. All the other cases remain as in Optimized Semantics 1.

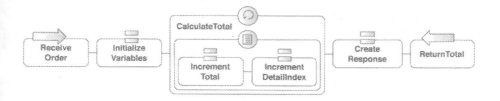

Fig. 3. The *While* sample BPEL process

version of *Dynamo* is based on ActiveBPEL Community Edition 4.1; it was deployed on Apache Tomcat 5.5.27. Profiling data have been acquired by means of the profiler integrated in the NetBeans IDE.

For sake of simplicity and repeatability we chose to test our system with the *While* sample process, bundled with the ActiveBPEL distribution and shown in Fig. 3. This process uses an index variable to iterate over a list of order items and calculate the total cost of the order. The iteration is realized by means of *while* activity, and thus the name of the example. We made two simple modifications to the process: 1) Extending the number of iterations to 100, to increase the amount of time taken by the execution of the *while* activity. This can be seen as a simple way to simulate, using a simple toy example, the long asynchronous interactions that typically occur between a process and its partner services in the real-world. 2) Inserting copies of the index variable, to allow for writing several formulae of the same type, as explained below.

We chose to consider only properties containing *Until* formulae, to represent the worst-case execution scenario, where the number of duplications of the corresponding alternating automaton (and thus the number of threads required to evaluate the properties) is potentially infinite. The properties have the form

$$\bigwedge_{i=1}^{n} Until(\$\texttt{detailIndex}_i \geq 1, onEvent(\texttt{start\_ReturnTotal}))$$

where n, ranging from 1 to 10, represents the number of *Until* formulae to be evaluated at each run of the process, and the variables of the form $\$\texttt{detailIndex}_i$ are used by the process to implement the iteration. They are set to 1 when the process starts and are incremented once per iteration, meaning that the first sub-formula of the *Until* operator of the formula is always true. The second sub-formula, on the other hand, becomes true when the process executes the `ReturnTotal` *reply* activity.

The process has been executed on two different implementations: a non-optimized one based on the standard semantics defined in Sect. 3.2, and an optimized one, based on the definition of Optimized Semantics 2. On each implementation, we executed 11 experiments, one for each different size of the property (i.e., number of *Until* operators) plus one corresponding to the base case, with no properties to verify. For each experiment, the application container was restarted. Due to the complexity of the middleware infrastructure, measurements are not exactly reproducible; this is a well-known phenomenon, for example in Java-based

Table 2. Number of thread activations and time for the evaluation of the sample formulae

size of the property	non-optimized		optimized	
	# threads	time (ms)	# threads	time (ms)
0	49	155	48	160
1	324	8208	132	458
2	648	19061	217	711
3	1064	31628	358	748
4	1640	48550	371	952
5	N/A	N/A	579	1044
6	N/A	N/A	670	1358
7	N/A	N/A	794	1940
8	N/A	N/A	876	1879
9	N/A	N/A	1007	2254
10	N/A	N/A	1070	2180

environments, where measurement variances due to application-inherent non-determinism are often amplified by differences in thread scheduling, dynamic just-in-time compilation, or garbage collection [7]. In order to compensate for the measurement variances, we repeated each experiment 10 times (under the same settings) and reported the geometric mean of the 10 trials.

Table 2 shows the number of thread activations and the time required for the evaluation of the properties, each one with a different, increasing number of *Until* operators. In the non-optimized implementation, the number of threads continuously grows until the system runs out of memory and experiences failures (reported as Java exceptions) in the attempt to create new threads, thus making the number of threads and the evaluation time become irrelevant (and thus marked as N/A in the table). On the other hand, the optimized version behaves much better and terminates as expected. Notice that the optimized version still has some spurious threads that make the total number of threads greater than the value estimated by the theoretical model. These threads derive from implementation constraints that do not interfere with the proposed optimizations and that we plan to address in future versions of our prototype.

These results prove that the optimized implementation, which is based on the optimized semantics, is better than the non-optimized implementation, which is based on the standard semantics, since it allowed us to check for properties that we could not have checked using the other version.

6   Related Work

The approach most similar to ours is the one described in [8], which deals with the on-line monitoring of Service Level Agreements. The main difference lies in the kind of observable properties that are supported by the two frameworks, which impacts both on the underlying theoretical model and on the corresponding implementation. [8] supports only the specification of latency, reliability and throughput requirements, which are a subset of the properties that can be expressed with ALBERT. A consequence of this limitation is that they can lay the approach on the top of a simpler theoretical model (timed automata).

[9] proposes a complementary approach to the previous one, as it focuses on the run-time monitoring of safety and liveness properties of Web service interactions, and does not consider timeliness constraints. Properties are specified by means of UML 2.0 Sequence Diagrams (SD) that are then translated into non-deterministic finite automata, whose size is polynomial in the number of events and the number of processes described by an SD. This is comparable to the spatial complexity of our approach, as the size of an LASA is polynomial in the number of temporal operators of the corresponding formula.

In [2] we provided a detailed comparison of various approaches for the run-time verification of Web service compositions. None of them describes a formal model to reason about the efficiency of the proposed approach.

To the best of our knowledge, alternating automata (and their variations) have not been used before for the run-time verification of service interactions, i.e., in the context of multi-parties, distributed applications. However, they have been proposed for the run-time verification of stand-alone applications. For example, [10] uses Metric Temporal Logic (MTL), which shares many constructs with ALBERT, and represents a formula in terms of an evolving computation tree equivalent to the original alternating automaton corresponding to the formula. The proposed optimization, which identifies and eliminates redundant sub-structures of a computation tree, is somehow equivalent to our proposal of reducing the duplications of an automaton. [11] presents three algorithms, based on alternating automata, to check both Past and Future Time Linear Temporal Logic (LTL). The only algorithm suitable to work on-line, however, has an exponential space complexity in the size of the input formula.

All the approaches mentioned above work with infinite program traces. However, in some cases the execution traces may be finite and therefore special-purpose algorithm can be used. [12] proposes an approach for automata-based run-time verification, where the standard algorithm to convert (Future Time) LTL formulae to Büchi automata is modified to generate finite-state automata that check finite program traces. [13] uses non-deterministic Büchi automata to verify formulae written in TLTL, the timed version of LTL: in this case, the size of the automaton is exponential in the length of the corresponding formula as well as its largest constant.

7   Conclusions

The work presented in this paper demonstrates that ALBERT formulae can be represented by concise alternating automata with a bounded number of duplicates. This is achieved by introducing an extension of alternating automata and by providing the definition of an operational semantics of ALBERT formulae in terms of this model.

Presented results not only have mere theoretical consequences, but also are the basis for a concrete and efficient implementation of our run-time verification framework. Our future work will focus on the refinement of the current prototype implementation and on a thorough quantitative analysis of the run-time verification framework.

Acknowledgments. The authors wish to thank Carlo Ghezzi for his insightful comments on earlier versions of the paper. Part of this work has been supported by the Swiss NSF project "CLAVOS" and by the ERC grant 227977 "SMScom".

References

1. Andrews, T., et al.: Business Process Execution Language for Web Services, Version 1.1. BPEL4WS specification (2003)
2. Baresi, L., Bianculli, D., Ghezzi, C., Guinea, S., Spoletini, P.: Validation of web service compositions. IET Softw. 1(6), 219–232 (2007)
3. Bianculli, D., Ghezzi, C., Spoletini, P., Baresi, L., Guinea, S.: A guided tour through SAVVY-WS: a methodology for specifying and validating web service compositions. In: Börger, E., Cisternino, A. (eds.) Advances in Software Engineering. LNCS, vol. 5316, pp. 130–161. Springer, Heidelberg (2008)
4. Chandra, A.K., Kozen, D.C., Stockmeyer, L.J.: Alternation. J. ACM 28(1), 114–133 (1981)
5. Vardi, M.Y.: An automata-theoretic approach to linear temporal logic. In: Moller, F., Birtwistle, G. (eds.) Logics for Concurrency. LNCS, vol. 1043, pp. 238–266. Springer, Heidelberg (1996)
6. Baresi, L., Bianculli, D., Guinea, S., Spoletini, P.: Keep it small, keep it real: Efficient run-time verification of web service compositions. Technical Report 2009.9, Politecnico di Milano - Dipartimento di Elettronica e Informazione (2009)
7. Georges, A., Buytaert, D., Eeckhout, L.: Statistically rigorous Java performance evaluation. In: Proceedings of OOPSLA 2007, pp. 57–76. ACM, New York (2007)
8. Raimondi, F., Skene, J., Emmerich, W.: Efficient online monitoring of web-service SLAs. In: Proc. of SIGSOFT 2008/FSE-16, pp. 170–180. ACM, New York (2008)
9. Simmonds, J., Chechik, M., Nejati, S.: Property patterns for runtime monitoring of web service conversations. In: Proc. of RV 2008 (2008)
10. Drusinsky, D.: On-line monitoring of metric temporal logic with time-series constraints using alternating finite automata. JUCS 12(5), 482–498 (2006)
11. Finkbeiner, B., Sipma, H.B.: Checking finite traces using alternating automata. Electr. Notes Theor. Comput. Sci. 55(2), 44–60 (2001)
12. Giannakopoulou, D., Havelund, K.: Runtime analysis of linear temporal logic specifications. In: Proc. of ASE 2001, pp. 412–416. IEEE Computer Society, Los Alamitos (2001)
13. Bauer, A., Leucker, M., Schallhart, C.: Monitoring of real-time properties. In: Arun-Kumar, S., Garg, N. (eds.) FSTTCS 2006. LNCS, vol. 4337, pp. 260–272. Springer, Heidelberg (2006)

Approximated Context-Sensitive Analysis for Parameterized Verification

Parosh Aziz Abdulla[1], Giorgio Delzanno[2], and Ahmed Rezine[3]

[1] Uppsala University, Sweden
parosh@it.uu.se
[2] Università di Genova, Italy
giorgio@disi.unige.it
[3] University of Paris 7, France
rezine.ahmed@liafa.jussieu.fr

Abstract. We propose a verification method for parameterized systems with global conditions. The method is based on *context-sensitive constraints*, a symbolic representation of infinite sets of configurations defined on top of words over a finite alphabet. We first define context-sensitive constraints for an exact symbolic backward analysis of parameterized systems with global conditions. Since the model is Turing complete, such an analysis is not guaranteed to terminate. To turn the method into a verification algorithm, we introduce context-sensitive constraints that over-approximate the set of backward reachable states and show how to symbolically test entailment and compute predecessors. We apply the resulting algorithm to automatically verify parameterized models for which the exact analysis and other existing verification methods either diverge or return false positives.

1 Introduction

We consider verification of safety properties for parameterized systems with universal and existential global conditions. Typically, such a system consists of an arbitrary number of processes organized in a linear array. Global conditions are used as guards. An example of a universally quantified global condition is that all processes to the left of a given process i should satisfy a property φ. Process i can perform the transition only if all processes with indices $j < i$ satisfy φ. In an existential condition we require that *some* (rather than *all*) processes satisfy φ. The task is to verify correctness regardless of the number of processes.

In [3] we have proposed a light-weight verification method for parameterized systems based on *monotonic abstraction* with the aim of avoiding the use of the full power of automata and regular languages (which require heavy manipulations like the use of transducers [21,14,7,9]). The main idea of the method in [3] is to consider a transition relation that is an over-approximation of the one induced by the parameterized system. To do that, we modify the semantics of universal quantifiers by eliminating the processes that violate the given condition (*downward closed semantics*). The obtained approximate transition

D. Lee et al. (Eds.): FMOODS/FORTE 2009, LNCS 5522, pp. 41–56, 2009.

system is *monotonic* with respect to the subword relation (larger configurations are able to simulate smaller ones). Since the approximate transition relation is monotonic, it can be analyzed using a symbolic backward reachability algorithm based on a generic method introduced in [2]. The algorithm operates on upward closed sets of configurations (with respect to the subword relation) and uses symbolic operations that are much simpler than transducers and regular languages. The PFS tool [3] that implements this technique can thus be applied to verify safety properties for configurations with any number of processes. Monotonic abstraction has proven successful in verifying a wide range of parameterized, distributed, and heap manipulating systems [3,5,4,6,1]. However, it may return false positives due to a loss of precision in the representation of special witness processes. We give an example of a system where such a situation occurs.

An example in which monotonic abstraction may return false positives is the parameterized system where processes are represented in Fig. 1. Each process has five local states $q_0, \ldots, q_4$. All processes are initially in state q_0. A process in the critical section is at state q_4. Note that the set of configurations violating mutual exclusion contains exactly configurations with at least two occurrences of symbol q_4. Processes start crossing from q_0 to q_1, and then to state q_2.

Once the first process has crossed to state q_2 it "closes the door" on the processes which are still in q_0. These processes will no longer be able to leave q_0 until the door is opened again (when no process is in state q_2 or q_3). Furthermore, a process is allowed to cross from q_3 to state q_4 only if there is at least one process still in state q_2 (i.e., the door is still closed on the processes in state q_0). This is to prevent a process first reaching

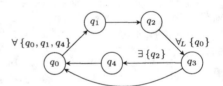

Fig. 1. State diagram of an individual process

q_4 and then a process to its left starting to move from q_0 all the way to state q_4 (thus violating mutual exclusion). From the set of processes which have left state q_0 (and which are now in state q_1 or q_2) the leftmost process has the highest priority. This is encoded by the global condition that a process may move from q_2 to q_3 only subject to the global condition that all processes to its left are in state q_0 (this condition is encoded by the universal quantifier $\forall_L$, where "L" stands for "Left"). A typical run of the system is of the form $q_0q_0q_0q_0 \longrightarrow q_0q_1q_0q_0 \longrightarrow q_0q_1q_1q_0 \longrightarrow q_0q_2q_1q_0 \longrightarrow q_0q_2q_2q_0 \longrightarrow q_0q_3q_2q_0 \longrightarrow q_0q_4q_2q_0 \longrightarrow q_0q_0q_2q_0$. The protocol satisfies mutual exclusion. Consider now the abstract transition system computed by applying monotonic abstraction. From the next-to-last configuration, the left most process can move (in the abstract system) to q_1. More precisely, the run may continue as follows in the abstract system. $q_0q_4q_2q_0 \longrightarrow q_1q_4q_0 \longrightarrow q_2q_4q_0 \longrightarrow q_3q_4q_0 \longrightarrow q_4q_4q_0$. Notice that monotonic abstraction removes the guard (the process in state q_2) since it does not satisfy the global condition of the rule $q_0 \rightarrow q_1 : \forall\{q_0, q_1, q_4\}$. With this abstraction the door is opened again. This allows processes in q_0 to move again, enabling one of them to reach q_4. This gives a false positive.

This kind of false positives arise typically in systems where correctness depends on the existence of a witness process. For this reason, it is relevant to study new approximations that can be used for more precise analysis than that provided by monotonic abstraction. The challenge here is to preserve the positive features of the latter approach such as the use of simple data structures and of a generic verification algorithm based on well-quasi orderings.

New Contribution. We propose a new verification algorithm based on an approximated context sensitive analysis that improves the precision of monotonic abstraction. The method is guaranteed to terminate, and is based on relatively simple symbolic data structures. We build the verification method in two steps.

We first define a symbolic representation, namely *context-sensitive constraints*, that are a natural generalization of the constraints used in the monotonic abstraction framework. In monotonic abstraction a word w of process states (referred to as the *basis*) is used as a symbolic representation of its upward closure computed with respect to word inclusion. This implies that any type of processes is allowed in between two consecutive states of the basis w (these allowed processes are referred to as *context*). Context-sensitive constraints generalize this idea by introducing constraints on the type of processes that are allowed to occur in each context. For each pair of consecutive states in the basis, constraints are expressed by using a subset R of states: only processes with states in R are allowed in this context. This kind of constraints can be used to exactly represent (one-step) predecessor configurations of a parameterized system with global conditions. An analysis based on this kind of constraints is not guaranteed to terminate in general. Furthermore, when testing in practice, even on simple examples the number of generated constraints often explodes after a few steps. Therefore, approximations are necessary to ensure both theoretical (e.g. using wqo theory) and practical termination (e.g. using more compact representations).

The approximated method we propose in this paper works on constraints of a special form, called *simple* context-sensitive constraints. In a simple context-sensitive constraint we use a single subset of states, called the *padding set*, to over-approximate the constraints on processes in each context. For this new symbolic representation, we have the following properties. The entailment ordering turns out to be a well-quasi ordering. The computation of predecessors is guaranteed to terminate and to return a finite representation of an over-approximation of the exact set of predecessor configurations. Our abstract predecessor operator incorporates accelerations in the computation of predecessors for ordered system that are similar in spirit to widening operators used in the unordered case (as those used in relation analysis for counter systems e.g. in [12,27,28]). Finally, the constraint operations are much simpler and more efficient than those used in the exact context-sensitive analysis. Since simple context-sensitive constraints can represent upward closed sets of configuration computed with respect to word inclusion, the resulting over-approximation is guaranteed to be at least as precise as monotonic abstraction. However, in several practical examples it gives more precise results (eliminates false positives).

As a first set of experiments, we have considered benchmark examples of parameterized systems taken from [15,7,3,8]. The performance of the new verification algorithm is comparable with that of the PFS tool based on monotonic abstraction [3]. We remark that in these examples exact analysis often diverges or suffers from the symbolic state explosion problem. Furthermore, we also consider several new case-studies that include both ordered systems like formulations of Szymanski's algorithm with non-atomic updates (semi-automatically verified in [18,22,23]), and unordered concurrent systems like synchronization skeletons [12,27,28] and reference counting schemes for virtual memory [16]. For these examples monotonic abstraction often returns spurious error traces due to a loss of precision in the representation of *special processes* (as in Szymanski) or in the representation of *counters*. Our new verification algorithm eliminates all the false positives and verifies the new case studies for any number of processes/unbounded value of counters. We are not aware of other tools that can automatically verify the same class of ordered/unordered parameterized models.

Plan of the paper. We describe our model of parameterized systems in the next Section. Then, we introduce context-sensitive constraints in Section 3, and simple-context sensitive constraints in Section 4. In Section 5, we discuss experimental results. Finally, in Section 6 we discuss related and future work.

2   Model

For a set A, we use A^* to denote the set of finite words over A, and use $w_1 w_2$ to denote the concatenation of two words w_1 and w_2 in A^*. For a natural number n, we use $\bar{n}$ to denote the set $\{1, \ldots, n\}$.

Formally, a *parameterized system* is a pair $\mathcal{P} = (Q, T)$, where Q is a finite set of *local states*, and T is a finite set of *transitions*. A transition is either *local* or *global*. A local transition is of the form $q \to q'$, where a process changes state from q to q' independently of the states of the other processes. A global transition is of the form $q \to q' : \mathbb{Q}P$, where $\mathbb{Q} \in \{\exists_L, \exists_R, \exists_{LR}, \forall_L, \forall_R, \forall_{LR}\}$ and $P \subseteq Q$. Here, the process checks the states of the other processes. For instance, the condition $\forall_L P$ means "all processes to the left are in states belonging to P"; the condition $\forall_{LR} P$ means "all other processes (whether to the left or to the right) are in states belonging to P"; and so on.

A parameterized system $\mathcal{P} = (Q, T)$ induces an infinite-state transition system $(C, \longrightarrow)$ where $C = Q^*$ is the set of *configurations* and $\longrightarrow$ is a transition relation on C. For a configuration $c = q_1 q_2 \cdots q_n$, we define $c^\bullet := \{q_1, \ldots, q_n\}$. For configurations $c = c_1 q c_2$, $c' = c_1 q' c_2$, and a transition $t \in T$, we write $c \xrightarrow{t} c'$ to denote that one of the following conditions is satisfied:

- t is a local transition of the form $q \to q'$.
- t is a global transition of the form $q \to q' : \mathbb{Q}P$, and one of the following conditions is satisfied:

- either $\mathbb{Q}P = \exists_L P$ and $c_1{}^\bullet \cap P \neq \emptyset$, $\mathbb{Q}P = \exists_R P$ and $c_2{}^\bullet \cap P \neq \emptyset$, or $\mathbb{Q}P = \exists_{LR} P$ and $(c_2{}^\bullet \cup c_2{}^\bullet) \cap P \neq \emptyset$.
- either $\mathbb{Q}P = \forall_L P$ and $c_1{}^\bullet \subseteq P$, $\mathbb{Q}P = \forall_R P$ and $c_2{}^\bullet \subseteq P$, or $\mathbb{Q}P = \forall_{LR} P$ and $(c_1{}^\bullet \cup c_2{}^\bullet) \subseteq P$.

We use $\xrightarrow{*}$ to denote the reflexive transitive closure of $\longrightarrow$.

We define an ordering $\preceq$ on configurations as follows. Let $c = q_1 \cdots q_m$ and $c' = q_1' \cdots q_n'$ be configurations. Then, $c \preceq c'$ if c is a subword of c', i.e., there is a strictly increasing injection h from $\overline{m}$ to $\overline{n}$ such that $q_i = q_{h(i)}$ for all $i : 1 \leq i \leq n$.

Given a parameterized system, we assume that, prior to starting the execution of the system, each process is in an (identical) *initial* state q_{init}. We use *Init* to denote the set of *initial* configurations, i.e., configurations of the form $q_{init} \cdots q_{init}$ (all processes are in their initial states). The set *Init* is infinite.

A set of configurations $U \subseteq C$ is *upward closed* with respect to $\preceq$ if $c \in U$ and $c \preceq c'$ implies $c' \in U$. For a configuration c, we use $\widehat{c}$ to denote the upward closure of c, i.e., the set $\{c' \mid c \preceq c'\}$. For sets of configurations $D, D' \subseteq C$ we use $D \longrightarrow D'$ to denote that there are $c \in D$ and $c' \in D'$ with $c \longrightarrow c'$. The *coverability problem* for parameterized systems is defined as follows:

PAR-COV
Instance

 – A parameterized system $\mathcal{P} = (Q, T)$.
 – A finite set C_F of configurations.
Question *Init* $\xrightarrow{*} \widehat{C_F}$?

It can be shown, using standard techniques (see e.g. [26]), that checking safety properties (expressed as regular languages) can be translated into instances of the coverability problem. Typically, $\widehat{C_F}$ is used to characterize sets of *bad* configurations which we do not want to occur during the execution of the system. The system is safe iff $\widehat{C_F}$ is not reachable. Therefore, checking safety properties amounts to solving PAR-COV (i.e., to the reachability of upward closed sets). In Example 1 the set of bad configurations is $\widehat{q_4 q_4}$.

3   Exact Context-Sensitive Symbolic Analysis

Assume a parameterized system $\mathcal{P} = (Q, T)$, where Q is a finite set of states. In order to finitely represent infinite sets of system configurations (e.g. configurations of arbitrary size) we use the *context-sensitive constraints* defined in this section. For the sake of clarity, we first present a simplified version of our constraints and then discuss extensions we use in our implementation. We work with words in $\mathbb{A}^*$, where $\mathbb{A} = Q \cup \mathbb{P}(Q)$ and $\mathbb{P}(Q)$ denotes the set of subsets of Q. We use $p, q, \ldots$ to denote states in Q, and $P, R, \ldots$ to denote sets of states in $\mathbb{P}(Q)$. Furthermore, for $w \in \mathbb{A}^*$ we use $w^\bullet$ to denote the union of all states in Q occurring in w either as one of its letters or listed in one of its sets. As an example, for $R = \{q_1, q_2\}$ we have that $(R q_3 R)^\bullet = \{q_1, q_2, q_3\}$.

Definition 1. *A context-sensitive (CC-)constraint is a word in $\mathbb{A}^*$ of the form $R_0 q_1 R_1 \ldots q_n R_n$, where $q_i \in Q$ for $i : 1 \le i \le n$ and $R_i \subseteq Q$ for $i : 0 \le i \le n$. The configuration $q_1 \ldots q_n$ is called the* basis *and each set R_i is called a* context. *The denotation of a context-sensitive constraint ϕ, written $\llbracket \phi \rrbracket$, is the set of configurations of the form $c_0 q_1 c_1 \ldots q_n c_n$ where $c_i \in R_i^*$ for $i : 0 \le i \le n$.*

As an example, assume $Q = \{q_1, q_2, q_3\}$, $R_0 = R_1 = \{q_2, q_3\}$ and $R_2 = \{q_1, q_3\}$. The constraint ϕ defined as $R_0 q_1 R_1 q_2 R_2$ denotes all configurations of the form $c_0 q_1 c_1 q_2 c_2$ such that sub-configurations c_0 and c_1 cannot contain processes q_1 and sub-configuration c_2 cannot contain occurrences of processes q_2. Therefore, configurations $q_3 q_1 q_3 q_2 q_1$ and $q_3 q_1 q_3 q_3 q_2 q_1$ belong to $\llbracket \phi \rrbracket$, whereas $q_1 q_1 q_2$ and $q_1 q_3 q_2 q_2$ do not belong to $\llbracket \phi \rrbracket$. Notice that CC's of the form $Q q_1 Q \ldots q_n Q$ denote upward closed sets of states with respect to word inclusion (there are no constraints on the contexts). For instance, the set of bad states in Example 1 can be characterized by the CC $Q q_4 Q q_4 Q$ where $Q = \{q_0, q_1, q_2, q_3, q_4\}$.

We now define the symbolic operations we use in our analysis, namely the entailment and the predecessors computation on context-sensitive constraints. These respectively correspond to the application, without any loss of precision, of the inclusion and the predecessor operations on the associated denotations.

Entailment. For constraints $\phi = R_0 q_1 \ldots q_n R_n$ and $\phi' = R_0' q_1' \ldots q_m' R_m'$, we define $\phi \sqsubseteq \phi'$ iff there exists a monotonic injection $h : \overline{n} \to \overline{m}$ such that $q_i = q_{h(i)}'$ for $i : 1 \le i \le n$ and the following conditions hold:

- $(R_0' q_1' \ldots q_{h(1)-1}' R_{h(1)-1}')^\bullet \subseteq R_0^\bullet$
- $(R_{h(i)}' q_{h(i)+1}' \ldots q_{h(i+1)-1}' R_{h(i+1)-1}')^\bullet \subseteq R_i^\bullet$ for $i : 1 \le i \le n-1$;
- $(R_{h(n)}' q_{h(n)+1}' \ldots q_m' R_m')^\bullet \subseteq R_n^\bullet$.

We have that $\phi_1 \sqsubseteq \phi_2$ if and only if $\llbracket \phi_2 \rrbracket \subseteq \llbracket \phi_1 \rrbracket$ (ϕ_1 is weaker than ϕ_2).

Computing Predecessors. Given a set S of CC's, it is possible to define a *symbolic predecessor operator* Pre that effectively computes, when applied to S, a set $S' = Pre(S)$ of CC's such that $\llbracket S' \rrbracket$ is the set of configurations from which one can reach configurations in $\llbracket S \rrbracket$ using $\xrightarrow{*}$ (i.e. predecessors).

We first introduce the symbolic predecessor computation for a $\forall_L$-rule, and then describe the case of the other transitions. Consider a transition t of the form $q \to q' : \forall_L P$ with $P \subseteq Q$. Then, $Pre_t(\phi)$ is the set $\{\phi' \mid \phi \leadsto_t \phi'\}$ where $\leadsto_t$ is the minimal relation that satisfies one of the following conditions. Let $\phi = R_0 q_1 \ldots q_n R_n$:

1. if there exists i s.t. $q_i = q'$ with $q_j \in P$ for each $j : 1 \le j < i$, then
   $$\phi \leadsto_t (R_0 \cap P) q_1 \ldots q_{i-1}(R_{i-1} \cap P) q R_i q_{i+1} \ldots q_n R_n$$
2. if there exists i s.t. $q' \in R_i$ with $q_j \in P$ for each $j : 1 \le j \le i$, then
   $$\phi \leadsto_t (R_0 \cap P) q_1 \ldots q_i (R_i \cap P) q R_i q_{i+1} \ldots q_n R_n$$

Notice that: in (1) the length of the new basis and the number of contexts are the same as in ϕ, whereas in the new constraint produced in (2) we add a new process as well as a new context. The case of $\forall_R$-rules is similar to that for $\forall_L$-rules. The remaining cases are given below.

Forall. Let $\phi = R_0 q_1 \ldots q_n R_n$. Consider a transition t of the form $q \to q' : \forall_{LR} P$ with $P \subseteq Q$. Then, $\leadsto_t$ is the minimal relation that satisfies one of the following conditions.

1. if there exists i s.t. $q_i = q'$ with $q_j \in P$ for each $j : (1 \le j \ne i \le n)$, then
   $\phi \leadsto_t (R_0 \cap P)q_1 \ldots q_{i-1}(R_{i-1} \cap P)q(R_i \cap P)q_{i+1} \ldots q_n(R_n \cap P)$.
2. if there exists i s.t. $q' \in R_i$ with $q_j \in P$ for each $j : 1 \le j \le n$, then
   $\phi \leadsto_t (R_0 \cap P)q_1 \ldots q_i(R_i \cap P)q(R_i \cap P)q_{i+1} \ldots q_n(R_n \cap P)$.

Local. Let t be a local rule $q \to q'$, $\leadsto_t$ is the minimal relation that satisfies one of the following conditions:

1. if there exists $E_1, E_2 \in \mathbb{A}^*$ s.t. $\phi = E_1 q' E_2$, then $\phi \leadsto_t E_1 q E_2$.
2. if there exists $E_1, E_2 \in \mathbb{A}^*$ and $R \subseteq Q$ s.t. $\phi = E_1 R E_2$, $q' \in R$, and $q \notin R$, then $\phi \leadsto_t E_1 R q R E_2$.

Exist. Let t be the rule $q \to q' : \exists_L P$, $\leadsto_t$ is the minimal relation that satisfies one of the following conditions:

1. if there exists $E_1, E_2, E_3 \in \mathbb{A}^*$ s.t. $\phi = E_1 p E_2 q' E_3$, then $\phi \leadsto_t E_1 p E_2 q E_3$.
2. if there exists $E_1, E_2, E_3 \in \mathbb{A}^*$, $R \subseteq Q$ s.t. $p \in R$, and $\phi = E_1 R E_2 q' E_3$, then
   $\phi \leadsto_t E_1 R p R E_2 q E_3$.
3. if there exists $E_1, E_2, E_3 \in \mathbb{A}^*$, $R \subseteq Q$ s.t. $p \in R$, $q' \in R$, $q \notin R$ and
   $\phi = E_1 p E_2 R E_3$, then $\phi \leadsto_t E_1 p E_2 R q R E_3$.
4. if there exists $E_1, E_2, E_3 \in \mathbb{A}^*$, $R, S \subseteq Q$ s.t. $p \in S$, $q' \in R$, $q \notin R$ and
   $\phi = E_1 S E_2 R E_3$, then $\phi \leadsto_t E_1 S p S E_2 R q R E_3$.
5. if there exists $E_1, E_2 \in \mathbb{A}^*$, $R \subseteq Q$ s.t. $p, q' \in R$, $q \notin R$ and $\phi = E_1 R E_2$,
   then $\phi \leadsto_t E_1 R p R q R E_3$.

The rules for computing predecessors with respect to rules with $\exists_R, \exists_{LR}$ can be derived in a manner similar to the above described cases.

Symbolic Backward Reachability. Context expressions can be used for an exact representation of predecessor configurations. Each application of Pre is effectively computable. Let Φ_0 be a set of CC's that represent an upward closed set of configurations (unsafe states). Starting from Φ_0, we compute the sequence of sets of CC's-constraints $\Phi_0, \ldots, \Phi_i, \ldots$ such that $\Phi_{i+1} = \Phi_i \cup \bigcup_{t \in T, \phi \in \Phi_i} Pre_t(\phi)$. Each step of this sequence can be effectively computed. Furthermore, we can apply the entailment $\sqsubseteq$ to discharge CC's that do not add new information (i.e. stronger than an already computed constraint). If we reach a fixpoint at step k, then Φ_k gives us an exact representation of the predecessors of configurations in $[\![\Phi_0]\!]$. Thus, we can potentially use this fixpoint computation to solve PAR-COV, i.e., to verify/falsify safety properties for configurations of arbitrary size. However, since our model is Turing complete (e.g. we can encode two counter machines using universally quantified conditions) the resulting CC's-based symbolic backward reachability analysis is not guaranteed to terminate. Therefore, in order to obtain a terminating verification procedure, we need to introduce some approximation. We discuss this point in the next section.

4   Approximated Context-Sensitive Symbolic Algorithm

In this section, we present an approximated representation of context-sensitive constraints that we use to turn the (possibly non-terminating) CC-based verification procedure into an approximated verification algorithm. For this purpose, we first define a special class of constraints.

Definition 2. *A simple context-sensitive (SCC-)constraint is a word in* $\mathbb{A}^*$ *of the form* $Rq_1R\ldots q_nR$ *in which* $\{q_1,\ldots,q_n\} \subseteq R \subseteq Q$.

Since the same constraint is uniformly applied to each context in the basis, we can simplify the notation and represent an SCC as a pair (c, R), where $c \in Q^*$ and $c^\bullet \subseteq R \subseteq Q$. We refer to R as the *padding set*. As we discuss later in this section, the requirement that the basis c in included is the padding set has two consequences: it allows us to apply the theory of well-quasi ordering to ensure termination of the backward analysis (see Lemma 1); it gives us a natural way to define *accelerations* to speed up the symbolic computation of predecessors (see Section 4.1). Notice that an SCC need not represent an upward closed set of configurations. Indeed, the environment R may be a strict subset of the set of all states. For instance, if $Q = \{a, b, c\}$ then the denotation of the SCC $(aa, \{a, b\})$ contains strings like $aa, aba, abab, \ldots$ but it does not include any strings with c even if they contain aa as a substring (i.e. $aca, abac, \ldots$ are not in its denotation).

A CC $\phi = R_0q_0\ldots q_nR_n$ can naturally be approximated by the following SCC:

$$\phi^\# = (q_0\ldots q_n, \phi^\bullet)$$

Indeed, it is immediate to check that $[\![\phi]\!] \subseteq [\![\phi^\#]\!]$. Let us now reconsider the symbolic operations (discussed in Section 3 for CC's) needed for implementing an SCC-based symbolic backward analysis.

Entailment. The entailment relation for SCC's can now be simplified as follows. For $\phi = (c, R)$ and $\phi' = (c', R')$, we have that $\phi \sqsubseteq \phi'$ iff $c \preceq c'$ and $R \supseteq R'$. We recall that $\phi \sqsubseteq \phi'$ implies $[\![\phi']\!] \subseteq [\![\phi]\!]$.

Furthermore, we can prove that $\sqsubseteq$ is a *Well Quasi-Ordering (WQO)* for SCC's, i.e., for any infinite sequence $\phi_0, \phi_1, \phi_2, \ldots$, of constraints, there are $i < j$ such that $\phi_i \sqsubseteq \phi_j$. Indeed, let ϕ_i be of the form (c_i, R_i). Since Q is finite and $R_i \subseteq Q$ for all i, it follows that there is an infinite subsequence $\phi_{i_0}, \phi_{i_1}, \phi_{i_2}, \ldots$ such that $R_{i_j} = R_{i_k}$ for all j, k. By Higman's lemma [20] (which implies that $\preceq$ is a WQO on Q^*), there are $j < k$ such that $c_{i_j} \preceq c_{i_k}$, and hence $\phi_{i_j} \sqsubseteq \phi_{i_k}$. This gives the following lemma which we use later to prove termination of our algorithm.

Lemma 1. $\sqsubseteq$ *is a WQO on the set of SCC's.*

We extend the relation $\sqsubseteq$ to sets of SCC's such that $\Phi_1 \sqsubseteq \Phi_2$ if for each $\phi_2 \in \Phi_2$ there is a $\phi_1 \in \Phi_1$ with $\phi_1 \sqsubseteq \phi_2$. Notice that $\Phi_1 \sqsubseteq \Phi_2$ implies that $[\![\Phi_2]\!] \subseteq [\![\Phi_1]\!]$.

As an example, consider the SCC $\phi = (pq, \{p, q, r\})$. Examples of configurations in $[\![\phi]\!]$ are prq and $rprprqr$. The set of bad states in Example 1 can be characterized by the SCC's $(q_4q_4, \{q_0, q_1, q_2, q_3, q_4\})$. Also, for the SCC $\phi = (pq, \{p, q, r, s\})$ and $\phi' = (qpprqp, \{p, q, r\})$, we have $\phi \sqsubseteq \phi'$.

4.1   Computing Predecessors

The abstract predecessor operator $Pre^{\#}$ is obtained as the composition of Pre and of the abstraction $\#$, i.e., $Pre^{\#}(\phi) = (Pre(\phi))^{\#}$. However, it would be inefficient to implement it in this way. Indeed, in general Pre requires the analysis and generation of several cases (as for $\exists_L$-rules). As we discuss in Section 5, the large number of generated constraints makes the exact analysis unfeasible even on simple examples. For this reason, we show next how to directly define $Pre^{\#}$ as an operator working on SCC's-constraints.

First, we introduce some notations. For a basis c and a state q, we write $c \otimes q$ to denote the set $\{c_1 q c_2 \mid c = c_1 c_2\}$. The operation adds the singleton q in an arbitrary position inside c. We define $Pre^{\#}$ by means of a set of relations $\overset{t}{\leadsto}$ defined as follows. For a transition t, we define $\overset{t}{\leadsto}$ to be the smallest relation on constraints containing the following elements:

Local. If t is a local transition of the form $q \to q'$ then

- $(c_1 q' c_2, R) \overset{t}{\leadsto} (c_1 q c_2, R \cup \{q\})$.
- $(c, R) \overset{t}{\leadsto} (c_1, R \cup \{q\})$ if $q' \in R$ and $c_1 \in (c \otimes q)$

In the first case, a process in the basis of the constraint performs a local transition from q to q'. We add q to the padding set as required by the well-formedness of SCC's-constraints. From an operational perspective, augmenting the padding set with q has an effect similar to *widening* operators used in relational analysis for unordered parameterized systems (e.g. based on polyhedra in [15]). To illustrate this, consider the rule $p \to q$ and the constraint (r, R) where $R = \{q, r\}$. The exact predecessor computation would compute an infinite sequence of the form $RpRrR$, $RrRpR$ (one occurrence of p), $RrRpRpR$, $RpRrRpR$, $RpRpRrR$ (two occurrences of p), ... Our approximated operator computes the limit of the sequence, i.e., $(rp, R \cup \{p\})$, $(pr, R \cup \{p\})$ (*at least* one occurrence of p). Thus, our abstraction plays here the role of a *widening* step for *ordered* configurations.

Exists. if t is a global transition of the form $q \to q' : \exists_L P$ then

- $(c_1 q' c_2, R) \overset{t}{\leadsto} (c_1 q c_2, R \cup \{q\})$ if $P \cap c_1^{\bullet} \neq \emptyset$.
- $(c_1 q' c_2, R) \overset{t}{\leadsto} (c_3 q c_2, R \cup \{q\})$ if $p \in P \cap R$, $p \notin c_1^{\bullet}$, $c_3 \in (c_1 \otimes p)$.
- $(c_1 p c_2, R) \overset{t}{\leadsto} (c_1 p c_3, R \cup \{q\})$ if $p \in P$, $q' \in R$, $q \notin R$, and $c_3 \in (c_2 \otimes q)$.
- $(c_1 c_2, R) \overset{t}{\leadsto} (c_1 p c_3, R \cup \{q\})$ if $p \in P$, $p \notin c_1^{\bullet}$, $q' \in R$, $q \notin R$, and $c_3 \in (c_2 \otimes q)$.

In the first case, a process in the basis of the constraint performs an existential global transition from q to q'. The transition is performed if there is a witness which is to the left of the process and which is inside the basis of the constraint. The second case is similar to the first case, except that the witness is in the padding set (and not in the left part of the basis). Therefore, we add the witness explicitly in an arbitrary position to the left of the process. In the third case, a number of processes (at least one process) in the padding set perform the transition. There is a witness which enables the transition inside the basis. The witness should be to the left of the process making the transition. In the fourth case, both the witness and the process making the transition are in the padding set. This case is similar to the third case, except that we need to add the process making the transition explicitly in the basis. In a similar manner to the local transition case, we add q to the padding to reflect the abstraction.

If t is a global transition of the form $q \to q' : \exists_R P$ or $q \to q' : \exists_{LR} P$, then analogous conditions to the previous case hold.

Forall. t is a global transition of the form $q \to q' : \forall_{LR} P$, then

- $(c_1 q' c_2, R) \stackrel{t}{\leadsto} (c_1 q c_2, (R \cap P) \cup \{q\})$, if $(c_1 c_2)^\bullet \subseteq P$.
- $(c_1 c_2, R) \stackrel{t}{\leadsto} (c_1 q c_2, (R \cap P) \cup \{q\})$, if $q' \in R$, $q \notin R$ and $(c_1 c_2)^\bullet \subseteq P$.

In the first case, a process in the basis moves from q to q'. The remaining processes in the basis must be in R. Furthermore, we restrict the padding set to those processes within R. In the second case, a process of type q in the padding set moves to q'. Notice that in both cases, the state q is added to the padding to reflect the abstraction.

If t is a global transition of the form $q \to q' : \forall_L P$, then

- $(c_1 q' c_2, R) \stackrel{t}{\leadsto} (c_1 q c_2, R \cup \{q\})$, if $c_1^\bullet \subseteq P$.
- $(c_1 c_2, R) \stackrel{t}{\leadsto} (c_1 q c_2, R \cup \{q\})$, if $q' \in R$ and $c_1^\bullet \subseteq P$.

In the first case, a process in the basis moves from q to q'. The remaining processes in the basis belong to R. In our constraints we use a single padding set to define the constraints on processes to the left and to the right of the process that makes the transition. Thus, to compute the precondition of the universal condition on the padding set we have to apply an over-approximation and use R as constraints on contexts (processes to the left should be restricted to $R \cap P$). In the second case, a process q from the padding set moves to q'. Notice that in both cases, the state q is added to the padding to reflect the abstraction. The second case is similar to the first case, except that the process that performs the transition is selected from the padding set.

If t is a global transition of the form $q \to q' : \forall_R P$, then analogous conditions to the previous case hold.

Now let $\leadsto := \bigcup_{t \in T} \stackrel{t}{\leadsto}$ and define for a constraint ϕ the set $(\phi \leadsto) := \{\phi' \mid \phi \leadsto \phi'\}$.

Lemma 2. *For any constraint ϕ, we have $Pre(\llbracket \phi \rrbracket) \subseteq \llbracket (\phi \leadsto) \rrbracket = \llbracket Pre^{\#}(\phi) \rrbracket$.*

Backward Reachability Algorithm. We use the relation $\leadsto$ to define a symbolic backward reachability algorithm for approximating solutions to PAR-COV. We start with a finite set Φ_F of SCC's denoting $\widehat{C_F}$ (notice that we can always define SCC's that describe an upward-closed set). We generate a sequence $\Phi_0 \sqsupseteq \Phi_1 \sqsupseteq \Phi_2 \sqsupseteq \cdots$ of finite sets of constraints such that $\Phi_0 = \Phi_F$, and $\Phi_{j+1} = \Phi_j \cup (\Phi_j \leadsto)$. Since $\llbracket \Phi_0 \rrbracket \subseteq \llbracket \Phi_1 \rrbracket \subseteq \llbracket \Phi_2 \rrbracket \subseteq \cdots$, the procedure terminates when we reach a point j where $\Phi_j \sqsubseteq \Phi_{j+1}$. Thus, termination of the algorithm is guaranteed by Lemma 1. Notice that the termination condition implies that $\llbracket \Phi_j \rrbracket = (\bigcup_{0 \le i \le j} \llbracket \Phi_i \rrbracket)$. By Lemmas 2, Φ_j denotes an over-approximation of the set of all predecessors of $\llbracket \Phi_F \rrbracket$. This means that if $(Init \cap \llbracket \Phi_j \rrbracket) = \emptyset$, then there exists no $c \in \llbracket \Phi_F \rrbracket$ with $Init \xrightarrow{*} c$. Thus, the algorithm can be used as a semi-test for checking PAR-COV.

Extensions. We discuss here possible extensions of the symbolic representation and of the model. The basic form of SCC's can be enriched in order to provide a more compact representation of sets of configurations. More specifically, as in [3], let us assume that individual processes have a state in Q and a set of local Boolean variables in V. Let $\mathbb{B}$ be the set of Boolean formulas with predicates in $Q \cup V$. We can work on CC-constraints of the form $R_0 b_0 R_1 \ldots b_n R_n$ $((b_0, \ldots, b_n, R)$ for SCC-constraints) where b_i is a formula in $\mathbb{B}$ and R_i (R) is a subset of formulas in $\mathbb{B}$. Now the basis describes a finite set of configurations with n processes and each set R_i gives constraints either on the state or on the local variables for processes occurring in the context. Furthermore, we can extend the exact/approximated symbolic computation of predecessors to rules with other synchronization mechanisms like *broadcast* communication and read/write operations on globally shared variables either with range in a finite domain or in the natural numbers. Operations on the latter type of shared variables can be obtained by using synchronization with special processes with state *zero*/*one*: increment is modelled via synchronization with a *zero* process that moves to *one*, decrement via synchronization with a *one* process that moves to *zero*, and zero test is modelled via a global condition "*there are no processes with state one*". The current value of the shared variable is the number of occurrence of processes in state *one*. Thus, this kind of variables may range over an unbounded set of natural numbers.

5   Experimental Results

We have implemented the verification procedures based on CC and SCC (see Table 1) and compared them to PFS (monotonic abstraction). To this purpose, we used examples of cache coherence protocols, mutual exclusion algorithms, and counter based synchronization problems. In the following, we briefly discuss some of the case studies.

The examples consist of the Illinois and the DEC Firefly cache coherence protocols from [15]; the Bakery and Burns mutual exclusion algorithms used in [3]; a compact model of Szymanski algorithm with atomicity conditions from [8,25], a refinement of Szymanski algorithm from [23] (see Fig. 2), and the Gribomont-Zenner mutex from [18]. Several synchronization and reference counting examples using unbounded integer counters are also considered. These include an abstract model of the *reference counting* example for page allocation in [16], and solutions to the readers/writers problem from [27] with priorities to readers or writers. We remark that in all examples global conditions are evaluated atomically. The results are summarized in Table 2. For each example, we give

Table 1. Methods and tools listed in order of precision in the analysis

Tool	Method	Approximation	Precision	Termination
CC	backward reach.	none	exact	not guaranteed
SCC	backward reach.	abstraction of CC's	over-approx	always guaranteed
PFS	backward reach.	monotonic abst.	over-approx	always guaranteed

<table>
<tr><td>

```
var flag : array[N] of [0 − 4]
flag := (0, . . . , 0);
process p[i] =
1   non critical;
2   f[i] := 1;
3   await ∀j ≠ i.f[j] < 3;
4   f[i] := 3;
5   if ∃j ≠ i.f[j] = 1
    then
6       f[i] := 2;
7       await ∃ j ≠ i.f[j] = 4;
8       f[i] := 4;
9   else  f[i] := 4;
10 await ∀j < i.f[j] < 2;
11 critical section;
12 await ∀j > i.f[j] < 2 ∨ f[j] > 3;
13 f[i] := 0;
```

</td><td>

$States: \ Q = \{s_0, s_1, \ldots, s_{11}\}$
$Transitions:$
$instruction: \ transition$
$\quad 1: \ s_0 \to s_1$
$\quad 2: \ s_1 \to s_2$
$\quad 3: \ s_2 \to s_3 : \forall_{LR}\{s_0, s_1, s_2, s_3, s_7, s_8\}$
$\quad 4: \ s_3 \to s_4$
$5 \ then \ \ 5: \ s_4 \to s_6 : \exists_{LR}\{s_2, s_3\}$
$\quad 6: \ s_6 \to s_7$
$\quad 7: \ s_7 \to s_8 : \exists_{LR}\{s_9, s_{10}, s_{11}\}$
$\quad 8: \ s_8 \to s_9$
$5 \ else \ \ 5: \ s_4 \to s_5 : \forall_{LR}\neg\{s_2, s_3\}$
$\quad 9: \ s_5 \to s_9$
$\quad 10: \ s_9 \to s_{10} : \forall_L\{s_0, s_1, s_2, s_3\}$
$\quad 11: \ s_{10} \to s_{11} : \forall_R\neg\{s_4, s_5, s_6, s_7, s_8\}$
$\quad 12: \ s_{11} \to s_0$

$Initial \ state: \ s_0$
$Bad \ states: \ \phi = (s_{10}s_{10}, Q^*)$

</td></tr>
</table>

Fig. 2. Algorithm of Szymanski [23] (left), and its parameterized model (right)

the number of iterations performed by the reachability algorithm, the number of constraints upon termination of the algorithm, and the time (in seconds or minutes). We use _ in the appropriate fields to indicate that we had to stop the analysis after several hours.

In the simplest examples like the Bakery algorithm, each of the three methods (PFS,SCC,CC) automatically verifies mutual exclusion. However, exact analysis may diverge even on simple examples. Such a case occurs when testing mutual exclusion for the *dirty* cache line state in the DEC Firefly model of [15]. A similar behavior was already observed with HyTech [19] (a tool manipulating polyhedra that can be used for unordered models) in [15]. In more complicated examples like the algorithms of Burns and Szymanski exact analysis does not terminate.

Monotonic abstraction proved to be precise for a wide range of parameterized systems [3,5,4,6,1]. However, it returned false positives for some of the protocols in Table 2. These are the fine grained formulations of Szymanski algorithm, the reference counting model, and particular versions of readers/writers. The main steps of the spurious error trace returned by PFS (monotonic abstraction) on the algorithm of Fig. 2 are described below.

$$(s_0, s_0, s_0) \to^* (s_1, s_1, s_1) \to^* (s_1, s_1, s_3) \to (s_2, s_1, s_3) \to (s_3, s_1, s_3) \to (s_3, s_1, s_4)$$
$$\to^* (s_5, s_2, s_4) \to (s_9, s_2, s_4) \to^* (s_9, s_2, s_7) \longrightarrow_0 (s_3, s_7) \to^* (s_{10}, s_{10})$$

Table 2. Experimental results

Model	Method	# iter	# constr	ex-time	spurious trace	verified
Bakery [3]	PFS	2	2	0.01s		✓
	CC	4	3	0.01s		✓
	SCC	3	2	0.01s		✓
Illinois [15]	PFS	5	33	0.02s		✓
	CC	2	17	0.05s		✓
	SCC	7	53	0.18s		✓
Burns [3]	PFS	14	40	0.05s		✓
	CC	--	--	--	--	--
	SCC	15	48	0.02s		✓
DEC Firefly [15]	PFS	3	11	0.01s		✓
	CC	--	--	--	--	--
	SCC	5	10	0.03s		✓
Compact Szymanski [8,25]	PFS	10	17	0.1s		✓
	CC	--	--	--	--	--
	SCC	24	162	3.35s		✓
Refined Szymanski [23]	PFS	24	658	1.5 s	✓	
	CC	--	--	--	--	--
	SCC	34	641	1m		✓
Gribomont-Zenner [18]	PFS	36	197	0.2 s	✓	
	CC	--	--	--	--	--
	SCC	56	863	5m		✓
Ref. counting [16]	PFS	7	15	0.02s	✓	
	CC	--	--	--	--	--
	SCC	7	8	0.01s		✓
Readers/writers[27] (locks:no locks)	PFS	(10:5)	(31:28)	(0.05s:0.2s)	(:✓)	(✓:)
	CC	--	--	--	--	--
	SCC	(7:7)	(12:8)	(0.02s:0.01s)		(✓:✓)
Readers/writers (locks:no locks) refined, priority to readers	PFS	(21:7)	(125:67)	(0.4s:0.6s)	(:✓)	(✓:)
	CC	--	--	--	--	--
	SCC	(25:12)	(128:34)	(1.7s:0.06s)		(✓:✓)
Readers/writers (locks:no locks) refined, priority to writers	PFS	(22:9)	(683:219)	(9.4s:0.3s)	(:✓)	(✓:)
	CC	--	--	--	--	--
	SCC	(27:9)	(646:19)	(17.2s:0.03s)		(✓:✓)
Light control [27]	PFS	13	96	0.06s	✓	
	CC	--	--	--	--	--
	SCC	9	29	0.02s		✓

The step indicated with $\longrightarrow_0$ corresponds to the deletion of a process violating the universal condition of the third instruction in Fig. 2(right). The spurious error trace is due to the fact that the denotation of the constraints manipulated by PFS contain every local state. When applied to this model, the approximated SCC-based algorithm terminates without detecting error traces, i.e., mutual exclusion is verified for the refined model for any number of processes. Notice that the compact model studied in [8,25], can be verified using both PFS and SCC.

6 Conclusions and Related Work

We have presented a new algorithm for parameterized verification based on special constraints, called SCC's, that retain approximated context-sensitive information on the type of processes executing in parallel with a finite set of completely specified individuals. We apply the new algorithm to several nontrivial examples in which other types of analysis fail. Furthermore, the new algorithm performs well on most of the examples that can be verified with existing parameterized verification techniques. In this paper, we consider protocols where variable updates are non-atomic. On the other hand, we consider in [4] models where global conditions are performed non-atomically. We plan to further investigate verification methods and efficient data structures for SCC's-like context-sensitive constraints that can help to lift the non-atomicity assumptions on both variable updates and global conditions.

Related Work. The constraints used for the exact analysis are similar to the APC regular expressions studied in [11]. The verification method proposed in [11] is complementary to ours. Indeed, it is based on symbolic forward exploration with accelerations and without guarantying termination; whereas we consider here an over-approximation (based on simple context-sensitive constraints) that ensures the termination of symbolic backward exploration.

Other parameterized verification methods based on reductions to finite-state models have been applied to safety properties of mutual exclusion protocols like Szymanski's algorithm. Among these, we mention the *invisible invariants* method [8,24] and the *environment abstraction* method [13,25]. In [25] environment abstraction is applied to a formulation of Szymanski with the same assumptions as the model in [8], called *compact Szymanski* in Table 2. This model can be verified using monotonic abstraction as discussed in Section 5. The refined model [23] we consider is different in that atomic instructions do not contain both tests and assignments. This potentially introduces new race conditions making verification a harder task. It is not clear whether the refined models of Szymanski's algorithm considered in the present paper can be automatically verified using the methods suggested in [8,13].

The infinite-state reference counting example we consider in this paper is inspired by a finite-state abstraction studied in [16]: in contrast to the predicate-abstraction approach used in [16], we model reference counting for a physical page under observation via an unbounded integer shared variable, with increment, decrement, and zero-test.

Unordered models with counters can be modelled with systems working on unbounded integer variables such as in ALV [27,28] (based on the Omega library) and HyTech [19] (based on Halbwachs's polyhedra library). In these approaches extrapolation and widening operators are needed to enforce termination. This is typical for polyhedra-based methods when applied to models like DEC firefly and readers/writers. In contrast to methods like HyTech and ALV, the algorithm presented in this paper incorporates accelerations that can be applied both to ordered and unordered parameterized systems without losing termination.

References

1. Abdulla, P.A., Bouajjani, A., Cederberg, J., Haziz, F., Rezine, A.: Monotonic abstraction for programs with dynamic memory heaps. In: Gupta, A., Malik, S. (eds.) CAV 2008. LNCS, vol. 5123, pp. 341–354. Springer, Heidelberg (2008)
2. Abdulla, P.A., Čerāns, K., Jonsson, B., Tsay, Y.-K.: General decidability theorems for infinite-state systems. In: LICS 1996, pp. 313–321 (1996)

3. Abdulla, P.A., Ben Henda, N., Delzanno, G., Rezine, A.: Regular model checking without transducers. In: Grumberg, O., Huth, M. (eds.) TACAS 2007. LNCS, vol. 4424, pp. 721–736. Springer, Heidelberg (2007)
4. Abdulla, P.A., Ben Henda, N., Delzanno, G., Rezine, A.: Handling parameterized systems with non-atomic global conditions. In: Logozzo, F., Peled, D.A., Zuck, L.D. (eds.) VMCAI 2008. LNCS, vol. 4905, pp. 22–36. Springer, Heidelberg (2008)
5. Abdulla, P.A., Delzanno, G., Rezine, A.: Parameterized verification of infinite-state processes with global conditions. In: Damm, W., Hermanns, H. (eds.) CAV 2007. LNCS, vol. 4590, pp. 145–157. Springer, Heidelberg (2007)
6. Abdulla, P.A., Delzanno, G., Haziza, F., Rezine, A.: Parameterized tree systems. In: Suzuki, K., Higashino, T., Yasumoto, K., El-Fakih, K. (eds.) FORTE 2008. LNCS, vol. 5048, pp. 69–83. Springer, Heidelberg (2008)
7. Abdulla, P.A., Jonsson, B., Nilsson, M., d'Orso, J.: Regular model checking made simple and efficient. In: Brim, L., Jančar, P., Křetínský, M., Kucera, A. (eds.) CONCUR 2002. LNCS, vol. 2421, pp. 116–130. Springer, Heidelberg (2002)
8. Arons, T., Pnueli, A., Ruah, S., Xu, J., Zuck, L.: Parameterized verification with automatically computed inductive assertions. In: Berry, G., Comon, H., Finkel, A. (eds.) CAV 2001. LNCS, vol. 2102, pp. 221–234. Springer, Heidelberg (2001)
9. Boigelot, B., Legay, A., Wolper, P.: Iterating transducers in the large. In: Hunt Jr., W.A., Somenzi, F. (eds.) CAV 2003. LNCS, vol. 2725, pp. 223–235. Springer, Heidelberg (2003)
10. Bouajjani, A., Habermehl, P., Vojnar, T.: Abstract regular model checking. In: Alur, R., Peled, D.A. (eds.) CAV 2004. LNCS, vol. 3114, pp. 372–386. Springer, Heidelberg (2004)
11. Bouajjani, A., Muscholl, A., Touili, T.: Permutation Rewriting and Algorithmic Verification. Inf. and Comp. 205(2), 199–224 (2007)
12. Bultan, T., Gerber, R., Pugh, W.: Model-checking concurrent systems with unbounded integer variables: symbolic representations, approximations, and experimental results. TOPLAS 21(4), 747–789 (1999)
13. Clarke, E., Talupur, M., Veith, H.: Environment abstraction for parameterized verification. In: Emerson, E.A., Namjoshi, K.S. (eds.) VMCAI 2006. LNCS, vol. 3855, pp. 126–141. Springer, Heidelberg (2005)
14. Dams, D., Lakhnech, Y., Steffen, M.: Iterating transducers. In: Berry, G., Comon, H., Finkel, A. (eds.) CAV 2001. LNCS, vol. 2102, pp. 286–297. Springer, Heidelberg (2001)
15. Delzanno, G.: Constraint-Based Verification of Parameterized Cache Coherence Protocols. FMSD 23(3), 257–301 (2003)
16. Emmi, M., Jhala, R., Kohler, E., Majumdar, R.: Verifying reference counted objects. In: Kowalewski, S., Philippou, A. (eds.) TACAS 2009. LNCS, vol. 5505, pp. 352–367. Springer, Heidelberg (2009)
17. Finkel, A., Schnoebelen, P.: Well-structured transition systems everywhere! TCS 256(1-2), 63–92 (2001)
18. Gribomont, E., Zenner, G.: Automated verification of Szymanski's algorithm. In: Steffen, B. (ed.) TACAS 1998. LNCS, vol. 1384, pp. 424–438. Springer, Heidelberg (1998)
19. Henzinger, T.A., Ho, P.-H., Wong-Toi, H.: HyTech: A Model Checker for Hybrid Systems. STTT 1, 110–122 (1997)
20. Higman, G.: Ordering by divisibility in abstract algebras. London Math. Soc. 2(7) (3), 326–336 (1952)
21. Kesten, Y., Maler, O., Marcus, M., Pnueli, A., Shahar, E.: Symbolic model checking with rich assertional languages. TCS 256, 93–112 (2001)

22. Manna, Z., et al.: STEP: the Stanford Temporal Prover (1994)
23. Manna, Z., Pnueli, A.: An exercise in the verification of multi – process programs. Beauty is Our Business, 289–301 (1990)
24. Pnueli, A., Ruah, S., Zuck, L.: Automatic deductive verification with invisible invariants. In: Margaria, T., Yi, W. (eds.) TACAS 2001. LNCS, vol. 2031, pp. 82–97. Springer, Heidelberg (2001)
25. Talupur, M.: Abstraction techniques for parameterized verification. Ph.D thesis, CMU (2006)
26. Vardi, M.Y., Wolper, P.: An automata-theoretic approach to automatic program verification. In: LICS 1986, pp. 332–344 (1986)
27. Yavuz-Kahveci, T., Bultan, T.: A symbolic manipulator for automated verification of reactive systems with heterogeneous data types. STTT 5(1), 15–33 (2003)
28. Yavuz-Kahveci, T., Bultan, T.: Verification of parameterized hierarchical state machines using action language verifier. In: MEMOCODE 2005, pp. 79–88 (2005)

Verification of Parameterized Systems with Combinations of Abstract Domains

Naghmeh Ghafari[1], Arie Gurfinkel[2], and Richard Trefler[1]

[1] David R. Cheriton School of Computer Science, University of Waterloo
[2] Software Engineering Institute, Carnegie Mellon University

Abstract. We present a framework for verifying safety properties of parameterized systems. Our framework is based on a combination of Abstract Interpretation and a backward-reachability algorithm. A parameterized system is a family of systems in which n processes execute the same program concurrently. The problem of parameterized verification is to decide whether for all values of n the system with n processes is correct. Despite well-known difficulties in analyzing such systems, they are of significant interest as they can describe a wide range of protocols from mutual-exclusion to transactional memory. We assume that neither the number of processes nor their statespaces are bounded a priori. Hence, each process may be *infinite-state*. Our key contribution is an abstract domain in which each element (a) represents the lower bound on the number of processes at a control location and (b) employs a numeric abstract domain to capture arithmetic relations between variables of the processes. We also provide an extrapolation operator for the domain to guarantee sound termination of the backward-reachability algorithm. Our abstract domain is generic enough to be instantiated by different well-known numeric abstract domains such as octagons and polyhedra. This makes the framework applicable to a wide range of parameterized systems.

1 Introduction

A parameterized system is a family of systems in which n processes execute the same program concurrently. The problem of parameterized verification is to verify whether for all values of n the system with n processes is correct. Such systems arise naturally in many important applications ranging from communication protocols such as mutual-exclusion and leader election, to distributed systems such as web-services, to cache coherence, resource sharing, transactional memory, and others.

Parameterized system verification is highly undecidable. Apt and Kozen [3] showed that even verification of parameterized systems of finite-state processes is undecidable. This negative result has naturally directed the research in parameterized analysis towards two directions: (i) studying decidability of restricted subclasses (e.g. [15,16,17]), and (ii) developing generally applicable but semi-automated proof principles that utilize induction (e.g. [10,20]). In all of the cases above, it is assumed that each process is *finite-state*.

In this paper, we focus on the analysis of parameterized systems of infinite-state processes. This is a common setting in practice. For example, even in Lamport's bakery

D. Lee et al. (Eds.): FMOODS/FORTE 2009, LNCS 5522, pp. 57–72, 2009.

protocol [19] each process maintains an integer ticket, and, hence, has an infinite state-space. In this paper, we are interested in a sound, automated, and terminating procedure for verifying safety properties of such systems. Since this problem is undecidable, such a procedure is necessarily incomplete.

Incomplete, but sound and terminating algorithms are commonly used for reasoning about single-process infinite-state programs. They are typically developed in the framework of Abstract Interpretation [13] (AI). In this paper, we apply such a technique to parameterized systems. We present a framework that combines AI-style reasoning with a backward-reachability algorithm. Our key contribution is an abstract domain in which each element (a) represents the lower bound on the number of processes at a control location and (b) employs a numeric abstract domain to capture arithmetic relations between variables of the processes. Our abstract domain is generic enough to be instantiated by different well-known numeric abstract domains such as octagons [22] and polyhedra [14].

We present an algorithm to over-approximate backward-reachability in a parameterized system using our abstract domain. In its initial form, the algorithm is sound but it is not guaranteed to terminate. We show that there are two reasons for divergence: one comes from the fact that the numeric domain is infinite, and the other is due to the existence of an unbounded number of processes in a parameterized system. We show that it is possible to enforce sound termination of the algorithm by combining numeric widening with a new approximation operator developed especially for our purpose. This results in an algorithm that is incomplete but sound and terminating. That is, if the algorithm does not find an error state, then the system is correct. However, if the algorithm finds an error state, it is uncertain that the error actually is present in the system and is not introduced by the over-approximation. We illustrate an implementation of our algorithm on a variant of Lamport's bakery mutual-exclusion protocol (Alg. 2 in [21]).

Related work. In recent years there has been substantial interest in verification of parameterized systems over a finite (or boolean) data domain. The proposed solutions range from exact model-checking and reachability analysis for restricted classes of systems [15,16,17], to generally applicable, sound, but incomplete procedures, e.g., network invariants [20,11], and regular model checking [5,6,18]. Only a handful deal with both an infinite data domain and unbounded parameterization of processes [1,2,4,7,8].

Abdulla and Jonsson [2] consider the case of 1-clock timed systems. They show that the verification of a class of safety properties is decidable under some restrictions on the constraints used. Inspired by [2], Bozzano and Delzanno [8] present a safety verification technique for parameterized systems with unbounded *local* data variables. Their approach is based on assertions that combine multiset rewriting over first order formulas and constraints. Decidability is achieved by restricting constraints to a constant-free subclass of *difference constraints* (itself a subclass of linear arithmetic). In [1], the method of [8] is extended to GAP constraints. GAP constraints are linear constraints of the form: $x = y$, $x \leq y$, or $x + k < y$, where x and y are variables and k is a *positive* constant.

The method of [8] is generalized into an analysis framework in [4,7] by using a constrained (multiset) rewriting system on words over an infinite alphabet. In this framework, each configuration is composed from a label over a finite set of symbols and a vector of data in a potentially infinite domain. The constraints are expressed in a logic that is an extension of a monadic first order theory of the natural ordering on positive integers (corresponding to positions on the word). This logic is also parameterized with a first order theory on the considered data domain such as Presburger arithmetics. In [4,7] the authors present decidability results for satisfiability of a particular fragment of this logic. They also prove that this fragment is closed under the computations of post- and pre-images. This result together with the decidability of the satisfiability problem can be used for deciding whether a given assertion is an inductive invariant of a system.

In this paper, we present an alternative framework to the multiset rewriting framework of [4,7]. In our framework, we delegate the reasoning about constraints to Abstract Interpretation. The advantage is two-fold. First, our technique can use any constraints for which there are efficient abstract domains available. Second, the termination of the analysis is guaranteed by combining the widening operator of the abstract domain with a new approximation operator.

Many of the techniques above are based on *counter abstraction* (e.g. [12,23]). The key idea of this abstraction is to keep track only of the upper bound on the number of processes that satisfy a certain property. For example, the number of processes in the critical section. To ensure that the abstract system is finite-state, the work of [23] restricts the value of counters to either 0, 1 or infinity. In [12], counter abstraction and predicate abstraction are combined together to achieve more flexibility. However, the system model is more restrictive than ours. Our abstract domain PD can be seen as a *variant* of counter abstraction that maintains the *lower* bound on the number of processes satisfying a certain condition.

In contrast to symbolic methods for finite collections of processes with local integer variables [9], our abstract domains are defined over an unbounded collection of variables. The number of variables during the backward-search is not bounded a priori. This allows us to reason about systems with global conditions over any number of processes.

Outline of the paper. The rest of the paper is organized as follows. Syntax and semantics of parameterized systems are defined in Sec. 2. The abstract domain for parameterized systems is introduced in Sec. 3, and is followed by the backward-reachability algorithm in Sec. 4. We discuss techniques to ensure termination of our algorithm and illustrate our algorithm on Lamport's bakery protocol in Sec. 5, followed by concluding remarks in Sec. 6.

2   Parameterized Systems

We describe the system model used in the rest of the paper.

Syntax. A parameterized system $\mathcal{P}$ is a triple (Q, V, T), where Q is a finite set of control locations, V is a finite set of variables, and T is a finite set of guarded commands (or rules). Each $\tau \in T$ is of the form:

$$\tau : q \xrightarrow{g} q' \qquad\qquad \text{(guarded command)}$$

where $q, q' \in Q$, and g is a guard. We allow for three types of guards: local, universal global, and existential global that are defined below.

$$\tau_1 : q_1 \xrightarrow{g_1} q_2, \ g_1 : (\texttt{self}.x' = \texttt{self}.x + 1) \wedge (\texttt{self}.y' = \texttt{self}.y)$$

$$\tau_2 : q_1 \xrightarrow{g_2} q_3, \ g_2 : \forall \texttt{other} \neq \texttt{self} : (\texttt{other}.\mathbf{pc} = q_3) \wedge (\texttt{self}.x' = \texttt{self}.x) \wedge$$
$$(\texttt{self}.y' = \texttt{self}.y - 2) \wedge (\texttt{other}.x > 0)$$

$$\tau_3 : q_3 \xrightarrow{g_3} q_1, \ g_3 : \exists \texttt{other} \neq \texttt{self} : (\texttt{other}.\mathbf{pc} = q_3) \wedge (\texttt{self}.x' = \texttt{self}.x) \wedge$$
$$(\texttt{self}.y' = \texttt{self}.y) \wedge (\texttt{other}.y - \texttt{other}.x > 2) \wedge$$
$$(\texttt{other}.x > 1)$$

Fig. 1. An example of a parameterized system $\mathcal{P}_1 = (\{q_1, q_2, q_3\}, \{x, y\}, \{\tau_1, \tau_2, \tau_3\})$

We write V' for the set $\{x' \mid x \in V\}$, and $\texttt{self}.V$ and $\texttt{other}.V$ for the set $\{\texttt{self}.x \mid x \in V\}$ and $\{\texttt{other}.x \mid x \in V\}$, respectively. A *local guard* is an expression on $\texttt{self}.(V \cup V')$ constraining current and next local states of a single process. The *universal* and *existential global guards* are, respectively, expressions of the following form:

$$\forall \texttt{other} \neq \texttt{self} : (\texttt{other}.\mathbf{pc} = q_o) \wedge \theta \qquad \exists \texttt{other} \neq \texttt{self} : (\texttt{other}.\mathbf{pc} = q_o) \wedge \theta$$

where q_o is a control location in Q, $\texttt{other}.\mathbf{pc}$ is a special variable, and θ is an expression over $\texttt{self}.(V \cup V') \cup \texttt{other}.V$ variables. Intuitively, commands with local guards express how a process behaves independently of other processes in the system, commands with global guards allow a process to reference variables and control locations of the other processes in either universal or existential form. These three types of guarded commands are sufficient to express a wide variety of parameterized systems [1].

An example of a parameterized system where each process manipulates integer variables is shown in Fig. 1. It consists of three commands: τ_1 with a local guard g_1, τ_2 with a universal guard g_2, and τ_3 with an existential guard g_3. Informally, a process executing τ_1 changes its control location from q_1 to q_2, increments local variable x, and does not change local variable y. Similarly, a process executing τ_2 goes from q_1 to q_3 but only if all other currently executing processes are in q_3 and the value of their copies of the variable x are positive. Furthermore, execution of τ_2 decrements the y variable of the current process by 2. Finally, a process executing τ_3 changes its control location from q_3 to q_1 but only if there exists another process that is at q_3 and whose variable x is greater than 1 and the difference between variables y and x of that process is greater than 2. During this transition, variables x and y of the executing process do not change.

We formalize the semantics of parameterized systems using transition systems.

Semantics. A *process state* is a pair (q, v), where $q \in Q$ and v is a valuation assigning values to variables in V. We often treat a process state $u = (q, v)$ as a valuation of variables $V \cup \{\mathbf{pc}\}$ such that $u(\mathbf{pc}) = q$, and $u(y) = v(y)$ for all $y \in V$. An n-*process configuration* is a tuple $\langle u_1, \ldots, u_n \rangle$, where each u_i is a process state. We refer to the first (left-most) process in a configuration as P_1, to the second as P_2, etc, and refer to the number of the process as a process id (PID). So PID of P_1 is 1, PID of P_2 is 2, etc. For two configurations $c_1 = \langle u_1, \ldots, u_n \rangle$ and $c_2 = \langle w_1, \ldots, w_m \rangle$, we use $c_1 \cdot c_2$ to denote their concatenation $\langle u_1, \ldots, u_n, w_1, \ldots, w_m \rangle$.

For an expression θ, we write $\theta[x \leftarrow y]$ for the result of substituting y for x in θ. A valuation σ is a model of an expression θ over V, written $\sigma \models \theta$, if θ is satisfied by σ, i.e., $\theta[x \leftarrow \sigma(x) \mid x \in X]$ is valid. For example, let $\sigma = \{x \mapsto 5, y \mapsto 10\}$, then $\sigma \models (x < y)$, and $\sigma \not\models (x + y = 10)$. For a triple of valuations σ_c, σ_n, and σ_o over V, we write $(\sigma_c, \sigma_n, \sigma_o)$ for a valuation σ over $\texttt{self}.V \cup \texttt{self}.V' \cup \texttt{other}.V$ defined as $\sigma(\texttt{self}.y) \triangleq \sigma_c(y)$, $\sigma(\texttt{self}.y') \triangleq \sigma_n(y)$, and $\sigma(\texttt{other}.y) \triangleq \sigma_o(y)$. We write (σ_c, σ_n) for short when σ_o is irrelevant.

Let n be a natural number and $\mathcal{P} = (Q, V, T)$ a parameterized system. An n-process instance of $\mathcal{P}$ is a transition system $\mathcal{T}_n(\mathcal{P}) = (C_n, \Delta_n)$, where C_n is the set of all n-process configurations, and $\Delta_n \subseteq C_n \times C_n$ is a transition relation. Intuitively, a pair of configurations c and c' are in Δ_n if c' is reachable from c via an execution of a guarded command by a single process. For each $\tau \in T$ of the form $q \xrightarrow{g} q'$, let Δ_n^τ be defined such that $(c, c') \in \Delta_n^\tau$ iff $c = c_1 \cdot \langle u \rangle \cdot c_2$, $c' = c_1 \cdot \langle u' \rangle \cdot c_2$, and the following holds:

- g is a local guard and $(u, u') \models g$, or
- g is a universal global guard and $\forall u_o \in (c_1 \cdot c_2) : (u, u', u_o) \models g$, or
- g is an existential global guard and $\exists u_o \in (c_1 \cdot c_2) : (u, u', u_o) \models g$.

Then, $\Delta_n \triangleq \bigcup_{\tau \in T} \Delta_n^\tau$.

For example, consider the parameterized system $\mathcal{P}_1$ given in Fig. 1. Let $c_1 = \langle (q_1, (x \mapsto 4, y \mapsto 6)) \rangle$ and $c_2 = \langle (q_2, (x \mapsto 5, y \mapsto 6)) \rangle$ be 1-process configurations. Then, $(c_1, c_2) \in \Delta_1^{\tau_1}$. Let $c_3 = \langle (q_3, (x \mapsto 4, y \mapsto 5)), (q_3, (x \mapsto 2, y \mapsto 7)) \rangle$ and $c_4 = \langle (q_1, (x \mapsto 4, y \mapsto 5)), (q_3, (x \mapsto 2, y \mapsto 7)) \rangle$ be 2-process configurations. Then, $(c_3, c_4) \in \Delta_2^{\tau_3}$.

In this paper, we work with a single transition system instead of many instances. We use $\mathcal{T}(\mathcal{P}) \triangleq (C, \Delta)$, where $C \triangleq \bigcup_{n \in \mathbb{N}} C_n$, and $\Delta \triangleq \bigcup_{n \in \mathbb{N}} \Delta_n$. Note that $\mathcal{T}(\mathcal{P})$ contains all n-instantiations of $\mathcal{P}$ as sub-systems.

Reachability Problem. The reachability problem of parameterized systems is: given a set of *initial* states $I \subseteq C$, and a set of *error* states $E \subseteq C$, decide whether there exist two configurations $c_i \in I$ and $c_e \in E$ such that there is a path from c_i to c_e in $\mathcal{T}$. This formulation is equivalent to a more common one of deciding whether there exists an $n \in \mathbb{N}$, such that an error configuration is reachable from an initial configuration in $\mathcal{T}_n(\mathcal{P})$. It is well-known that the verification of any safety property can be reduced to a reachability problem.

A backward-reachability-based algorithm is: given a set of error configurations E, compute an over-approximation of the set of all configurations that can reach E, denoted by R, then, decide whether the intersection of I and R is empty. In the rest of the paper, we only focus on computing R. All of the computation of our algorithm is done using a specialized abstract domain that we describe in the next section.

3   Abstract Domains for Parameterized Systems

We give a brief overview of numeric abstract domains and introduce our new domains for representing configurations of parameterized systems.

Abstract Domains. We provide a brief overview of the basics of Abstract Interpretation [13]. For the purpose of this paper, an *abstract domain* [13] A is a collection of elements equipped with a concretization function γ_A that maps each element of A to a set of concrete elements. We assume that A is equipped with two computable functions: an *abstract ordering* $\sqsubseteq_A$: $A \times A \rightarrow \{\text{true}, \text{false}\}$, and a *join* $\sqcup_A : A \times A \rightarrow A$ that over-approximate subset ordering and union, respectively:

$$a \sqsubseteq_A b \Rightarrow \gamma_A(a) \subseteq \gamma_A(b) \qquad a \sqcup_A b = c \Rightarrow (\gamma_A(a) \cup \gamma_A(b)) \subseteq \gamma(c) \qquad \text{(soundness)}$$

A well-known class of *numerical abstract domains* captures arithmetic (typically linear) relations between variables in a concrete domain. We use octagon [22] as an example of a numeric domain. For a set of variables V, elements of the *octagon* domain [22] $\text{OCT}(V)$ are conjunctions of constraints of the form $(\pm x \pm y \leq c)$, where $x, y \in V$ and c is a constant. The concretization γ_{OCT} maps a conjunction of constraints to a set of valuations, e.g., $\gamma_{\text{OCT}}(x \leq 3) = \{\sigma \in V \rightarrow \mathbb{N} \mid \sigma(x) \leq 3\}$. Abstract ordering is implemented with implication, e.g., $(x \leq 3) \sqsubseteq_{\text{OCT}} (x \leq 4)$ since $x \leq 3 \Rightarrow x \leq 4$. Join of two octagons is the smallest octagon containing their union. For example, $(x = 3) \sqcup_{\text{OCT}} (x = 5)$ is an octagon $3 \leq x \leq 5$ that can also be written as $-x \leq -3 \wedge x \leq 5$. We use this domain for all of the examples in the paper. However, our results extend to other domains such as polyhedra [14] (conjunctions of linear inequalities) and sets of octagons or polyhedra as well.

Parametric Abstract Domain PD. In this section, we define an abstract domain PD, called the *parametric domain*, that captures information about control locations of configurations of a parameterized system. In the rest of this section, we fix a parameterized system $\mathcal{P}$, and use Q to denote its control locations. Elements of PD are called *abstract locations*. Each element $s \in \text{PD}$ is a map $Q \rightarrow 2^{\mathbb{N}}$ such that $s[q]$ is finite for all $q \in Q$ and for $q, q' \in Q$, if $q \neq q'$ then $s[q] \cap s[q'] = \emptyset$. Intuitively, $s[q]$ represents the processes that are currently at q. For example, let

$$s_1 = (q_1 \mapsto \{1\}, q_2 \mapsto \{2, 3\}) \qquad (\star)$$

Intuitively, s_1 represents all concrete configurations in which there are *at least* three processes: one at q_1, and two at q_2. Note that the actual numeric PIDs are irrelevant and are only used for reference as we show below.

Let s be in PD. We write $\text{PROC}(s)$ for the set of all PIDs appearing in s. Formally, $\text{PROC}(s) \triangleq \bigcup_{q \in Q} s[q]$. We write $|s|$ for $|\text{PROC}(s)|$, and $\text{PC}(i, s)$ for the control location of process i, i.e., $\text{PC}(i, s) = q$ iff $i \in s[q]$. For example, for s_1 above, $\text{PROC}(s_1) = \{1, 2, 3\}, |s_1| = 3$, and $\text{PC}(1, s_1) = q_1$. Without loss of generality, we assume whenever $|s| = m$, then $\text{PROC}(s) = \{1, .., m\}$.

In the rest of this section, we formalize the definitions of concretization, abstract ordering, and join for this domain. Intuitively, $\gamma_{\text{PD}}(s)$ is the set of all configurations that have at least $|s[q]|$ processes at q, for all $q \in Q$. Formally, let $c = \langle (q_1, v_1), \ldots, (q_n, v_n) \rangle$ be a configuration, $s \in \text{PD}$ such that $|s| = m \leq n$, and $h : \{1, .., m\} \rightarrow \{1, .., n\}$ be an injection. We say that c satisfies s under h, written $c \models_h s$ iff

$$\forall i \in \text{PROC}(s) : \text{PC}(i, s) = q_{h(i)}$$

We define $\gamma_{\text{PD}}(s) \triangleq \{c \mid \exists h : c \models_h s\}$. It is easy to see that this definition captures our intuition. For example, let $c_1 = \langle (q_1, v_1), (q_2, v_2), (q_1, v_3), (q_2, v_4) \rangle$, where $\{v_i\}$ are arbitrary valuations, and $h = \{1 \mapsto 1, 2 \mapsto 2, 3 \mapsto 4\}$. Then, $c_1 \models_h s_1$; thus, $c_1 \in \gamma_{\mathrm{PD}}(s_1)$.

For two abstract locations s and t, if for all $q \in Q$, $|t[q]| \leq |s[q]|$, then t approximates more concrete configurations. We define the ordering $\sqsubseteq_{\mathrm{PD}}$ as:

$$s \sqsubseteq_{\mathrm{PD}} t \Leftrightarrow (\forall q \in Q : |t[q]| \leq |s[q]|)$$

For example, let $s_2 = (q_1 \mapsto \{2\}, q_2 \mapsto \{1\})$ and $s_3 = (q_1 \mapsto \{1,2\}, q_2 \mapsto \{3\})$. Then, $s_3 \sqsubseteq_{\mathrm{PD}} s_2$, but $s_3 \not\sqsubseteq_{\mathrm{PD}} s_1$ and $s_1 \not\sqsubseteq_{\mathrm{PD}} s_3$. Note that the abstract domain PD is not a lattice. Thus, the Galois connection framework of AI (Example 4.6 in [13]) is not applicable. Therefore, we follow a more general framework of Abstract Interpretation [13] that allows for an abstract domain to be a pre-order.

Let $\top_{\mathrm{PD}}$ be defined as an element s such that for all $q \in Q, s[q] = \emptyset$. Then, $\top_{\mathrm{PD}}$ is the $\sqsubseteq_{\mathrm{PD}}$-largest element of PD. For $s, t \in$ PD, we define the join as $s \sqcup_{\mathrm{PD}} t = t$ if $s \sqsubseteq_{\mathrm{PD}} t$ and $\top_{\mathrm{PD}}$ otherwise. At a first glance, our definition of join may look too imprecise. However, our analysis algorithm (see BACKREACH in Sec. 4) only applies the join $s \sqcup_{\mathrm{PD}} t$ under the assumption that $s \sqsubseteq_{\mathrm{PD}} t$.

Theorem 1. *The abstract ordering $\sqsubseteq_{\mathrm{PD}}$ and the join $\sqcup_{\mathrm{PD}}$ are sound.*

The proof of the theorems can be found in the appendix. In the next section, we show how to extend the domain PD with a numeric (or even an arbitrary) abstract domain.

Abstract Domain PD(A). We combine the parametric domain PD with an abstract domain A. The new domain is called PD(A). For clarity of presentation, we assume that A is a numerical abstract domain. We call elements of PD(A) *abstract global states* (AGS). An AGS is of the form (s, ψ), where $s \in$ PD and $\psi \in A$. Intuitively, s captures the control location information and ψ captures numerical constraints on process variables. For an AGS $r = (s, \psi)$, we write $\mathrm{loc}(r)$ for the abstract location s.

In the rest of the section, we fix a parameterized system $\mathcal{P} = (Q, V, T)$. For $x \in V$, we write $P_i.x$ to refer to the variable x of process i. We require that for every element $(s, \psi) \in$ PD(A), ψ is an expression over variables in the set $\{P_i.x \mid x \in V, i \in \mathrm{PROC}(s)\}$. For example, an AGS $(s_1, P_1.x < P_2.y)$, where s_1 is as defined in ($\star$), represents all concrete configurations that satisfy s_1 and, additionally, have a process i in state q_1 and a process j in state q_2 such that $P_i.x < P_j.y$. Note that i and j are not necessarily 1 and 2, since the PIDs in the abstract global states are only used for reference and do not directly correspond to PIDs in concrete configurations.

We now proceed to define $\gamma_{\mathrm{PD(A)}}$ formally. For a function $h : \mathbb{N} \to \mathbb{N}$ and an expression ψ, we write $h(\psi)$ for the result of permuting all process references in ψ according to h, i.e., $h(\psi) \triangleq \psi[P_i \leftarrow P_{h(i)} \mid i \in \mathbb{N}]$. Let $c = \langle u_1, \ldots, u_n \rangle$ be a concrete configuration. We write σ_c for a valuation corresponding to the configuration c, defined as follows: $\sigma_c(P_j.x) \triangleq u_j(x)$. Let (s, ψ) be an AGS, such that $|s| = m$ and $m \leq n$, and $h : \{1, .., m\} \to \{1, .., n\}$ be an injection. We say that c satisfies (s, ψ) under h, written, $c \models_h (s, \psi)$ iff $c \models_h s \wedge \sigma_c \models h(\psi)$. Finally, we define $\gamma_{\mathrm{PD(A)}}((s, \psi)) \triangleq \{c \mid \exists h : c \models_h (s, \psi)\}$.

We now describe the ordering $\sqsubseteq_{\mathrm{PD(A)}}$. Let s, t be in PD, such that $s \sqsubseteq_{\mathrm{PD}} t$. We write, $\mathcal{U}(s, t)$ for the set of all functions h such that (a) h is an injection from $\{1, .., |t|\}$ to $\{1, .., |s|\}$, and (b) for all $i \in \mathrm{PROC}(t) : i \in t[q] \Rightarrow h(i) \in s[q]$. That is, h maps each process of t to an equivalent process of s. For example, let $s_4 = (q_1 \mapsto \{1, 2\})$, and $s_5 = (q_1 \mapsto \{1\})$, then $\mathcal{U}(s_4, s_5) = \{h_1, h_2\}$, where $h_1 = \{1 \mapsto 1\}$ and $h_2 = \{1 \mapsto 2\}$. Note that if $s \sqsubseteq_{\mathrm{PD}} t$, then $\mathcal{U}(s, t)$ is not empty. The ordering $\sqsubseteq_{\mathrm{PD(A)}}$ is defined as:

$$(s, \psi) \sqsubseteq_{\mathrm{PD(A)}} (t, \varphi) \Leftrightarrow s \sqsubseteq_{\mathrm{PD}} t \wedge \exists h \in \mathcal{U}(s, t) : \psi \sqsubseteq_A h(\varphi)$$

For example, let $\psi_1 = ((P_1.x > 0) \wedge (P_2.x > 4))$, and $\psi_2 = (P_1.x > 1)$, then $(s_4, \psi_1) \sqsubseteq_{\mathrm{PD(A)}} (s_5, \psi_2)$, since ψ_1 implies $h_2(\psi_2) = (P_2.x > 1)$.

The $\sqsubseteq_{\mathrm{PD(A)}}$-largest element is $(\top_{\mathrm{PD}}, \top_A)$, where $\top_A$ is the $\sqsubseteq_A$-largest element of A. The join $\sqcup_{\mathrm{PD(A)}}$ is defined as:

$$(s, \psi) \sqcup_{\mathrm{PD(A)}} (t, \varphi) \triangleq \begin{cases} (s, \psi \sqcup_A h(\varphi)) & s \sqsubseteq_{\mathrm{PD}} t \wedge t \sqsubseteq_{\mathrm{PD}} s \\ \top_{\mathrm{PD(A)}} & \text{otherwise} \end{cases}$$

where h is any injection in $\mathcal{U}(s, t)$. Intuitively, we use the join $\sqcup_A$ of A to join the constraints of the variables, while aligning PIDs between s and t. Note that a different choice for h affects precision but not soundness of the join. In practice, it is best to pick an h that leads to the $\sqsubseteq_{\mathrm{PD(A)}}$-least result. As with PD, it is possible to define join more precisely, but it was not needed for our algorithm.

Theorem 2. *The abstract ordering $\sqsubseteq_{\mathrm{PD(A)}}$ and the join $\sqcup_{\mathrm{PD(A)}}$ are sound.*

Elements of PD(A) concisely represent (possibly infinite) sets of configurations of a concrete parameterized system. This domain is the basis of our backward-reachability algorithm that we present in the next section.

4   Backward-Reachability Analysis

We present the BACKREACH algorithm for over-approximating the backward-reachability in parameterized systems. We begin with an overview of the algorithm, then discuss its main step, i.e. computation of the pre-image, and conclude with an example.

Overview. The algorithm BACKREACH is shown in Fig. 2. As inputs, it takes a set Trans of guarded commands and an AGS e. The output is a set of AGSs that over-approximates all concrete configurations from which e is reachable.

The algorithm uses the list RL to keep track of all states seen so far, and a work list WL to keep track of all states to be explored. When WL becomes empty, the algorithm terminates. In each iteration, a state (s, ψ) is chosen from WL (lines 3–4), its predecessors are computed (lines 6–7), and are added to RL and WL lists if needed (lines 8–19). The computation of the predecessors is done using the function Pre, which is described in details below. The algorithm ensures that RL contains only one state for each abstract location by joining the AGSs with the same abstract locations (line 17).

In the rest of this section, we describe the implementation of the pre-image computation (line 7 of BACKREACH algorithm). First, we describe the operation for the domain PD, and then extend it to PD(A).

Pre-Image for PD. Let s be an element of PD, $\tau : q \xrightarrow{g} q'$ a guarded command, and i a PID. The result of pre-image operation $\mathrm{Pre}_{\mathrm{PD}}(s, \tau, i)$ is a set B of elements of PD that over-approximates all states from which a state in $\gamma(s)$ is reachable by process i executing τ. There are three cases, based on the type of the guard g.

```
 1: Set of AGS BACKREACH (Set Trans, AGS e)
 2:    WL ← {e}, RL ← {e}
 3:    forall (s, ψ) ∈ WL do
 4:        WL ← WL \ {(s, ψ)}
 5:        P ← ∅
 6:        forall {τ ∈ Trans, i ∈ PROC(s) | τ = (q →ᵍ q') and i ∈ s[q']} do
 7:            P ← P ∪ Pre((s, ψ), τ, i)
 8:        forall r ∈ P do
 9:            skip ← false, saved ← null
10:            forall u ∈ RL do
11:                if r ⊑_PD(A) u then
12:                    skip ← true, break
13:                if loc(r) = loc(u) then
14:                    saved ← u
15:            if skip = false then
16:                if saved ≠ null then
17:                    RL ← (RL \ {saved}) ∪ {saved ⊔_PD(A) r}, WL ← WL ∪ {saved ⊔_PD(A) r}
18:                else
19:                    RL ← RL ∪ {r}, WL ← WL ∪ {r}
20:    return RL
```

Fig. 2. The BACKREACH algorithm

Case 1. g is a local guard. If s is an abstract location obtained by process P_i executing τ, then, P_i is in state q' in s. Furthermore, P_i must have been in state q before executing τ. To formalize this, we define a helper function $\text{MOVEPROC}(s, i, q_1, q_2)$ that moves process i in s from location q_1 to location q_2: $\text{MOVEPROC}(s, i, q_1, q_2) \triangleq t$, where $t[q_1] = s[q_1] \setminus \{i\}$, $t[q_2] = s[q_2] \cup \{i\}$, and $t[q] = s[q]$ otherwise. Then,

$$\text{Pre}_{\text{PD}}(s, \tau, i) \triangleq \begin{cases} \{\text{MOVEPROC}(s, i, q', q)\} & \text{if } i \in s[q'] \\ \emptyset & \text{otherwise.} \end{cases}$$

For example, let $s_1 = (q_1 \mapsto \{1\}, q_2 \mapsto \{2, 3\})$, and $\tau = q_1 \overset{true}{\to} q_2$. Then, $\text{Pre}_{\text{PD}}(s_1, \tau, 1) = \emptyset$, and $\text{Pre}_{\text{PD}}(s_1, \tau, 2) = (q_1 \mapsto \{1, 2\}, q_2 \mapsto \{3\})$.

Case 2. g is a universal global guard: $\forall \text{other} \neq \text{self} : (\text{other.pc} = q_o) \wedge \theta$. Then, the pre-image computation is similar to Case 1 except that all processes other than i must be in control location q_o in s. Thus, $\text{Pre}_{\text{PD}}(s, \tau, i) \triangleq \{\text{MOVEPROC}(s, i, q', q)\}$, if $i \in s[q']$ and $\forall j \in \text{PROC}(s) \setminus \{i\} : \text{PC}(s, j) = q_o$, and $\emptyset$ otherwise.

Case 3. g is an existential global guard: $\exists \text{other} \neq \text{self} : (\text{other.pc} = q_o) \wedge \theta$. Then, τ can only be executed from an abstract location that has a process different from i at location q_o. The computation of Pre_{PD} is partitioned based on the choice of that other process. The other process can be either a process in $\text{PROC}(s)$, or a new process with PID $(|s| + 1)$. Let

$$\text{Pre}_{\text{PD}}(s, \tau, i) \triangleq \bigcup_{j \in s[q_o] \setminus \{i\}} \text{OPre}_{\text{PD}}(s, \tau, i, j) \cup \text{OPre}_{\text{PD}}(s, \tau, i, |s| + 1)$$

where $\text{OPre}_{\text{PD}}(s, \tau, i, j)$ is the pre-image under the assumption that P_j is the other process. We define another helper function called $\text{MOVEADDPROC}(s, i, q_1, q_2, j, q_3)$ that in addition to moving process i from q_1 to q_2 adds a new process j to q_3: $\text{MOVEADDPROC}\ (s, i, q_1, q_2, j, q_3) \triangleq t$, where $t[q_1] = s[q_1] \setminus \{i\}$, $t[q_2] = s[q_2] \cup \{i\}$, $t[q_3] = s[q_3] \cup \{j\}$, and $t[q] = s[q]$ otherwise. Then,

$$\text{OPre}_{\text{PD}}(s, \tau, i, j) \triangleq \begin{cases} \{\text{MOVEPROC}(s, i, q', q)\} & \text{if } j \in s[q_o] \setminus \{i\} \\ \{\text{MOVEADDPROC}(s, i, q', q, j, q_o)\} & \text{if } j = |s| + 1 \\ \emptyset & \text{otherwise.} \end{cases}$$

For example, let $\tau_1 = q_1 \xrightarrow{g_1} q_2$ and $g_1 : \exists\text{other} \neq \text{self} : (\text{other.pc} = q_2) \wedge \theta$. Then, $\text{Pre}_{\text{PD}}(s_1, \tau_1, 2)$ is the union of $\text{OPre}_{\text{PD}}(s, \tau, 2, 3)$ and $\text{OPre}_{\text{PD}}(s, \tau, 2, 4)$ where $\text{OPre}_{\text{PD}}(s, \tau, 2, 3) = (q_1 \mapsto \{1, 2\}, q_2 \mapsto \{3\})$ and $\text{OPre}_{\text{PD}}(s, \tau, 2, 4) = (q_1 \mapsto \{1, 2\}, q_2 \mapsto \{3, 4\})$.

Theorem 3. *The pre-image operation of* PD *is sound.*

Pre-Image for PD(A). We assume that the domain A has a pre-image operation $\text{Pre}_A(\psi, R)$ that takes an element of the domain $\psi \in A$, and a relation R described by an expression over primed and unprimed variables. It returns an abstract element that over-approximates the pre-image of $\gamma_A(\psi)$ over R. Many numeric domains satisfy this assumption. For example, in OCT, $\text{Pre}_{\text{OCT}}(x \geq 1, x' = x + 1)$ is $x \geq 0$.

Let (s, ψ) be an element of PD(A) and $\tau : q \xrightarrow{g} q'$ a guarded command. The pre-image operation in PD(A) is defined using the following templates. If g is either local or universal, then

$$\text{Pre}_{\text{PD(A)}}((s, \psi), \tau, i) \triangleq \text{Pre}_{\text{PD}}(s, \tau, i) \times \text{Pre}_A(\psi, R_i)$$

and if g is existential then $\text{Pre}_{\text{PD(A)}}((s, \psi), \tau, i)$ is defined similar to Pre_{PD} where

$$\text{OPre}_{\text{PD(A)}}((s, \psi), \tau, i, j) \triangleq \text{OPre}_{\text{PD}}(s, \tau, i, j) \times \text{Pre}_A(\psi, R_{i,j})$$

where i, j are PIDs, and $R_i, R_{i,j}$ are relations defined based on g as described below.

Case 1. g is a local guard. Assume $g = \theta$, where θ is an expression over $\text{self.}(V \cup V')$. Let Θ_i and Γ_i be defined as follows:

$$\Theta_i \triangleq \theta[\text{self} \leftarrow P_i] \qquad \Gamma_i \triangleq \bigwedge_{j \in (\text{PROC}(s) \setminus \{i\})} \bigwedge_{x \in V} P_j.x' = P_j.x$$

Then, $R_i \triangleq \Theta_i \wedge \Gamma_i$. Intuitively, Θ_i instantiates the guard to process i, and Γ_i ensures that the variables of processes other than i are not affected. For example, let (s_1, ψ_1) be an AGS where s_1 is as defined in $(\star)$ and $\psi_1 = ((P_1.x > 0) \wedge (P_2.x > 1) \wedge (P_3.x > 2))$. Let $\tau_1 = q_1 \xrightarrow{g_1} q_2$ and $g_1 : x' = x + 1$. Then, $\text{Pre}_{\text{PD(A)}}((s_1, \psi_1), \tau, 2) = ((q_1 \mapsto \{1, 2\}, q_2 \mapsto \{3\}), ((P_1.x > 0) \wedge (P_2.x > 0) \wedge (P_3.x > 2))$ since process P_2 is the self process.

Case 2. g is a universal global guard: $\forall\text{other} \neq \text{self} : (\text{other.pc} = q_o) \wedge \theta$, where θ is an expression over $\text{self.}(V \cup V') \cup \text{other.}V$ variables. We need to instantiate θ with two PIDs: one for self, and one for other. Let $\Theta_{i,j}$ be defined as:

Table 1. An example of a computation of BACKREACH

Name	Location	Constraints
1	$(q_2 \mapsto \{1\})$	$(P_1.x > 1) \wedge (P_1.y > 3)$
2	$(q_1 \mapsto \{1\})$	$(P_1.x > 0) \wedge (P_1.y > 3)$
3	$(q_3 \mapsto \{1, 2\})$	$(P_1.x > 0) \wedge (P_1.y > 3) \wedge (P_2.y - P_2.x > 2) \wedge (P_2.x > 1)$
4	$(q_1 \mapsto \{1\}, q_3 \mapsto \{2\})$	$(P_1.x > 0) \wedge (P_1.y > 5) \wedge (P_2.y - P_2.x > 2) \wedge (P_2.x > 1)$
5	$(q_1 \mapsto \{2\}, q_3 \mapsto \{1\})$	$(P_1.x > 0) \wedge (P_1.y > 3) \wedge (P_2.y - P_2.x > 4) \wedge (P_2.x > 1)$

$$\Theta_{i,j} \triangleq \theta[\texttt{self} \leftarrow P_i, \texttt{other} \leftarrow P_j]$$

Then, $R_i \triangleq \bigwedge_{j \in (\text{PROC}(s) \setminus \{i\})} \Theta_{i,j} \wedge \Gamma_i$. Intuitively, R_i ensures that all processes other than i satisfy the global guard but only values of process i are affected during the transition.

Case 3. g is an existential guard: $\exists \texttt{other} \neq \texttt{self} : (\texttt{other.pc} = q_o) \wedge \theta$, where θ is again an expression over $\texttt{self}.(V \cup V') \cup \texttt{other}.V$ variables. However, in this case, the pre-image operator provides a PID j to instantiate the $\texttt{other}$ process. Thus, $R_{i,j}$ is defined as $R_{i,j} \triangleq \Theta_{i,j} \wedge \Gamma_i$.

Theorem 4. *The pre-image operation of* PD(A) *is sound.*

An Example. In this section, we illustrate a run of the BACKREACH algorithm on an example using abstract domain PD(OCT). We use the parameterized system shown in Fig. 1, and let e be $((q_2 \mapsto \{1\}), ((P_1.x > 1) \wedge (P_1.y > 3)))$.

We present the AGSs computed by the algorithm in Table 1. Each row in the table represents a single AGS (s, ψ) where the first column is a numeric reference, the second is the abstract location l, and the third is the octagon constraint ψ. Row 1 of the table corresponds to e defined above. We refer to the rows of Table 1 by numeric references.

In the first iteration, the algorithm computes $\text{Pre}(e, \tau_1, 1)$ that results in the AGS (s_2, ψ_2) shown in row 2. In the second iteration, the algorithm computes $(s_3, \psi_3) = \text{Pre}((s_2, \psi_2), \tau_3, 1)$ shown in row 3. In the third iteration, τ_2 is enabled twice: once for process P_1, and once for process P_2. Row 4 shows (s_4, ψ_4), the result of pre-image of τ_2 with respect to process P_1, i.e., $\text{Pre}((s_3, \psi_3), \tau_2, 1)$. This state is subsumed by (s_2, ψ_2) since $s_4 \sqsubseteq_{\text{PD}} s_2$ and $\psi_4 \Rightarrow \psi_2$. Thus, it is not added to the list RL. Row 5 shows (s_5, ψ_5), the result of pre-image of τ_2 with respect to process P_2, i.e., $\text{Pre}((s_3, \psi_3), \tau_2, 2)$. This state is subsumed by (s_2, ψ_2) as well. The reason is slightly more complicated. First, $s_5 \sqsubseteq_{\text{PD}} s_2$. Second, the process P_2 of s_5 corresponds to the process P_1 of s_2 and $\psi_5 \Rightarrow \psi_2[P_1 \leftarrow P_2]$. Thus, this AGS is not added to the list RL.

At this point, the work list WL becomes empty and the algorithm terminates. Thus, the RL contains only the AGSs shown in the first three rows of Table 1.

BACKREACH is sound: if it terminates, it always computes the correct result.

Theorem 5. *Let* $\mathcal{P} = (Q, V, T)$ *be a parameterized system and* e *be an abstract global state. If* BACKREACH(T, e) *terminates, it returns an over-approximation of the set of backward-reachable states from* $\gamma_{\text{PD(A)}}(e)$.

BACKREACH is incomplete and may run forever. In the next section, we show how sound termination can be enforced.

5 Enforcing Convergence

There are two reasons for a possible divergence of BACKREACH. First, the numeric abstract domain A may be infinite (like octagons or polyhedra), thus BACKREACH may get stuck in an infinite numeric computation. Second, successive applications of pre-image to a transition with an existential guard may introduce unbounded numbers of processes. Here, we illustrate divergence of the BACKREACH algorithm through a set of examples and show how to enforce termination.

Numeric Divergence. We begin with an example that illustrates numeric divergence in the abstract domain $PD(OCT)$. Let $\mathcal{P} = (Q, V, T)$ where $Q = \{q\}$, $V = \{x\}$, and $T = \{\tau\}$ where τ is $q \overset{g}{\to} q$, $g : (x \geq 0) \Rightarrow (x' = x - 1)$. Let e be $((q \mapsto \{1\}), (P_1.x = 5))$. Consider the execution of BACKREACH(T, e). In the first iteration, the algorithm computes the state $((q \mapsto \{1\}), (P_1.x = 6))$. It is joined to e at line 17, resulting in

$$((q \mapsto \{1\}), ((P_1.x = 5) \sqcup_{OCT} (P_1.x = 6))) = ((q \mapsto \{1\}), (5 \leq P_1.x \leq 6))$$

Similarly, the result of the second iteration is $((q \mapsto \{1\}), (5 \leq P_1.x \leq 7))$, etc. Thus, the BACKREACH(T, e) diverges.

In AI, a common approach to force sound convergence is to use *widening* instead of join to combine the reachable states. A *widening* operator [13], denoted by ∇_A, is an operator that over-approximates join, i.e., $\forall x, y \in A : x \sqcup_A y \sqsubseteq_A x \nabla_A y$; additionally, for any increasing chain $x_0 \sqsubseteq_A x_1 \sqsubseteq_A \cdots \sqsubseteq_A x_n \cdots$ in A, the increasing chain $y_0 = x_0, \ldots, y_{n+1} = y_n \nabla_A x_{n+1}, \ldots$ stabilizes after a finite number of terms. Thus, replacing join with widening forces convergence of any least fixpoint computation.

We extend the widening operator of A to $PD(A)$ in the following way. Given two abstract global states (s, ψ) and (t, φ), then

$$(s, \psi) \nabla_{PD(A)} (t, \varphi) \triangleq \begin{cases} (s, \psi \nabla_A h(\varphi)) & \text{if } s \sqsubseteq_{PD} t \wedge t \sqsubseteq_{PD} s \\ \top_{PD(A)} & \text{otherwise.} \end{cases}$$

Theorem 6. *The operator $\nabla_{PD(A)}$ is a widening on $PD(A)$.*

In order to use this widening operator in our algorithm, we replace saved $\sqcup_{PD(A)}$ r with saved $\nabla_{PD(A)}$ (saved $\sqcup_{PD(A)}$ r) at line 17. We refer to the resulting algorithm as BACKREACH with widening.

Consider the previous example. With widening, the result of the first iteration is computed as follows:

$$\begin{aligned} &((q \mapsto \{1\}), (P_1.x = 5)) \nabla_{PD(OCT)} ((q \mapsto \{1\}), (5 \leq P_1.x \leq 6)) \\ =\ &((q \mapsto \{1\}), (P_1.x = 5) \nabla_{OCT} (5 \leq P_1.x \leq 6)) \\ =\ &((q \mapsto \{1\}), (5 \leq P_1.x)) \end{aligned}$$

The algorithm converges after a single iteration. In this case, the result happens to be the exact set of all reachable states.

Successive applications of pre-image to transitions with only local or universal guards do not increase the number of processes in the reachable abstract global states. Therefore, systems with no existential guards may only experience numerical divergence. In such systems adding widening is sufficient to enforce convergence.

Table 2. An example of a divergent computation of BACKREACH

Name	Location	Constraints
1	$(q_2 \mapsto \{1\})$	$(2 \leq P_1.x \leq 5)$
2	$(q_1 \mapsto \{1\}, q_2 \mapsto \{2\})$	$(2 \leq P_1.x \leq 5) \wedge (5 \leq P_2.x \leq 8)$
3	$(q_1 \mapsto \{1,2\}, q_2 \mapsto \{3\})$	$(2 \leq P_1.x \leq 5) \wedge (5 \leq P_2.x \leq 8) \wedge (8 \leq P_3.x \leq 11)$
4	$(q_1 \mapsto \{1,2,3\}, q_2 \mapsto \{4\})$	$(2 \leq P_1.x \leq 5) \wedge (5 \leq P_2.x \leq 8) \wedge (8 \leq P_3.x \leq 11) \wedge (11 \leq P_4.x \leq 14)$

Theorem 7. *Let $\mathcal{P} = (Q, V, T)$ be a parameterized system with no existential transition and $e \in PD(A)$. The BACKREACH(T, e) with widening terminates and returns an over-approximation of the set of backward-reachable configurations from $\gamma_{PD(A)}(e)$.*

Parametric Divergence. Consider the following example. Assume the abstract domain is PD(OCT). Let $\mathcal{P} = (Q, V, T)$ where $Q = \{q_1, q_2\}$, $V = \{x\}$, and $T = \{\tau\}$ where

$$\tau : q_1 \xrightarrow{g} q_2 \ , \ g : \exists \texttt{other} \neq \texttt{self} : (\texttt{other.pc} = q_2) \wedge (\texttt{other}.x = \texttt{self}.x - 3)$$

Let $e = ((q_2 \mapsto \{1\}), (2 \leq P_1.x \leq 5))$ as shown in row 1 of Table 2. The first iteration of BACKREACH(T, e) computes an AGS shown in row 2 of Table 2, the second, computes the AGS shown in row 3 of Table 2, etc. The algorithm does not terminate – each iteration adds a new AGS with one more process than in any AGS seen so far.

To mitigate this, we introduce an approximation operator called k-*compact*, $\rhd_k$, where $k \in \mathbb{N}$. Given an AGS (s, ψ) where $|s| > k$, $\rhd_k$ computes an AGS (t, φ) such that $(s, \psi) \sqsubseteq_{PD(A)} (t, \varphi)$ and $|t| = k$. The operator k-compact, $\rhd_k((s, \psi))$, is implemented by: (a) choosing a process, say i, in s, (b) removing i from s, and (c) existentially projecting away all variables of the form $P_i.x$ from ψ. Note that the choice of which process to drop only affects the precision and not the soundness of k-compact.

Theorem 8. *The approximation operator k-compact is sound.*

To incorporate $\rhd_k$ in the BACKREACH algorithm, we apply it after the pre-image computation at line 7. This ensures that the number of processes in each AGS never becomes larger than k.

Consider the previous example. Assume $k = 3$. Let ϕ denote the AGS computed in the third iteration (row 4 of Table 2). Assume $\rhd_3$ drops process P_3, then $\rhd_3(\phi)$ is

$$((q_1 \mapsto \{1,2\}, q_2 \mapsto \{3\}), ((2 \leq P_1.x \leq 5) \wedge (5 \leq P_2.x \leq 8) \wedge (11 \leq P_3.x \leq 14)))$$

The algorithm joins this AGS with the AGS computed in the second iteration (row 3 of Table 2) using widening and obtains

$$((q_1 \mapsto \{1,2\}, q_2 \mapsto \{3\}), ((2 \leq P_1.x \leq 5) \wedge (5 \leq P_2.x \leq 8) \wedge (8 \leq P_3.x)))$$

The algorithm terminates with an over-approximation of the set of reachable states.

Theorem 9. *Let $\mathcal{P} = (Q, V, T)$ be a parameterized system and $e \in PD(A)$. The BACKREACH(T, e) algorithm with widening and k-compact operator always terminates and returns an over-approximation of the set of backward-reachable configurations from $\gamma_{PD(A)}(e)$.*

$\tau_1 : idle \xrightarrow{g_1} choose$, $g_1 : \forall other \neq \texttt{self} : (other.\textbf{pc} \neq choose) \wedge (next' = next + 1)$

$\tau_2 : choose \xrightarrow{g_2} wait$, $g_2 : \forall other \neq \texttt{self} : (other.\textbf{pc} \neq choose) \wedge (\texttt{self}.tick' = next)$

$\tau_3 : wait \xrightarrow{g_3} pause$, $g_3 : (\texttt{self}.d' = \texttt{self}.tick - serv)$

$\tau_4 : pause \xrightarrow{g_4} pause$, $g_4 : ((\texttt{self}.d > 0) \Rightarrow (\texttt{self}.d' = \texttt{self}.d - 1))$

$\tau_5 : pause \xrightarrow{g_5} wait$, $g_5 : (\texttt{self}.d \leq 0) \wedge (\texttt{self}.tick > serv)$

$\tau_6 : pause \xrightarrow{g_6} use$, $g_6 : (serv = \texttt{self}.tick) \wedge (\texttt{self}.d \leq 0)$

$\tau_7 : use \xrightarrow{g_7} idle$, $g_7 : (next \geq serv + 1) \wedge (serv' = serv + 1)$

Fig. 3. Lamport's bakery mutual-exclusion protocol with proportional back-off

Lamport's Bakery Mutual-Exclusion Protocol. Fig. 3 shows a variant of Lamport's bakery mutual-exclusion protocol (Alg. 2 in [21]). The algorithm maintains two shared counters: *next* and *serv*, where *next* is the value of the next available ticket, and *serv* is the value of the ticket of the next process to be served. The shared variables belong to neither self nor other. We extend our framework to accommodate shared variables.

To enter the critical section, a process (i) obtains a ticket by incrementing *next* (as shown in τ_1), and storing its value in a local variable named *tick* (τ_2), (ii) picks a delay (τ_3) and spins for d steps (τ_4) and (τ_5), and (iii) enters its critical section when its ticket is being served (τ_6), i.e. its ticket value is equal to *serv*. When a process leaves the critical section, it goes back to the *idle* state and increments *serv* (τ_7).

The guards on τ_1 and τ_2 ensure that no other process changes *next* while a process is acquiring a ticket. A delay between consecutive reads of the *serv* is added to reduce network contention due to the polling of the common shared variable *serv*. In [21], the authors suggest that a reasonable delay is the number of processes already waiting to enter their critical section. The protocol ensures FIFO service by serving the processes in the same order in which they first requested it.

We have implemented the BACKREACH algorithm in JAVA using APRON library for octagon abstract domain[1].We have used this implementation to validate that the state $(idle \mapsto \{1, 2\})$ is not reachable from $(use \mapsto \{1, 2\})$. The experiments were performed on a P4 3.2 GHz machine running Linux SUSE 10.3. The computation with widening converges after 56 iterations and takes 3.475 seconds. The widening is crucial for handling τ_4 that is similar to the example in the beginning of this section.

6   Conclusion

We present a framework based on Abstract Interpretation for the analysis of safety properties of parameterized systems where each of the individual processes may be infinite-state. We introduce a new abstract domain for the parameterized systems that employs a numeric abstract domain. We describe an algorithm that over-approximates backward-reachability. We combine widening with an extrapolation operator developed for this abstract domain to enforce sound termination of the algorithm. We illustrate

---

[1] Available at http://www.swen.uwaterloo.ca/~nghafari/AIPMCTool

our technique by automatically verifying the mutual-exclusion property in a variant of Lamport's bakery protocol.

Safety verification of parameterized systems using AI-based frameworks introduces a whole family of new, sound, automatic, and terminating static analyses procedures for parameterized systems, each procedure varying the chosen abstraction and widening operator. We have implemented the BACKREACH algorithm and are currently investigating other protocols to which our analysis framework is applicable. One direction for future research is to consider other possible operators like k-compact that increase the precision of approximation by choosing the process to drop based on heuristics derived from the features of the analyzed system.

Acknowledgments. Ghafari and Trefler are supported in part by grants from the Natural Sciences and Engineering Research Council of Canada.

References

1. Abdulla, P.A., Delzanno, G., Rezine, A.: Parameterized Verification of Infinite-State Processes with Global Conditions. In: Damm, W., Hermanns, H. (eds.) CAV 2007. LNCS, vol. 4590, pp. 145–157. Springer, Heidelberg (2007)
2. Abdulla, P.A., Jonsson, B.: Verifying Networks of Timed Processes (Extended Abstract). In: Steffen, B. (ed.) TACAS 1998. LNCS, vol. 1384, pp. 298–312. Springer, Heidelberg (1998)
3. Apt, K.R., Kozen, D.C.: Limits for Automatic Verification of Finite-State Concurrent Systems. Information Processing Letters 22(6), 307–309 (1986)
4. Bouajjani, A., Habermehl, P., Jurski, Y., Sighireanu, M.: Rewriting Systems with Data. In: Csuhaj-Varjú, E., Ésik, Z. (eds.) FCT 2007. LNCS, vol. 4639, pp. 1–22. Springer, Heidelberg (2007)
5. Bouajjani, A., Habermehl, P., Vojnar, T.: Abstract Regular Model Checking. In: Alur, R., Peled, D.A. (eds.) CAV 2004. LNCS, vol. 3114, pp. 372–386. Springer, Heidelberg (2004)
6. Bouajjani, A., Jonsson, B., Nilsson, M., Touili, T.: Regular Model Checking. In: Emerson, E.A., Sistla, A.P. (eds.) CAV 2000. LNCS, vol. 1855, pp. 403–418. Springer, Heidelberg (2000)
7. Bouajjani, A., Jurski, Y., Sighireanu, M.: A Generic Framework for Reasoning About Dynamic Networks of Infinite-State Processes. In: Grumberg, O., Huth, M. (eds.) TACAS 2007. LNCS, vol. 4424, pp. 690–705. Springer, Heidelberg (2007)
8. Bozzano, M., Delzanno, G.: Beyond Parameterized Verification. In: Katoen, J.-P., Stevens, P. (eds.) TACAS 2002. LNCS, vol. 2280, pp. 221–235. Springer, Heidelberg (2002)
9. Bultan, T., Gerber, R., Pugh, W.: Model-Checking Concurrent Systems with Unbounded Integer Variables: Symbolic Representations, Approximations and Experimental Results. ACM Trans. on Programming Languages and Systems 21(4), 747–789 (1999)
10. Clarke, E.M., Grumberg, O., Browne, M.C.: Reasoning about Networks with Many Identical Finite-State Processes. In: PODC 1986, pp. 240–248 (1986)
11. Clarke, E.M., Grumberg, O., Jha, S.: Verifying Parameterized Networks. ACM Trans. Program. Lang. Syst. 19(5), 726–750 (1997)
12. Clarke, E.M., Talupur, M., Veith, H.: Environment Abstraction for Parameterized Verification. In: Emerson, E.A., Namjoshi, K.S. (eds.) VMCAI 2006. LNCS, vol. 3855, pp. 126–141. Springer, Heidelberg (2005)
13. Cousot, P., Cousot, R.: Abstract Interpretation Frameworks. J. of Logic and Computation 2(4), 511–547 (1992)

14. Cousot, P., Halbwachs, N.: Automatic Discovery of Linear Restraints Among Variables of a Program. In: POPL 1978, pp. 84–97 (1978)
15. Emerson, E.A., Kahlon, V.: Reducing Model Checking of the Many to the Few. In: McAllester, D. (ed.) CADE 2000. LNCS, vol. 1831, pp. 236–254. Springer, Heidelberg (2000)
16. Emerson, E.A., Namjoshi, K.S.: On Model Checking for Non-Deterministic Infinite-State Systems. In: LICS 1998, pp. 70–80 (1998)
17. German, S.M., Sistla, A.P.: Reasoning about Systems with Many Processes. J. of the ACM 39(3); 675–735 (1992)
18. Kesten, Y., Maler, O., Marcus, M., Pnueli, A., Shahar, E.: Symbolic Model Checking with Rich Assertional Languages. In: Grumberg, O. (ed.) CAV 1997. LNCS, vol. 1254, pp. 424–435. Springer, Heidelberg (1997)
19. Lamport, L.: "A New Solution of Dijkstra's Concurrent Programming Problem". Communication of ACM 17(8), 453–455 (1974)
20. Lesens, D., Halbwachs, N., Raymond, P.: Automatic Verification of Parameterized Linear Networks of Processes. In: POPL 1997, pp. 346–357 (1997)
21. Mellor-Crummey, J.M., Scott, M.L.: Algorithms for scalable synchronization on shared-memory multiprocessors. ACM Trans. on Computer Systems 9(1), 21–65 (1991)
22. Miné, A.: The Octagon Abstract Domain. Higher-Order and Symbolic Computation 19(1), 31–100 (2006)
23. Pnueli, A., Xu, J., Zuck, L.D.: Liveness with (0, 1, ∞)-Counter Abstraction. In: Brinksma, E., Larsen, K.G. (eds.) CAV 2002. LNCS, vol. 2404, pp. 107–122. Springer, Heidelberg (2002)

On Model-Checking Optimistic Replication Algorithms

Hanifa Boucheneb[1] and Abdessamad Imine[2]

[1] Laboratoire VeriForm, École Polytechnique de Montréal, Canada
`hanifa.boucheneb@polymtl.ca`
[2] INRIA Grand-Est & Nancy-Université, France
`imine@loria.fr`

Abstract. Collaborative editors consist of a group of users editing a shared document. The Operational Transformation (OT) approach is used for supporting optimistic replication in these editors. It allows the users to concurrently update the shared data and exchange their updates in any order since the convergence of all replicas, *i.e.* the fact that all users view the same data, is ensured in all cases. However, designing algorithms for achieving convergence with the OT approach is a critical and challenging issue. In this paper, we address the verification of OT algorithms with a model-checking technique. We formally define, using tool *UPPAAL*, the behavior and the convergence requirement of the collaborative editors, as well as the abstract behavior of the environment where these systems are supposed to operate. So, we show how to exploit some features of such systems and the tool *UPPAAL* to attenuate the severe state explosion problem. We have been able to show that if the number of users exceeds 2 then the convergence property is not satisfied for five OT algorithms. A counterexample is provided for every algorithm.

1 Introduction

Collaborative editors are a class of distributed systems, where two or more users (sites) may manipulate simultaneously some objects like texts, images, graphics, etc. In order to achieve an unconstrained group work, the shared objects are replicated at the local memory of each participating user. Every operation is executed locally first and then broadcast for execution at other sites. So, the operations are applied in different orders at different replicas of the object. This potentially leads to divergent (or different) replicas, an undesirable situation for replication-based collaborative editors. *Operational Transformation* (OT) is an approach which has been proposed to overcome the divergence problem [4]. This approach consists of an algorithm which transforms an operation (previously executed by some other site) according to local concurrent ones in order to achieve convergence. It has been used in many collaborative editors such as Joint Emacs [9] (an Emacs collaborative editor), CoWord [14] (a collaborative version of MicroSoft Word) and CoPowerPoint [14] (a collaborative version of MicroSoft PowerPoint).

D. Lee et al. (Eds.): FMOODS/FORTE 2009, LNCS 5522, pp. 73–89, 2009.
© IFIP International Federation for Information Processing 2009

As established in [12], an OT algorithm consists of two parts: (i) an *integration procedure* that is responsible for generating and propagating local operations as well as executing remote operations; (ii) a *transformation function* (called IT function) that determines how an operation is transformed against another. This function depends on the semantics of the shared document. However, if an OT algorithm is not correct then the consistency of shared data is not ensured. Thus, it is critical to verify such an algorithm in order to avoid the loss of data when broadcasting operations. According to [9], only the transformation function of a shared data needs to fulfill two properties $TP1$ and $TP2$ (explained in Section 2) in order to ensure convergence. Finding such a function and proving that it satisfies $TP1$ and $TP2$ is not an easy task. This proof is often unmanageably complicated due to the fact that an OT algorithm has infinitely many states.

In this paper, we investigate the use of a model-checking technique [1] to verify whether an OT algorithm satisfies the convergence property or not. Model-checking is a very attractive and automatic verification technique of systems. It is applied by representing the behavior of a system as a finite *state transition system*, specifying properties of interest in a temporal logic and finally exploring the state transition system to determine whether they hold or not. The main interesting feature of this technique is the production of counterexamples in case of unsatisfied properties. Several Model-checkers have been proposed in the literature. The well known are $SPIN^1$, $UPPAAL^2$ and $NuSMV^3$. Among these Model-checkers, we consider here the tool $UPPAAL$.

$UPPAAL$ is a tool suite for validation and symbolic model-checking of real-time systems. It consists of a number of tools including a graphical editor for system descriptions, a graphical simulator, and a symbolic model-checker. This choice is motivated by the interesting features of $UPPAAL$ tools [8], especially the powerful of its description model, its simulator and its symbolic model-checker. Indeed, its description model is a set of timed automata [1] extended with binary channels, broadcast channels, C-like types, variables and functions (functions can be used to abstract some complicated treatments). Its simulator is useful and convivial as it allows to get and replay, step by step, counterexamples obtained by its symbolic model-checker. Its model-checker[4], based on a forward on-the-fly method, allows to compute over 5 millions of states.

In this work, we deal with OT algorithms that have the same integration procedure but differ only by their transformation functions. To verify these algorithms, we formally describe, using $UPPAAL$, the behavior and the requirements of the replication-based collaborative editors, as well as the abstract behavior of the environment where these systems are supposed to operate. Two main models are studied and proposed for the verification of the convergence properties of OT algorithms: the *concrete model* and the *symbolic model*. The concrete model is very close to the system implementation in the sense that the selection and the

---

[1] http://spinroot.com

[2] http://www.uppaal.com

[3] http://nusmv.irst.itc.it

[4] The model-checker is used without the graphical interface.

effective execution of editing operations are performed during the construction of execution traces. However, this model runs up against a severe explosion of states (the number of signatures increases exponentially with the number of operations). We have not been able to verify some OT algorithms. The symbolic model aims to overcome the limitation of the concrete model by delaying the effective selection and execution of editing operations until the construction of symbolic execution traces of all sites is completed. Using the symbolic model, we have been able to show that if the number of sites exceeds 2 then the convergence property is not satisfied for all OT algorithms considered here. A counterexample is provided for every algorithm.

The paper starts with a presentation of the OT approach and one of the known OT algorithms proposed in the literature for synchronizing shared text documents (Section 2). Section 3 is devoted to the description of the symbolic model and its model-checking. Related work and conclusion are presented respectively in sections 4 and 5.

2   Operational Transformation Approach

2.1   Background

OT is an optimistic replication technique which allows many users (or sites) to concurrently update the shared data and next to synchronize their divergent replicas in order to obtain the same data. The updates of each site are executed on the local replica immediately without being blocked or delayed, and then are propagated to other sites to be executed again. Accordingly, every update is processed in four steps: (i) *generation* on one site; (ii) *broadcast* to other sites; (iii) *reception* on one site; (iv) *execution* on one site.

The shared object. We deal with a shared object that admits a linear structure. To represent this object we use the *list* abstract data type. A *list* is a finite sequence of elements from a data type $\mathcal{E}$. This data type is only a template and can be instantiated by many other types. For instance, an element may be regarded as a character, a paragraph, a page, a slide, an XML node, etc. Let $\mathcal{L}$ be the set of lists.

The primitive operations. It is assumed that a list state can only be modified by the following primitive operations: (i) $Ins(p, e)$ which inserts the element e at position p; (ii) $Del(p)$ which deletes the element at position p. We assume that positions are given by natural numbers. The set of operations is defined as follows:

$$\mathcal{O} = \{Ins(p, e) | e \in \mathcal{E} \text{ and } p \in \mathbb{N}\} \cup \{Del(p) | p \in \mathbb{N}\} \cup \{Nop\}$$

where Nop is the idle operation that has null effect on the list state. Since the shared object is replicated, each site will own a local state l that is altered only by local operations. The initial state, denoted by l_0, is the same for all sites. The function $Do : \mathcal{O} \times \mathcal{L} \to \mathcal{L}$, computes the state $Do(o, l)$ resulting from applying

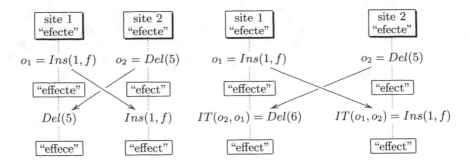

Fig. 1. Incorrect integration   **Fig. 2.** Integration with transformation

operation o to state l. We say that o is *generated* on state l. We denote by $[o_1; o_2; \ldots; o_n]$ an operation sequence. Applying an operation sequence to a list l is defined as follows: (i) $Do([], l) = l$, where $[]$ is the empty sequence and; (ii) $Do([o_1; o_2; \ldots; o_n], l) = Do(o_n, Do(\ldots, Do(o_2, Do(o_1, l))))$. Two operation sequences seq_1 and seq_2 are *equivalent*, denoted by $seq_1 \equiv seq_2$, iff $Do(seq_1, l) = Do(seq_2, l)$ for all lists l.

Definition 1. *(Causality Relation) Let an operation o_1 be generated at site i and an operation o_2 be generated at site j. We say that o_2 causally depends on o_1, denoted $o_1 \rightarrow o_2$, iff: (i) $i = j$ and o_1 was generated before o_2; or, (ii) $i \neq j$ and the execution of o_1 at site j has happened before the generation of o_2.*

Definition 2. *(Concurrency Relation) Two operations o_1 and o_2 are said to be concurrent, denoted by $o_1 \parallel o_2$, iff neither $o_1 \rightarrow o_2$ nor $o_2 \rightarrow o_1$.*

As a long established convention in OT-based collaborative editors [4, 12], the *timestamp vectors* are used to determine the causality and concurrency relations between operations. Every timestamp is a vector V of integers with a number of entries equal to the number of sites. For a site j, each entry $V[i]$ returns the number of operations generated at site i that have been already executed on site j. Let o_1 and o_2 be two operations issued respectively at sites s_{o_1} and s_{o_2} and equipped with their respective timestamp vectors V_{o_1} and V_{o_2}. The causality and concurrency relations are detected as follows: (i) $o_1 \rightarrow o_2$ iff $V_{o_1}[s_{o_1}] > V_{o_2}[s_{o_1}]$; (ii) $o_1 \parallel o_2$ iff $V_{o_1}[s_{o_1}] \leq V_{o_2}[s_{o_1}]$ and $V_{o_1}[s_{o_2}] \geq V_{o_2}[s_{o_2}]$.

2.2   Transformation Principle

A crucial issue when designing shared objects with a replicated architecture and arbitrary messages communication between sites is the *consistency maintenance* (or *convergence*) of all replicas.

Example 1. Consider the following group text editor scenario (see Fig.1): there are two users (on two sites) working on a shared document represented by a sequence of characters. These characters are addressed from 0 to the end of the document. Initially, both copies hold the string " *efecte*". User 1 executes operation $o_1 = Ins(1, f)$ to insert the character f at position 1. Concurrently, user 2 performs $o_2 = Del(5)$ to delete the character e at position 5. When o_1 is received and executed on site 2, it produces the expected string "*effect*". But, when o_2 is received on site 1, it does not take into account that o_1 has been executed before it and it produces the string "*effece*". The result at site 1 is different from the result of site 2 and it apparently violates the intention of o_2 since the last character e, which was intended to be deleted, is still present in the final string. Consequently, we obtain a *divergence* between sites 1 and 2. It should be pointed out that even if a serialization protocol [4] was used to require that all sites execute o_1 and o_2 in the same order (*i.e.* a global order on concurrent operations) to obtain an identical result *effece*, this identical result is still inconsistent with the original intention of o_2.

To maintain convergence, the OT approach has been proposed by [4]. When User X gets an operation op that was previously executed by User Y on his replica of the shared object User X does not necessarily integrate op by executing it "as is" on his replica. He will rather execute a variant of op, denoted by op' (called a *transformation* of op) that *intuitively intends to achieve the same effect as* op. This approach is based on a transformation function IT, called *Inclusive Transformation*, that applies to couples of concurrent operations defined on the same state.

Example 2. In Fig.2, we illustrate the effect of IT on the previous example. When o_2 is received on site 1, o_2 needs to be transformed according to o_1 as follows: $IT((Del(5), Ins(1, f)) = Del(6)$. The deletion position of o_2 is incremented because o_1 has inserted a character at position 1, which is before the character deleted by o_2. Next, op'_2 is executed on site 1. In the same way, when o_1 is received on site 2, it is transformed as follows: $IT(Ins(1, f), Del(5)) = Ins(1, f)$; o_1 remains the same because f is inserted before the deletion position of o_2.

2.3 Transformation Function

We present here an IT function known in the literature for synchronizing linear objects [10] altered by insertion and deletion operations. In this work, the signature of insert operation is extended by two parameters *pre* and *post*. These parameters store the set of concurrent delete operations. The set *pre* contains operations that have deleted a character before the insertion position p. As for *post*, it contains operations that have removed a character after p. When an insert operation is generated the parameters *pre* and *post* are empty. They will be filled during transformation steps.

In Fig.3, we give the four transformation cases for Ins and Del proposed by Suleiman and *al* [10]. There is an interesting situation in the first case (Ins and Ins), called *conflict situation*, where two concurrent $Ins(p_1, c_1, pre_1, post_1)$ and $Ins(p_2, c_2, pre_2, post_2)$ have the same position (*i.e.* $p_1 = p_2$). To resolve this conflict, three cases are possible:

1. $(pre_1 \cap post_2) \neq \emptyset$: character c_2 is inserted before character c_1,
2. $(pre_1 \cap post_2) \neq \emptyset$: character c_2 is inserted after character c_1,
3. $(pre_1 \cap post_2) = (post_1 \cap pre_2) = \emptyset$: in this case function $code(c)$, which computes a total order on characters ($e.g.$ lexicographic order), is used to choose among c_1 and c_2 the character to be added before the other. Like the site identifiers, $code(c)$ enables us to tie-break conflict situations [3].

Note that when two concurrent operations insert the same character ($e.g.$ $code(c_1) = code(c_2)$) at the same position, the one is executed and the other one is ignored by returning the idle operation Nop. In other words, only one character is kept. The remaining cases of IT are quite simple.

2.4   Transformation Properties

Definition 3. *Let seq be a sequence of operations. Transforming any editing operation o according to seq is denoted by $IT^*(o, seq)$ and is recursively defined as follows:*

$$IT^*(o, []) = o \text{ where } [] \text{ is the empty sequence;}$$
$$IT^*(o, [o_1; o_2; \ldots; o_n]) = IT^*(IT(o, o_1), [o_2; \ldots; o_n])$$

We say that o has been concurrently generated according to all operations of seq.

Using an IT function requires us to satisfy two properties [9]. For all o, o_1 and o_2 pairwise concurrent operations:

- **Condition** $TP1$: $[o_1; IT(o_2, o_1)] \equiv [o_2; IT(o_1, o_2)]$.
- **Condition** $TP2$: $IT^*(o, [o_1; IT(o_2, o_1)]) = IT^*(o, [o_2; IT(o_1, o_2)])$.

Property $TP1$ defines a *state identity* and ensures that if o_1 and o_2 are concurrent, the effect of executing o_1 before o_2 is the same as executing o_2 before o_1. This property is necessary but not sufficient when the number of concurrent operations is greater than two. As for $TP2$, it ensures that transforming o along equivalent and different operation sequences will give the same operation.

Properties $TP1$ and $TP2$ are sufficient to ensure the convergence for *any number* of concurrent operations which can be executed in *arbitrary order* [9]. Accordingly, by these properties, it is not necessary to enforce a global total order between concurrent operations because data divergence can always be repaired by operational transformation. However, finding an IT function that satisfies $TP1$ and $TP2$ is considered as a hard task, because this proof is often unmanageably complicated.

It should be noted that, using our model-checking technique, we detected subtle flaws in the IT function of Fig.3. These flaws lead to divergence situations (see Section 3).

2.5   Consistency Criteria

A stable state in an OT-based collaborative editor is achieved when all generated operations have been performed at all sites. Thus, the following criteria must be ensured [4, 9, 12]:

$$\mathrm{IT}(Ins(p_1, c_1, pre_1, post_1), Ins(p_2, c_2, pre_2, post_2)) =$$

$$
\begin{cases}
Ins(p_1, c_1, pre_1, post_1) & \text{if } p_1 < p_2 \\
Ins(p_1 + 1, c_1, pre_1, post_1) & \text{if } (p_1 > p_2) \vee (p_1 = p_2 \wedge pre_1 \cap post_2 \neq \emptyset) \\
Ins(p_1, c_1, pre_1, post_1) & \text{if } p_1 = p_2 \wedge post_1 \cap pre_2 \neq \emptyset \\
Ins(p_1, c_1, pre_1, post_1) & \text{if } (pre_1 \cap post_2 = \emptyset \vee pre_1 \cap post_2 = \emptyset) \wedge \\
& \quad p_1 = p_2 \wedge code(c_1) > code(c_2) \\
Ins(p_1 + 1, c_1, pre_1, post_1) & \text{if } (pre_1 \cap post_2 = \emptyset \vee post_1 \cap pre_2 = \emptyset) \wedge \\
& \quad p_1 = p_2 \wedge code(c_1) < code(c_2) \\
Nop() & \text{otherwise}
\end{cases}
$$

$$\mathrm{IT}((Ins(p_1, c_1, pre_1, post_1), Del(p_2))) = \begin{cases} Ins(p_1, c_1, pre_1, post_1 \cup \{Del(p_2)\}) & \text{if } p_1 \leq p_2 \\ Ins(p_1 - 1, c_1, pre_1 \cup \{Del(p_2)\}, post_1) & \text{otherwise} \end{cases}$$

$$\mathrm{IT}((Del(p_1), Ins(p_2, c_2, pre_2, post_2))) = \begin{cases} Del(p_1) & \text{if } p_1 < p_2 \\ Del(p_1 + 1) & \text{otherwise} \end{cases}$$

$$\mathrm{IT}(Del(p_1), Del(p_2)) = \begin{cases} Del(p_1) & \text{if } p_1 < p_2 \\ Del(p_1 - 1) & \text{if } p_1 > p_2 \\ Nop() & \text{otherwise} \end{cases}$$

Fig. 3. IT function of Suleiman and *al*

Definition 4. *(Consistency Model) An OT-based collaborative editor is con-sistent iff it satisfies the following properties:*

1. Causality preservation: *if $o_1 \to o_2$ then o_1 is executed before o_2 at all sites.*
2. Convergence: *when all sites have performed the same set of updates, the copies of the shared document are identical.*

To preserve the causal dependency between updates, timestamp vectors are used. The concurrent operations are serialized by using IT function. As this technique enables concurrent operations to be serialized in any order, the convergence depends on $TP1$ and $TP2$ that IT function must verify.

2.6 Operational Transformation Algorithms

Every site is equipped by an OT algorithm that consists of two main compo-nents [4, 9]: the *integration procedure* and the *transformation component*. The integration procedure is responsible for receiving, broadcasting and executing operations. It is rather *independent* of the type of the shared objects. Several integration procedures have been proposed in the groupware research area, such as dOPT [4], adOPTed [9], SOCT2,4 [11, 15] and GOTO [12]. The transforma-tion component is commonly an IT function which is responsible for merging two concurrent operations defined on the same state. This function is *specific* to the semantics of a shared object. Every site generates operations sequentially and stores these operations in a stack also called a *history* (or *execution trace*). When a site receives a remote operation o, the integration procedure executes the following steps:

1. From the local history *seq* it determines the equivalent sequence *seq'* that is the concatenation of two sequences seq_h and seq_c where (i) seq_h contains

all operations happened before o (according to Definition 1), and; (ii) seq_c consists of operations that are concurrent to o. For more details, see [3].

2. It calls the transformation component in order to get operation o' that is the transformation of o according to seq_c (*i.e.* $o' = IT^*(o, seq_c)$).
3. It executes o' on the current state.
4. It adds o' to local history seq.

The integration procedure allows history of executed operations to be built on every site, provided that the causality relation is preserved. At stable state, history sites are not necessarily identical because the concurrent operations may be executed in different orders. Nevertheless, these histories must be equivalent in the sense that they must lead to the same final state. This equivalence is ensured iff the used IT function satisfies properties $TP1$ and $TP2$.

In this work, we deal with OT algorithms that have the same integration procedure but differ only by their transformation functions. Five IT functions have been considered (see [3]).

The rest of the paper is devoted to the specification and analysis of OT algorithms, by means of model-checker *UPPAAL*. We show how to exploit some features of OT algorithms and the specification language of *UPPAAL* to attenuate the state explosion problem of the execution environment of such algorithms.

3   Modelling OT Algorithms with UPPAAL

3.1   UPPAAL's Model

In *UPPAAL*, a system consists of a collection of processes which can communicate via some shared data and synchronize through binary or broadcast channels [8]. Each process is an automaton extended with finite sets of clocks, variables (bounded integers), guards and actions. In such automata, locations can be labelled by clock conditions and edges are annotated with selections, guards, synchronization signals and updates. Selections bind non-deterministically a given identifier to a value in a given range (type). The other three labels of an edge are within the scope of this binding. An edge is enabled in a state if and only if the guard evaluates to true. The update expression of the edge is evaluated when the edge is fired. The side effect of this expression changes the state of the system. Edges labelled with complementary synchronization signals over a common channel must synchronize. Two or more processes synchronize through channels with a sender/receiver syntax [2]. For a binary channel, a sender can emit a signal through a given binary channel Syn ($Syn!$), if there is another process (a receiver) ready to receive the signal ($Syn?$). Both sender and receiver synchronize on execution of complementary actions $Syn!$ and $Syn?$. For a broadcast channel, a sender can emit a signal through a given broadcast channel Syn ($Syn!$), even if there is no process ready to receive the signal ($Syn?$). When a sender emits such a signal via a broadcast channel, it is synchronized with all processes ready to receive the signal. The updates of synchronized edges are executed starting with the one of the sender followed by those of the receiver(s). The execution order of updates of receivers complies with their creation orders.

3.2 Modelling Execution Environment of OT Algorithms

A collaborative editor is composed of two or more sites (users) which communicate via a network and use the principle of multiple copies, to share some object (a text). Initially, each user has a copy of the shared object. It can afterwards modify its copy by executing operations generated locally and those received from other users. When a site executes a local operation, it is broadcast to all other users. The execution of a non local operation consists of integration and transformation steps as explained in the previous section (see sub-section 2.6).

Two main models are proposed for the verification of the convergence properties of OT algorithms: the *concrete model* and the *symbolic model*. The main difference between these models concerns the effective execution of operation signatures. Indeed, in the concrete model, effective execution of editing operations is performed during the generation of traces (see Fig. 4) while, in the symbolic model, it is delayed until the construction of symbolic execution traces of all sites is completed (see Fig 5). In this paper, we focus on the symbolic model. For further details about the concrete model and the different variants of the concrete and symbolic models, we refer to [3].

System definition. A collaborative editor is modelled as a set of variables, functions, processes (one per user) and a broadcast channel. Note that the network is abstracted and not explicitly represented. This is possible by putting visible (in global variables) all operations generated by different sites and timestamp vectors of sites. In this way, there is no need to represent and manage queues of messages. Behaviors of sites are similar and represented by a type of process named *Site*. The only parameter of the process is the site identifier named *pid*. With *UPPAAL*, the definition of the system is given by the following declarations which mean that the system consists of *NbSites* sites of type *Site*:
Sites(const pid_t pid) = Site(pid);
system Sites;

Input data and Variables. Variables are of two kinds: those used to store input data and those used to manage the execution of operations. Note that almost all variables are defined as global to be accessible by any site (avoiding duplication of data in the representation of the system state). In addition, this eases the specification of the convergence property and allows to force the execution, in one step, some edges of different sites. The system model has the following inputs and variables:

1. The number of sites (*const int NbSites*); Each site has its own identifier, denoted *pid* for process identifier (*pid* $\in [0, NbSites - 1]$).
2. The initial text to be shared by users and its alphabet. The text to be shared by users is supposed to be infinite but the attribute *Position* of operations is restricted to the window $[0, L - 1]$ of the text. The length of the window is set in the constant L (*const int L*).
3. The number of local operations of each site, given in array *Iter[NbSites]* (*const int Iter[NbSites]*, *Iter[i]* being the number of local operations of

site i). We also use and set in constant named $MaxIter$ the total number of operations ($const\ int\ MaxIter = \sum\limits_{i \in [0, NbSites-1]} Iter[i]$);

4. The IT function ($const\ int\ algo$).
5. The timestamp vectors of different sites ($V[NbSites][NbSites]$).
6. Vector $Operations[MaxIter]$ to store the owner and the timestamp vector of each operation.
7. Vectors $Trace[NbSites][MaxIter]$ to save the symbolic execution traces of sites (the execution order of operations).
8. Boolean variable $Detected$ to recuperate the truth value of the convergence property.
9. Vector $Signatures[MaxIter]$ to get back signatures ($operator, position, character$) of operations which violate the convergence property.
10. $List[2][MaxIter]$ to save operation signatures as they are exactly executed in two sites (after integration steps).
11. The broadcast channel Syn.

Behavior of each site. The process behavior of each site is depicted by the automaton shown in Fig.5. Each user executes *symbolically*, one by one, all operations (local and non local ones), on its own copy of the shared text. The symbolic execution of an operation (local or non local) is represented by the loop on location $l0$ which consists of 3 parts: the selection of a process identifier ($k:\ pid\_t$), the guard $guard(k)$ and the update $SymbolicExecution(k)$. The guard part verifies whether a site pid can execute an operation of site k. The update part is devoted to the symbolic execution of an operation of a site k. The execution order of operations must, however, respect the causality principle. The causality principle is ensured by the timestamp vectors of sites $V[NbSites][NbSites]$. For each pair of sites (i, j), element $V[i][j]$ is the number of operations of site j executed by site i. $V[i][i]$ is then the number of local operations executed in site i. Note that $V[i][j]$ is also the rank of the next operation of site j to be executed by site i. Timestamp vectors are also used to determine whether operations are concurrent or dependent. Initially, entries of the timestamp vector of every site i are set to 0. Afterwards, when site i executes an operation of a site j ($j \in [0, NbSites - 1]$), it increments the entry of j in its own timestamp vector (i.e., $V[i][j] + +$).

Symbolic execution of a local operation. A local operation can be executed by a site pid if the number of local operations already executed by site pid does not yet reach its maximal number of local operations (i.e. $V[pid][pid] < Iter[pid]$). In this case, its timestamp vector is set to the timestamp vector of its site. Its owner and the timestamp vector are stored in array $Operations$. Its entry in $Operations$ is stored in $Trace[pid]$. Its broadcast to other sites is simulated by incrementing the number of local operations executed ($V[pid][pid] + +$).

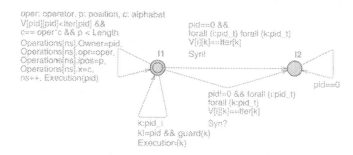

Fig. 4. The concrete model

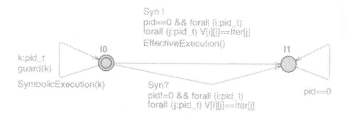

Fig. 5. The symbolic model

Symbolic execution of non local operations. A site *pid* can execute an operation of another site k if there is an operation of k executed by k but not yet executed by *pid* (i.e.: $V[pid][k] < V[k][k]$) and its timestamp vector is less or equal to the timestamp vector of site *pid* (i.e.: $\forall j \in [0, NbSites-1], V[pid][j] >= Operations[num].V[j]$, *num* being the identifier of the operation). Recall that, the transformation and effective execution of operations (Insert and Delete) are not performed at this level. They are realized when the construction of all traces is completed.

Effective execution of operations. When all sites complete the construction of their respective traces, they are forced to perform synchronously, via the broadcast channel *Syn*, their respective edges connecting locations *l0* and *l1* (synchronization on termination). The update part of edge connecting locations *l0* and *l1* of site 0 is devoted to testing all signatures possibilities of operations and then verifying the convergence property. The test of all these possibilities is encapsulated in a C-function, called *EffectiveExecution* which is stopped as soon as the violation of the convergence property is detected. This property is violated if there exist two sites which have completed the same set of operations but their texts are not identical. In this case, signatures of operations and exact traces of both sites which violate the convergence property are returned in vectors *Signatures* and *List*, and the variable *Detected* is set to *true*. The integration steps (see sub-section 2.6) are treated at this level (i.e., in this function).

3.3   Verification of the Convergence Property

The convergence property states that whenever two sites complete the execution of the same set of operations, their resulting texts must be identical. A stable state of the system is a situation where all sent operations are received and executed (there is no operation in transit). A site i is in a stable state if all operations sent to site i are received and executed by i (i.e. $forall(k : pid\_t) \ V[i][k] == V[k][k]$). The convergence property can be rewritten using the notion of stable state as follows: "Whenever two sites i and j are in stable state, they have identical texts". For the concrete model [3], we use the negation of this property specified by the following $UPPAAL$'s CTL formula ϕ_1:

$$E\diamond \ (exists(i : pid\_t) \ exists(j : pid\_t)$$

$$i! = j \ \&\& \ forall(k : pid\_t) \ V[i][k] == V[k][k] \ \&\& \ V[j][k] == V[k][k])$$

$$\&\& \ exists(l : int[0, L-1]) \ text[i][l]! = text[j][l]$$

This formula means that there is an execution path leading to some situation where two sites i and j are in stable states and their copies of text $text[i]$ and $text[j]$ are different. For the symbolic model, the verification of the convergence propriety is based on a variable named $Detected$. This variable is set to $true$ when the convergence propriety is violated. Therefore, the convergence propriety is violated iff UPPAAL's CTL formula $\phi_1' : E\diamond \ Detected$ is satisfied.

We have tested five IT functions known in the literature for synchronizing linear objects. Each IT function produces a new instance of OT algorithm, where only the transformation function changes. These OT algorithms are denoted respectively: $Ellis$ [4], $Ressel$ [9], Sun [13], $Suleiman$ [10] and $Imine$ [6]. Two models are used : concrete and symbolic models.

We report in Table 1 the results obtained, for two properties: absence of deadlocks ($\phi_2 : A[] \ notdeadlock$) and the violation of the convergence property

Table 1. Model-checking the concrete and the symbolic models

Alg.	Prop.	Val.	Expl./Comp./Time	Val.	Expl./Comp./Time
Ellis 3 3	ϕ_1/ϕ_1'	true	825112/1838500/121.35	true	1625/1739/0.14
Ellis 3 3	ϕ_2	?	?	true	1837/1837/0.68
Ressel 3 3	ϕ_1/ϕ_1'	true	833558/1851350/122.76	true	1637/1751/0.25
Ressel 3 3	ϕ_2	?	?	true	1837/1837/1.63
Sun 3 3	ϕ_1/ϕ_1'	true	836564/1897392/122.33	true	1625/1739/0.14
Sun 3 3	ϕ_2	?	?	true	1837/1837/0.38
Suleiman 3 3	ϕ_1/ϕ_1'	false	3733688/3733688/365.06	false	1837/1837/0.83
Suleiman 3 3	ϕ_2	?	?	true	1837/1837/2.22
Suleiman 3 4	ϕ_1/ϕ_1'	?	?	true	18450/19380/2.45
Imine 3 3	ϕ_1/ϕ_1'	false	3733688/3733688/361.16	false	1837/1837/0.81
Imine 3 3	ϕ_2	?	?	true	1837/1837/2.18
Imine 3 4	ϕ_1/ϕ_1'	?	?	true	18401/19331/2.45

(ϕ_1 or ϕ_1') defined above, in case of 3 sites ($NbSites = 3$), 3 or 4 operations ($MaxIter = 3$ or $MaxIter = 4$), and a window of the observed text of length $L = 2 * MaxIter$. A state q of a model is in deadlock iff there is no edge enabled in q nor in states reachable from q by time progression. Property ϕ_2 is always satisfied and allows us to compute the size of the entire state space. Note that all tests are performed using the version 4.0.6 of UPPAAL 2k on a 3 Gigahertz Pentium-4 with 1GB of RAM. We give, in column 4, for each algorithm and each property, the number of explored states, the number of computed states and the execution time (CPU time in seconds). A question mark indicates a situation where the verification was aborted due to a lack of memory. We report in Table 2, the counterexamples obtained for the convergence property and the symbolic model (each operation oi, for $i = 1, 3$, is generated by $Sitei$, $o11$ and $o12$ are generated in this order by $Site1$). Note that counterexamples obtained for the concrete and the symbolic models may be different. These results show that the symbolic model allows a significant gain in both time and space comparatively to the concrete model. With the symbolic model, we have been able to prove that the convergence property is not satisfied for five OT algorithms and to provide counterexamples.

Table 2. Counterexamples obtained for the tested IT functions

Alg.	Operations	Traces
Ellis	o1: Ins(1,0), o2: Ins(1,1), o3: Ins(1,0)	Site1: o1; o2; o3 Site3: o3; o2; o1
Ressel	o1: Ins(2,0), o2: Ins(1,1), o3: Del(1)	Site1: o1; o2; o3 Site3: o3; o2; o1
Sun	o1: Ins(1,0), o2: Ins(2,0), o3: Ins(2,1)	Site1: o1; o2; o3 Site3: o3; o1; o2
Suleiman	o11: Del(1), o12: Ins(1,0), o2: Ins(1,0), o3: Ins(2,0)	Site2 : o2; o3; o11; o12 Site3 : o3; o2; o11; o12
Imine	o11: Ins(1,0), o12: Ins(2,0), o2: Ins(2,0), o3: Del(1)	Site1 : o11; o12; o2; o3 Site3 : o3; o2; o11; o12

For instance, in Fig.6, we report a divergence scenario for OT algorithm based on transformation function proposed by Suleiman and *al* [10] (see Fig.3), where o_0, o_2 and o_3 are pairwise concurrent and $o_0 \rightarrow o_1$.

State space reduction. To reduce the size of the state space to be explored, we propose some reductions (see [3] for more details) which preserve the convergence property. The first reduction consists of synchronization of the execution of non local operations in sites which have finished the execution of their local operations. This synchronization preserves the convergence property since when a site completes the execution of all local operations, it does not send any information to other sites and the execution of non local operations affects only the state of the site. With this synchronization, intermediate states resulting from different interleavings of these operations are not accessible. This reduction has been implemented in the variant models of the concrete and the symbolic models [3].

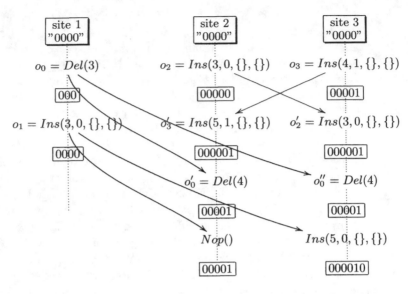

Fig. 6. Complete divergence scenario for Suleiman's algorithm

The second reduction forces to stop the construction of concrete/symbolic traces as soon as two any sites have completed the construction of their own traces. As sites have symmetrical behaviors, this reduction does not alter the convergence property. In the concrete and the symbolic models, edges connecting location $l0$ to $l1$ and the broadcast channel Syn, implement this reduction.

Another factor which contributes to the state explosion problem is the timestamp vectors of different sites and operations. These vectors are used to ensure the causality principle. To attenuate this state explosion problem, we offer the possibility to replace the timestamp vectors by a relation of dependence over operations. This model allows to test whether an OT algorithm works or not under some relation of dependence (see [3] for more details).

4 Related Work

To our best knowledge, there exists only one work on analyzing OT algorithms [7]. In this work, the authors proposed a formal framework for modelling and verifying IT functions with algebraic specifications. For checking the properties $TP1$ and $TP2$, they used a theorem prover based on advanced automated deduction techniques. For all IT functions considered here, they showed that: (i) $TP1$ is only satisfied for Suleiman's and Imine's IT functions; (ii) $TP2$ is always violated.

For example, consider the IT function proposed by Suleiman et *al.* [10] (see Fig.3). A theorem prover-based verification revealed a $TP2$ violation in this function [5], as illustrated in Fig.7. As this is related to $TP2$ property, there are

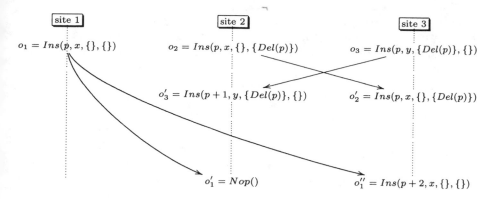

Fig. 7. $TP2$ violation for Suleiman's algorithm

three concurrent operations (for all positions p and all characters x and y such that $Code(x) < Code(y)$):

$o_1 = Ins(p, x, \{\}, \{\})$, $o_2 = Ins(p, x, \{\}, \{Del(p)\})$ and $o_3 = Ins(p, y, \{Del(p)\}, \{\})$ with the transformations $o'_3 = IT(o_3, o_2)$, $o'_2 = IT(o_2, o_3)$, $o'_1 = IT^*(o_1, [o_2; o'_3])$ and $o''_1 = IT^*(o_1, [o_3; o'_2])$.

However, the theorem prover's output gives no information about whether this $TP2$ violation is reachable or not. Indeed, we do not know how to obtain o_2 and o_3 (their pre_1 and $post_2$ parameters are not empty respectively) as they are necessarily the results of transformation against other operations that are not given by the theorem prover. Using our model-checking-based technique, we can get a complete and informative scenario when a bug is detected. Indeed, the output contains all necessary operations and the step-by-step execution that lead to divergence situation. Thus, by model-checking verification, the existence of the $TP2$ violation depicted in Fig.7 is proved (or certified) by the complete scenario given in Table 2.

As they are the basis cases of the convergence property, $TP1$ and $TP2$ are sufficient to ensure the data convergence for any number of concurrent operations which can be performed in any order. Thus, a theorem prover-based approach remains better for proving that some IT function satisfies $TP1$ and $TP2$. But it is partially automatable and, in the most cases, less informative when divergence bugs are detected. A model-checking-based approach is fully automatable for finding divergence scenarios. Nevertheless, it is more limited as the convergence property can be exhaustively evaluated on only a specific finite state space.

5   Conclusion

We proposed here a model-checking technique, based on formalisms used in tool UPPAAL, to model the behavior of replication-based collaborative editors.

To cope with the severe state explosion problem of such systems, we exploited their features and those of tool UPPAAL to establish and apply some abstractions and reductions to the model. The verification has been performed with the model-checking module of UPPAAL. An interesting and useful feature of this module is to provide, in case of failure of the tested property, a trace of an execution for which the property is not satisfied. We used this feature to give counterexamples for five OT algorithms, based on different transformation functions proposed in the literature to ensure the convergence property. Using our model-checking technique we found an upper bound for ensuring the data convergence in such systems. Indeed, when the number of sites exceeds 2 the convergence property is not achieved for all OT algorithms considered here. We think that our work is a forward step towards an efficient framework for formally developing shared objects based on the OT approach.

However, the serious drawback of the model-checking is the state explosion. So, in future work, we plan to investigate the following directions: (i) It is interesting to find, under which conditions, the model-checking verification problem can be reduced to a finite-state problem. (ii) Combining theorem-prover and model-checking approaches in order to attenuate the severe state explosion problem.

References

1. Alur, R., Dill, D.: A theory of timed automata. Theoretical Computer Science 126(2), 183–235 (1994)
2. Bérard, B., Bouyer, P., Petit, A.: Analysing the pgm protocol with uppaal. International Journal of Production Research 42(14), 2773–2791 (2004)
3. Boucheneb, H., Imine, A.: Experiments in model-checking optimistic replication algorithms. Research Report 6510, INRIA (April 2008)
4. Ellis, C.A., Gibbs, S.J.: Concurrency control in groupware systems. In: SIGMOD Conference, vol. 18, pp. 399–407 (1989)
5. Imine, A.: Conception formelle d'algorithmes de réplication optimiste. Vers l'édition Collaborative dans les réseaux Pair-à-Pair. Ph.d thesis, University of Henri Poincaré, Nancy, France (December 2006)
6. Imine, A., Molli, P., Oster, G., Rusinowitch, M.: Proving correctness of transformation functions in real-time groupware. In: ECSCW 2003, Helsinki, Finland, September 14-18 (2003)
7. Imine, A., Rusinowitch, M., Oster, G., Molli, P.: Formal design and verification of operational transformation algorithms for copies convergence. Theoretical Computer Science 351(2), 167–183 (2006)
8. Larsen, K., Pettersson, P., Yi, W.: Uppaal in a nutshell. Journal of Software Tools for Technology Transfer 1(1-2), 134–152 (1997)
9. Ressel, M., Nitsche-Ruhland, D., Gunzenhauser, R.: An integrating, transformation-oriented approach to concurrency control and undo in group editors. In: ACM CSCW 1996, Boston, USA, November 1996, pp. 288–297 (1996)
10. Suleiman, M., Cart, M., Ferrié, J.: Serialization of concurrent operations in a distributed collaborative environment. In: ACM GROUP 1997, November 1997, pp. 435–445 (1997)

11. Suleiman, M., Cart, M., Ferrié, J.: Concurrent operations in a distributed and mobile collaborative environment. In: IEEE ICDE 1998, pp. 36–45 (1998)
12. Sun, C., Ellis, C.: Operational transformation in real-time group editors: issues, algorithms, and achievements. In: ACM CSCW 1998, pp. 59–68 (1998)
13. Sun, C., Jia, X., Zhang, Y., Yang, Y., Chen, D.: Achieving convergence, causality-preservation and intention-preservation in real-time cooperative editing systems. ACM Trans. Comput.-Hum. Interact. 5(1), 63–108 (1998)
14. Sun, C., Xia, S., Sun, D., Chen, D., Shen, H., Cai, W.: Transparent adaptation of single-user applications for multi-user real-time collaboration. ACM Trans. Comput.-Hum. Interact. 13(4), 531–582 (2006)
15. Vidot, N., Cart, M., Ferrié, J., Suleiman, M.: Copies convergence in a distributed real-time collaborative environment. In: ACM CSCW 2000, Philadelphia, USA (December 2000)

Recursive Parametric Automata and ϵ-Removal*

Lin Liu[1] and Jonathan Billington[2]

[1] School of Computer and Information Science
[2] Computer Systems Engineering Centre
University of South Australia
{lin.liu,jonathan.billington}@unisa.edu.au

Abstract. This work is motivated by and arose from the parametric verification of communication protocols over unbounded channels, where the channel capacity is the parameter. Verification required the use of finite state automata (FSA) reduction, including ϵ-removal, for a specific infinite family of FSA. This paper generalises this work by introducing Recursive Parametric FSA (RP-FSA), an infinite family of FSA that can be represented recursively in a single parameter. Further, the paper states and proves a necessary and sufficient condition regarding the transformation of a RP-FSA to its language equivalent ϵ-removed family of FSA that is also a RP-FSA in the same parameter. This condition also guarantees a further structural property regarding the RP-FSA and its ϵ-removed family.

Keywords: Parametric Automata, Protocol Verification, Automata Reduction, Language Equivalence.

1 Introduction

The Capability Exchange Signalling (CES) protocol [9] is a multimedia control protocol that allows a communication party to inform its peer of its multimedia (e.g. audio and/or video) transmission and reception capabilities. To verify the CES protocol against its service specification, we need to obtain the CES service language: the set of allowable sequences of CES service primitives (i.e. user observable events). Our approach [4] is to extract service languages from state spaces of Coloured Petri Net (CPN) [10] models of service specifications by using automata reduction [2]. The CES service CPN has transitions that model CES service primitives and a transition that models message loss, an internal event that is not to be included in the CES service language (but is needed to capture sequences of primitives). We derive a Finite State Automaton (FSA) from the state space [4] by designating initial and final states and mapping the CPN transition modelling message loss to an ϵ-transition. Then we use FSA reduction to remove ϵ-transitions and non-determinism as steps towards proving language equivalence or inclusion (with respect to the protocol).

Our CPN model [11] of the CES service is parameterised by a positive integer (channel capacity), so it has an infinite family of state spaces. To verify the

---

* This work was partially supported by ARC Discovery Grant, DP0559927.

D. Lee et al. (Eds.): FMOODS/FORTE 2009, LNCS 5522, pp. 90–105, 2009.

CES protocol against its service for any value of the parameter, we firstly obtain symbolic representations for the state spaces and the associated FSAs. In [11] we exploit regularities in the state spaces to obtain a recursive representation. We then derive an infinite family of FSAs from the state spaces. In [12,14] we proved that the language equivalent ϵ-removed (LE-ER) family of automata can also be represented recursively. Furthermore, after removing non-determinism, we obtain a language equivalent recursively represented family of automata that represents the CES service language for arbitrary capacity [13]. These results lead us to the following generalisation: if a parametric FSA can be represented recursively, under what conditions can its LE-ER (or determinised) family also be represented recursively? In this paper, we determine a sufficient condition for a recursively represented parametric FSA to retain its recursive representation under ϵ-removal. We also determine a necessary condition to satisfy another structural property regarding these families of automata.

We firstly define a (first order) Recursive Parametric FSA (RP-FSA) in terms of a system parameter $l \in \mathcal{N}^+$ (the positive integers). Intuitively, FSA_l comprises a *base component*, FSA_{l-1}, plus another component, ADD_l. We then consider the LE-ER family derived from a RP-FSA, which we denote FSA_l^{ER}. We identify and prove the necessary and sufficient condition for a) FSA_l^{ER} to be a RP-FSA in l and b) the base component of FSA_l^{ER} to be identical to FSA_{l-1}^{ER}. The result contributes to the development of automata theory which we believe will be applicable to the verification of a class of parametric systems, as already demonstrated for the CES service [12,13,14].

There has been work on Recursive State Machines [1] and Unrestricted Hierarchical State Machines [3] where nodes correspond to ordinary states or to recursive invocations of other state machines. In contrast, we develop recursive representations of an *infinite family* of FSAs in an integer parameter and examine its related LE-ER family. We are not aware of any other work in this area.

The rest of the paper is organised as follows. Section 2 defines a RP-FSA. A theorem regarding transforming a RP-FSA to its LE-ER family is given in Section 3 with its proof in Section 4. Section 5 summarises the paper and suggests future work.

2   Definition of a Recursive Parametric FSA

Our work on the CES service has motivated us to define an infinite family of FSAs over a parameter $l \in \mathcal{N}^+$. Members of the family are related in that the FSA for l includes the FSA for $(l-1)$, and the alphabet and initial state are the same for all members of the family.

Definition 1. *A Recursive Parametric FSA is an infinite family of FSAs in a system parameter $l \in \mathcal{N}^+$, where its lth member, $FSA_l = (V_l, \Sigma, A_l, v_0, F_l)$, is given by*

- V_l *is a finite set of states or nodes that depends on l,*
- Σ *is a finite set, known as the alphabet,*

- $A_l \subseteq V_l \times (\Sigma \cup \{\epsilon\}) \times V_l$, is the transition relation, where ϵ is the empty string,
- $v_0 \in V_l$ is the initial state, and every state in V_l is accessible from v_0,
- F_l is the set of final states.

Given $FSA_1 = (V_1, \Sigma, A_1, v_0, F_1)$, the family, FSA_l (for $l \geq 2$) is obtained recursively as follows.

$$V_l = V_{l-1} \cup V_l^{add} \tag{1}$$
$$A_l = A_{l-1} \cup A_l^{add} \tag{2}$$
$$F_{l-1} \subseteq F_l \tag{3}$$

where

$$V_{l-1} \cap V_l^{add} = \emptyset \tag{4}$$
$$A_l^{add} \subseteq (V_{l-1} \times (\Sigma \cup \{\epsilon\}) \times V_l^{add}) \cup (V_l^{add} \times (\Sigma \cup \{\epsilon\}) \times V_l) \tag{5}$$

An example of a RP-FSA is the parametric FSA, FSA_{CES_l}, derived from the state space of our parameterised CES service CPN [12,14]. Fig. 1 shows FSA_{CES_3}. The subgraph that ignores the shaded nodes (13 to 20) and their associated arcs is FSA_{CES_1}. It has 12 nodes and 33 arcs, including 4 dashed arcs (ϵ-transitions). The initial state and the only final state of FSA_{CES_1} are both node 1. The alphabet, $\Sigma = \{Treq, Tind, Tres, Tcnf, Rreq, Rind, RindU, RindP\}$, is the set of (abbreviated) names of the CES service primitives. From Fig. 1, by ignoring the darkly shaded nodes (17 to 20) and their associated arcs, we obtain a subgraph that is FSA_{CES_2}. We see that FSA_{CES_2} can be constructed from FSA_{CES_1} by adding the 4 grey nodes (13 to 16) and the 16 grey arcs. By denoting $v_2^{add_1} = 13$, $v_2^{add_2} = 14$, $v_2^{add_3} = 15$ and $v_2^{add_4} = 16$, and $v_1^{add_1} = 2$, $v_1^{add_2} = 10$, $v_1^{add_3} = 4$ and $v_1^{add_4} = 12$, the 16 additional arcs are given in Table 1 for $l = 2$. When looking at the whole graph in Fig. 1, FSA_{CES_3} can be constructed from FSA_{CES_2} by adding 4 nodes (17 to 20) and 16 arcs (Table 1 for $l = 3$), when denoting $v_3^{add_1} = 17$, $v_3^{add_2} = 18$, $v_3^{add_3} = 19$ and $v_3^{add_4} = 20$.

It has been shown in [12,14] that, for $l \geq 2$, FSA_{CES_l} can be recursively constructed in the following way:

$$V_l = V_{l-1} \cup V_l^{add}$$
$$A_l = A_{l-1} \cup A_l^{add}$$
$$F_l = F_{l-1} = \{v_0\} = \{1\}$$

where

$$V_l^{add} = \{v_l^{add_i} \mid i \in \{1, \ldots, 4\}\}, \ V_{l-1} \cap V_l^{add} = \emptyset$$

and A_l^{add} is given in Table 1, where $v_1^{add_1} = 2$, $v_1^{add_2} = 10$, $v_1^{add_3} = 4$, $v_1^{add_4} = 12$ (Fig. 1). From Definition 1, the family FSA_{CES_l} ($l \in \mathcal{N}^+$) is a RP-FSA.

3   RP-FSA and ϵ-Removal

In this section, we propose the necessary and sufficient condition for the LE-ER automata family derived from FSA_l ($l \in \mathcal{N}^+$) to be a RP-FSA in l, where its base component is the LE-ER automaton of FSA_{l-1}. We firstly provide some definitions related to FSA_l, where $l \geq 2$.

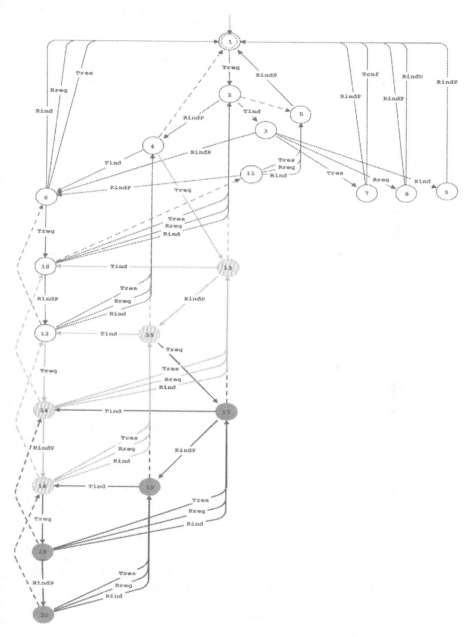

Fig. 1. FSA_{CES_3}

Definition 2. *A node $v \in V_{l-1}$ is an **entry node** to FSA_{l-1}, iff $\exists\, (v', t, v) \in A_l$ where $v' \in V_l^{add}$. The set of entry nodes of FSA_{l-1} is denoted by V_{l-1}^{EN}.*

Definition 3. *A node $v \in V_{l-1}$ is an **exit node** from FSA_{l-1}, iff $\exists\, (v, t, v') \in A_l$ where $v' \in V_l^{add}$. The set of exit nodes of FSA_{l-1} is denoted by V_{l-1}^{EX}.*

Table 1. A_l^{add} ($l \geq 2$)

Name	Arc	Name	Arc	Name	Arc
$a_l^{add_1}$	$(v_{l-1}^{add_3}, Treq, v_l^{add_1})$	$a_l^{add_2}$	$(v_{l-1}^{add_4}, Treq, v_l^{add_2})$	$a_l^{add_3}$	$(v_l^{add_1}, RindP, v_l^{add_3})$
$a_l^{add_4}$	$(v_l^{add_1}, Tind, v_{l-1}^{add_2})$	$a_l^{add_5}$	$(v_l^{add_1}, \epsilon, v_{l-1}^{add_1})$	$a_l^{add_6}$	$(v_l^{add_2}, RindP, v_l^{add_4})$
$a_l^{add_7}$	$(v_l^{add_2}, \epsilon, v_{l-1}^{add_2})$	$a_l^{add_8}$	$(v_l^{add_2}, Tres, v_l^{add_1})$	$a_l^{add_9}$	$(v_l^{add_2}, Rreq, v_l^{add_1})$
$a_l^{add_{10}}$	$(v_l^{add_2}, Rind, v_l^{add_1})$	$a_l^{add_{11}}$	$(v_l^{add_3}, Tind, v_{l-1}^{add_4})$	$a_l^{add_{12}}$	$(v_l^{add_3}, \epsilon, v_{l-1}^{add_3})$
$a_l^{add_{13}}$	$(v_l^{add_4}, Tres, v_l^{add_3})$	$a_l^{add_{14}}$	$(v_l^{add_4}, Rreq, v_l^{add_3})$	$a_l^{add_{15}}$	$(v_l^{add_4}, Rind, v_l^{add_3})$
$a_l^{add_{16}}$	$(v_l^{add_4}, \epsilon, v_{l-1}^{add_4})$				

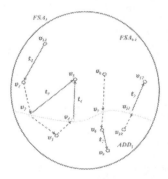

Fig. 2. An illustration of the definitions related to a RP-FSA

Definition 4. *The* **base component** *of* FSA_l *is* FSA_{l-1}, *and the* **added component** *of* FSA_l *is a labelled directed graph,* $ADD_l = (V_l^{add} \cup V_{l-1}^{EN} \cup V_{l-1}^{EX}, A_l^{add})$.

Definition 5. *A node of* FSA_l *is a* **candidate node** *(denoted* v^C*), iff* $\exists\,(v', t, v^C) \in A_l$ *and* $t \in \Sigma$. *We denote the set of candidate nodes of* FSA_l, V_l^C, *which comprises* $V_{l-1}^C = \{v^C \mid (v, t, v^C) \in A_{l-1}, t \in \Sigma\}$ *and* $V_l^{addC} = V_l^C \setminus V_{l-1}^C = \{v^C \mid (v, t, v^C) \in A_l^{add}$ *and* $(v', t', v^C) \notin A_{l-1}, t, t' \in \Sigma\}$.

Definition 6. *A finite sequence of transitions of* FSA_l *that starts at node vs and ends at node ve is a* **candidate sequence** *(denoted* $s_{(vs,ve,t)}^C$*), iff for* $n \geq 1$

$$s_{(vs,ve,t)}^C = vs \xrightarrow{\epsilon} v_1 \xrightarrow{\epsilon} \ldots \xrightarrow{\epsilon} v_n \xrightarrow{t} ve \qquad (6)$$

where $t \in \Sigma$. *The set of candidate sequences of* FSA_l *is denoted by* S_l^C.

Definition 7. *A finite sequence of transitions of* FSA_l *that starts at node vs and ends at node ve is a* **return sequence** *(denoted* $s_{(vs,ve,t)}^R$*), iff for* $n \geq 1$, $s_{(vs,ve,t)}^R \in S_l^C$, $vs, ve \in V_{l-1}$ *and* $\exists\, v_i \in \{v_1, \ldots, v_n\}$ *such that* $v_i \in V_l^{add}$. *The set of return sequences of* FSA_l *is denoted by* S_l^R.

Definition 8. *An empty cycle of a FSA is a sequence of ϵ-transitions that starts and ends in the same state.*

Fig. 2 illustrates the definitions, where dashed arcs show ϵ-transitions. The base component and added components of FSA_l are the parts above and under the curly grey line respectively. v_4 and v_{11} are entry nodes, v_2 and v_7 are exit nodes, and they are drawn at the boundary of the base and added components. v_1, v_5, v_9 and v_{12} are candidate nodes. $s_1 = v_1 \xrightarrow{\epsilon} v_2 \xrightarrow{\epsilon} v_3 \xrightarrow{\epsilon} v_4 \xrightarrow{t_1} v_5$, $s_2 = v_1 \xrightarrow{\epsilon} v_2 \xrightarrow{t_1} v_5$, $s_3 = v_6 \xrightarrow{\epsilon} v_7 \xrightarrow{\epsilon} v_8 \xrightarrow{t_2} v_9$, $s_4 = v_{10} \xrightarrow{\epsilon} v_{11} \xrightarrow{t_3} v_{12}$, are candidate sequences, and s_1 is a return sequence while the other three are not.

Another example is FSA_{CES_l}. In Table 1, $v_{l-1}^{add_3}$ and $v_{l-1}^{add_4}$ are exit nodes because, from each of them, there is a transition to a node in V_l^{add}, i.e. $a_l^{add_1}$ and $a_l^{add_2}$. $v_{l-1}^{add_1}$, $v_{l-1}^{add_2}$, $v_{l-1}^{add_3}$ and $v_{l-1}^{add_4}$ are entry nodes because there are transitions that start at nodes of V_l^{add} and end at each of them (i.e. transitions $a_l^{add_4}$, $a_l^{add_5}$, $a_l^{add_7}$, $a_l^{add_{11}}$, $a_l^{add_{12}}$, and $a_l^{add_{16}}$). FSA_{CES_l} contains candidate sequences, but it does not have return sequences because a return sequence requires at least one ϵ-transition that starts at a node in V_{l-1} and ends at a node in V_l^{add}. From Table 1 and Fig. 1 (FSA_{CES_1} only), FSA_{CES_l} does not have such ϵ-transitions.

Now we formalise the necessary and sufficient condition in the theorem below.

Theorem 1. *For $l \in \mathcal{N}^+$, let $FSA_l = (V_l, \Sigma, A_l, v_0, F_l)$ be a RP-FSA without empty cycles, and $FSA_l^{ER} = (V_l^{ER}, \Sigma, A_l^{ER}, v_0, F_l^{ER})$ its family of LE-ER automata. FSA_l^{ER} is a RP-FSA in l, where, for $l \geq 2$, its base component is FSA_{l-1}^{ER} iff for $vs, ve \in V_{l-1}^C$, $s_{(vs,ve,t)}^R \in S_l^R \Rightarrow (s_{(vs,ve,t)}^C \in S_{l-1}^C$ or $(vs, t, ve) \in A_{l-1})$.*

The theorem states that when the presence of a return sequence ($s_{(vs,ve,t)}^R$) between two candidate nodes in FSA_l, implies the presence of either a corresponding candidate sequence ($s_{(vs,ve,t)}^C$) between the same candidate nodes in the base component of FSA_l (i.e. FSA_{l-1}) or a direct transition between them ($(vs, t, ve) \in A_{l-1}$), then the LE-ER automaton of FSA_l is also a RP-FSA in l, with its base component being the LE-ER automaton of FSA_{l-1}. The converse also holds.

Referring to Fig. 2 and assuming that s_1 is the only return sequence, this RP-FSA satisfies the condition as a candidate sequence s_2 that belongs to FSA_{l-1} is between v_1 and v_5 and the last transitions of s_2 and s_1 are both t_1. If s_2 did not exist (assuming no other candidate sequences from v_1 to v_5 with t_1 as their last transition and that (v_1, t_1, v_5) does not exist), the FSA would not satisfy the condition. As mentioned earlier, FSA_{CES_l} does not have return sequences, so the condition is satisfied, and its LE-ER FSA can be represented recursively based on the LE-ER FSA of $FSA_{CES_{l-1}}$, a result that we proved in [12,14].

4   Proving the Necessary and Sufficient Condition

4.1   Preliminaries

We can remove ϵ-transitions by constructing ϵ-closures [15]. The ϵ-closure of a state or a set of states is the set of all states that are accessible by only

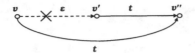

Fig. 3. Removing an ϵ-transition using Algorithm 1

ϵ-transitions from that state or set of states. Our goal is to determine the condition under which the LE-ER automaton of FSA_l is also a RP-FSA, where the base component of the LE-ER automaton is the LE-ER automaton of the base component of FSA_l. To derive the condition we remove ϵ-transitions in the base component (FSA_{l-1}) and the added component (ADD_l) separately, so that it is easier to identify if the LE-ER automaton of FSA_{l-1} is included in the LE-ER automaton of FSA_l. When an ϵ-closure includes ϵ-transitions of FSA_{l-1} and ADD_l, the above approach removes all the ϵ-transitions in an ϵ-closure at one time, and is thus not appropriate for our procedure.

Barrett et al [2] present an incremental approach. To transform a FSA to its LE-ER automaton, we firstly remove empty cycles (Definition 8), then remove all the remaining ϵ-transitions one by one. The algorithm for removing ϵ-transitions from a FSA without empty cycles is formalised as follows, based on [2].

Algorithm 1. *For $FSA = (V, \Sigma, A, v_0, F)$ without empty cycles, its LE-ER automaton, $FSA^{ER} = (V^{ER}, \Sigma, A^{ER}, v_0, F^{ER})$ is created as follows:*

1. *Initially, let $V^{ER} = V$, $A^{ER} = A$, $F^{ER} = F$.*
2. **While** $A_\epsilon^{ER} = \{(v, \epsilon, v') \mid (v, \epsilon, v') \in A^{ER}\} \neq \emptyset$, **do:**
   (a) *choose any $(v, \epsilon, v') \in A_\epsilon^{ER}$*
   (b) *update A^{ER} to $(A^{ER} \setminus \{(v, \epsilon, v')\}) \cup \{(v, t, v'') \mid (v', t, v'') \in A^{ER}, \ t \in (\Sigma \cup \{\epsilon\})\}$*
   (c) *if $v' \in F^{ER}$, update F^{ER} to $F^{ER} \cup \{v\}$.*
3. *Update V^{ER} to $V^{ER} \setminus \{v \mid \nexists s = v_0 \xrightarrow{t_0} \dots v_n \xrightarrow{t_n} v, n \geq 0, t_i \in \Sigma, 0 \leq i \leq n\}$*
4. *Update A^{ER} to $A^{ER} \setminus \{(v, t, v') \mid v \notin V^{ER} \text{ or } v' \notin V^{ER}\}$*

As shown in Fig. 3, when using the algorithm to remove (v, ϵ, v'), if $(v', t, v'') \in A^{ER}$, (v, t, v'') is included in A^{ER} (step 2(b)). Furthermore, if v' is a final state of FSA, v is included in F^{ER} (step 2(c)). After all the ϵ-transitions are removed by following step 2, some nodes of V^{ER} may become inaccessible from the initial state v_0, so in steps 3 and 4, we exclude inaccessible states and their associated transitions from V^{ER} and A^{ER} respectively.

We now state three lemmas to be used in the proof of the theorem. Lemma 1 gives the result of removing a sequence of ϵ-transitions. Lemma 2 states the necessary and sufficient condition for adding a non-ϵ-transition when removing ϵ-transitions from FSA_l. Lemma 3 presents the necessary and sufficient condition for a node of FSA_l to remain accessible after all ϵ-transitions are removed.

Lemma 1. *Let $FSA = (V, \Sigma, A, v_0, F)$ be an FSA that includes ϵ-transitions. Consider a transition sequence $s = vs \xrightarrow{\epsilon} v_1 \xrightarrow{\epsilon} \dots \xrightarrow{\epsilon} v_n \xrightarrow{t} ve$ where $n \geq 1$ and*

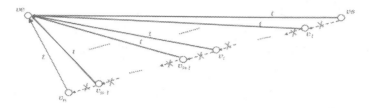

Fig. 4. Removing ϵ-transitions from the transition sequence in Lemma 1

$t \in \Sigma$. *After the n ϵ-transitions are removed from this sequence using steps 1 and 2 of Algorithm 1, transitions $\{(v, t, ve) \mid v \in \{vs, v_1, \ldots, v_n\}\}$ are in A^{ER}.*

Proof. Referring to Fig. 4, we firstly remove the second last transition in s, (v_{n-1}, ϵ, v_n), then the preceding ϵ-transition, and keep moving backwards until the first ϵ-transition, (vs, ϵ, v_1) is removed.

On removing (v_{n-1}, ϵ, v_n), arc (v_{n-1}, t, ve) is added according to Algorithm 1. When the third last transition $(v_{n-2}, \epsilon, v_{n-1})$ (if $n \geq 3$) is removed, because (v_{n-1}, t, ve) has just been added, (v_{n-2}, t, ve) has to be added. In general, when removing any ϵ-transition (v_i, ϵ, v_{i+1}) ($1 \leq i < n - 1$) in this way, because (v_{i+1}, t, ve) exists, (v_i, t, ve) has to be added. This process is continued until (vs, ϵ, v_1) is removed while (vs, t, ve) is added because (v_1, t, ve) has been added previously or was the last in the sequence if $n = 1$.

So after the n ϵ-transitions are removed, the set of arcs $\{(v, t, ve) \mid v \in \{vs, v_1, \ldots, v_n\}\}$, $n \geq 1$ are added to A^{ER}. Hence, Lemma 1 is proved. □

Lemma 2. *For $t \in \Sigma$ and $(vs, t, ve) \notin A_l$, when applying Algorithm 1 to FSA_l, after steps 1 and 2 are completed, a non-ϵ-transition (vs, t, ve) is in A_l^{ER} iff $s_{(vs, ve, t)}^C \in S_l^C$.*

Proof. The sufficient condition follows immediately from Lemma 1 as (vs, t, ve) is one of the arcs added when removing ϵ-transitions from $s_{(vs, ve, t)}^C$.

The necessary condition states that if transition (vs, t, ve) is added then there must be a candidate sequence $s_{(vs, ve, t)}^C$ (and $(vs, t, ve) \notin A_l$). To show this holds, we prove its contrapositive, i.e. if there does not exist $s_{(vs, ve, t)}^C \in S_l^C$, (vs, t, ve) can not be added when removing ϵ-transitions from FSA_l.

From Algorithm 1 if there does not exist a transition sequence from vs to ve at all, no new arc (vs, t, ve) can be added. So we only need to show that, (vs, t, ve) still can not be added when none of sequences from vs to ve are candidate sequences, i.e. any sequence from vs to ve is of the form $s' = vs \xrightarrow{t_1} v_1 \xrightarrow{t_2} \ldots \xrightarrow{t_{n-1}} v_n \xrightarrow{t} ve$, where $n \geq 1$, $t \in \Sigma$, and $\exists t' \in \{t_1, \ldots, t_{n-1}\}$ such that $t' \neq \epsilon$, a sequence that can only be made up of a chain of non-ϵ-transitions, or of both ϵ-transitions and non-ϵ-transitions.

In the first case, s' contains only non-ϵ-transitions, no ϵ-transitions to be removed from s', hence no arcs can be added. For the second case, assume that (vs, t', v_1) is a non-ϵ-transition. According to Algorithm 1, when removing any of the ϵ-transitions between v_1 and v_n, it is not possible to add an arc that starts from vs because vs is not the source node of an ϵ-transition. Now assume that (v_m, t', v_{m+1}) $(1 \leq m \leq n-1)$ is the first non-ϵ-transition we encounter in the chain (i.e. all preceding transitions are ϵ-transitions), then from Lemma 1, arcs $\{(v, t', v_{m+1}) \mid v \in \{vs, v_1, \ldots, v_{m-1}\}\}$ will be added when all the ϵ-transitions from vs to v_m are removed. However, these added arcs are not ϵ-transitions because $t' \neq \epsilon$. When removing any ϵ-transitions between v_{m+1} and v_n, again according to Algorithm 1, it is not possible to add an arc starting from vs. Therefore, for the transition sequence s' described above, arc (vs, t, ve) cannot be added.

Since we have used s' to represent any of the possible transition sequences existing from vs to ve, we have proved that if all of the transition sequences from vs to ve are not candidate sequences, then (vs, t, ve) can not be added. So the necessary condition is proved as well.

Therefore Lemma 2 holds.   □

Lemma 3. *When applying Algorithm 1 to FSA_l, after steps 1 and 2 are completed, a state v $(v \neq v_0)$ remains accessible iff $v \in V_l^C$ (a candidate node).*

Proof. Because all the states of FSA_l are accessible, there must exist at least one transition sequence from v_0 to a state v. It can be seen that a transition sequence from v_0 to a predecessor of v, v', may be of one of the 3 types: Type 1: a sequence that comprises ϵ-transitions only; Type 2: a sequence that comprises non-ϵ-transitions only; Type 3: a sequence that comprises both ϵ and non-ϵ-transitions.

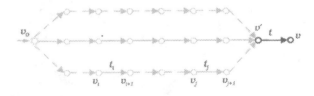

Fig. 5. Example transition sequences from v_0 to a predecessor (v') of node v

Fig. 5 shows an example for each of the 3 types of transition sequences from v_0 to v'. In this figure, an ϵ-transition is drawn as a dashed arc and a non-ϵ-transition is shown as a solid arc. The sequence on the top that comprises dashed arcs only is a type 1 sequence. The sequence in the middle that has solid arcs only is a type 2 sequence, and the sequence at the bottom that has two solid arcs and some dashed arcs is of type 3.

In the following we prove the sufficient condition first, i.e. if there exists (v', t, v) and $t \in \Sigma$, v is still accessible after ϵ-removal.

With a type 1 sequence, from Lemma 1, on the removal of ϵ-transitions the transition (v_0, t, v) is added, making v directly accessible.

For a type 2 sequence no ϵ-transitions are removed and the sequence remains ensuring v is accessible.

For a type 3 sequence, consider the example sequence shown at the bottom of Fig. 5. It has two non-ϵ-transitions (v_i, t_i, v_{i+1}) and (v_j, t_j, v_{j+1}), and $t_i \neq \epsilon$, $t_j \neq \epsilon$. When removing all the ϵ-transitions before v_i in the sequence, according to Lemma 1, from each node in the sequence before v_i, an arc labelled with t_i and pointing to v_{i+1} is added. So we have (v_0, t_i, v_{i+1}) in A_l^{ER}. When ϵ-transitions between v_{i+1} and v_j are removed, similarly from each node in the sequence from v_{i+1} to v_{j-1} an arc labelled with t_j and pointing to v_{j+1} is added. So we have (v_{i+1}, t_j, v_{j+1}) in A_l^{ER}. Finally when the ϵ-transitions between v_{j+1} and v' are removed, from each node of this part of the sequence (including v_{j+1} but excluding v'), a non-ϵ-transition that points to v and is labelled with t is added, including (v_{j+1}, t, v). Therefore, from v_0, via three non-ϵ-transitions (v_0, t_i, v_{i+1}), (v_{i+1}, t_j, v_{j+1}) and (v_{j+1}, t, v), we can reach v. So v must be accessible after all of the ϵ-transitions of FSA_l are removed.

The necessary condition states if v remains accessible after ϵ-removal, then there must exist $(v', t, v) \in A_l$ and $t \in \Sigma$. To show that this statement is correct, we prove its contrapositive, that is, if there does not exist $(v', t, v) \in A_l$ where $t \in \Sigma$, v is inaccessible after ϵ-removal.

As v is accessible before removing ϵ-removal, there must be a set of arcs $A_l^{2v} \subseteq A_l$ such that $A_l^{2v} = \{a \mid a = (v', t, v) \in A_l\}$. Because $\nexists (v', t, v) \in A_l$ and $t \in \Sigma$, all the arcs in A_l^{2v} are ϵ-transitions. Furthermore, as no empty cycles are allowed in FSA_l, so we have $A_l^{2v} = \{a \mid a = (v', \epsilon, v) \in A_l, v' \neq v\}$. Then if applying Algorithm 1 to FSA_l, transitions $\{(v', t', v'') \mid \exists (v, t', v'') \in A_l, v'' \neq v'\}$ are added, and none of the added arcs pointing to v. Meanwhile, all the arcs of A_l^{2v} are removed. So no arcs will point to v after ϵ-removal, i.e. v has become inaccessible. The necessary condition has been proved.

Therefore Lemma 3 holds. $\square$

From Lemma 2, when removing ϵ-transitions, transitions are added only between starting and ending nodes of candidate sequences (Definition 6). So such sequences are candidates for adding new transitions, that is why we call them candidate sequences. From Lemma 3 the destination node of a non-ϵ-transition is a candidate to be kept in the LE-ER automaton of FSA_l as it remains accessible after ϵ-removal, so we call such a node a candidate node (Definition 5).

4.2   Proving the Sufficient Condition

Lemma 4. *For $l \in \mathcal{N}^+$, let $FSA_l = (V_l, \Sigma, A_l, v_{0_l}, F_l)$ be a RP-FSA without empty cycles, and $FSA_l^{ER} = (V_l^{ER}, \Sigma, A_l^{ER}, v_0, F_l^{ER})$ its LE-ER automata family. If for $vs, ve \in V_{l-1}^C$, $s_{(vs,ve,t)}^R \in S_l^R \Rightarrow (s_{(vs,ve,t)}^C \in S_{l-1}^C$ or $(vs, t, ve) \in A_{l-1})$, then for $l \geq 2$,*

$$V_l^{ER} = V_{l-1}^{ER} \cup (V_l^{ER})^{add} \tag{7}$$

$$A_l^{ER} = A_{l-1}^{ER} \cup (A_l^{ER})^{add} \tag{8}$$

$$F_{l-1}^{ER} \subseteq F_l^{ER} \tag{9}$$

where

$$V_{l-1}^{ER} \cap (V_l^{ER})^{add} = \emptyset \tag{10}$$

$$(A_l^{ER})^{add} \subseteq (V_{l-1}^{ER} \times \Sigma \times (V_l^{ER})^{add}) \cup ((V_l^{ER})^{add} \times \Sigma \times V_l^{ER}) \qquad (11)$$

Proof. The proof is structured into 3 lemmas concerning the states of FSA_l^{ER} (Lemma 5), its arcs (Lemma 6) and its final states (Lemma 7).

Lemma 5. *Let FSA_l and FSA_l^{ER} be the automata referred to in Lemma 4, then for $l \geq 2$, the set of states of FSA_l^{ER} is given by Equations (7) and (10).*

Proof. From step 3 of Algorithm 1, V_l^{ER} comprises states of FSA_l that remain accessible after ϵ-removal. Based on Lemma 3, a state of FSA_l is accessible after ϵ-removal iff it is a candidate node, i.e. $V_l^{ER} = V_l^C$, for $l \in \mathcal{N}^+$. Thus we have $V_{l-1}^{ER} = V_{l-1}^C$. From Definition 5, $V_l^C = V_{l-1}^C \cup V_l^{addC}$ and $V_{l-1}^C \cap V_l^{addC} = \emptyset$. Let $(V_l^{ER})^{add} = V_l^{addC}$, then $V_l^{ER} = V_{l-1}^{ER} \cup (V_l^{ER})^{add}$ and $V_{l-1}^{ER} \cap (V_l^{ER})^{add} = \emptyset$. So Equations (7) and (10) always hold, thus Lemma 5 is proved.   □

Lemma 6. *Let FSA_l and FSA_l^{ER} be the automata referred to in Lemma 4. If for $vs, ve \in V_{l-1}^C$, $s_{(vs,ve,t)}^R \in S_l^R \Rightarrow (s_{(vs,ve,t)}^C \in S_{l-1}^C$ or $(vs, t, ve) \in A_{l-1})$, then for $l \geq 2$, the set of arcs of FSA_l^{ER} is given by (8) and (11).*

Proof. As A_l^{ER} is obtained from A_l by removing and adding transitions, we have

$$A_l^{ER} = (A_l \cup A_l^A) \setminus A_l^D \qquad (12)$$

where A_l^A represents the set of non-ϵ-transitions added and A_l^D the set of transitions that are removed. From Algorithm 1, the set of transitions removed from A_l comprises ϵ-transitions of FSA_l and the transitions whose source and/or destination nodes become inaccessible. From Lemma 3, the set of inaccessible states is $(V_l \setminus V_l^C)$. Therefore we have,

$$\begin{aligned} A_l^D = &\{(v, \epsilon, v') \in A_l\} \\ &\cup \{(v, t, v') \in A_l \mid t \in \Sigma,\ v \in (V_l \setminus V_l^C)\ \text{or}\ v' \in (V_l \setminus V_l^C)\} \qquad (13) \end{aligned}$$

Note that if the source and/or destination nodes of a transition added in step 2 become inaccessible, this transition is removed in step 4. However, we do not include these transitions in A_l^D as we use A_l^A to only represent the non-ϵ-transitions that are added between candidate nodes (which remain accessible after ϵ-removal).

Because $A_l = A_{l-1} \cup A_l^{add}$ (Equation (2)), A_l^D can be represented as $A_l^D = A_{l-1}^D \cup (A_l^{add})^D$, where

$$\begin{aligned} A_{l-1}^D = &\{(v, \epsilon, v') \in A_{l-1}\} \\ &\cup \{(v, t, v') \in A_{l-1} \mid t \in \Sigma,\ v \in (V_{l-1} \setminus V_{l-1}^C)\ \text{or}\ v' \in (V_{l-1} \setminus V_{l-1}^C)\} \\ (A_l^{add})^D = &\{(v, \epsilon, v') \in A_l^{add}\} \\ &\cup \{(v, t, v') \in A_l^{add} \mid t \in \Sigma,\ v \in (V_l \setminus V_l^C)\ \text{or}\ v' \in (V_l \setminus V_l^C)\} \qquad (14) \end{aligned}$$

From Definition 5, V_{l-1}^C comprises all the states in V_{l-1} that remain accessible via states in V_{l-1}, i.e. $(V_{l-1} \setminus V_{l-1}^C)$ is the set of states of V_{l-1} that are inaccessible when only considering V_{l-1}. So A_{l-1}^D comprises all the transitions removed from A_{l-1} when transforming FSA_{l-1} to FSA_{l-1}^{ER} by itself. So we can revise Equation (12) to:

$$A_l^{ER} = (A_{l-1} \setminus A_{l-1}^D) \cup (A_l^{add} \setminus (A_l^{add})^D) \cup A_l^A \qquad (15)$$

We now look at the details of A_l^A. From Lemma 2, a non-ϵ-transition is added between vs and ve iff there is $s_{(vs,ve,t)}^C \in S_l^C$. So we have:

$$A_l^A = \{(vs, t, ve) \mid vs, ve \in V_l^C, t \in \Sigma \text{ and } s_{(vs,ve,t)}^C \in S_l^C\} \qquad (16)$$

As $V_l^C = V_{l-1}^C \cup V_l^{addC}$, there are four cases for the location of the starting and ending nodes of $s_{(vs,ve,t)}^C$. They are **case 1**: $vs, ve \in V_{l-1}^C$; **case 2**: $vs \in V_{l-1}^C$, $ve \in V_l^{addC}$; **case 3**: $vs \in V_l^{addC}$, $ve \in V_{l-1}^C$; and **case 4**: $vs, ve \in V_l^{addC}$.

We use A_l^{A1} to represent all the transitions in A_l^A that are added based on case 1 candidate sequences, and A_l^{A234} for all the transitions that are added based on cases 2, 3 and 4. So $A_l^A = A_l^{A1} \cup A_l^{A234}$, where

$$A_l^{A1} = \{(vs, t, ve) \in A_l^A \mid vs, ve \in V_{l-1}^C\} \qquad (17)$$
$$A_l^{A234} = \{(vs, t, ve) \in A_l^A \mid vs \in V_l^{addC} \text{ or } ve \in V_l^{addC}\} \qquad (18)$$

We have proved $V_l^{ER} = V_{l-1}^{ER} \cup (V_l^{ER})^{add}$, with $V_{l-1}^{ER} = V_{l-1}^C$, $(V_l^{ER})^{add} = V_l^{addC}$. So

$$A_l^{A234} \subseteq (V_{l-1}^{ER} \times \Sigma \times (V_l^{ER})^{add}) \cup ((V_l^{ER})^{add} \times \Sigma \times V_l^{ER}) \qquad (19)$$

That is, a transition in A_l^{A234} is in $(A_l^{ER})^{add}$ (see (11)).

The candidate sequence, based on which a transition in A_l^{A1} is added, can belong to FSA_{l-1}, denoted **case 1a** (see the example sequence from v_1 to v_5 in Fig. 6(a)), or be a return sequence. When it is a return sequence, $s_{(vs,ve,t)}^R$, there are two cases. In the first case (**case 1b**) there is also either a direct transition $(vs, t, ve) \in A_{l-1}$ or a candidate sequence, $s_{(vs,ve,t)}^C$ that belongs to FSA_{l-1}. Fig. 6(b) provides an example where $s_1 = v_1 \xrightarrow{\epsilon} v_6 \xrightarrow{\epsilon} v_7 \xrightarrow{\epsilon} v_8 \xrightarrow{\epsilon} v_9 \xrightarrow{t_1} v_4$ is a return sequence, and $s_2 = v_1 \xrightarrow{\epsilon} v_2 \xrightarrow{\epsilon} v_3 \xrightarrow{t_1} v_4$ belongs to FSA_{l-1}. s_1 and s_2 have the same starting and ending nodes and their last transitions are both labelled by t_1. In the second case (**case 1c**), there is neither a direct transition $(vs, t, ve) \in A_{l-1}$ nor a candidate sequence, $s_{(vs,ve,t)}^C$ that belongs to FSA_{l-1} ($s_{(vs,ve,t)}^C \notin S_{l-1}^C$). Fig. 6(c) illustrates case 1c, where $s_1 = v_1 \xrightarrow{\epsilon} v_2 \xrightarrow{\epsilon} v_3 \xrightarrow{\epsilon} v_4 \xrightarrow{\epsilon} v_5 \xrightarrow{t_1} v_6$ and $s_2 = v_1 \xrightarrow{\epsilon} v_2 \xrightarrow{\epsilon} v_3 \xrightarrow{\epsilon} v_8 \xrightarrow{t_3} v_9$ are return sequences. From v_1 to v_6 there is no direct transition nor a candidate sequence of FSA_{l-1}. From v_1 to v_9, there is no direct transition and only one candidate sequence in FSA_{l-1} but its last transition is labelled by t_2, rather than t_3, so it is not a corresponding candidate sequence.

In case 1a, (vs, t, ve) is added and must be in A_{l-1}^{ER}, because when using Algorithm 1 to transform FSA_{l-1} to FSA_{l-1}^{ER} (by itself), (vs, t, ve) is included in A_{l-1}^{ER}, from Lemma 1. For case 1b, if $(vs, t, ve) \in A_{l-1}$, then Algorithm 1 will not remove it (as $t \in \Sigma$ and from Lemma 3) so it must be in A_{l-1}^{ER}. Alternatively, if

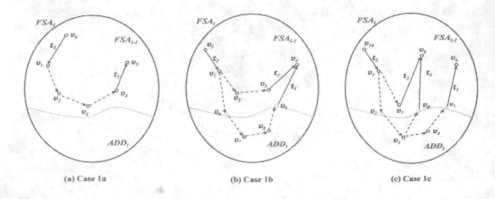

(a) Case 1a   (b) Case 1b   (c) Case 1c

Fig. 6. An illustration of Case 1 sequences

$s^C_{(vs,ve,t)} \in S^C_{l-1}$, then by Lemma 2, $(vs, ve, t) \in A^{ER}_{l-1}$. Hence the return sequences from vs and ve only add transitions that are already in A^{ER}_{l-1} and therefore have no effect. So far the transitions added in cases 1a and 1b are all in A^{ER}_{l-1} and the transitions added in cases 2 to 4 are in $(A^{ER}_l)^{add}$.

For case 1c, since $(vs, t, ve) \notin A_{l-1}$ it will only be included in A^{ER}_{l-1} if $s^C_{(vs,ve,t)} \in S^C_{l-1}$ from Lemma 2. Since there is no such candidate sequence, (vs, t, ve) is not in A^{ER}_{l-1}. For example, referring to Fig. 6(c), (v_1, t_3, v_9) is added when using Algorithm 1 on FSA_l, but it is not in A^{ER}_{l-1} because, when removing ϵ-transitions from FSA_{l-1}, $s^C_{(v_1,v_9,t_3)}$ is not in S^C_{l-1} (Lemma 2). Similarly, (v_1, t_1, v_6) is added when transforming FSA_l based on Lemma 2, but it is also not in A^{ER}_{l-1} as $s^C_{(v_1,v_6,t_1)}$ is not in S^C_{l-1}. The added transition (vs, t, ve) is not in $(A^{ER}_l)^{add}$ either because a transition of $(A^{ER}_l)^{add}$ must have its source and/or destination node in $(V^{ER}_l)^{add}$ (see (11)). Thus if we exclude case 1c, so that for $vs, ve \in V^C_{l-1}$, $s^R_{(vs,ve,t)} \in S^R_l \Rightarrow (s^C_{(vs,ve,t)} \in S^C_{l-1}$ or $(vs, t, ve) \in A_{l-1})$, then the base component of the LE-ER FSA_l will be FSA^{ER}_{l-1} because its set of transitions will be A^{ER}_{l-1} (rather than a superset). This is the condition stated in Lemma 4 (and Theorem 1). Thus we have shown that under this condition, all the added arcs during ϵ-removal for FSA_l are in A^{ER}_{l-1} or $(A^{ER}_l)^{add}$, and we can revise the representation of A^{ER}_l from Equation (15) to:

$$A^{ER}_l = (A_{l-1} \setminus A^D_{l-1}) \cup (A^{add}_l \setminus (A^{add}_l)^D) \cup A^{A1ab}_l \cup A^{A234}_l$$
$$= ((A_{l-1} \setminus A^D_{l-1}) \cup A^{A1ab}_l) \cup ((A^{add}_l \setminus (A^{add}_l)^D) \cup A^{A234}_l) \quad (20)$$

where

$$A^{A1ab}_l = \{(vs, t, ve) \mid vs, ve \in V^C_{l-1}, t \in \Sigma \text{ and} \quad (21)$$
$$s^R_{(vs,ve,t)} \in S^R_l \Rightarrow (s^C_{(vs,ve,t)} \in S^C_{l-1} \text{ or } (vs, t, ve) \in A_{l-1})\}$$

comprises all the transitions added when transforming FSA_{l-1} to FSA^{ER}_{l-1}. A^D_{l-1} comprises all transitions removed in the same context, so under this condition,

$(A_{l-1} \backslash A_{l-1}^D) \cup A_l^{A1ab}$ consists of all the transitions of FSA_{l-1}^{ER}, i.e.

$$A_{l-1}^{ER} = (A_{l-1} \backslash A_{l-1}^D) \cup A_l^{A1ab} \tag{22}$$

Now consider $(A_l^{add} \backslash (A_l^{add})^D) \cup A_l^{A234}$, the second half of Equation (20). Transitions in A_l^{add} have source and/or destination nodes in V_l^{add}. $(A_l^{add})^D$ comprises all the ϵ-transitions of A_l^{add} and all the transitions that are removed from A_l^{add} because their source and/or destination nodes are not in $(V_l^{ER})^{add}$. So all the transitions in $(A_l^{add} \backslash (A_l^{add})^D))$ have source and/or destination nodes in $(V_l^{ER})^{add}$. A_l^{A234} satisfies (19), thus

$$((A_l^{add} \backslash (A_l^{add})^D) \cup A_l^{A234}) \subseteq ((V_{l-1}^{ER} \times \Sigma \times (V_l^{ER})^{add}) \cup ((V_l^{ER})^{add} \times \Sigma \times V_l^{ER}))$$

If we let $(A_l^{ER})^{add} = (A_l^{add} \backslash (A_l^{add})^D)) \cup A_l^{A234}$, then (11) is satisfied. From this and Equations (20) and (22), $A_l^{ER} = A_{l-1}^{ER} \cup (A_l^{ER})^{add}$, so Equation (8) holds. Therefore Lemma 6 is proved.   □

Lemma 7. *Let FSA_l and FSA_l^{ER} be the automata referred to in Lemma 4, then for $l \geq 2$, the set of final states of FSA_l^{ER} is given by (9).*

Proof. From Algorithm 1, the final states of FSA_l^{ER} are obtained by adding new final states and keeping accessible states in F_l. That is $F_l^{ER} = F_l^A \cup F_l^K$, where $F_l^A = \{v \in V_l^C \mid (v, \epsilon, v') \in A_l \text{ where } v' \in F_l\}$, and $F_l^K = F_l \cap V_l^C$. As $A_l = A_{l-1} \cup A_l^{add}$ and $V_l^C = V_{l-1}^C \cup V_l^{addC}$, we have

$$F_l^A = \{v \in V_{l-1}^C \mid (v, \epsilon, v') \in A_{l-1} \text{ where } v' \in F_{l-1}\} \tag{23}$$
$$\cup \{v \in V_l^{addC} \mid (v, \epsilon, v') \in A_l^{add} \text{ where } v' \in F_l\}$$
$$F_l^K = (F_{l-1} \cap V_{l-1}^C) \cup (F_l \cap V_l^{addC}) \tag{24}$$

Using the same argument for FSA_{l-1}, we get

$$F_{l-1}^{ER} = \{v \in V_{l-1}^C \mid (v, \epsilon, v') \in A_{l-1} \text{ where } v' \in F_{l-1}\} \cup (F_{l-1} \cap V_{l-1}^C)$$

so that $F_{l-1}^{ER} \subseteq F_l^{ER}$, i.e. (9) holds, and Lemma 7 is proved.   □

Thus (7) to (11) hold under the condition of the lemma and hence Lemma 4 is proved.   □

4.3   Proving the Necessary Condition

Lemma 8. *For $l \in \mathcal{N}^+$, if FSA_l^{ER} is a RP-FSA as specified in (7) to (11), then FSA_l satisfies for $vs, ve \in V_{l-1}^C$, $s_{(vs,ve,t)}^R \in S_l^R \Rightarrow (s_{(vs,ve,t)}^C \in S_{l-1}^C$ or $(vs, t, ve) \in A_{l-1})$.*

Proof. To prove the lemma, we prove its contrapositive, i.e. for $vs, ve \in V_{l-1}^C$ when $s_{(vs,ve,t)}^R \in S_l^R \not\Rightarrow (s_{(vs,ve,t)}^C \in S_{l-1}^C$ or $(vs, t, ve) \in A_{l-1})$ then FSA_l^{ER} is *not* a RP-FSA as specified in (7) to (11).

From the proof of Lemma 6, if case 1c is not excluded, i.e. for $vs, ve \in V_{l-1}^C$ when $s_{(vs,ve,t)}^R \in S_l^R \not\Rightarrow (s_{(vs,ve,t)}^C \in S_{l-1}^C$ or $(vs, t, ve) \in A_{l-1})$, then (vs, t, ve) is added where $vs, ve \in V_{l-1}^{ER}$. However, this transition is not in A_{l-1}^{ER} or $(A_l^{ER})^{add}$ as explained in the proof of Lemma 6. This means $A_l^{ER} \neq A_{l-1}^{ER} \cup (A_l^{ER})^{add}$, so Equation (8) does not hold. Hence FSA_l^{ER} is *not* a RP-FSA as specified in (7) to (11), and the contrapositive is true. Hence Lemma 8 is proved.   □

Therefore, based on Lemma 4 and Lemma 8, Theorem 1 holds.

5   Conclusion and Future Work

In this paper we have defined an infinite family of FSA related by an integer parameter, called Recursive Parametric FSA (RP-FSA). We considered the removal of ϵ-transitions from this family and identified (and proved) the necessary and sufficient condition for which this transformation results in another family which is RP-FSA in the same parameter, where the transformed family's base component is the ϵ-removed base component of the original RP-FSA. This is of theoretical interest and may provide the basis for an algebra of RP-FSA where ϵ-removal and graph addition are operators. However, this work was motivated by the verification of a multimedia protocol. We have developed a more general theory that we believe can be applied to other practical systems. In [5], a structural regularity has been discovered in the data transfer service of the Internet's Transmission Control Protocol (TCP) operating over unbounded channels. This can lead to a recursive (or closed form) expression for the state space in terms of the channel capacity. We have also observed similar regular behaviour in the state space of a simulator model [8]. The symbolic FSAs derived from the state spaces of these systems are RP-FSA. When the RP-FSA contains ϵ-transitions we can use the condition identified in this paper to check if the corresponding LE-ER RP-FSA can be obtained. If this is the case and this ϵ-removed RP-FSA is (or can be transformed to) a deterministic RP-FSA, then we have a recursive representation of a specification against which the system can be verified.

Future work will include developing the theory on the condition under which an RP-FSA is closed under FSA determinisation, i.e. the determinised family of FSA can also be represented in the same recursive style, and applying it and the result presented in this paper to the verification of industrial systems. We will also consider extending the theory to two integer parameters for protocols with two parameters, as illustrated in the verification of the Stop and Wait Protocol class [6,7].

References

1. Alur, R., Etessami, K., Yannakakis, M.: Analysis of Recursive State Machines. In: Berry, G., Comon, H., Finkel, A. (eds.) CAV 2001. LNCS, vol. 2102, pp. 207–220. Springer, Heidelberg (2001)
2. Barrett, W.A., Bates, R.M., Gustafson, D.A., Couch, J.D.: Compiler Construction: Theory and Practice, 2nd edn. Science Research Associates (1986)

3. Benedikt, M., Godefroid, P., Reps, T.: Model Checking of Unrestricted Hierarchical State Machines. In: Orejas, F., Spirakis, P.G., van Leeuwen, J. (eds.) ICALP 2001. LNCS, vol. 2076, pp. 652–666. Springer, Heidelberg (2001)
4. Billington, J., Gallasch, G.E., Han, B.: A Coloured Petri Net Approach to Protocol Verification. In: Desel, J., Reisig, W., Rozenberg, G. (eds.) Lectures on Concurrency and Petri Nets. LNCS, vol. 3098, pp. 210–290. Springer, Heidelberg (2004)
5. Billington, J., Han, B.: Formalising TCP's Data Transfer Service Language: A Symbolic Automaton and its Properties. Fundamenta Informaticae 80(1-3), 49–74 (2007)
6. Gallasch, G.E., Billington, J.: A Parametric State Space for the Analysis of the Infinite Class of Stop-and-Wait Protocols. In: Valmari, A. (ed.) SPIN 2006. LNCS, vol. 3925, pp. 201–218. Springer, Heidelberg (2006)
7. Gallasch, G.E., Billington, J.: Parametric Language Analysis of the Class of Stop-and-Wait Protocols. In: van Hee, K.M., Valk, R. (eds.) PETRI NETS 2008. LNCS, vol. 5062, pp. 191–210. Springer, Heidelberg (2008)
8. Gordon, S., Billington, J.: Analysing a Missile Simulator with Coloured Petri Nets. Int. J. on Software Tools for Technology Transfer 2(2), 144–159 (1998)
9. ITU: Recommendation H.245, Control protocol for multimedia communication (2005)
10. Jensen, K.: Coloured Petri Nets: Basic Concepts, Analysis Methods and Practical Use, 2nd edn., vol. 1. Springer, Heidelberg (1997)
11. Liu, L., Billington, J.: Tackling the Infinite State Space of a Multimedia Control Protocol Service Specification. In: Esparza, J., Lakos, C.A. (eds.) ICATPN 2002. LNCS, vol. 2360, pp. 273–293. Springer, Heidelberg (2002)
12. Liu, L., Billington, J.: A Proof of the Recursive Formula for the Infinite Service Language of the CES Protocol. Technical report, CSEC-13, Computer Systems Engineering Centre, University of South Australia (2004)
13. Liu, L., Billington, J.: Obtaining the Service Language for H.245's Multimedia Capability Exchange Signalling Protocol: the Final Step. In: 10th Int. Multi-Media Modelling Conference, pp. 323–328. IEEE, Los Alamitos (2004)
14. Liu, L., Billington, J.: Reducing Parametric Automata: A Multimedia Protocol Service Case Study. In: Wang, F. (ed.) ATVA 2004. LNCS, vol. 3299, pp. 483–486. Springer, Heidelberg (2004)
15. Louden, K.C.: Compiler Construction: Principles and Practice. PWS Publishing Company (1997)

A Software Platform for
Timed Mobility and Timed Interaction

Gabriel Ciobanu and Călin Juravle

Institute of Computer Science, Romanian Academy, Iaşi
"A.I.Cuza" University of Iaşi, Romania
gabriel@iit.tuiasi.ro, calin.juravle@info.uaic.ro

Abstract. TiMo is a process algebra using timeouts for interactions
and adaptable migration between explicit locations. Starting from this
formalism, we have implemented a software platform for agent migration, separating the migration mechanism such that it can be reused for
other systems with mobility. We describe the platform architecture and
functionalities, the software modules and some implementation details,
emphasizing the novel aspects and comparing with similar implementations. The implementation corresponds rigorously to the semantics of
TiMo. An example illustrates the use of the migration platform for a
simple problem.

1 Introduction

Mobile applications represents an important topic in distributed system field.
Mobility is difficult in both the modeling part and in implementation, especially when time is also considered. To address the modeling part, many formalisms have been proposed over the years such as π-calculus [8], distributed
π-calculus [6], timed distributed π-calculus [4], TiMo [3]. Concerning the implementation, there are several architectures and different programming languages
(Telescript [11], Java) which support or facilitate code mobility or mobile agents
programming. Although there are several papers on both aspects (theoretical
and practical) addressing mobility, the link between the theoretical specification
and effective implementation is not clearly defined.

Our aim is to provide a platform for agent migration which corresponds to a
formal model. Starting from TiMo, we implement such a platform. To ensure
that it corresponds with the high-level operational semantics of TiMo, we define
a formal notion of configuration and use it to describe and reason about the
evolution of a system.

Since mobility is the main concept, we separate the low-level mobility concerns
and the high-level model aspects into two layers. Thus, our implementation consists of an extensible basic framework which can be used to implement various
systems based on mobility and a framework inspired by TiMo which facilitates to
specify mobile agents. The lower layer is named *MobileCalculi framework* and,
besides a migration mechanism, it offers generic implementations of common
concepts needed to implement mobile systems. The upper layer is inspired by

D. Lee et al. (Eds.): FMOODS/FORTE 2009, LNCS 5522, pp. 106–121, 2009.
© IFIP International Federation for Information Processing 2009

TiMo and it is referred as the *software framework for TiMo*; it also provides a compiler for an intermediate language in which someone can specify systems of mobile agents. In order to prove the extensibility of *MobileCalculi* framework we also implemented a software framework for dπ-calculus [6]. The whole system is named *MCTools*. Thus, *MCTools* represents a software platform for mobile calculi implementation.

MCTools system is developed according to a choreography based distributed architecture. It is working without a central coordinator. Agents are free to roam and travel in a network of machines which have the system installed, without being orchestrated by a central entity.

The paper is structured as follows. We first briefly present the TiMo model in Section 2, then we describe some implementation details in Sections 3 and 4. We present the correspondence between TiMo and the implementation in Section 5. Before ending with conclusion and related works, an illustrating example is presented in Section 6.

2   TiMo

TiMo [3] is a simple process algebra in which one can formally model distributed systems with explicit locations, migration and temporal constraints. It is a part of the π-calculus family [8], close to the distributed π-calculus [6] and timed distributed π-calculus [4]. TiMo features a simple syntax, dropping the type aspects of distributed π-calculus and focusing on interaction and migration. The time is local and modeled by timers which are associated with basic actions. The result is that the interaction and migration time is no longer indefinite. Moreover, if an action does not happen in a predefined time, then the process continues with a "safety" alternative.

TiMo Syntax is given below. It is assumed that *Chan* is a set of channels, *Loc* is a set of locations, *Var* is a set of location variables and *Ident* is a finite set of process identifiers (each identifier $I \in Ident$ has a fixed arity $m_I \geq 0$).

$$P, Q ::= 0 \mid a^{\Delta t} \,!\, \langle v \rangle \,\textbf{then}\, P \,\textbf{else}\, Q \mid a^{\Delta t} \,?\, (u) \,\textbf{then}\, P \,\textbf{else}\, Q \mid$$
$$\textbf{go}^{lt \Delta mt} \, v \,\textbf{then}\, P \,\textbf{else}\, Q \mid I(v_1, \ldots, v_{m_I}) \mid P \mid Q \mid \#P$$
$$M, N ::= k[\![P]\!] \mid M \mid N$$

In the above description it is assumed that $a \in Chan$; $t, lt, mt \in \mathbb{N}$,; $v, v_1, \ldots,$ $v_{m_I} \in Loc \cup Var$; $k \in Loc$ and $u \in Var$. Moreover, each process identifier $I \in Ident$ has a unique definition of form $I(u_1, \ldots, u_{m_I}) = P_I$ where $u_i \neq u_j$ (for $i \neq j$) are variable acting here as parameters.

Process $a^{\Delta t} \,!\, \langle v \rangle \,\textbf{then}\, P \,\textbf{else}\, Q$ attempts to send v over channel a for t units of time. If the communication takes place then it continues as P, otherwise it continues as Q. Input process $a^{\Delta t} \,?\, \langle u \rangle \,\textbf{then}\, P \,\textbf{else}\, Q$ has a similar behaviour. Process $\textbf{go}^{lt \Delta mt} \, v \,\textbf{then}\, P \,\textbf{else}\, Q$ implements mobility. It first waits lt units of time which represents the *local time* dedicated to local work, then it moves to location v in mt units of time (mt stands for *migration time*). If the move is accomplished within the specified time, then the process behaves as P (at v), otherwise it continues as Q at current location. Processes are further constructed from the basic processes together with the terminating process 0 by using the parallel composition $P \,|\, Q$. A located process $k[\![P]\!]$ is a process running at location k. The symbol $\#$ from $\#P$ is a purely technical notation used in the formalization of structural operational semantics of TiMo. Intuitively, it says that the process has finished its action and it is temporally waiting for the next tick of the clock.

Operational Semantics of TiMo is given by the rules presented in Table 1.

Table 1. TiMo operational semantics

$$
\text{GO:} \qquad k[\![\mathbf{go}^{0\Delta mt}\, l\, \mathbf{then}\, P\, \mathbf{else}\, Q]\!] \xrightarrow{k:l} l[\![\#P]\!]
$$

$$
\text{COM:} \qquad l[\![a^{\Delta t}\,!\,\langle l\rangle\, \mathbf{then}\, P\, \mathbf{else}\, Q
$$

$$
|\; a^{\Delta t'}\,?\,(u)\, \mathbf{then}\, P'\, \mathbf{else}\, Q'\,]\!] \xrightarrow{k:a(l)}
$$

$$
l[\![\#P \,|\, \#\{l/u\}P']\!]
$$

$$
\text{PAR:} \qquad \frac{N \xrightarrow{\beta} N'}{N\,|\,M \xrightarrow{\beta} N'\,|\,M}
$$

$$
\text{STRUC:} \qquad \frac{N \equiv N' \quad N \xrightarrow{\beta} M \quad M \equiv M'}{N' \xrightarrow{\beta} M'}
$$

$$
\text{TIME:} \qquad \frac{N \not\rightarrow}{N \xrightarrow{\surd} \phi(N)}
$$

Looking to the labels of the transitions, there are two kinds of transition rules: $M \xrightarrow{\beta} N$ and $M \xrightarrow{\surd} N$. The first one corresponds to the execution of an action β, while the second one represents a timing tick. The action β can be either $k:l$ or $k:a(l)$, where k is the location where the action takes place, l is either the location where the process goes, or the location transmitted along the channel a. In rule TIME, $N \not\rightarrow$ denotes that no other rule can be applied.

ϕ is the time-passing function which acts in the following way. Each top-level expression $I(l_1, \ldots, l_{m_I})$ is replaced by the corresponding definition $\{l_1/u_1, \ldots, l_{m_I}/u_{m_I}\}P_I$. Each top-level expression of the form $a^{\Delta 0}\ldots \mathbf{then}\, P\, \mathbf{else}\, Q$ or $\mathbf{go}^{0\Delta 0}\ldots \mathbf{then}\, P\, \mathbf{else}\, Q$ is replaced by $\#Q$. For the top-level communication expressions with $\Delta t > 0$, t is decreased by 1. Each top-level expression of the form $\mathbf{go}^{lt\Delta mt}\, \mathbf{then}\, P\, \mathbf{else}\, Q$ is replaced by $\mathbf{go}^{lt'\Delta(mt')}\, \mathbf{then}\, P\, \mathbf{else}\, Q$ where $lt' = \max\{0, lt - 1\}$ and $mt' = mt$ if $lt > 0$ or $mt' = max\{0, mt - 1\}$ if $lt = 0$. All occurrences of the special symbol $\#$ are deleted.

A top-level expression is not containing a symbol $\#$. Note that only after the lt timer reaches 0, the process migrates to the destination.

3 MobileCalculi Framework

As stated in the introduction *MobileCalculi* framework represents the lower level of the *MCTools* system. Its purpose is to be the low-level link between the theoretical part of mobility (represented by various formalisms such as those from π-calculus family) and the practical part which deals with mobile code and mobile systems implementations. It was designed to abstract the concepts used in the formal models, and to handle low-level details such as network or location management. The correspondence between location names and physical locations, represented by an IP address plus a port, is done at this level.

The framework serves as a base for implementation of models for mobility, dealing with the common part of such formalisms: names, locations, agents, migration, fresh name generation, etc. It provides a default mechanism for migration which makes possible to migrate an agent by its code and data. Moreover, it provides the architecture of an engine for simulation of the formal evolution of a process. It also handles communications with other machines, and thus it can create and initialize a distributed environment from a global specification, making it a useful tool for distributed experiment. The global specification of a system is represented by the agent distribution at their initial locations.

The framework is based on an extensible architecture so that the majority of components can be customized according to needs. It is implemented in Java language, the main reason being the infrastructure offered by Java for working with mobile code and dynamic classes. A formalism is implemented by extending structures from the framework and adapting them to its specific features. The software framework for TiMo serves as an example, but we can also use other formalism implementation. To prove the extensibility of the *MobileCalculi* framework we also implemented a software framework for dπ-calculus.

We developed a generic purpose GUI in order to ease the user interaction with *MCTools* platform, in particular with the *MobileCalculi* framework. Using the GUI one can easily access the majority of framework functionalities without any coding. It is possible to start or stop the system, change the active formalism (the upper layer), compile, load and execute specific formalism specifications and interact with other *MCTools* platforms.

We describe the implementation from a functional viewpoint. A global view of the platform architecture can be seen in Figure 1, where it is presented the interaction between the two layers, the lower layer represented by *MobileCalculi* framework, and the upper layer represented by a formalism framework (in particular TiMo framework). It also present the dependency inside the layers.

The functionality of *MobileCalculi* framework is divided into several modules. The most important ones are the *core* module which deals with common functionalities and general patterns, and the *mobility* module which encapsulates the mobility mechanism. These modules are presented below. To keep the presentation clear and simple the rest of the modules are omitted.

Core Module. The *core* module is the heart of the *MobileCalculi* framework. It contains the main functionalities and propose the patterns which must be

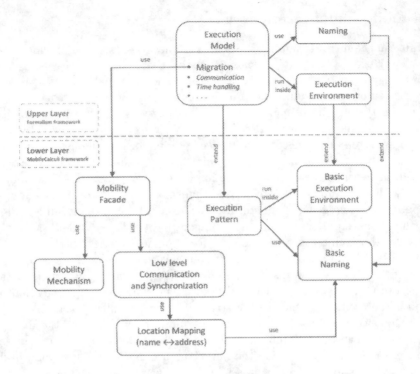

Fig. 1. MCTools Functional Architecture

followed by a formalism implementation. The implementation of a formalism either extends these patterns and enhances agent execution with specific features, or just uses some of the basic functionalities.

The main entities in a formalism for mobility are agents, locations and names. An agent is represented by an object which contains a main method with its actions/instructions. This representation defines an execution pattern by assuming that agent execution is equivalent with its main method execution. The agent runs at a specific location, in a private thread. The location acts as an execution environment for agents. It keeps a list with resources, such as communication channels, which can be used by agents. All the entities (including resources) are referred by name, so the name concept is also defined as a separate entity.

A formalism implementation must provide at least an *execution model* and an *execution environment*. The *execution model* is defined by the formalism primitives (such as migration, communication) which have to be described according to the formal specification. One must focus only on these primitives since the basic ones such as starting or stooping the execution, joining with other execution threads or spawning addition workers are implemented in the default pattern. This model runs inside a specific *execution environment* and uses a naming structure. For example the execution environment for TiMo defines a virtual clock and the agents defined in TiMo are governed by this clock. Again, some basic functionalities of an execution environment are implemented at the framework low-level (adding or removing new agents, generating unique names).

Since the framework is built for mobility formalism, it assumes that migration primitives are present in every formalism implementation. Considering this, the *core* module facilitate the use of the mobility mechanism presented in Section 3, by managing the low level details and acting as a mobility façade.

It is worth noting that this module also incorporates many other functionalities which are transparent to the developer of a certain formalism implementation. It handles communication with other machine, not just for transmitting agents, but also for synchronization and control. It manages the execution environment, and it sets up a distributing environment from a global specification. Moreover, it manages the several formalisms providing a way to switch between them dynamically; this enable the possibility to change the execution model (in other words the upper layer of *MCTools* system) without shutting down the platform and independently of other platforms.

Another important functionality which can be use directly by the upper layer is the formal evolution engine. Given a formal specification, this engine enables to execute locally the evolution of a formal specification corresponding to the formalism semantic rules. Using this feature one can detect possible discrepancies between formal specifications and their implementations.

Mobility Module. This module creates the needed infrastructure for agent migration. It also provides a default migration mechanism based on bytecode migration. This module abstracts the migration objects by providing an interface which must be implemented by all the entities which want to migrate. This maintains a decoupled architecture and makes it possible to easily change the migration mechanism. The main feature of this module is the proposed migration architecture.

Among the possible alternatives we consider the solution based on bytecode migration. It ensure the dependencies migration by using special class loaders. The main idea is to retain the bytecode of agents in a local repository. In order to access a class bytecode, the class must be loaded with a special class loader which saves the bytecode at loading. At migration the agent definition and dependencies are searched in this repository. The definitions of agent and its dependencies are stored at destination in a similar repository from where they can be loaded. After loading the agent, data can be recovered.

Note that we preferred to migrate the dependencies together with the agent rather than implementing a lazy mechanism. The motivation behind this is given by the fact that after a valid migration the agent should work correctly independent of other locations. In a lazy situation it is possible that the location containing the dependencies does not work when the agent needs a certain dependency. Thus, bringing the dependency in a lazy way determines the failure of the agent. Having all the dependencies transported together with the agent, we avoid this scenario and let the agent to execute independently of previous locations. Our choice has also the advantage of simplifying the handling of disconnected operations (the agent can execute even if the owner is not connected).

4   Software Framework for TiMo

The main features of TIMO implementation are:

- creating and executing TIMO agents in a distributed environment;
- the possibility of introducing native Java code into the agents body;
- an intermediate language *TLang* and a (typed) compiler which can generate the Java code from a simple syntax;
- an operational correspondence between implementation and its formal model.

In order to help writing the TIMO agents, we develop a language called *TLang* to intermediate between the high-level TIMO and the low-level Java code. *TLang* uses only a limited set of Java types and instructions. Even if TLang does not include all Java functionalities, it provides several important advantages like type checking, syntax for agents distribution, possibility to embed Java code, mechanisms for simulation of strong mobility. We also create a compiler which translates TIMO agents (written in a simple syntax) into the appropriate Java

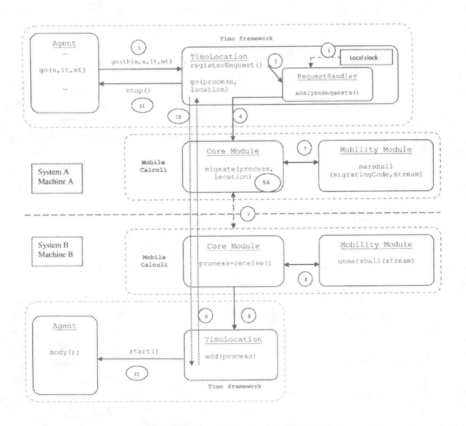

Fig. 2. Migration of a TIMO agent

code. The compiler also builds the objects necessary to run the agents in a distributed environment using *MobileCalculi* framework.

Before presenting the implementation, we analyze some constraints imposed by the transition from theory to practice. We allow other values than locations to be transmitted on channels. Only allowing locations to be transmitted, our implementation would serve mainly for theoretical simulation and not for practical use. The communication values can be of any Java type if the agent is written directly in Java, and of some restricted type if it is developed with *TLang*. Communication on channel is well typed. This means that a channel has an associated type. For instance, if an agent wants to sent or receive a *location* on a channel dedicated to *strings*, an error appears (more exactly, a compile error if the compiler is used, or a runtime error if Java is used). The safety process is activated either when time expires for a communication (as in the formalism), or when an exception is thrown out and the agent is about to fail.

More implementation details are presented in [2]. Here we briefly summarize TiMo primitives and temporal aspects. The temporal aspects are implemented with the help of a *virtual clock*. The clock is local to each location, and so has a predefined frequency. At each tick it triggers an event, and the subscribers take the appropriate actions. One subscriber is the *TimoLocation* which analyzes at every tick the requests it has received.

Migration uses the infrastructures provided by the *MobileCalculi* framework. Since the framework implements a "weak" mobility mechanism, it falls to the programmer to retain the program counter and manage the point from which the execution of agents is restarted at destination. The semantic of migration timers is implemented by using a distributed protocol. The local timer lt is represented as the waiting time before the migration. It is the first one which is decremented. The migration timer mt is implemented as a distributed protocol. After the local time reaches 0, the migration procedure is initiated and the migration timer starts to be decremented. After the agent arrives at its destination, a *receive message* is sent back. If the message is receive before the migration timer becomes 0 the agent is remove from its initial location and another message, a *confirmation message* is sent to destination; otherwise the agent activates its safety process at the current location. At destination the agent restarts only after receiving the *confirmation message*. The default behaviour if this message is not received is to remove the agent (at destination). A successful migration can be visualized in Figure 2.

Communication between agents respects faithfully the TiMo definition, and it is based on the *rendez-vous* mechanism [7].

5   Implementation Soundness

In this section we show that our implementation corresponds with TiMo high-level semantics. We first define an abstract notion of *configuration* and then use it to reason about the implementation soundness with respect to TiMo semantics.

Table 2. Process Stack Definition

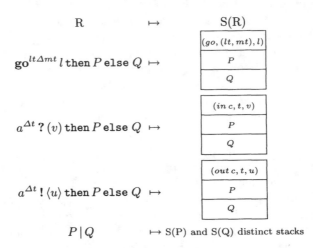

R	$\mapsto$	S(R)

$\mathbf{go}^{lt \triangle mt} \, l \, \mathbf{then} \, P \, \mathbf{else} \, Q \; \mapsto$

$(go, (lt, mt), l)$
P
Q

$a^{\triangle t} \, ? \, (v) \, \mathbf{then} \, P \, \mathbf{else} \, Q \; \mapsto$

$(in \, c, t, v)$
P
Q

$a^{\triangle t} \, ! \, \langle u \rangle \, \mathbf{then} \, P \, \mathbf{else} \, Q \; \mapsto$

$(out \, c, t, u)$
P
Q

$P \, | \, Q \qquad \mapsto S(P)$ and $S(Q)$ distinct stacks

Definition 1. *Given a process R specified in TiMO, we define the process stack $S(R)$, or simply S, as in Table 2.*

Remark 1. This definition is consistent with both the theoretical view which presents the process as a sequence of actions, and the practical view where each process has a stack from where the next action is executed. Moreover, it is consistent with the software framework for TiMo. In implementation, only the primitives of communication and migration are considered when the virtual clock ticks. All the other actions are internal. Thus, from a temporal point of view, we can abstract the process as being composed only from primitives of communication and migration presented as a stack.

The configuration of a location is represented by the set of stacks $S_1^1, S_2^2, ..., S_n^n$ of the processes which run at that location l, and it is written as $l[S_1^1, S_2^2, ..., S_n^n]$. The configuration of a distributed system is a network of location configurations where each node contains the set of stacks corresponding to the local processes. We denote by $l_1[S_1^1, ..., S_{n_1}^1] \times ... \times l_n[S_1^n, ..., S_{n_n}^n]$ a network with n locations, where for each location l_i the number of processes is provided by n_i.

We denote by $Config$ the set of all possible configurations, and usually refer to a configuration only thinking to the top of its stacks. We write 0 for the empty stack corresponding to a terminated process. When it is not explicitly specified, by configuration we understand the configuration of a system.

Definition 2. *Over the configuration set, we define the transition function δ : $Config \times CT \to Config$, where $CT = \{tick, subst, go, fail_{com}, fail_{go}\}$.*

In the following we write $\delta(c, ctype) = c'$ as $c \xrightarrow{ctype} c'$.

- $l[S_1, ..., \#(chAct \, a, t, x), ..., S_n] \xrightarrow{tick} l[S_1, ..., (chAct \, a, t-1, x), ..., S_n]$
  where $chAct \in \{in, out\}$ and $x \in Val \cup Var$.

- $l[S_1, ..., \#(go, (lt, mt), l), ..., S_n] \xrightarrow{tick} l[S_1, ..., (go, (lt - 1, mt), l), ..., S_n]$
  provided that $lt > 0$ and $l \in Loc$.
- $l[S_1, ..., \#(go, (0, mt), l), ..., S_n] \xrightarrow{tick} l[S_1, ..., (go, (0, mt - 1), l), ..., S_n]$
  provided that $mt \geq 0$ and $l \in Loc$.
- $l[S_1, ..., (in\, a, t, v), ..., (out\, a, t', u), ..., S_n] \xrightarrow{subst} l[S_1, ..., \#S(\{u/v\}P), ...,$
  $\#S(P'), ..., S_n]$ provided that $min(t, t') \geq 0$, the stack of in action is $[(in\, a, t, v), P, Q]$ and that of out action is $[(out\, a, t', u), P', Q']$.
- $l[S_1, ..., (in\, a, t, x), ..., S_n] \xrightarrow{fail_{com}} l[S_1, ..., \#S(Q), ..., S_n]$
  provided that $t < 0$ and the stack of in action is $[(in\, a, t, v), P, Q]$.
- $l[S_1, ..., (out\, a, t, u), ..., S_n] \xrightarrow{fail_{com}} l[S_1, ..., \#S(Q), ..., S_n]$
  provided that $t < 0$ and the stack of out action is $[(out\, a, t, u), P, Q]$.
- $l[S_1^l, ..., (go, (0, mt), k), ..., S_{nl}^l] \times k[S_1^k, ... S_{nk}^k] \xrightarrow{go}$
  $l[S_1^l, ..., 0, ..., S_{nl}^l] \times k[S_1^k, ..., S_{nk}^k, \#S(P)]$
  provided that $mt \geq 0$ and the stack of go at l is $[(go, (0, mt), l), P, Q]$.
- $l[S_1^l, ..., (go, (0, mt), k), ..., S_{nl}^l] \xrightarrow{fail_{go}} l[S_1^l, ..., \#S(Q), ..., S_{nl}^l]$
  provided that $mt < 0$, location k is unreachable and the stack of go at l is $[(go, (0, mt), l), P, Q]$.
- if none of the above rules can be applied, we apply one of the following rules:

  - $l[S_1, ..., (chAct\, a, t, x), ..., S_n] \xrightarrow{tick} l[S_1, ..., (chAct\, a, t - 1, x), ..., S_n]$
    provided that $t \geq 0$, $chAct \in \{in, out\}$ and $x \in Val \cup Var$.
  - $l[S_1, ..., (go, (lt, mt), l), ..., S_n] \xrightarrow{tick} l[S_1, ..., (go, (lt - 1, mt), l), ..., S_n]$
    provided that $lt > 0$ and $l \in Loc$.
  - $l[S_1, ..., (go, (0, mt), l), ..., S_n] \xrightarrow{tick} l[S_1, ..., (go, (0, mt - 1), l), ..., S_n]$
    provided that $mt \geq 0$ and $l \in Loc$.

Note that the rules are maximally applied for all possible stacks of a configuration.

Proposition 1. *The implementation of migration and communication primitive corresponds operationally to the rules GO and COM of the TIMO formalism.*

Proof. We prove this by showing that for each process R and for each possible evolution rule of type GO or COM which takes R into R', there exists a sequence of transitions which takes the configuration corresponding to R into a configuration which corresponds to R'. This is summarized in the following diagram, where $\beta = k : l$ or $k : a(l)$.

$$
\begin{array}{ccc}
R & \xrightarrow{\beta} & R' \\
\downarrow & & \downarrow \\
config & \longrightarrow^* & config'
\end{array}
$$

There are several cases which must be analyzed including success actions, failed actions, and actions that come right next after a blocking.

- We first consider the communication case: $k[\![a^{\Delta t} ? (v) \, \mathbf{then} \, P \, \mathbf{else} \, Q \,|\, a^{\Delta t'} \, !$
  $(u) \, \mathbf{then} \quad P' \, \mathbf{else} \, Q']\!] \xrightarrow{k:a(u)} k[\![\#\{u/v\}P \,|\, \#P']\!]$. The configuration

$k[(in\,a,\,t,\,v),\,(out\,a,\,t',\,u)]$ corresponds to process R. We apply *subst* rule: $k[(in\,a,\,t,\,v),\,(out\,a,\,t',\,u)] \xrightarrow{subst} k[\#S(P),\,\#S(P')]$. It is easy to see that the resulting configuration corresponds to the process R'.

- The migration case is as follows: $k[\![\mathbf{go}^{0\,\Delta mt}m\,\mathbf{then}\,P\,\mathbf{else}\,Q]\!] \xrightarrow{k:l} m[\![\#P]\!]$. The corresponding configuration of the left-hand side is $k[(go,\,(0,\,mt),\,m)]$. We apply *go* rule and get $k[(go,\,(0,\,mt),\,m)] \times m[0] \xrightarrow{go} k[0] \times m[\#P]$. The resulting configuration is the corresponding one for the right-hand side which proves this case.
- The failure cases are similarly treated, and not presented here.
- When an action comes after a #, we add an extra *tick* transition in order to keep the consistency between processes and configurations. Suppose that we have the following case: $k[\![\mathbf{go}^{0\,\Delta mt}m\,\mathbf{then}\,P\,\mathbf{else}\,Q]\!] \xrightarrow{k:m} m[\![\#P]\!]$ with $P = a^{\Delta t}?(v)\,\mathbf{then}\,P_1\,\mathbf{else}\,Q_1 \mid a^{\Delta t'}!(u)\,\mathbf{then}\,P_1'\,\mathbf{else}\,Q_1'$. The evolution continues with the *tick* rule: $m[\![\#P]\!] \xrightarrow{tick} m[\![a^{\Delta t-1}?(v)\,\mathbf{then}\,P_1\,\mathbf{else}\,Q_1 \mid a^{\Delta t'-1}!(u)\,\mathbf{then}\,P_1'\,\mathbf{else}\,Q_1']\!] \xrightarrow{m:a(u)} m[\![\#P_1 \mid \#P_1']\!]$. The corresponding configuration transitions are: $k[(go,\,(0,\,mt),\,m)] \times m[0] \xrightarrow{go} k[0] \times m[\#S(P)]$. Expanding $S(P)$ we get: $m[\#S(P)] = m[\#(in\,a,\,t,\,v),\#(out\,a,\,t',\,u] \xrightarrow{subst} m[\#S(P_1),\,\#S(P_1')]$ which corresponds to the resulting process.
- The other cases are similarly treated, and not presented here.

Remark 2. Each syntactic structure from TiMo can be represented in *TLang* (the compiler language) which then can be translated into a Java implementation.

Table 3. *timo2lang* function

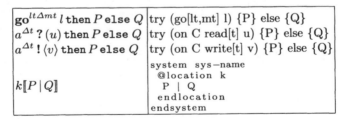

$\mathbf{go}^{lt\Delta mt}\,l\,\mathbf{then}\,P\,\mathbf{else}\,Q$	try (go[lt,mt] l) {P} else {Q}
$a^{\Delta t}\,?\,(u)\,\mathbf{then}\,P\,\mathbf{else}\,Q$	try (on C read[t] u) {P} else {Q}
$a^{\Delta t}\,!\,\langle v\rangle\,\mathbf{then}\,P\,\mathbf{else}\,Q$	try (on C write[t] v) {P} else {Q}

$k[\![P\mid Q]\!]$	system sys-name
	  @location k
	   P | Q
	  endlocation
	endsystem

We show how a high-level structure from TiMo becomes a low-level implementation by defining two functions, *timo2lang* and *lang2impl*, which translate a process expression into a *TLang* program, and then a *TLang* program into a Java implementation. Let *TimoProc* be the set of all TiMo processes, *TLangProg* the set of all programs/specifications which can be written in *TLang* language, and *JavaCode* the set of correct Java programs. The functions are defined as follows:

$$timo2lang : TimoProc \rightarrow TLangProg$$
$$lang2impl : TLangProg \rightarrow JavaCode$$

Since the TiMo processes are built structurally, it is enough to show how the basic syntactic structures are handled. For the basic cases, functions *timo2lang*

Table 4. *lang2impl* function

| try (go[lt,mt] l){P} else {Q} | ```
try{
  if(!moved){
    moved = true;go(l, lt, mt);
  } else {
    try {
      //P body
    }catch(Exception e){
    // agent failed
    }
  }catch(Exception e1){//Q body}
``` |
| try (on C read[t] u){P} else {Q} | ```
try {
  u = in(c,u.getClass(), t);
  // P code
}catch(Exception e){// Q code}
``` |
| try (on C write[t] v){P} else {Q} | ```
try {
  out(c, v, t);
  // P code
}catch(Exception e){// Q code}
``` |
| ```
system sys-name
  @location k
  P | Q
  endlocation
endsystem
``` | specific functions which create an object containing the system description (agents and their distribution). |

and *lang2impl* are presented in Tables 3 and 4. The left column represents the argument, and the right one is the result of function application.

TıMo processes can also be encoded directly in Java without using the intermediate language *TLang*. This can easily be proved by composing the functions *lang2impl* and *timo2lang*; *lang2impl* ∘ *timo2lang* takes a process expression and returns its Java program. Note that *timo2lang(TimoProc)* ⊂ *TLangProg* and *timo2lang(TLangProg)* ⊂ *JavaCode*, thus not every program written in TLang or Java encodes a TıMo process.

Proposition 1 and Remark 2 show a sound way of deriving Java code for mobility starting from TıMo specification. Thus we conclude with the following statement.

Remark 3. Each agent specified in TıMo can be implemented by the software platform defined by *MCTools*, and its execution reflects the operational semantics of TıMo.

6   Example

We present a simple problem which demonstrates the usability of the migration platform and timing constraints. The scenario is given by the discovery of a specific resource, in our case a shop location (though it could be any other like a printer, a scanner etc). We first describe the problem, then we show how it can be encoded into TıMo. Then, we briefly discuss the *TLang* implementation, and the running Java code.

Suppose that we have a *Client* who wishes to find the best *Shop* for a specific product. Although the client does not know where to find the specific product, it knows a location where a *Broker* may inform about the right place. The problem is that the *Broker* is available only for some limited amount of time. Moreover, the best shop changes over time in such a way that in the first 4 units of time the best one is *shopA* and then, in the next 7 units of time the best one is *shopB*. Besides, the *Client* has to do some internal work and cannot leave its location in the first 2 units of time. After that, it may move in 3 units of time to the *Broker* location, and it cannot afford to spend more than 2 units of time at the *Broker* location. The communication channel between the *Client* and the *Broker* is *A*. The *Client* is located initially at *home*, and the *Broker* at location *info*. The whole system is named *Shops*. The TiMo specification for *Shops* is as follows:

$$Client = \mathbf{go}^{2\Delta3}\ info\ \mathbf{then}\ (A^{\Delta2}\ ?\ (u)\ \mathbf{then}\ \mathbf{go}^{0\Delta0}\ u\ \mathbf{else}\ \mathbf{go}^{0\Delta3}\ home\,)$$

$$Broker = A^{\Delta4}\ !\ \langle shopA\rangle\ \mathbf{then}\ 0\ \mathbf{else}\ A^{\Delta7}\ !\ \langle shopB\rangle$$

$$Shops = home[\![Client]\!]\ |\ info[\![Broker]\!]$$

Minimally, the *Shops* system may be encoded in *TLang* as in Figure 3. We say minimally because we do not see any result from this, and the agent does not do anything besides communicating and migrating. A possible running result of this system, completed with some output, is presented in Figure 4. We say "a possible running" because if the agent does not arrive in time at location *info*, or a destination is unreachable, then the output would be different.

```
#extended-language                        agent Broker
#location home(192.168.1.2:9000,0);         try (on A write[4] shopA)
#location info(192.168.1.2:9009,0);         {
#location shopA(192.168.1.2:9099,0);        } else {
#location shopB(192.168.1.2:9999,0);          try (on A write[7] shopB)
                                              {
const channel<location> A;                    }
                                            }
agent Client                              endagent
  location shop;
  try (go[2,3] info){                     system Shops
    try (on A read[2] shop) {               @location home
      try (go[0,0] shop){}                    Client
    } else {                                endlocation
      try (go[0,3] home){}                  @location info
    }                                         Broker
  }                                         endlocation
endagent                                  endsystem
```

Fig. 3. *TLang* encoding of *Shops* system

Some explanations are needed in order to understand the implementation. The first line tells the compiler that the program will use Java types and instructions. The next line describes the location addresses and communication ports. For example *home (192.168.1.2: 9000, 0)* tells that *home* location has the IP address *192.168.1.2*, it runs the basic framework at port *9000* and has no preferred port for receiving agents. The next line declare a global channel named *A* for messages of type *location*. The rest of the specification deals with agents code and distribution.

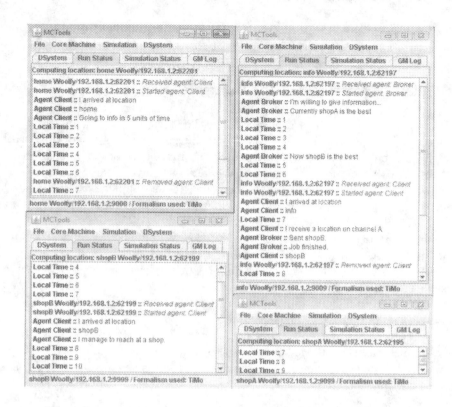

Fig. 4. Running of the *Shops* system

Figure 4 presents the result of system execution after the agents were completed with some text output. Each window corresponds to a location which is written in the status bar. The text boxes contains system messages and agents output, providing useful information about the system evolution. The *Client* starts at location *home*, and after 5 units of time it moves to location *info*. At *info* he communicates with the *Broker* and receives the name *shopB* along channel A. It is important to observe that he does not interact at local time 6, when he arrives, but after another tick. To understand why this happens it is enough to follow the *Client* configuration evolution: $home[(go, (2, 3), info)] \xrightarrow{tick}^5 \xrightarrow{go} info[\#(in\,A, 2\,shop)] \xrightarrow{tick} info[(in\,A, 2, shop)]$. This emphasizes the correspondence between the implementation and the TIMO semantics. Then the agent moves to location *shopB* where it prints a confirmation message. Location *shopA* remains empty during the entire period of time. If we describe the system by a configuration perspective, we get the following evolution which abstracts the system execution and follows the TIMO semantics:

$$home[(go, (2,3), info)] \times info[(out\,A, 4, shopA)] \xrightarrow{tick}^4 \xrightarrow{com_{fail}} home[(go, (0, 1),$$
$$info)] \times info[\#(out\,A, 7, shopB)] \xrightarrow{tick} \xrightarrow{go} \xrightarrow{tick} home[0] \times info[(out\,A, 6,$$
$$shopB), (in\,A, 2, shop)] \xrightarrow{com} \xrightarrow{tick} info[(go, (0, 0), shopB), 0_B] \xrightarrow{go} \xrightarrow{tick}$$

$info[0_B] \times shopB[0_C]$. By 0_C we denote the terminated *Client* process and by 0_B the terminated *Broker* process. We omit the empty location configuration.

7 Related Work and Concluding Remarks

The paper presents a software platform for timed migration. We develop this platform starting from a process algebra which uses time constraints to control both the communication between processes and movement between locations.

We design this platform in two layers. The lower layer deals with low-level details and provides the migration mechanism. It also implements the general concepts used in process algebra of the upper layer, and so it can be re-used for the implementation of other formalisms with mobility. We emphasize the upper layer implementing TiMo, a process algebra with communication, migration and temporal aspects. An intermediate language called *TLang* is used to specify a TiMo distributed systems. The novel features of the lower layer are given by a reusable mobility mechanism using various Java class-loading techniques, as well as the possibility to see the formal evolutions (defined by their semantics) for both TiMo and dπ-calculus which can emphasize possible discrepancies between formal specifications and their implementations. Another feature is represented by the implementation of a distributed protocol without a central coordinator; it allows a sound development methodology of agents on a single machine followed by their distribution among locations.

In TiMo the novelty is provided by the use of two timers lt and mt, and a safety process depending on the the migration timer mt. This aspects are reflected in the corresponding implementation of TiMo.

A similar platform called IMC is presented in [1]. Based on this platform, the authors have implemented the distributed π-calculus. *MCTools* lower layer corresponds to IMC, and offers more functionalities based on a different architecture. Let us mention few differences: the naming mechanism, an integrated formal evolution engine, remote actions which allow to initialize a distributed environment based on a specification. Moreover, using two layers, *MCTools* implements a handling mechanism of various formalism which is not available with IMC.

Several formalisms and implementations have been proposed in the recent years. Among them, we mention Facile [10], join calculus [5] and nomadic π-calculus [9]. Compared to these works, *MCTools* provide a flexible migration layer which could be used by several formalisms. The migration is based on the movement of the agent class and its dependencies from each location to any other location using *MCTools* lower layer.

References

1. Bettini, L., De Nicola, R., Falassi, D., Loreti, M.: Implementing a Distributed Mobile Calculus Using the IMC Framework. Electronic Notes in Theoretical Computer Science 181, 63–79 (2007)

 2. Ciobanu, G., Juravle, C.: MCTools: A Software Platform for Mobility and Timed Interaction. Technical Report FML-09-01, Romanian Academy (2009)
 3. Ciobanu, G., Koutny, M.: Modelling and Verification of Timed Interaction and Migration. In: Fiadeiro, J.L., Inverardi, P. (eds.) FASE 2008. LNCS, vol. 4961, pp. 215–229. Springer, Heidelberg (2008)
 4. Ciobanu, G., Prisacariu, C.: Timers for Distributed Systems. Electronic Notes in Theoretical Computer Science 164, 81–99 (2006)
 5. Fournet, C., Gonthier, G., Levy, J.-J., Maranget, L., Remy, D.: A Calculus of Mobile Agents. In: Sassone, V., Montanari, U. (eds.) CONCUR 1996. LNCS, vol. 1119, pp. 406–421. Springer, Heidelberg (1996)
 6. Hennessy, M., Riely, J.: Resource Access Control in Systems of Mobile Agents. Information and Computation 173, 82–120 (2002)
 7. Magee, J., Krame, J.: Concurrency: State Models and Java Programs. Wiley, Chichester (2006)
 8. Milner, R.: Communicating and Mobile Systems: the π-calculus. Cambridge University Press, Cambridge (1991)
 9. Sewell, P., Wojciechowski, P.T., Pierce, B.C.: Location-independent Communication for Mobile Agents: a Two-level Architecture. In: Bal, H.E., Cardelli, L., Belkhouche, B. (eds.) ICCL-WS 1998. LNCS, vol. 1686, pp. 1–31. Springer, Heidelberg (1999)
10. Thomsen, B., Leth, L., Kuo, T.-M.: A Facile Tutorial. In: Sassone, V., Montanari, U. (eds.) CONCUR 1996. LNCS, vol. 1119, pp. 278–298. Springer, Heidelberg (1996)
11. White, J.E.: Telescript Technology: The Foundation for the Electronic Marketplace. White Paper, General Magic (1994)

Modeling, Validation, and Verification of PCEP Using the IF Language*

Iksoon Hwang[1], Mounir Lallali[1], Ana Cavalli[1], and Dominique Verchere[2]

[1] TELECOM & Management SudParis, 9 Rue Charles Fourier,
91011 Évry Cedex, France
{Iksoon.Hwang,Mounir.Lallali,Ana.Cavalli}@it-sudparis.eu
[2] Alcatel-Lucent R&I, Route de Villejust, 91620 Nozay, France
Dominique.Verchere@alcatel-lucent.com

Abstract. In this paper, we present the modeling, validation, and verification of an industrial protocol for constraint-based path computation, called PCEP. From the PCEP specification defined by IETF, we divide the functionalities of PCEP into two parts: application and protocol. The protocol part of PCEP is then described in the IF language which is based on communicating timed automata. A number of basic requirements are identified from the PCEP specification and then described as properties in the IF language. Based on these properties, the validation and verification of the formal specification are carried out using the IF toolset. Test cases are generated by using an automatic test generation tool, called TestGen-IF, which uses partial state space exploration guided by test purposes. As a result of the modeling, validation, and verification, some errors and ambiguities are found in the PCEP specification. Also a number of test cases are obtained which will be used for testing implementations.

1 Introduction

Formal methods are mathematically rigorous techniques that can be used to describe and analyze the behavior of systems. A number of advantages arise from the use of formal methods during the software development procedure. Less ambiguous specifications are provided and these can be used in model checking and model-based testing. Validation is the process of evaluating software during or at the end of the development process to determine whether it satisfies specified requirements [1]. Model checking and model-based testing have been widely used for validation and verification of systems. Recently, there have been a number of industrial case studies that use formal methods in validation and verification. Bozga *et al.* [2] presented the verification and test generation for the SSCOP protocol and Jia and Graf [3] performed the verification experiments on the MASCARA protocol using IF (Intermediate Format) [4]. Hessel and Pettersson [5] provides model-based testing of a WAP gateway using UPPAAL [6].

---

* This work has been supported by the French competitiveness cluster SYSTEM@TIC, through CARRIOCAS project.

D. Lee et al. (Eds.): FMOODS/FORTE 2009, LNCS 5522, pp. 122–136, 2009.
© IFIP International Federation for Information Processing 2009

The CARRIOCAS project [7] aims at providing a distributed pilot network for industrial applications with high complexity, scope, and scale. A number of hardware and software components are developed in the project in order to provide the connectivity services for such large-scale distributed, data, and computing intensive applications. One of the important activities of the CARRIOCAS project is the validation experiment on the proposed pilot network. As a part of the validation activities, a communication protocol for constraint-based path computation which is called Path Computation Element Communication Protocol (PCEP) [8] is chosen for validation and verification.

In this paper, we present the modeling, validation, and verification of PCEP, which are carried out in the CARRIOCAS project. From the PCEP specification defined by IETF (Internet Engineering Task Force), we divide the functionalities of PCEP into two parts: application and protocol. The protocol part is then described in the IF language. A number of basic requirements are identified from the PCEP specification and then described as properties in IF. Based on these properties, the validation and verification of the formal specification are carried out using the IF toolset [9]. From the basic requirements, a number of test purposes are defined and test cases are generated by using an automatic test generation tool, called TestGen-IF [10]. As a result of the modeling, validation, and verification, we found some errors and ambiguities in the PCEP specification. Also we obtained a number of test cases which will be used for testing implementations in the CARRIOCAS project.

The paper is organized as follows. In Section 2, we explain briefly about the CARRIOCAS project and PCEP. The IF language and the IF toolset are explained in Section 3. In Section 4, we describe how to model PCEP in the IF language and the validation of the formal specification is carried out in Section 5. The test generation methods and results are discussed in Section 6 and finally Section 7 concludes the paper.

2   CARRIOCAS Project and PCEP

2.1   CARRIOCAS Project

Large scale distributed applications (often termed as Grid applications) challenge the performance of the existing telecom network infrastructures. In the CARRIOCAS project, a number of research and industrial applications are considered such as car design with crash simulations for safety analysis and energy production with atomic reactor models for central problem simulations. These applications require ultra-high performance computers to execute their simulation application workflows during the life-cycle of the project and also need exchange of massive amounts of data in order to enable local and distant groups of engineers to work collaboratively while viewing and analyzing their results.

The purpose of the CARRIOCAS project is to design and develop the components of high-throughput capacity system and flexible network architectures that can adapt its connectivity services dynamically for the data-intensive and delay sensitive distributed applications. The pilot network aggregates the Ethernet data flows issued from client networks to be transported by carrier grade Ethernet Virtual Circuits. The CARRIOCAS project is attempting to develop a common service management component based on the Scheduling, Reconfiguration, and Virtualization (SRV) functions to allow the compositions of different connection service elements from a network infrastructure. The SRV functions can be extended above different types of infrastructures including computational servers and data storage centers to deliver bundles of service elements. These extensions require advanced Network Management capabilities based on Path Computation Element (PCE) functions which provide the routes of the connection services, e.g. the routes on GMPLS (Generalized Multi-Protocol Label Switching)-capable carrier grade Ethernet switches.

In addition to the design and development of the network, one of the important activities of the CARRIOCAS project is the validation experiment on the proposed pilot network. As a part of the validation activities, a communication protocol for constraint-based path computation which is called PCEP is chosen for validation and verification.

2.2   Path Computation Element Communication Protocol

In large scale and multi-domain networks, path computation can be complex and may require specific computational components and cooperation between elements in different nodes. In order to address these problems, an architecture based on PCE model has been proposed [8]. In this PCE-based architecture, a PCE is an entity that computes a network path based on a network graph and computational constraints and a Path Computation Client (PCC) is any kind of client application requesting a path computation to be performed by a PCE. PCEP is a communication protocol between a PCC and a PCE, or between two PCEs in order to exchange path computation requests and path computation replies as well as notifications of specific events related to the use of a PCE. PCEP operates over TCP [11] which provides reliable messaging and flow control. The following PCEP messages are defined:

- *Open* message is used to initiate and negotiate a PCEP session.
- *Keepalive* message is used to establish and maintain a PCEP session.
- *PCReq* message is sent to request a path computation.
- *PCRep* message is sent in reply to a path computation request.
- *PCNtf* message is sent to notify a specific event.
- *PCErr* message is sent upon the occurrence of a protocol error condition.
- *Close* message is used to close a PCEP session.

A PCC may have PCEP sessions with more than one PCE and similarly a PCE may have PCEP sessions with multiple PCCs. Once the TCP connection is established between a PCC and a PCE, the PCC and the PCE (also referred to as "PCEP peers") initiate PCEP session establishment. Various session parameters including the Keepalive timer, the Deadtimer, other detailed capabilities,

and policy rules are carried within *Open* messages. If the session parameters
are agreed, *Keepalive* messages are used to acknowledge *Open* messages. Once
the PCEP session has been successfully established, *Keepalive* messages may be
exchanged between PCEP peers to ensure the liveness of the PCEP session. If
the session parameters are not acceptable but negotiable, session negotiation
can be performed where the proposed session parameters are contained within
PCErr messages. If the PCEP peers disagree on the session parameters or one
of the PCEP peers does not answer after the expiration of the establishment
timer, the TCP connection is immediately closed. Figure 1 shows the scenario
of PCEP session establishment after negotiation.

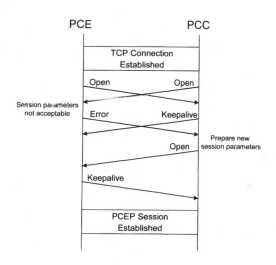

Fig. 1. PCEP session establishment after negotiation

After establishment of a PCEP session, when an event is triggered that requires the computation of a set of paths, the PCC sends a *PCReq* message which
contains a set of constraints and attributes for the path for computing. Upon
receiving a path computation request from a PCC, the PCE triggers a path computation, the results are sent back to the PCC in a *PCRep* message where they
can be either positive (one or more computed paths) or negative (no path found).
When a PCE wants to notify a specific event to PCCs such as possible unacceptable delay because of overload, it sends a *PCNtf* message to PCCs. Similarly,
a PCC may desire to notify a PCE of a particular event such as the cancelation of pending requests. A *PCErr* message is sent in several situations: when
a protocol error condition is met or when the request is not compliant with the
PCEP specification, e.g. reception of malformed messages or unexpected messages. When one of the PCEP peers desires to terminate a PCEP session, it first
sends a *Close* message and then closes the TCP connection. When the PCEP
session is terminated, the PCC and the PCE cancel all pending operations and
clear corresponding resources.

3   IF Language

3.1   IF Model

IF [4] is a formal method based on communicating timed automata in order to model asynchronous communicating real-time systems. In IF, a system is expressed by a set of parallel processes communicating asynchronously through a set of buffers. A process instance can be created and destroyed dynamically during system execution. An IF process is described as a timed automaton extended with discrete data variables. A process has a set of control states and a private buffer for input messages, and can have local data such as discrete variables and clocks. There are two types of control states: stable states and unstable states. An unstable state is a temporary state where no interleaving between processes is possible. In other words, if a process moves to an unstable state by an action, the atomicity of the execution is guaranteed until it reaches a stable state.

Transitions describe the behavior of a process on stimuli. A transition can be triggered either by (timed) guards or by an input message where an urgency attribute (*eager*, *delayable* or *lazy*) defines the priority of the transition over time progress. When an *eager* transition is executable, time progress is blocked until the transition is executed. If there is an executable *delayable* transition, time can progress as long as the transition is executable. If time progress makes the *delayable* transition non-executable, time progress is blocked until the transition is executed. For *lazy* transitions, time can progress although the transitions become non-executable. The action of a transition may include sending output messages, setting/resetting clocks, assignment of variable values, and creation/destruction of processes.

3.2   IF Toolset

The IF toolset [9] provides an environment for modeling and validation of an IF specification. The core components of the toolset are the IF static analyzer and the IF exploration platform. The IF static analyzer transforms an IF specification into an abstract syntax tree which is a collection of C++ objects. The IF exploration platform performs the simulation of process executions by using the abstract syntax trees. A set of APIs is provided by the IF exploration platform, which allows implementation of user-specific exploration. Through these APIs, CADP [12], a tool for validation of LTS models and TGV [13], for test case generation using on-the-fly technique can be connected to the IF toolset.

In the IF toolset, it is possible to check if given properties hold for an IF specification by using observers. Once a property is described in the IF language using a specific syntax for observers, e.g. monitoring of events and cutting off generation of irrelevant states, it is executed in parallel with the target system. The communication between the system and the observer process is synchronous and the observer process has always the highest priority during exploration so that monitoring of an event is triggered immediately when the event occurs.

4   Formal Description of PCEP

4.1   Overall Architecture

In our experiments, we divide the functionalities of PCEP into two parts: application and protocol. The functionalities of the application part include session initiation, session parameter negotiation, request/reply of path computation, notification of specific events, closing the session, etc. The functionalities of the protocol part include the handling of finite state machines including local variables and timers, collision resolution procedure, keeping the current session by exchanging *Keepalive* messages, etc. In our formal specification of PCEP, the protocol part is modeled by a system. PCEP applications and the lower layer (TCP) are, therefore, considered to be an environment. A complete set of service primitives are defined between PCEP applications and the system and between the system and the lower layer. As a PCEP application can communicate with more than one peer PCEP applications, it is necessary to model multiple instances of the PCEP protocol. The system consists of a main process and multiple instances of a child process where each instance of the child process handles a PCEP session. The Figure 2 shows the overall architecture.

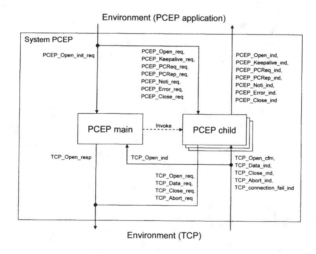

Fig. 2. Overall architecture of the formal specification of PCEP

In TCP, function interfaces are defined to provide a certain minimum set of services to guarantee that all TCP implementations can support the same protocol hierarchy [11]. The service primitives between the system and TCP are based on those function interfaces. For exchange of user data, i.e. exchange of the PCEP messages through Send and Receive user calls, we introduce parameterized service primitives, TCP_Data_PCEP_xxx_req and TCP_Data_PCEP_xxx_ind. The TCP_Data_PCEP_Unknown_ind service primitive represents an unknown PCEP message from its peer and the TCP_connection_fail_ind service primitive represents TCP connection failures such as the failure of sending a message. The service primitives between the system and PCEP applications are based on the PCEP messages. In order to model session initiation request from a PCEP application, the PCEP_Open_init_req service primitive is introduced. When the main process receives a session initiation request by receiving either the TCP_Open_ind message from a PCEP peer or the PCEP_Open_init_req message from a PCEP application, it creates a child process which manages the PCEP session.

4.2   States, Internal Variables, and Timers

As mentioned in Section 4.1, we have two kinds of processes in our model: a main process and a child process. Since the purpose of the main process is to create instances of a child process when there are session initiation requests, the main process has only one stable state, Idle. In a child process the following four stable states are defined based on the PCEP specification: TCPPending, Open-Wait, KeepWait, and SessionUP. In addition to the stable states, we introduce a number of unstable states in order to branch off the control flow of a process. If the behavior is decided by internal variable values or clock values, each case can be represented by a transition. If the decision should be made by the parameter values of an input message, however, it is necessary to have more than one transition, one to receive a message and the others to check the parameter values. In this case, the parameter values are checked in unstable states in order to guarantee the atomicity of the behavior. The following shows an example.

```
state TCPPending;
  deadline lazy;
  input TCP_Open_cfm(tcpConnectResult);
    nextstate TCPPending_TCP_Open_cfm_decision;
  ...
endstate;

state TCPPending_TCP_Open_cfm_decision #unstable ;
  provided (tcpConnectResult = ConnectSuccess);
    ...
      nextstate OpenWait;

  provided (tcpConnectResult = ConnectFail) and
           (tcpConnectRetry < TCPConnectMaxRetry);
    ...
      nextstate TCPPending;
  ...
endstate;
```

In our model, four internal variables and five timers are defined based on the PCEP specification: tcpConnectRetry, pcepOpenRetry, remoteOK, and localOK for internal variables, and tcpConnectTimer, pcepOpenWaitTimer, pcepKeepWaitTimer, pcepKeepaliveTimer, and pcepDeadTimer for timers. In addition to the above internal variables, the main process manages a childInfoTable which contains information on the current ongoing sessions in order to manage the number of active sessions and duplicated session initiation requests. Also the childInfoTable is used for collision resolution procedure when there are simultaneous session initiation requests between PCEP peers.

As mentioned in Section 4.1, a decision on session parameter negotiation is carried out by PCEP applications in our model. When a child process in OpenWait state receives an *Open* message from its peer, it sends the received information to its PCEP application and then waits for a reply from the application. If there is no reply for a given time, the child process should release the corresponding PCEP resources and close the TCP connection. A new timer, internalKeep-WaitTimer is introduced for that purpose. Similarly, internalOpenWaitTimer is introduced for waiting a reply from applications when a *PCErr* message is received from its peer for session negotiation. The SyncTimer is not included in our model because the cancelation of path computation request is considered to be the functionality of PCEP applications.

4.3 Abstraction of Information

In PCEP, each PCEP message has a common header and may have a number of PCEP objects. In our service primitives, the number of parameters is minimized in order to reduce the problem size of the model. A minimum set of parameters to decide the behavior of the system is defined for each service primitive as follows: Keepalive and Deadtimer for an *Open* message, a list of pairs of errorType and errorValue for a *PCErr* message, the existence of rpObject and endPointObject for a *PCReq* message, and the existence of rpObject for a *PCRep* message. The Keepalive parameter value is used to send a *Keepalive* message periodically in SessionUP state. A PCEP session is closed if there is no PCEP message from its peer during the time given in the Deadtimer parameter. The errorType and errorValue are necessary since the behavior of the system can be different according to these values. The existence of rpObject and endPointObject is used to send proper *PCErr* messages when these mandatory parameters are missing.

In our model, we assume that the PCEP messages received from PCEP peers may have errors such as missing mandatory objects and unknown objects. In order to model any errors in the received PCEP message which cannot be modeled by other parameters, a boolean type parameter, errorInPCEPMessage is defined in TCP_Data_PCEP_XXX_ind service primitives. For example, receiving an unknown object is modeled by "errorInPCEPMessage=true" while missing rpObject by "rpObjectExist=false". Since the errorInPCEPMessage parameter represents most erroneous messages, some cases are missing in our model, e.g. the system should send a *PCErr* message with "errorType=3" when it receives an unknown object from its peer. When there is a TCP connection request from its peer, the decision whether accept it or not is usually made by system calls without interaction with its applications. Therefore, the tcpConnectResult parameter, which contains the result of this decision, is included in TCP_Open_ind service primitive.

4.4 Remarks

In this section, we explain two issues that we have faced when modeling.

How to make time progress in a system? In IF, it is assumed that time does not progress during execution of transitions, i.e. the time spent during execution of transitions is always zero. Time can progress only in stable configurations as long as there is no executable *eager* transition. In our model, there is always at least one executable transition enabled by an input message from environment at any stable state as we designed the system in such a way that the interaction between the system and environment is possible at any instance. Therefore, if the transitions enabled by an input message from environment have *eager* deadline, time in the system will never progress. In order to solve this problem, we used *lazy* deadline for every transition enabled by an input message from environment.

Is the first incoming message served first in a process? In IF, the communication between two processes is asynchronous, i.e. messages from other processes are stored in a buffer before being consumed. However, messages from environment are handled in a different way. The Figure 3 shows how incoming messages are handled in a process.

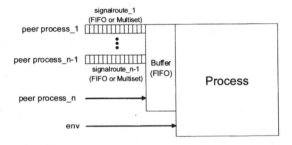

Fig. 3. Handling of incoming messages in a process

As shown in the figure, there is a FIFO buffer for each process. The messages sent from other processes arrive at the buffer either through a signalroute or directly from the peer process. Each signalroute has its own property such as fifo/multiset, reliable/lossy, etc. When a message is passed to a receiver process from a signalroute, it is stored in the buffer. The order of passing messages from signalroute to the buffer can be either FIFO or random according to the property of the signalroute. When a process sends a message to a receiver process directly by using the destination process ID, it is stored in the buffer immediately. When a message is sent from environment to a process, the message is not stored in the buffer and is consumed immediately by the process although there are messages in the buffer waiting for being consumed. Therefore, the communication between environment and a process is synchronous while the communication between two processes is asynchronous.

In our model, in the beginning, there was an internal communication between the main process and a child process. When an instance of a child process is to terminate, it sends a *done* message to the main process and the main process clears all internal information related to that child process. In order to keep the consistency of resources, the main process should consume the *done* message as soon as it receives. However, this cannot be guaranteed since the main process can receive messages from environment at any time. As a result, we had resource mismatch problem, i.e. the child information was not cleared in the main process although the child process had already been terminated. In order to solve this problem, we removed the internal communication and the internal information related to a child process is cleared by the child process itself. Note that our solution is a temporary one and only applicable to limited cases. A general solution is required for the above problem.

5   Validation of the Formal Description

5.1   Validation with IF Observers

IF observers can be used to check if given properties hold for an IF specification. Properties are based on observable actions such as input and output messages, and also include checking variable values and clock values. Once a property is described in the IF language, an exhaustive state space exploration using either breadth first search or depth first search is carried out by the IF simulator. During the simulation, the observer process checks if it can observe the expected behavior. In our experiments, first, we define the following three general properties.

- Property G1: The specification must be deadlock-free.
- Property G2: In any state, there must be at least one active timer.
- Property G3: In any state, the value of any active timer must be no greater than its maximum.

The purpose of the property G2 is to avoid infinite time progress waiting for some events[1]. The property G3 checks if the system stops timers appropriately either by timeout or by cancelation. Second, the properties specific to PCEP are identified from the PCEP specification. In order to facilitate the modeling, we define a state transition table that describes the behavior of the system for a given set of state, input, and conditions. Table 1 shows an example.

According to Table 1, if the system is in KeepWait state where the Keepalive timer is active and remoteOK=0 and it receives a TCP_Data_PCEP_Keepalive_ind message without error, it should send a PCEP_Keepalive_ind message and move to OpenWait state. The above information represents an atomic behavior that the system should follow and it can be considered to be a requirement. In our experiments, 101 basic requirements are identified from a complete state transition table and then 66 requirements are described as properties in the IF language. For each requirement, it is considered that the property holds for the formal specification if the system sends the expected output messages and moves to the expected next state for the given set of state, input, and conditions.

---

[1] In the case of PCEP, the property G2 may not hold if the Keepalive timer and the Deadtimer have zero values.

Table 1. State transition table

Input	KeepWait			
	Index	Condition	Output	Next state
TCP_Data_PCEP_Keepalive_ind	56	Keepalive timer active, No error in msg, remoteOK=0	PCEP_Keepalive_ind	OpenWait

In order to reduce the problem size during the validation, first, the timer values and retry numbers are limited. The maximum values of the tcpConnect-Timer, the pcepOpenWaitTimer, and the pcepKeepWaitTimer are limited to 2 instead of 60 seconds[2]. The maximum values of the pcepKeepaliveTimer and the pcepDeadTimer are limited to 2 and 8 respectively as the recommended value for the pcepDeadTimer is four times the value of the pcepKeepaliveTimer used by the remote peer. The tcpConnectMaxRetry is limited to 1 instead of 5. Second, we limit the range of parameter values. The values of the Keepalive and the Deadtimer parameters in an *Open* message are fixed to have 2 and 8, respectively. The number of error objects that can be carried within a *PCErr* message is limited to 1 and the values of errorType and errorValue parameters are limited to 1 and from 1 to 6 respectively.

5.2   Validation Results

With the limited timer values, retry numbers, and parameter values, the system with one instance of a child process was completely explored with 410 states and 12010 transitions. When we allowed all possible values for the input parameters while the timer values and retry numbers were limited, we had extremely large number of transitions. The system was completely explored with 3095 states and 55355305 transitions. When we used the timer values and retry numbers as given in the PCEP specification, e.g. 60 seconds for the tcpConnectTimer, while the parameter values were limited, we could explore the system with 85750 states and 3945670 transitions. In the case of two instances of a child process with the limited timer values, retry numbers, and parameter values, the simulator completed state space exploration with 74476 states and 4294788 transitions. For most properties, the validation is carried out where the timer values, retry numbers, and parameter values are limited. If it is necessary to have other parameter values, the ranges of those parameters are changed appropriately in the formal specification. For the property 29, the validation is carried out with two instances of a child process as it checks if the current PCEP connection is released by the collision resolution procedure. Table 2 shows the validation results.

Among 69 properties (three general and 66 specific to PCEP), 66 properties were successfully validated where most simulations were terminated within 15

---

[2] It is possible to consider that timer values are abstracted such that 0 represents no time progress, 1 time progress up to 59 seconds, and 2 represents 60 seconds.

Table 2. Validation results

Properties	# of states	# of trans	Time (hh:mm:ss)	Results
Prop. G1	85514	2855179	12:26:09	Interrupted (No failure)
Prop. G2	1568	54981	6	Validated
Prop. G3	51923	1050744	3:47	Validated
Prop. 18	2516	55929	9	Failed (No success)
Prop. 29	108111	2629793	9:58:28	Interrupted (Success, No failure)
Others	< 33500	< 867000	< 2:25	Validated

seconds. For two properties (property G1 and property 29), the simulations were interrupted after around 10 hours because of state explosion problem[3]. Although we observed the expected behavior and no failure was found for those two properties, we cannot say that the validation was successful since we could not explore all possible state space. We found that the property 18 does not hold for our formal specification. Although we explored all possible state space, we could not observe the expected behavior. This was due to the problem that was found in the original PCEP specification. There exists a case in the PCEP specification that never happens.

5.3   Remarks

One of the difficulties during the validation was the large size of state space. In our model, some internal variables, e.g. internal variables for receiving parameter values, are used temporarily. During the validation, we found that a number of redundant states were generated due to those internal variables. In order to remove those redundant states, we initialized those internal variables by the end of each transition. For example, once we check the value of the tcpConnectResult variable in TCPPending_TCP_Open_cfm_decision state as presented in Section 4.2, the variable is initialized as it is not used in other states. As a result, the numbers of states and transitions explored after exhaustive state space exploration reduced from 30329 states and 941313 transitions to 410 states and 12010 transitions.

In IF observers, internal variable values and the parameter values of messages can be checked after the execution of each transition. Therefore, if a property includes checking variable values or parameter values while those values are initialized after the execution of the transition, e.g. by going back to Idle state, it is not possible to check the property. The main reason why only 66 requirements are described as properties while 101 basic requirements are identified is due to this limitation.

---

[3] In our experiments, it is considered to have the state explosion problem either when the simulation proceeds very slowly where the memory usage reaches almost its maximum or when the simulator crashes due to lack of memory.

6   Test Generation of PCEP

6.1   Testgen-IF

The TestGen-IF generates timed test cases from an IF specification and a set of test purposes. Partial state space exploration guided by test purposes is carried out, which is called the Hit-or-Jump algorithm [14]. A test purpose is a set of (ordered) conditions. A condition is a conjunction of a process instance constraint, state constraints, action constraints, variable constraints, and clock constraints. A process instant constraint indicates the identifier of a process instance. A state constraint indicates source state or target state of a transition. Action constraints describe observable actions such as sending or receiving messages as well as non-observable actions such as informal statements. A variable constraint gives conditions on variable values and a clock constraint conditions on either clock values or status of clocks, e.g. active/inactive. The following shows the test purpose which corresponds to the requirement given in Table 1.

$$
\begin{aligned}
tp_{56} &= \{cond_1\} \\
cond_1 &= constraint_1 \wedge constraint_2 \wedge \ldots \wedge constraint_7 \\
constraint_1 &= \text{``}process : instance = \{\texttt{PCEPChild}\}\texttt{0}\text{''} \\
constraint_2 &= \text{``}state : source = \texttt{KeepWait}\text{''} \\
constraint_3 &= \text{``}state : target = \texttt{OpenWait}\text{''} \\
constraint_4 &= \text{``}action : \texttt{input TCP\_Data\_PCEP\_Keepalive\_ind(f)}\text{''} \\
constraint_5 &= \text{``}action : \texttt{output PCEP\_Keepalive\_ind()}\text{''} \\
constraint_6 &= \text{``}variable : \texttt{remoteOK = false}\text{''} \\
constraint_7 &= \text{``}clock : \texttt{pcepKeepWaitTimer is active}\text{''}
\end{aligned}
$$

The state exploration starts from a given state s_i, which is the initial state in the beginning, using breadth first search with a given *depth limit*. Initially, all conditions in a test purpose are unmarked. If an unmarked condition is satisfied in a transition during exploration where the target state is s_j, which is called a *Hit*, the condition is marked, the path from s_i to s_j is stored, the buffer that stores visited state information is cleared, and then the exploration starts again from s_j. If no unmarked condition is satisfied during the exploration until the given *depth limit*, which is called a *Jump*, one of leaf nodes, e.g. the state s'_j is chosen for the start state, the path from s_i to s'_j is stored, the buffer that stores visited state information is cleared, and then exploration starts again from s'_j. The state space exploration terminates either when all conditions are marked or when all state space is explored within the *depth limit*. Once all conditions are satisfied during the exploration, i.e. all conditions are marked, the path from the initial state to the target state of the transition where the last condition is satisfied becomes a test sequence for the test purpose. A test sequence consists of observable actions such as input and output messages and delays which represent time intervals between observable actions.

6.2   Test Generation and Results

As mentioned in Section 5.1, 101 basic requirements are identified from the PCEP specification. In our experiments, for simplicity, we generate a test case for each requirement. Among 101 requirements, 98 requirements are described as test purposes. Three requirements are missing because of the following reasons. As explained in Section 5.2, there is a requirement that our formal specification does not meet (property 18). For the other two requirements, they are not considered because the atomicity of the behavior cannot be guaranteed in our description of test purposes since two processes are involved in the behavior.

Similar to the case of validation, the timer values, retry numbers, and parameter values are limited for most test purposes. If it is necessary to have other parameter values, the ranges of those parameters are changed appropriately. The following shows an example test sequence which is generated by the test purpose given in Section 6.1

```
?TCP_Open_ind{1,ConnectSuccess} !TCP_Open_resp{ConnectSuccess}
!TCP_Data_PCEP_Open_req{{{2,8}}}
?TCP_Data_PCEP_Open_ind{f,{{2,8}}} !PCEP_Open_ind{{{2,8}}}
?PCEP_Error_req{{1,{{1,4},}}} !TCP_Data_PCEP_Error_req{{1,{{1,4},}}}
?TCP_Data_PCEP_Keepalive_ind{f} !PCEP_Keepalive_ind{}
```

For all 98 test purposes, the test sequences are generated successfully. After deleting the test sequences which are the prefix of another one, we finally obtain 90 test sequences where the total number of test inputs is 353. The generated test sequences will be used for testing PCEP implementation developed by one of the partners of the CARRIOCAS project.

7   Conclusions

In this paper, we presented the modeling, validation, and verification of PCEP which is a protocol for constraint-based path computation defined by IETF. The protocol part of PCEP is described in the IF language. A number of basic requirements are identified from the PCEP specification and then described as properties in the IF language. Based on these properties, the validation of the formal specification is carried out by using the IF toolset. From the basic requirements, a number of test purposes are defined and test cases are generated by using the TestGen-IF. The obtained test cases will be used for testing implementations developed by one of the partners of the CARRIOCAS project.

Our experiments showed very promising results concerning the use of formal methods for modeling, validation, and verification. A number of errors and ambiguities were found from the original specification including a wrong sentence that misleads the behavior of the protocol, a non-executable transition (related to the property 18 as explained in Section 5.2), and unclear descriptions such as when a timer should be started. It should be noted that most of these errors were found during the modeling phase. Therefore, we can conclude that if we describe specifications using formal methods, we can obtain higher quality of specifications, i.e. with less errors and ambiguities even before validation of the formal specifications.

References

1. Software Engineering Institute/Carnegie Mellon: Capability Maturity Model Integration (CMMISM) for Software Engineering Version 1.1 (2002)
2. Bozga, M., Fernandez, J.C., Ghirvu, L., Jard, C., Jron, T., Kerbrat, A., Morel, P., Mounier, L.: Verification and test generation for the SSCOP protocol. Journal of Science of Computer Programming 36, 27–52 (2000)
3. Jia, G., Graf, S.: Verification experiments on the MASCARA protocol. In: Dwyer, M.B. (ed.) SPIN 2001. LNCS, vol. 2057, pp. 123–142. Springer, Heidelberg (2001)
4. Bozga, M., Graf, S., Mounier, L.: IF-2.0: A validation environment for component-based real-time systems. In: Brinksma, E., Larsen, K.G. (eds.) CAV 2002. LNCS, vol. 2404, pp. 343–348. Springer, Heidelberg (2002)
5. Hessel, A., Pettersson, P.: Model-based testing of a WAP gateway: An industrial case-study. In: Brim, L., Haverkort, B.R., Leucker, M., van de Pol, J. (eds.) FMICS 2006 and PDMC 2006. LNCS, vol. 4346, pp. 116–131. Springer, Heidelberg (2007)
6. Larsen, K.G., Pettersson, P., Yi, W.: UPPAAL in a Nutshell. Int. Journal on Software Tools for Technology Transfer 1, 134–152 (1997)
7. Audouin, O., Cavalli, A., Chiosi, A., Leclerc, O., Mouton, C., Oksman, J., Pasin, M., Rodrigues, D., Thual, L.: CARRIOCAS project: an experimental high bit rate optical network tailored for computing and data intensive distributed applications. In: Society of Photo-Optical Instrumentation Engineers (SPIE) Conference Series (2007)
8. Vasseur, J.P., Le Roux, J.L.: Path Computation Element (PCE) Communication Protocol, IETF Internet draft, draft-ietf-pce-pcep-19.txt, work in progress (November 2008)
9. Bozga, M., Graf, S., Ober, I., Ober, I., Sifakis, J.: The IF toolset. In: Bernardo, M., Corradini, F. (eds.) SFM-RT 2004. LNCS, vol. 3185, pp. 237–267. Springer, Heidelberg (2004)
10. Cavalli, A.R., Montes De Oca, E., Mallouli, W., Lallali, M.: Two complementary tools for the formal testing of distributed systems with time constraints. In: Proceedings of the 12th IEEE/ACM International Symposium on Distributed Simulation and Real-Time Applications, Vancouver, Canada, pp. 315–318 (2008)
11. Postel, J.: Transmission Control Protocol. RFC 793 (Standard), Updated by RFCs 1122, 3168 (1981)
12. Fernandez, J.C., Garavel, H., Kerbrat, A., Mounier, L., Mateescu, R., Sighireanu, M.: CADP - A protocol validation and verification toolbox. In: Alur, R., Henzinger, T.A. (eds.) CAV 1996. LNCS, vol. 1102, pp. 437–440. Springer, Heidelberg (1996)
13. Fernandez, J.-C., Jard, C., Jéron, T., Viho, C.: Using on-the-fly verification techniques for the generation of test suites. In: Alur, R., Henzinger, T.A. (eds.) CAV 1996. LNCS, vol. 1102, pp. 348–359. Springer, Heidelberg (1996)
14. Cavalli, A.R., Lee, D., Rinderknecht, C., Zaïdi, F.: Hit-or-Jump: An algorithm for embedded testing with applications to in services. In: Proceedings of FORTE XII / PSTV XIX 1999, pp. 41–56. Kluwer, Dordrecht (1999)

Distinguing Non-deterministic Timed Finite State Machines

Maxim Gromov[1], Khaled El-Fakih[2], Natalia Shabaldina[1], and Nina Yevtushenko[1]

[1] Tomsk State University, 36 Lenin Str. Tomsk 634050, Russia
gromov@sibmail.com, snv@kitidis.tsu.ru,
ninayevtushenko@yahoo.com
[2] American University of Sharjah, P.O. Box 26666, UAE
kelfakih@aus.edu

Abstract. Conformance testing with the guaranteed fault coverage is based on distinguishing faulty system implementations from the corresponding system specification. We consider timed systems modeled by timed possibly non-deterministic finite state machines (TFSMs) and propose algorithms for distinguishing two TFSMs. In particular, we present a preset algorithm for separating two separable TFSMs and an adaptive algorithm for r-distinguishing two possibly non-separable TFSMs. The proposed techniques extend existing methods for untimed non-deterministic FSMs by dealing with the fact that unlike untimed FSMs in general, a TFSM has an infinite number of timed inputs. Correspondingly we state that the upper bounds on the length of distinguishing sequences are the same as for untimed FSMs.

1 Introduction

Timed systems are used in various application areas such as telecommunication systems, plant and traffic controllers and others. A number of formal models have been proposed for testing and verification of timed systems (see, for example, [1], [5], [22]) including systems modeled as timed Finite State Machines (FSMs) [9], [15], [16]. FSMs are widely used in many application areas; in particular, they are used as the underlying models for formal description techniques, such as SDL and UML State Diagrams, and many conformance test derivation methods are based on a specification given in the form of a finite state machine. For surveys see [3], [11] and for some related experiments see [4]. Most of the past work on FSM-based conformance testing has been done for deriving tests for deterministic FSMs w.r.t. the equivalence relation. In addition, there also exist methods for deriving tests for non-deterministic FSMs w.r.t. a number of conformance relations, such as the equivalence, reduction, and the non-separability relations [6], [7], [8], [12], [17], [18], [21]. Two FSMs are equivalent if they have the same input/output behavior and an FSM P is a reduction of FSM S if the behavior of P is contained in the behavior of S. Moreover, two FSMs are non-separable [23] if the sets of output responses of these machines to each input sequence intersect. If there exists an input sequence, called a *separating sequence*, such that the output responses of the two FSMs to the sequence are disjoint then the

D. Lee et al. (Eds.): FMOODS/FORTE 2009, LNCS 5522, pp. 137–151, 2009.
© IFIP International Federation for Information Processing 2009

machines are separable. Two complete FSMs are r-distinguishable if they have no common complete reduction. This fact can be checked by a finite set of sequences which is called an r-distinguishing set of the two FSMs. In this paper, we say that two FSMs are distinguishable if they are separable or r-distinguishable. Experiments that distinguish two FSMs can be classified as adaptive and preset [10]. In an adaptive experiment the next input of an experiment depends on the outputs to previous input sequences and in a preset experiment the whole input sequence is predetermined independently of the intermediate outcome of an experiment. Separating two FSMs can be done in a preset experiment; however, two non-separable FSMs can be still distinguished by an adaptive experiment using the r-distinguishability relation.

Testing based on timed FSM models is a difficult task since it requires checking the time constraints of the system in addition to input and output behavior. In the past few years some work has been carried out on deriving test suites based on timed automata. For example, Springintveld et al. [22] proposed a rigorous method that derives test suites with the guaranteed fault coverage w.r.t. the equivalence relation when the system specification and an Implementation Under Test (IUT) are deterministic. The results were extended in [5] to non-deterministic timed automata w.r.t. the equivalence relation under the assumption of "*all weather conditions*" [13], [14], also called *complete testing* assumption in [12]. According to this assumption, if an input sequence (a test case) is applied a number of times to a non-deterministic IUT, then all possible output sequences of the IUT to this test case are observed while testing. Similar to FSM-based methods, the methods in [5], [22] use so-called distinguishing sequences in test derivation; however, these sequences are derived for the equivalence relation. Recently, Merayo et al. [15], [16] considered a timed possibly non-deterministic FSM model. Time constrains limit a time elapsed when an output has to be produced after an input has been applied to the FSM. When an output is produced the clock variable is reset to zero. The model also takes into account time-outs; if no input is applied at a current state for some time-out period, the (timed) FSM moves from current state to another state using a time-out function. Various conformance relations are introduced for such a timed FSM model; however, the problem of deriving distinguishing sequences w.r.t. the proposed relations is not tackled in the papers. A timed model of a stochastic FSM is considered in [9] where the authors propose a method for deriving a complete test suite for the considered model w.r.t. the reduction relation. Distinguishing sets used for deriving a complete test suite extend corresponding sets for untimed FSMs based on related random variables.

When an IUT has a limited controllability, as happens, for instance, in remote testing, the complete testing assumption cannot be satisfied. In this case, the only relation that can be used for the preset testing with the guaranteed fault coverage is the separability relation [19], defined by Starke in [23], and the only relation that can be used for the adaptive testing with the guaranteed fault coverage is the r-distinguihability relation. Derivation methods and upper bounds on length of distinguishing sequences for untimed non-deterministic FSMs based on the separability relation can be found in [2], [20] and derivation methods based on the r-distinguishability relation can be found in [8], [17], [18]. However, methods given for the derivation of distinguishing sequence for untimed FSMs cannot be directly applied to timed FSMs, since in timed FSMs, in general, the number of timed inputs is infinite; thus, the extension of these methods is not a trivial problem. Accordingly, in this paper, we propose algorithms for distinguishing timed non-deterministic FSMs (TFSMs) w.r.t. the separability and r-distinguishability relations. In particular, given two TFSMs, we present a preset algorithm for deriving a shortest (timed) sequence that separates the two machines, when such a sequence exists. For two non-separable but r-distinguishable TFSMs, we present an adaptive algorithm for deriving sequences that r-distinguish these machines. We also state that upper bounds on the length of such distinguishing sequences coincide with those of untimed FSMs and similar to untimed FSMs those bounds are reachable. As usual, the algorithms presented in this paper can be used as well for fault diagnosis of timed FSMs.

We note that the TFSM model considered in this paper is somehow similar to that given in [15], [16]. In particular, as in [15], [16], we consider non-deterministic timed FSMs where time constraints are used to limit time elapsed at states and we also use one clock variable that is reset at every transition; however, unlike [15], [16], we do not consider time-outs at states. According to this fact, more complex time constraints can be described by the model in [15], [16]. Another timed model that is used as basis for test derivation is given in [5], [22]. This model is very close to the popular automaton based model presented by Alur and Dill [1]. However, we recall that the work in [22] considers only deterministic input/output behaviors of a timed I/O automaton while the authors in [5] consider non-deterministic behaviors only w.r.t. the equivalence relation under "all weather conditions" assumption. In comparison to the models used for test derivation in [5], [22], the models presented in this paper and in [15], [16] have less modeling capability since one clock is used and the clock is reset at every transition. However, unlike the timed model used in [5], [22], the timed models of this paper and in [15], [16] consider non-determinism and have an FSM as the underlying model. Correspondingly, for such TFSMs, FSM-based methods can be adapted for deriving distinguishing sequences as well as for deriving test suites with the guaranteed fault coverage.

This paper is organized as follows. Section 2 includes preliminaries. Sections 3 and 4 include algorithms, propositions and examples related to the derivation of separating and r-distinguishing sequences for timed non-deterministic FSMs. Section 5 concludes the paper.

2 Preliminaries

In this section, we introduce a timed non-deterministic Finite State Machine (TFSM) with some related notions and definitions.

Definition 1. An FSM S is a 5-tuple $(S, I, O, \lambda_S, s_0)$, where S, I, and O are finite sets of states, inputs and outputs, respectively, s_0 is the initial state and $\lambda_S \subseteq S \times I \times O \times S$ is a behavior relation.   □

A timed possibly non-deterministic and partial FSM (TFSM) is an FSM annotated with a *clock*, a time reset operation and time guards associated with transitions. The clock t is a real number that measures the time delay at a state and the time reset operation resets the value of the clock t to zero at the execution of a transition. A time guard g_i describes the time domain when a transition can be executed and is given in the form $\lceil min, max \rceil$, where $\lceil \in \{(, [\}, \rceil \in \{),]\}$ and min and max are non-negative rationales such that $min \leq max$. When $min = max$ we consider the only interval $[min, min] = \{min\}$. An output delay describes the time domain when an output has to be produced after an input is applied and is also given in the form $\lceil min, max \rceil$ over rational bounds min and max where $min \leq max$. Here we assume that the time reset operation is specified at every transition of a given TFSM.

Definition 2. A timed FSM (TFSM) S often called simply *a machine* throughout the paper, is a 5-tuple $(S, I, O, \lambda_S, s_0)$; the transition relation $\lambda_S \subseteq S \times I \times O \times S \times \Pi \times \aleph$ where Π is the set of time guards over $[0, \infty)$ and $\aleph$ is the set of output delay intervals over $[0, \infty)$. $\square$

The behavior of a TFSM S can be described as follows. If $(s, i, o, s', g_i = \lceil min, max \rceil, g_o = \lceil min', max' \rceil) \in S \times I \times O \times S \times \Pi \times \aleph$, we say that TFSM S when being at state s and accepting input i at time t satisfying the time guard $t \in \lceil min, max \rceil$, responds (after the input i has been applied) with output o within the time delay specified in g_o and moves to the state s'. The clock is reset to zero and starts advancing at s'.

A zero output delay, i.e. $g_o = [0, 0]$, indicates that the output is produced instantly at the time when the input is applied. For simplicity, for a transition with $g_o = [0, 0]$ and input guard g_i over $[0, \infty)$, we omit g_o and g_i from the description of the transition. Thus, a transition (s, i, o, s') indicates that being at state s and accepting input i at any time, S responds with output o instantly when i is applied. In this paper, we consider only functional distinguishability [15], [16] between TFSMs and thus, we do not consider output delays. In other words, the transition relation is a 5-tuple, $\lambda_S \subseteq S \times I \times O \times S \times \Pi$.

TFSM S is *well-defined* if for each two transitions $(s, i, o, s', \lceil min_1, max_1 \rceil)$, $(s, i, o', s'', \lceil min_2, max_2 \rceil) \in \lambda_S$ s.t. $min_2 \in \lceil min_1, max_1 \rceil$ or $min_1 \in \lceil min_2, max_2 \rceil$ it holds that $o \neq o'$ or $s' \neq s''$. In this paper, we consider only well-defined TFSMs. In this case, we cannot merge two guards, out of the same state and under the same input, without changing the behavior of the TFSM.

A TFSM S is *observable* if for each two transitions $(s, i, o, s', \lceil min_1, max_1 \rceil)$, $(s, i, o', s'', \lceil min_2, max_2 \rceil) \in \lambda_S$ it holds that if $\lceil min_1, max_1 \rceil \cap \lceil min_1, max_1 \rceil \neq \varnothing$ then $o' = o$ implies $s' = s''$.

The machine S is (time) *deterministic* if for each two transitions $(s, i, o, s, \lceil min_1, max_1 \rceil)$, $(s, i, o', s', \lceil min_2, max_2 \rceil) \in \lambda_S$, it holds that $\lceil min_1, max_1 \rceil \cap \lceil min_2, max_2 \rceil = \varnothing$; otherwise, the machine S is (time) *non-deterministic*. Each deterministic TFSM is observable.

The TFSM S is *input enabled* if the underlying FSM is complete, i.e., if for each pair $(s, i) \in S \times I$, λ_S has a transition $(s, i, o, s', \lceil min, max \rceil)$.

The TFSM S is *complete* if the underlying FSM is complete and for each pair $(s, i) \in S \times I$ of TFSM S, the union of time guards over all transitions $(s, i, o, s', \lceil min, max \rceil) \in \lambda_S$ equals to $[0, \infty)$; otherwise, the machine is called *partial*. Given a complete TFSM, the behavior of the TFSM is defined at each state for each input that can be applied at any time instance in $[0, \infty)$.

Definition 3. Given a TFSM $S = (S, I, O, \lambda_S, s_0)$, a pair (i, t), $i \in I$, t is a nonnegative rational, is a *timed input* that states that an input i is applied at time t. Given a state s, there is a *clocked transition* $(s, (i, t), o, s')$ in S if there exists a transition $(s, i, o, s', \lceil min, max \rceil) \in \lambda_S$ with $t \in \lceil min, max \rceil$. $\square$

A TFSM $S = (S, I, O, \lambda_S, s_0)$ is a *submachine* of TFSM $P = (P, I, O, \lambda_P, p_0)$ if $S \subseteq P$, $s_0 = p_0$ and each clocked transition $(s, (i, t), o, s')$ of S is a clocked transition of P.

Definition 4. Given TFSM $S = (S, I, O, \lambda_S, s_0)$, state s and a (time) guard $g = \lceil min, max \rceil$, state s' is an (i, g)-*successor* of state s if there exists $t \in g$ s.t. $(s, (i, t), o, s')$ is a clocked transition of S. Generally, the set of (i, g)-successors of state s can be empty as well as can have several states. Given a set of states $M \subseteq S$ and a timed guard $g = \lceil min, max \rceil$, the set M' of states is an (i, g)-*successor* of the set M if M' is the union of the sets of (i, g)-successors over all states of the set M.   □

Given a TFSM $S = (S, I, O, \lambda_S, s_0)$ and a pair $(s, i) \in S \times I$, let $G = \{j_1 = 0, j_2, ..., j_m\}$, $j_a < j_{a+1}$, $a = 1, ..., m - 1$, be the finite ordered set of boundaries of guards over all transitions $(s, i, o, s', g_j) \in \lambda_S$. We denote $\Pi_{(s, i)}$ the (finite) set $\{(j_1, j_2), ..., (j_{m-1}, j_m), (j_m, \infty), \{j_1\}, \{j_2\}, \{j_3\}, ..\{j_m\}\}$, i.e., the set $\Pi_{(s, i)}$ has singletons for all boundaries and all (infinite) domains with consecutive boundaries of the set G. By definition, the set $\Pi_{(s, i)}$ is finite and items of the set are very close to regions of the region graph in [1]. Each item of the set $\Pi_{(s, i)}$ describes a time domain (or region) where the TFSM has the same behavior for the pair (s, i). If there is no transition $(s, i, o, s', \lceil min, max \rceil) \in \lambda_S$ then, by definition, $\Pi_{(s, i)}$ is the empty set. By definition of the set $\Pi_{(s, i)}$, the following statement holds.

Proposition 1. Given a TFSM $S = (S, I, O, \lambda_S, s_0)$, a pair $(s, i) \in S \times I$ s.t. the set $\Pi_{(s, i)}$ is not empty, $g \in \Pi_{(s, i)}$ and $t_1, t_2 \in g$, the sets of (i, t_1)- and (i, t_2)-successors of state s coincide.   □

We note that a TFSM can have the same behavior for the pair (s, i) in different domains of the set $\Pi_{(s,i)}$. For example, suppose that λ_S has transitions $(s, i, o_1, s_1, [0, 2))$, $(s, i, o_2, s_2, [2, \infty))$, $(s, i, o_3, s_1, [0, 3))$, $(s, i, o_2, s_1, [3, \infty))$ for (s, i). The set $\Pi_{(s, i)} = \{(0, 2), (2, 3), (3, \infty), \{0\}, \{2\}, \{3\}\}$. The set of $(i, 1)$-successors of state s coincides with the set of $(i, 0.5)$-successors. Moreover, the TFSM at state s has the same behavior for timed inputs $(i, 0)$ and $(i, 1)$ despite of the fact that time instances 0 and 1 belong to different domains of the set $\Pi_{(s, i)}$.

Definition 5. Given a TFSM S, a sequence over the input (output) alphabet is called an *input (output) sequence*. A sequence $(i_1, t_1) ... (i_l, t_l)$ of timed inputs is a *timed input sequence*. The set of all timed sequences is denoted I_t^*. We also introduce the function out_S that maps the set $S \times I_t^*$ into the set of output sequences. Given state s and a timed input sequence $\alpha = (i_1, t_1) ... (i_l, t_l)$, an output sequence $o_1 ... o_l \in out_S(s, \alpha)$ if there exist states $s_1 = s, ..., s_{l+1}$ s.t. for each $j \in \{1, ..., l\}$ the TFSM S has a clocked transition $(s_j, (i_j, t_j), o_j, s_{j+1})$ and as usual, we say that the pair $(\alpha, out_S(s, \alpha))$ *can take* the machine S from state s to state s_{l+1}. A pair "timed_input_sequence_α/output_sequence_β" is a *timed I/O sequence* or a *timed trace* of S at state s if $\beta = out_S(s, \alpha)$.

If TFSM S is deterministic then for each state s and each timed input sequence α, the set $out_S(s, \alpha)$ has at most one item. If TFSM S is complete then the set $out_S(s, \alpha)$ is not empty.

The set of all timed traces of S at state s is denoted $TTr_S(s)$, also denoted TTr_S for short if s is the initial state of S. As usual, the TFSM S is *initially connected* if for each state s, there exists a timed trace that can take the machine from the initial state to state s.

As usual, the behavior of two TFSMs can be compared using their intersection. The intersection of two TFSMs S and P is not defined at state (s,p) for a timed input (i, t) when S and P at states s and p produce disjoint sets of outputs to this timed input.

Definition 6. Given TFSMs S and P, the *intersection* $S \cap P$ is the largest connected submachine of the TFSM $(S \times P, I, O, \lambda_{S \cap P}, (s_0, p_0))$ where $((s,p), i, o, (s',p'), \lceil min_1, max_1 \rceil) \in \lambda_{S \cap P}$ if there are transitions $(s, i, o, s', \lceil min_2, max_2 \rceil) \in \lambda_S$ and $(p, i, o, p', \lceil min_3, max_3 \rceil) \in \lambda_P$ s.t. $\lceil min_2, max_2 \rceil \cap \lceil min_3, max_3 \rceil \neq \varnothing$ and $\lceil min_1, max_1 \rceil = \lceil min_2, max_2 \rceil \cap \lceil min_3, max_3 \rceil$. □

Similar to untimed FSMs [18], a number of compatibility and distinguishability relations can be defined between two complete non-deterministic timed FSMs. The only difference is that these relations are defined w.r.t. timed input sequences.

Definition 7[1]

- TFSMs S and P are *equivalent* if $TTr_S = TTr_P$; otherwise, the machines are *distinguishable*. A timed input sequence α s.t. $out_S(s_0, \alpha) \neq out_P(p_0, \alpha)$ is said to *distinguish* machines S and P.

- TFSM S is a *reduction* of TFSM P if $TTr_S \subseteq TTr_P$; otherwise, S is not a *reduction* of TFSM P. If a complete TFSM S is not a *reduction* of a complete TFSM P then there exists a timed input sequence α such that $out_S(s_0, \alpha) \not\subseteq out_P(p_0, \alpha)$ and α is said to *r-distinguish* the TFSM S from the TFSM P.

- TFSMs S and P are *non-separable* if for each timed input sequence α it holds that $out_S(s_0, \alpha) \cap out_P(p_0, \alpha) \neq \varnothing$. If there exists a timed input sequence α s.t. $out_S(s_0, \alpha) \cap out_P(p_0, \alpha) = \varnothing$ then TFSMs S and P are *separable* and α is said to *separate* machines S and P.

- TFSMs S and P are *r-compatible* if there exists a complete TFSM that is a reduction of both machines S and P. If TFSMs S and P are not *r*-compatible then they are *r-distinguishable*. Similar to untimed FSMs, *r*-distinguishable TFSMs are not necessary *r*-distinguishable by a single sequence. □

In this paper, we propose methods for deriving separating and *r*-distinguishing sequences for two complete and observable TFSMs (when such sequences exist). As the number of timed inputs of a complete TFSM is infinite, the methods used for untimed FSMs cannot be directly used.

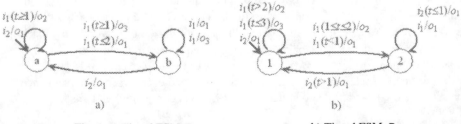

Fig. 1. a) Timed FSM S b) Timed FSM P

---

[1] In the same way, the compatibility and distinguishability relations can be introduced for two states of two TFSMs or for two states of a TFSM.

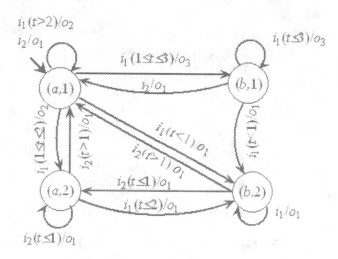

Fig. 2. Timed FSM $S \cap P$

3   Separability Relation and Separating Sequences

Similar to untimed FSMs, the separability of TFSMs S and P can be checked by using the intersection $S \cap P$. The following statement holds.

Proposition 2. Given complete TFSMs S and P, if the intersection $S \cap P$ is complete then the TFSMs S and P are non-separable.   □

In fact, state s of TFSM S and state p of TFSM P can be separated by a timed input (i, t) if and only if $out_S(s, (i, t)) \cap out_P(p, (i, t)) = \varnothing$. If the intersection $S \cap P$ is complete then for each state (s, p) and each timed input (i, t) it holds that $out_S(s, (i, t)) \cap out_P(p, (i, t)) \neq \varnothing$. Correspondingly, for each timed input sequence α it holds that $out_S(s_0, \alpha) \cap out_P(p_0, \alpha) \neq \varnothing$.

We now present an algorithm for deriving a minimum length separating sequence for two complete observable TFSMs. Algorithm 1 uses the intersection of two partitions. Given two partitions $\Pi_{(q, i)}$ and $\Pi_{(s, i)}$ over $[0, \infty)$, the intersection of these partitions contains non-empty intersections $g \cap h$, $g \in \Pi_{(q, i)}$, $h \in \Pi_{(s, i)}$.

Algorithm 1: Deriving a minimum length separating sequence of two TFSMs

Input: Complete observable TFSMs $S = (S, I, O, \lambda_S, s_0)$ and $P = (P, I, O, \lambda_P, p_0)$
Output: A separating sequence of TFSMs S and P (when such a sequence exists)
Derive the intersection $Q = S \cap P$,
If Q is a complete TFSM then END Algorithm 1. TFSMs S and P are non-separable.
Otherwise, assign
    $k : = 0$;
    $Edge : = \varnothing$;
    $Q_{k0} : = \{(s_0, p_0)\}$;

$Q_k := \{Q_{k0}\}$;
While

> (for some $Q_{kj} \in Q_k, j \ge 0$, there exists a timed input (i, t) such that for each state (s,p) of the set Q_{kj}, states s and p are separated by (i, t) (*Rule 1*)
> or
> for each $Q_{kj} \in Q_k$, there exists $Q_{am} \in Q_a, a < k$, s.t. each state $(s,p) \in Q_{kj}$ is a reduction of some state $(s',p') \in Q_{am}$ (*Rule 2*))

Do:

> $Q_{k+1} := \varnothing$;
> For each subset $Q_{kj} \in Q_k, j = 0, ..., |Q_k| - 1$, for which there is no $Q_{am} \in Q_a, a < k$, s.t. each state $(s,p) \in Q_{kj}$ is a reduction of some state $(s',p') \in Q_{am}$ and for each input i,
> Do:
>
>> Derive the set Π as the intersection of $\Pi_{(q, i)}$ over all state pairs $q \in Q_{kj}$;
>> For each guard $g \in \Pi$, derive the set M as the union of (i, g)-successors over all $q \in Q_{kj}$ of the TFSM Q ;
>> Add M to Q_{k+1};
>> Add a triple $(Q_{kj}, (i, g), M)$ to the set *Edge*;
>> Increment k by 1;

If for some $Q_{k\,j_k}$, $j \ge 0$, there exists a timed input (i, t) such that for each state (s,p) of the set Q_{kj}, states s and p are separated by (i, t) (*Rule 1*) then derive a timed sequence α as follows. Given the set *Edge*, derive the sequence $(Q_{00}, (i_1, g_1), Q_{1\,j_1})$, $(Q_{1\,j_1}, (i_2, g_2), Q_{2\,j_2})$, ..., $(Q_{(k-1)\,j_{k-1}}, (i_k, g_k), Q_{k\,j_k})$ such that $(Q_{(l-1)\,j_{l-1}}, (i_l, g_l), Q_{l\,j_l}) \in$ *Edge* for each $l \in \{1, ..., k\}$ and then derive a sequence of timed inputs $\alpha = (i_1, t_1) ... (i_k, t_k)$ s.t. $t_j \in g_j, j = 1, ..., k$. The sequence α is a shortest separating sequence of TFSMs S and P.

If for each $Q_{kj} \in Q_k$, there exists $Q_{am} \in Q_a, a < k$, s.t. each state $(s,p) \in Q_{kj}$ is a reduction of some state $(s',p') \in Q_{am}$ then TFSMs S and P are non-separable.   □

Proposition 3. If TFSMs S and P are separable then Algorithm 1 returns a shortest separating sequence of S and P.   □

In fact, in [20] an algorithm is given for deriving a shortest separating sequence for two untimed FSMs based on the successor tree of the intersection of two FSMs. Algorithm 1 uses also the intersection and successor tree when deriving a shortest separating sequence of two timed FSMs. However, for TFSMs, the number of timed inputs is infinite and thus, each state has an infinite number of timed successors. In order to make this number finite we introduce and then use in Algorithm 1 the notion of a partition $\Pi_{(q, i)}$. According to Proposition 1, given a state q of the intersection $S \cap P$, an input i, and a region $g \in \Pi_{(q, i)}$, for each $t_1, t_2 \in g$, the set of (i, t_1)- and (i, t_2)-successors of state q coincide. Correspondingly, all such successors coincide with the set of (i, g)-successors of state q.

Proposition 4. Given two complete TFSMs S and P with n and m states, if the machines are separable then there exists a separating sequence with length at most 2^{mn-1} and the upper bound 2^{mn-1} is reachable. □

The first part of the statement is implied by Algorithm 1, as by construction, according to Rule 2, k cannot be greater than $2^{mn-1} + 1$. The second part holds since the upper bound is reachable for untimed FSMs [20] which can be considered as a particular case of timed FSMs where for each pair (s, i) the set $\Pi_{(s, i)}$ has a singleton $[0, \infty)$.

In order to show that the upper bound in Proposition 4 is reachable it is enough to show that is reachable for untimed complete non-deterministic FSMs. For any n and m, there exist observable untimed FSMs S and P with n and m states which can be separated only by a timed input sequence of length 2^{nm-1}. As an example, we can consider such untimed FSMs from [20]; these machines have the input alphabet I, $|I| = 2^{nm-1}$, and the output alphabet O, $|O| = 2nm$. However, determining the minimal number of inputs, for separating two separable machines, such that the upper bound of Proposition 4 is reachable is still an unsolved problem.

Example. As an application example for Algorithm 1, consider TFSMs S (Fig. 1a) and P (Fig. 1b) with initial states **a** and **1** defined over inputs $\{i_1, i_2\}$, outputs $\{o_1, o_2, o_3\}$. The intersection $S \cap P$ is shown in Fig. 2. By definition, the set $Q_0 = \{Q_{00}\}$, where $Q_{00} = \{(a, 1)\}$. Given the intersection $S \cap P$, the set $\Pi_{(a1, i1)} = \{(0, 1), (1, 2), (2, 3), (3, \infty), \{0\}, \{1\}, \{2\}, \{3\}\}$, and thus, for Q_{00} and i_1, $\Pi = \{(0, 1), (1, 2), (2, 3), (3, \infty), \{0\}, \{1\}, \{2\}, \{3\}\}$, while for Q_{00} and i_2, $\Pi = \{(0, \infty), \{0\}\}$. Correspondingly, we obtain the set $Edge = \{(Q_{00}, (i_1, 0 < t < 1), \{(b,2)\}); (Q_{00}, (i_1, 1 < t < 2), \{(a,2), (b,1)\}); (Q_{00}, (i_1, 2 < t < 3), \{(a,1), (b,1)\}); (Q_{00}, (i_1, t > 3), \{(a,1)\}); (Q_{00}, (i_1, 0), \{(b,2)\}); (Q_{00}, (i_1, 1), \{(a,2), (b,1)\}); (Q_{00}, (i_1, 2), \{(a,2), (b,1)\}), (Q_{00}, (i_1, 3), \{(a,1), (b,1)\}), (Q_{00}, (i_2, t > 0), \{(a,1)\}), (Q_{00}, (i_2, \{0\}), \{(a,1)\})\}$. Therefore, the set $Q_1 = \{\{(b,2)\}, \{(a,2), (b,1)\}, \{(a,1), (b,1)\}, \{(a,1)\}, \{(b,2)\}, \{(a,1), (b,1)\}, \{(a,1)\}\}$.

For states $(a,1)$ and $(b,2)$, the union of time guards in the intersection $S \cap P$ is $[0, \infty)$ for both inputs i_1 and i_2, and thus, states a and 1 and states b and 2 are not 1-separable. However, we observe that the behavior of the intersection $S \cap P$ is not defined at states $(a,2)$ and $(b,1)$ for timed inputs $(i_1, t > 3)$. Thus, states a and 2 and states b and 1 are separable by a timed input $(i_1, 4)$. Given timed input $(i_1, 1)$, the intersection reaches from the initial state $(a,1)$ states $(a,2)$ and $(b,1)$ and thus, the sequence of timed inputs $(i_1, 1) (i_1, 4)$ separates TFSMs S and P.

In order to distinguish two separable timed FSMs we do not need the "all weather conditions" assumption. It is enough to apply a separating input sequence once since the sets of outputs of the machines to this sequence are disjoint. However, it is well-known that when a common reduction of non-separable complete non-deterministic untimed FSMs does not exist such machines can be distinguished without "all weather conditions" assumption [18] by a so-called r-distinguishing set. Similar to untimed non-deterministic FSMs, if two timed complete observable FSMs do not have a common complete reduction then these machines can be distinguished by an adaptive experiment using the r-distinguishability relation. In the following section, we present an algorithm for an adaptive experiment that checks the r-distinguishability of two observable TFMSs and if the machines are r-distinguishable an r-distinguishing set is derived.

4 R-Distinguishability Relation and r-Distinguishing Sets

Two complete TFSMs S and P which have no common complete reduction are *r-distinguishable*. If TFSMs S and P have a common complete reduction then these TFSMs are *r-compatible*. Generally the number of pair-wise non-equivalent complete reductions of a timed FSM is infinite and thus, it is not trivial to decide if two complete timed TFSMs are r-distinguishable. However, if TFSMs S and P are observable then, similar to observable untimed non-deterministic FSMs, we can use another (equivalent) definition of the r-distinguishability relation that helps us when checking r-distinguishability by an adaptive experiment.

Given observable timed FSMs S and P and their intersection $Q = S \cap P$, states s and p are 1-r-distinguishable if states s and p can be separated by a timed input, i.e. the intersection is partially specified at state $q = (s,p)$. In other words, there exists an input i s.t. in the intersection $S \cap P$ the union Ω of guards over all transitions $((s,p), i, o, (s',p'), g) \in \lambda_{S \cap P}$ is different from $[0, \infty)$. A set $R_{sp} = \{(i, t)/o: o \in out_S(s, (i, t))$ or $o \in out_P(p, (i, t))\}$ where $t \in [0, \infty) \backslash \Omega$, is an *r-distinguishing set* of states s and p. We note that one timed input (i, t) is sufficient for r-distinguishing 1-r-distinguishable states s and p.

Consider $k > 1$ and assume that all pairs of $(k-1)$-r-distinguishable states are determined and for each pair of $(k-1)$-r-distinguishable s and p an *r-distinguishing set* R_{sp} is also determined. States s and p are *k-r-distinguishable* if these states are $(k-1)$-r-distinguishable or for some input i there exists $t \in [0, \infty)$ such that for each transition $((s,p), i, o, (s',p'), g) \in T_{S \cap P}$, $g \ni t$, states s' and p' are $(k-1)$-r-distinguishable. In this case, an r-distinguishing set for states s and p is constructed as the concatenation of $(i, t)/o$, $t \in g$, $o \in out_{S \cap P}((s,p), (i, t))$, with each sequence of each set $R_{s'p'}$ such that $S \cap P$ has the transition $(s,p) \to (i, t)/o \to (s',p')$. We refer to such a timed input (i, t) as a *k-r-distinguishing timed input* of states s and p.

Similar to untimed FSMs, it can be shown that observable TFSMs S and P are r-distinguishable if there exists an integer k s.t. their initial states are k-r-distinguishable. A set of sequences that r-distinguish the initial states of TFSMs is an *r-distinguishing* set of TFSMs S and P.

Let observable TFSMs S and P be r-distinguishable. Then they can be distinguished based on an r-distinguishing set of TFSMs S and P by using an adaptive experiment. For TFSMs with n and m states length of each sequence in the r-distinguishing set is at most nm and this upper bound is reachable. Moreover, during an adaptive experiment only one sequence of timed inputs of an r-distinguishing set will be applied to r-distinguish considered machines. However, the following proposition shows that the total length of an r-distinguishing set can be exponential.

Proposition 5. Given integers n and m, $n \geq 1$, $m \geq 1$, there always exist r-distinguishable TFSMs S and P with n and m states s.t. the total length of all sequences of some r-distinguishing set is at most $(nm+2)2^{nm-3}$ and this upper bound is reachable. □

In fact, the proposition is a corollary to the similar proposition [24] for untimed FSMs which can be considered as a particular case of timed FSMs where for each pair (s, i) the set $\Pi_{(s, i)}$ has a singleton $[0, \infty)$. However, below we show that similar to untimed FSMs, an r-distinguishing set can be represented as the set of traces of a partial timed FSM that has at most $nm + 2$ states and thus, there exists a representation of an r-distinguishing set with the polynomial complexity.

Algorithm 2. Deriving an r-distinguishing set of two TFSMs

Input: Complete observable TFSMs $S = (S, I, O, \lambda_S, s_0)$ and $P = (P, I, O, \lambda_P, p_0)$

Output: Partial initially connected TFSM $R_{(S,P)}$ if TFSMs S and P are r-distinguishable

Derive the tuple $R = (R, I, O, \lambda_R)$ where, λ_R is empty and R contains two states which we call r_S and r_P;
Derive the intersection $Q = S \cap P$ of TFSMs S and P;
$k := 1$;
$Q_k := Q$, where Q is the set of states of $S \cap P$;
    While $((s_0,p_0) \in Q_k$ and the set Q_k has pairs of k-r-distinguishable states), do:
        Determine all pairs of the set Q_k which have k-r-distinguishable states;
        For each pair (s,p) of the set Q_k s.t. s and p are k-r-distinguishable
            Determine a k-r-distinguishing timed input (i, t) of states s and p;
            Add state (s,p) into set R;
            For each $o \in O$ s.t. there is the transition $((s,p), i, o, (s',p'), g) \in \lambda_Q$ where $g \ni t$, add the tuple $((s,p), i, o, (s',p'), [t])$ to λ_R;
            For each $o \in O$ s.t. there is no transition $((s, p), i, o, (s',p'), g) \in \lambda_Q$ where $g \ni t$, add to λ_R the tuple $((s,p), i, o, r_S, [t])$ if $o \in out_S(s, (i, t))$. If $o \in out_P(p, (i, t))$ add the tuple $((s,p), i, o, r_P, [t])$;
            Delete state (s,p) from the set Q_k;
        Increment k by 1;
        $Q_k := Q_{k-1}$;
    If $(s_0,p_0) \notin Q_k$ then convert the tuple R into TFSM by claiming state (s_0,p_0) as the initial state of the TFSM. The largest initially connected submachine of TFSM R is TFSM $R_{(S,P)}$; END Algorithm 2.
    If states of each pair of Q_k are not k-r-distinguishable then End Algorithm 2. TFSMs S and P are r-compatible, i.e. are not r-distinguishable. □
By construction of TFSM $R_{(S,P)}$, the following statement holds.

Proposition 6. Given two r-distinguishable observable TFSMs S and P with n and m states, Algorithm 1 returns an acyclic partial TFSM $R_{(S,P)}$ such that for each state (s,p) of $R_{(S,P)}$ there exists exactly one input i for which $\Pi_{(s,\ i)}$ is not empty. Moreover, no input is defined at states r_S and r_P.   □

According to Proposition 6, if Algorithm 2 returns a TFSM $R_{(S,P)}$ then an r-distinguishing set R of TFSMs S and P is the set of all timed traces, which take the TFSM $R_{(S,P)}$ from the initial state to states r_S and r_P. Correspondingly, the final state of an executed trace uniquely indicates which TFSM S or P is under experiment. In other words, if the final state of an executed trace is r_S (r_P) then the TFSM under experiment is $S(P)$.

Example. As an example of Algorithm 2, consider TFSM S with the initial state 1 and also TFSM S with the initial state 3 (Figure 3). Since in this example we consider two submachines of S starting from initial states 1 and 3, we denote the first machine as S_1 and the second as S_3 and we add into R two states r_{S1} and r_{S3} with subscripts indicating the initial states of the TFSMs. Part of the intersection $Q = S_1 \cap S_3$ is shown in Figure 4. Set $Q_1 = Q$ (for $k = 1$) includes all states of the TFSM Q. States 3 and 2 of Q_1 are 1-r-distinguishable by a timed input $(i_2, 1)$ and states 2 and 4 are 1-r-distinguishable by a timed input $(i_1, 2)$. Thus, we remove states $(3, 2)$ and $(2, 4)$ from Q_1 and obtain Q_2 which does not include states $(3, 2)$ and $(2, 4)$. States 1 and 3 of the initial state $(1, 3)$ in Q_2 are 2-r-distinguishable. By direct inspection, one can observe that states $(3, 2)$ and $(2, 4)$ are reached from the initial state by a timed input $(i_1, 3)$ and thus, TFSM $R_{(S1,\ S3)}$, shown in Figure 5, represents an r-distinguishing set $\{(i_1, 3)/o_1.(i_2, 1)/o_1, (i_1, 3)/o_1.(i_2, 1)/o_2, (i_1, 3)/o_2.(i_1, 2)/o_1, (i_1, 3)/o_2.(i_1, 2)/o_2\}$.

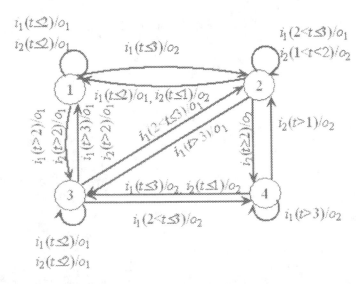

Fig. 3. TFSM S where states 1 and 3 are not separable but they are r-distinguishable

$Q = S_1 \cap S_3$	(1,3)	(3,2)	(2,4)	(2,2)
$i_1, t \leq 2$	(1,3) / o_1	(3,1) / o_1	-	(1,1) / o_1
$i_1, 2 < t \leq 3$	(3,2) / o_1 (2,4) / o_2	(2,2) / o_1	-	(2,2) / o_1
$i_1, t > 3$	(3,1) / o_1 (1,3) / o_1	(1,3) / o_1	(1,3) / o_2	(3,3) / o_1 (1,1) / o_2
$i_2, t \leq 1$				
$i_2, 1 < t < 2$	(1,3) / o_1	-	(2,2) / o_2	(2,2) / o_2
$i_2, t = 2$	(1,3) / o_1	-	(4,4) / o_2	(4,4) / o_2
$i_2, t > 2$	(1,3) / o_1	-	(4,4) / o_2	(4,4) / o_2

Fig. 4. Part of the intersection TFSM $Q = S \cap P$

$R_{(S1,S3)}$	(1,3)	(3,2)	(2,4)	r_{S1}	r_{S3}
$i_1, t=3$	(3,2) / o_1 (2,4) / o_2	-	r_{S1}/o_1	-	-
$i_1, t=2$			r_{S3}/o_2		
$i_2, t = 1$	-	r_{S1}/o_1 r_{S3}/o_2	-	-	-

Fig. 5. TFSM $R_{(S1,S3)}$

5   Conclusion and Further Research Work

In this paper, we present algorithms for distinguishing timed non-deterministic finite state machines (TFSMs). More precisely, we present a preset algorithm for separating two separable TFSMs and an adaptive algorithm for distinguishing two r-distinguishable possibly non-separable TFSMs. The algorithms take into account the fact that in general, unlike untimed FSMs, in a TFSM the number of timed inputs is usually infinite. We also state that the upper bounds on length of distinguishing sequences are as those of untimed FSMs. In this paper, we only consider complete TFSMs where for every state and input action of the TFSM the set of outgoing transitions of the state under the input action is not empty and the time guards of these outgoing transitions are defined over $[0, \infty)$. In order to apply our work to partial TFSMs, one can complete a TFSM in the well-known way: for every state and input action where there is no outgoing transitions under the input action at some time instance, add a self-loop transition to the state with the *Null* output and with a corresponding time guard.

The work presented in this paper can be extended in various ways. For example, the presented algorithms can be used as a basis for test derivation of TFSMs with the guaranteed fault coverage. In addition, the algorithms can be adapted for other distinguishability relations as those defined for untimed non-deterministic FSMs.

References

1. Alur, R., Dill, D.L.: A Theory of Timed automata. Theoretical Computer Science 126(2), 183–235 (1994)
2. Alur, R., Courcoubetis, C., Yannakakis, M.: Distinguishing Tests for Nondeterministic and Probabilistic Machines. In: Proc. the 27th ACM Symposium on Theory of Computing, pp. 363–372 (1995)
3. Bochmann, G.V., Petrenko, A.: Protocol Testing: Review of Methods and Relevance for Software Testing. In: International Symposium on Software Testing and Analysis, Seattle, pp. 109–123 (1994)
4. Dorofeeva, M., El-Fakih, K., Maag, S., Cavalli, A.R., Yevtushenko, N.: Experimental Evaluation of FSM-Based Testing Methods. In: Proc. IEEE Software Engineering and Formal Methods, pp. 23–32 (2005)
5. En-Nouaary, A., Dssouli, R., Khendek, F.: Timed Wp-Method: Testing Real-Time Systems. IEEE TSE 28(11), 1023–1038 (2002)
6. Hierons, R.M.: Testing from a Non-Deterministic Finite State Machine Using Adaptive State Counting. IEEE Transactions on Computers 53(10), 1330–1342 (2004)
7. Hierons, R.M.: Using Candidates to Test a Deterministic Implementation against a Non-Deterministic Finite State Machine. The Computer Journal 46(3), 307–318 (2003)
8. Hierons, R.M.: Adaptive Testing of a Deterministic Implementation Against a Nondeterministic Finite State Machine. The Computer Journal 41(5), 349–355 (1998)
9. Hierons, R.M., Merayo, M.G.: Nunez: Testing from a Stochastic Timed System with a Fault Model. Journal of Logic and Algebraic Programming 72(8), 98–115 (2009)
10. Kohavi, Z.: Switching and Finite Automata Theory. McGraw-Hill, New York (1978)
11. Lee, D., Yannakakis, M.: Principles and Methods of Testing Finite State Machines-A Survey. Proc. of the IEEE 84(8), 1090–1123 (1996)
12. Luo, G., Petrenko, A., Bochmann, G.V.: Selecting Test Sequences for Partially Specified Nondeterministic Finite State Machines. In: Proc. 7th International Workshop on Protocol Test Systems (1994)
13. Milner, R.: A Calculus of Communication Systems. LNCS, vol. 92. Springer, Heidelberg (1980)
14. Milner, R.: Communication and Concurrency. Prentice-Hall, Englewood Cliffs (1989)
15. Merayo, M.G., Nunez, M., Rodriguez, I.: Extending EFSMs to Specify and Test Timed Systems with Action Durations and Time-outs. IEEE Transactions on Computers 57(6), 835–844 (2008)
16. Merayo, M.G., Nunez, M., Rodriguez, I.: Formal Testing from Timed Finite State Machines. Computer Networks 52(2), 432–460 (2008)
17. Petrenko, A., Yevtushenko, N., Bochmann, G.V.: Testing Deterministic Implementations from their Nondeterministic Specifications. In: Proc. of the IFIP Ninth International Workshop on Testing of Communicating Systems, pp. 125–140 (1996)
18. Petrenko, A., Yevtushenko, N.: Conformance Tests as Checking Experiments for Partial Nondeterministic FSM. In: Grieskamp, W., Weise, C. (eds.) FATES 2005. LNCS, vol. 3997, pp. 118–133. Springer, Heidelberg (2006)
19. Spitsyna, N.: FSM-based test suite derivation strategies for discrete event systems. Ph.D. Thesis, Tomsk State University, pp. 1–158 (2005)
20. Spitsyna, N., El-Fakih, K., Yevtushenko, N.: Studying the Separability Relation between Finite State Machines. Software Testing, Verification and Reliability 17(4), 227–241 (2007)

21. Shabaldina, N., El-Fakih, K., Yevtushenko, N.: Testing Nondeterministic Finite State Machines with respect to the Separability Relation. In: Petrenko, A., Veanes, M., Tretmans, J., Grieskamp, W. (eds.) TestCom/FATES 2007. LNCS, vol. 4581, pp. 305–318. Springer, Heidelberg (2007)
22. Springintveld, J., Vaandrager, F., D'Argenio, P.: Testing Timed Automata. Theoretical Computer Science 254(1-2), 225–257 (2001)
23. Starke, P.: Abstract automata, pp. 3–419. American Elsevier, Amsterdam (1972)
24. Yevtushenko, N., Spitsyna, N.: On the Upper of Length of Separating and r-distinguishing Sequences for Observable Nondeterministic FSMs. In: Proc. of Artificial intelligence systems and computer sciences, pp. 124–126 (2006) (in Russian)

System Model-Based Definition of Modeling Language Semantics

Hans Grönniger, Jan Oliver Ringert, and Bernhard Rumpe

Lehrstuhl Informatik 3 (Softwaretechnik), RWTH Aachen, Germany

Abstract. In this paper, we present an approach to define the semantics for object-oriented modeling languages. One important property of this semantics is to support underspecified and incomplete models. To this end, semantics is given as predicates over elements of the semantic domain. This domain is called the system model which is a general declarative characterization of object systems. The system model is very detailed since it captures various relevant structural, behavioral, and interaction aspects. This allows us to re-use the system model as a domain for various kinds of object-oriented modeling languages. As a major consequence, the integration of language semantics is straight-forward. The whole approach is supported by tools that do not constrain the semantics definition's expressiveness and flexibility while making it machine-checkable.

1 Introduction

Modeling is an integral part of complex software system development projects. The purpose of models ranges from assisting developers and customers communicate to test case generation or (automatic) derivation of the developed system. A prominent example modeling language is UML [1]. Actually, it is a family of languages used to model various aspects of a software system. While UML is widely used, domain specific modeling languages emerged recently that allow developers and even customers to express solutions to well-defined problems in a concise way.

A complete definition of a modeling language consists of the description of its syntax, including well-formedness rules and its semantics (meaning) [2]. It is widely accepted that a commonly agreed formal semantics of a language is advantageous because it avoids problems like misunderstandings between people and lack of interoperability between tools. Additionally, semantics can also be used to formally reason about system properties for verification purposes. However, many languages are often specified through their syntax only and lack a precise semantics beyond informal explanations. UML is again a prominent example which has been standardized without a formal semantics, even though debate has started more than ten years ago [3,4].

Various efforts for the definition of a formal semantics for a modeling language like UML have shown that this really is a difficult task for the following reasons:

D. Lee et al. (Eds.): FMOODS/FORTE 2009, LNCS 5522, pp. 152–166, 2009.

- Multiple views and multiple models describe overlapping parts of the system. Thus, fundamentally different modelling concepts for structure, behavior and interaction have to be given an integrated semantics.
- As opposed to programming language semantics, modeling languages are used for specification. In particular high-level, abstract models are not necessarily executable. Instead, models tend to be incomplete and underspecified and thus their semantics must allow underspecification. A semantic definition has to provide a meaning for those models that cannot be described as an execution.
- The semantics has to be precise but not completely fixed. In UML terms, it should support semantic variation points that allow different stakeholders to provide a specialized interpretation for certain constructs.

Although UML is currently one of our main targets, the approach presented in this paper is not restricted to UML. Instead, the process of defining the semantics of a modeling language might even be more important for newly defined domain specific languages since it guides developers through the task of developing a formal semantics.

This paper presents our approach to define the semantics of object-oriented modeling languages which explicitly addresses the challenges mentioned above. The rest of the paper is structured as follows. Sect. 2 discusses our approach in general and motivates the usage of a single semantic domain that was carefully defined to capture the most important concepts of object-oriented systems. This domain is introduced in greater detail in Sect. 3 which also presents an implementation in the theorem prover Isabelle/HOL [5] as part of the proposed tool support. Sect. 4 is concerned with the precise definition of the syntax of a language using the framework MontiCore [6]. Furthermore, an automatic derivation of the abstract syntax as an Isabelle/HOL data type is outlined. With syntax and semantic domain specified and implemented in Isabelle/HOL, the process of defining the semantic mapping is described in Sect. 5. The mapping again is formalized in Isabelle/HOL. A running example is used throughout the paper for which a short verification application is also presented in Sect. 5. Related work is discussed in Sect. 6 and conclusions are drawn in Sect. 7.

2   General Approach

As indicated in Fig. 1, the semantics of a modeling language consists of the following basic parts [7]:

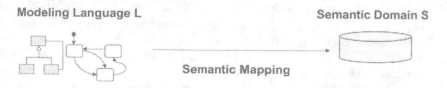

Fig. 1. Basic parts of a semantics definition

- the syntax of the language in question L – be it graphical or textual,
- the semantic domain S, a domain well-known and understood based on a well-defined mathematical theory, and
- the semantic mapping: a functional or relational definition that connects both, the elements of the syntax and the elements of the semantic domain.

This technique of giving meaning to a language is the basic principle of denotational semantics: every syntactic construct is mapped onto a semantic construct. As explained in [2] the semantic mapping has the form:

$$Sem : L \rightarrow \mathcal{P}(S)$$

and thus functionally relates any item in the syntactic domain to a set of constructs of the semantic domain. The semantics of a model $m \in L$ is therefore $Sem(m)$ denoting a set of elements in the domain S.

Given any two models $m, n \in L$ combined into a complex one $m \oplus n$ (for any composition operator $\oplus$ of the syntactic domain), the semantics of $m \oplus n$ is defined by $Sem(m \oplus n) = Sem(m) \cap Sem(n)$. This definition also works for sets of documents which allows an easy treatment of views on a system specified by multiple diagrams. The semantics of several views, e.g., several UML documents is given as $Sem(\{doc_1, \ldots, doc_n\}) = Sem(doc_1) \cap \ldots \cap Sem(doc_n)$. A set of models *docs* is consistent if elements of S exist that are described by the models, so $Sem(docs) \neq \emptyset$. As a consequence, the approach supports both view integration and model consistency verification.

In the same way, $n \in L$ is a (structural or behavioral) refinement of $m \in L$, exactly if $Sem(n) \subseteq Sem(m)$. Hence, refinement is nothing else than "n is providing at least the information about the system that m does". These general mechanisms provide a great advantage, as they simplify any reasoning about composition and refinement operators and also work for incomplete models.

Semantic Domain. We identify a single semantic domain S used as a target for the semantic mapping of various kinds of modeling languages. Since we are interested in object-oriented modeling languages, the domain should provide concepts commonly found in object-oriented systems. The system model, first defined in [8] and extended in [9], defines these concepts. Generally, the system model characterizes object-oriented systems using basic mathematical theories. The semantics of a model M is hence given as a set of all systems of the system model that are possible realizations of the model M. This way, we obtain an adequate and relatively easy to understand semantic domain which is crucial for the acceptance of a semantics definition.

To capture and integrate all the orthogonal aspects of a system modeled in, e.g., UML, the semantic domain necessarily has to have a certain complexity. Related approaches to UML semantics very often define a relatively small and specialized semantic domain and can therefore not capture the multitude of concepts typically found in a complex modeling language. More details on the system model are presented in Sect. 3.

Tool Support. Having the system model at hand, we could define the semantics of a language using pencil and paper. This was done for UML class diagrams [10] and Statecharts [11]. Tool support, however, is beneficial in two ways. First, we specify a machine-readable, checkable semantics that can directly be used for verification purposes. Second, the different artifacts can be better controlled and quality checked by using standard tools, e.g., version control.

Fig. 2 gives an overview of the default approach when defining the semantics of a language with tool support. First, the (domain specific) modeling language concepts are specified using a MontiCore grammar. MontiCore [6] is a framework for the textual definition of languages based on an extended context-free grammar format. This format enables a modular development of the syntax of a language by providing modularity concepts like language inheritance. Framework functionality helps developers also to define well-formedness rules and, for example, the implementation of generators.

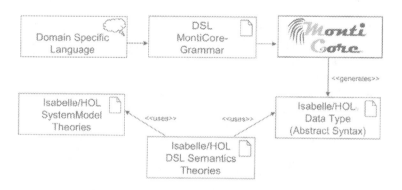

Fig. 2. Default Approach with Tool Support

To provide the semantics developer with maximum flexibility but also with some machine-checking (i.e., type checking) of the semantics and the potential for real verification applications, we use the theorem prover Isabelle/HOL for

- the formalization of the system model as a hierarchy of theories,
- the representation of the abstract syntax of the language as a deep embedding, and
- the semantic mapping which maps the generated abstract syntax to predicates over systems of the formalized system model.

The formalization of the system model as theories in Isabelle/HOL has to be done once and is described in Sect. 3. We have implemented a generator in MontiCore that produces an Isabelle/HOL data type representing the abstract syntax of the language, given a MontiCore grammar as input. Details on the derivation of the abstract syntax are explained in Sect. 4. The semantic mapping is also contained in Isabelle/HOL theories, an example is given in Sect. 5.

This approach of using a deep embedding has mainly two advantages over a shallow embedding. First, we can benefit from the sophisticated mathematical notation in Isabelle/HOL for defining the semantic mapping. Second, since both, the syntax and the mapping are formalized, we are able to reason about syntactic properties of concrete models and, more importantly, about properties of the mapping itself. This is in contrast to a shallow embedding where we would generate predicates directly from concrete models. This approach has some advantages when reasoning about concrete model properties but does not allow reasoning about the syntax or the mapping at all. Furthermore, we would have needed to invent another mathematical language to express the predicates outside Isabelle/HOL. As an extension to this approach (not shown in the figure), not only the abstract syntax data type is generated but also another generator that is able to translate concrete models to the abstract syntax representation as an instance of the generated data type. This is very useful when verifying properties of models and will be shown with the help of an example in Sect. 4.

Handling Semantic Variations. As mentioned in the introduction, the semantics of a modeling language should not be fixed but there should be explicit points where the interpretation of constructs can be specialized. These semantic variation points can be found in the system model but also in the semantic mapping or syntax. Variation points do not necessarily contradict interoperability: A comprehensive list of realization choices may serve tool builders as a definite reference when stating compliance to a given language.

In the system model [9] a large number of variation points has already been made explicit and different alternative configurations for variation points have been defined. Examples are the existence of multiple inheritance between classes, different realization strategies for associations, or different notions of type-safe overriding of methods. These semantic variations can be constrained prior to the semantic mapping but can also be left open.

For handling semantic variations in the syntax or in the mapping we propose to model these variations as stereotypes known from UML and to explicitly consider these stereotypes in the semantic mapping. The decisions of how particular syntactic elements should be interpreted can then be made by the modeler and need not be fixed beforehand. Additionally, there are dependencies between semantic variation points that have to be considered. A more complete account on how to handle semantic variations is however outside the scope of this paper.

3   System Model and Its Formalization

The system model is the universe of all possible object systems that can be modeled using an object-oriented modeling language like UML. It describes amongst other aspects the structural part of such systems, i.e., types, values, classes, objects and associations. Besides reasoning about the structure of systems it is also possible to specify or analyze behavior. The control part of the system model covers events and flow of information as well as execution of methods.

All systems are interpreted as timed or untimed global state machines (STS). Using the power of underspecification and variation points, the system model becomes very comprehensive but versatile in use. Due to space restrictions, we only present a small portion of structural definitions. To get a more complete picture of the system model features, the reader is referred to [9].

Main concepts of object-oriented modeling languages like types or classes appear in the system model grouped in corresponding universes, e.g., UTYPE or UCLASS. The universes contain only abstract identifiers. For example, classes are identified by elements of UCLASS and are only described by functions that yield information about their attributes, methods, or super-classes. They are never constructed from records or constructively represented in similar structures.

The system model itself is built in a modular and hierarchical way starting with a base theory about simple types and values. On top of this theory further theories define classes and objects as well as formalizations of the state of systems. The basic theories of the system model can be seen in Fig. 3.

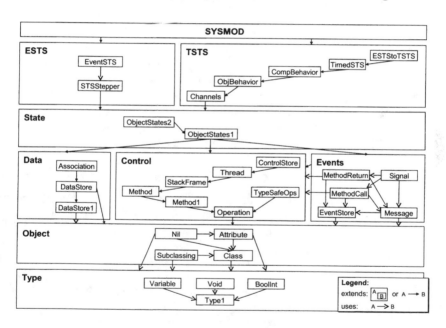

Fig. 3. Theories that constitute the system model

To support reasoning in the system model and the construction of the semantic mapping by tools, the proof assistant Isabelle is used for an implementation based on Isabelle/HOL. Isabelle's logic HOL [5] offers an implementation of functional programming and set theory.

Universes of the system model are implemented by corresponding data types since functions in Isabelle/HOL operate on data types. All introduced universes are universes of specific instances (systems) of the system model. They are retrieved from an instance of the system model with functions similar to selection functions on records [12]. For example, the function

```
consts UTYPE :: "SystemModel ⇒ iTYPE set"
```

maps systems to their universe UTYPE which is a set of type names from iType. Universes can comprise different sets of data type elements for concrete systems. An underlying data type (here iTYPE), is necessary since HOL sets have to be typed. Some universes contain others (e.g., $UCLASS \subseteq UTYPE$) which is modeled using wrapping constructors in the underlying type:

```
datatype iType = ...| TClass iClass | ...
```

The elements and sub-universes of a universe are defined as parametrized data type constructors yielding concrete values. This makes it possible to create and identify certain instances by names (here lists of characters). A class name in the system model can be created using the constructor Class Name of type iClass (with Name = "char list"). When reasoning about concrete instances this facilitates the creation and referencing of explicit names for elements.

All functions in Isabelle/HOL have to be total. Partial functions can be mimicked via the special type a' option = Some a' | None where a' is a type variable. Underspecified functions of the system model are introduced as constants of corresponding function types in Isabelle/HOL. Properties of functions or universes are given in definitions or predicates over systems. As an example, the underspecified function CAR is introduced as

```
consts CAR :: "SystemModel ⇒ (iTYPE ⇒ iVAL set)"
```

For every type name in UTYPE the function CAR yields all possible values an entity of the type can have in an instance of the system model. In its mathematical definition the function CAR fulfills the property

$$\forall u \in UTYPE : CAR(u) \neq \emptyset$$

This is realized by the predicate pCAR_Type1 that needs to hold for all valid systems sm of the system model:

```
pCAR_Type1 sm = (∀ u ∈ UTYPE sm . CAR sm u ≠ {})
```

The Isabelle implementation of the system model is split up in theories according to the structure in Fig. 3. Properties of system model instances as well as additional properties imposed by, e.g., variation points are declared in corresponding theories. These declarations have to be included as predicates when reasoning about instances. Predicates for elements of systems always have the signature "SystemModel ⇒ bool" (see Fig. 4 for a transitivity definition of the sub class relation) and thus are predicates on systems rather than on single functions or elements. This makes the combination and reuse of predicates much simpler.

```
1   constdefs pSubTrans :: "SystemModel ⇒ bool"
2   "pSubTrans sm == (
3     ∀ a b c . the (sub sm a b) ⟶  the (sub sm b c)
4               ⟶ the (sub sm a c))"
```

Fig. 4. Definition of a predicate about transitive sub class relations

To capture all systems sm ∈ SystemModel with non-empty universes $UTYPE$ and a transitive sub class relation sub one has to write:

$$\{\text{sm. pCAR\_Type1 sm} \wedge \text{pSubTrans sm}\}$$

The use and combination of theories and variation points is thus a partially manual composition task. This may be improved in the future when focusing more on the usability part of our implementation.

4   Concrete Syntax and Derivation of Abstract Syntax

In this section we briefly introduce MontiCore grammars to specify the syntax of a modeling language, explain its modularity concepts, and show how to derive the Isabelle/HOL abstract syntax data type. We present matters with the help of UML-like class diagrams as a shortened example sufficient to show the main concepts. Please note that the general idea can also be transferred to other tools that process context-free grammars or even metamodels.

In MontiCore, modeling languages are syntactically defined with context-free grammars like the one in Fig. 5. By language inheritance, the grammar re-uses productions of a super-grammar Common (l. 1) where, e.g., the commonly used non-terminals IDENT or Type are defined. The keyword external (l. 4) indicates that a second language for invariants is embedded. Later, this production can be mapped to any invariant language. Interface productions (l. 3) state that any implementing production (lines 10 and 18) can be parsed when the interface is expected (l. 8). Enumerations (l. 14) list possible alternative terminal symbols. Other than that, MontiCore grammars have terminal symbols enclosed in quotes (e.g., l. 7), alternatives (|), iteration (∗), and optional elements (?). Fig. 6 contains two simple concrete models that conform to the grammar of Fig. 5.

The MontiCore generator basically derives a set of Java classes representing the abstract syntax and an ANTLR-based parser that can process the models from Fig. 6. For our purpose, an additional generator has been implemented that produces an Isabelle/HOL theory that holds the abstract syntax as a set of data type definitions, see Fig. 7. The theory imports data types generated from super-grammars and the theory that fills the language parameters for externals (l. 2). Recursively dependent types are computed and generated as a single data type (not shown in this example). Iteration is translated to the built-in type list, optional elements to type option. The interface CDElement leads to a

```
1  grammar CDSimp extends mc.umlp.common.Common {
2
3    interface CDElement;
4    external Invariant;
5
6    CDDefinition =
7      "classdiagram" Name:IDENT
8      "{" ( CDElement | Invariant ";")* "}";
9
10   CDClass implements CDElement =
11     "class" Name:IDENT ("extends" scl:IDENT ("," scl:IDENT)*)?
12     ("{" (CDAttribute)* "}" | ";");
13
14   enum CDModifier = "public" | "private";
15
16   CDAttribute = CDModifier? Type Name:IDENT ";";
17
18   CDAssociation implements CDElement =
19     "association" Left:IDENT "--" Right:IDENT ";";
20 }
```

Fig. 5. MontiCore grammar of class diagrams

```
1  classdiagram ABC {          classdiagram CA {
2    class A;                    class C;
3    class B extends A;          class A extends C;
4    class C extends B;         }
5  }
```

Fig. 6. Two simple class models

data type with alternative constructors, one for each implementing type (l. 18). Enumerations become types with an alternative constructor for each possible value (l. 5).

The generated theory now holds a deep embedding of the syntax in Isabelle/ HOL and can be used to define the semantic mapping. Since we also want to be able to reason about concrete models, we also have to translate these to instances of the data type. For that purpose, our MontiCore generator additionally produces a specific generator that translates concrete models. Applied to the model ABC we obtain the theory shown in Fig. 8. The constant abc (l. 4) is a class diagram that has name ABC, an empty list of invariants, and three class diagram elements which are all classes. All classes have no attributes but some have a super-class, e.g., CDClass ''C'' has super-class ''B''.

Please note that the generator actually produces separate constants for each data type. It has been in-lined here for the sake of brevity.

```
1   theory CDSimpAS
2   imports "$UMLP/abstractSyntax/external/ExternalCDSimpAS" CommonAS
3   begin
4
5   datatype CDModifier =
6       CDModifierPRIVATE
7     | CDModifierPUBLIC
8
9   datatype CDAttribute =
10      CDAttribute "CDModifier option" Type IDENT
11
12  datatype CDClass =
13      CDClass IDENT "IDENT list" "CDAttribute list"
14
15  datatype CDAssociation =
16      CDAssociation IDENT IDENT
17
18  datatype CDElement =
19      CDElementCDClass CDClass
20    | CDElementCDAssociation CDAssociation
21
22  datatype CDDefinition =
23      CDDefinition IDENT "Invariant list" "CDElement list"
24
25  end
```

Fig. 7. Abstract syntax data type in Isabelle/HOL

```
1   theory ABC
2   imports "$UMLP/abstractSyntax/gen/CDSimpAS"
3   begin
4   constdefs "abc == CDDefinition  ''ABC'' []
5     [CDElementCDClass (CDClass  ''C'' [''B''] []),
6      CDElementCDClass (CDClass  ''B'' [''A''] []),
7      CDElementCDClass (CDClass  ''A'' [] []) ]"
8   end
```

Fig. 8. Concrete model representation

5   Semantic Mapping and Its Formalization

All necessary components for semantic mappings are now available for the use
in Isabelle: the language itself as a data type and a formalization of the system
model. Functions in Isabelle/HOL can be used to define mapping functions from
the implementation of the abstract syntax to the system model implementation.
Features like recursion, constructor pattern matching and functional decomposition can be incorporated. The domain of the mapping function is the generated top-level data type of the language to be mapped. Its range is the power

set of systems of the system model. Instances of systems are of the data type `SystemModel` in the Isabelle implementation.

From the UML class diagram grammar the data type `CDDefinition` in Fig. 7 is generated. The corresponding mapping function has the signature

$$\texttt{mCDDefinition :: "CDDefinition} \Rightarrow \texttt{SystemModel set"}$$

What the mapping function basically does is adding constraints to a set of systems. I.e., the mapping describes properties of the elements in its returned set of systems. Essential constraints are that every system has to fulfill a set of basic predicates like `pCAR_Type1` and `pSubTrans` from Sect. 3. This way the mapping only renders valid instances of the system model. Further constraints depend on the mapped modeling language. The mapping function can be decomposed to many short and compact functions each mapping one aspect of the abstract syntax. The function to map the data type `CDClass` (l. 15, Fig. 7) is shown in Fig. 9.

```
1   fun mCDClass :: "CDClass ⇒ SystemModel ⇒ bool"
2   where
3     "mCDClass (CDClass name supers attrs) sm = (
4     ∃ c ∈ UCLASS sm .
5        c = Class (mIDENT name) ∧
6        gall supers (mSuperClass c sm) ∧
7        gall attrs (mCDAttribute c sm)
8     )"
```

Fig. 9. Mapping of data type `CDClass`

This predicate on systems enforces that a class exists in `UCLASS` which has the specified class name and also fulfills further constraints given by the mapping of the super-classes `mSuperClass` and the mapping of the attributes `mCDAttribute`. The function `gall` feeds all elements of the list `supers` as a third parameter to the function `mSuperClass` which is called with the current class and system as parameters. These functional decompositions of the mapping make it easier to write comprehensible and maintainable code.

5.1   Example: Cyclic Inheritance Problem

To demonstrate the use of our implementation of the system model and the generation of instances from concrete models we present a short example. The textual models for this example were already given in Fig. 6. The semantic mapping renders a set of systems that fulfill the specifications given by the textual class diagrams. If a system complies to both specifications it is contained in the intersection of both mappings. Following the paradigm convention over configuration classes with same names in different systems share the same identity. Thus all systems in the intersection of the mappings contain a circular inheritance, i.e., `A extends C extends B extends A`.

```
1    constdefs pSubNonCirc :: "SystemModel ⇒ bool"
2    "pSubNonCirc sm ==
3        (∀ c1 c2 . (the (sub sm c2 c1) ∧  the (sub sm c1 c2)
4                    ⟶ c1 = c2))"
```

Fig. 10. Definition of a predicate for non-circular inheritance of classes

```
1    lemma SubNonCirc:
2        "⟦pSubNonCirc sm;the (sub sm c2 c1);the (sub sm c1 c2)⟧
3                    ⟹ c1 = c2"
4    by (unfold pSubNonCirc-def, auto)
```

Fig. 11. Rule to apply the predicate for non-circular inheritance

In this example we show a proof in our system model implementation that no system from the combined specification in Fig. 6 is compatible with the specification of non-circular inheritances given in Fig. 10. The lemma and the corresponding proof can be found in Fig. 12. The additional lemma in Fig. 11 is used to utilize the definition of pSubNonCirc in a more convenient way. The same is done for the definition pSubTrans from Fig. 4 in a corresponding lemma SubTrans.

```
1    lemma ABC-CA-circ: "mCDDefinition ABC.abc ∩ mCDDefinition CA.ca
2                    ∩ {sm . pSubNonCirc sm} = {}"
3    apply(unfold abc-def ca-def,auto)
4    apply(frule SubTrans, auto)
5    by(frule SubNonCirc,auto)
```

Fig. 12. Lemma and proof using generated UML models

First the definitions ABC.abc_def and CA.ac_def are unfolded replacing ABC.abc and CA.ac by their values (shown in Fig. 8 for the first model). To complete the proof the transitivity of the sub class relation (lemma SubTrans) is employed yielding that Class ''A'' is a sub class of Class ''B''. Afterwards the rule SubNonCirc leads to Class ''B'' = Class ''C'' which is an obvious contradiction here. Automatic simplification is done by the proof command auto throughout the proof.

In the example, two models of the same language are used. However, handling models of different languages is done in exactly the same way, since the semantics of a model is always given as predicates over the same type SystemModel.

6   Related Work

Quite a number of approaches to define a formal semantics for programming and modeling languages exist; a survey is given in [13,14]. These works deal with formalisms and mathematical frameworks that tend to be too complex or cumbersome to use for industrial applications. Efforts to bridge this gap led to reasoning tools to support using these formal/mathematical frameworks. Prominent works have shown that proof assistants can be used to define and verify semantics of programming languages [15,16,17,18]. But as discussed the execution semantics of programming languages is not directly suitable for underspecified modeling techniques.

Works around Java compilers [19] and virtual machines [20] show that the embedding of languages and the derivation of a proof environment are a tedious but crucial task. We automate the task of embedding modeling languages in a proof environment and offers the system model as a reasoning framework.

One of the earliest frameworks for designing and analyzing domain specific programming languages (DSPLs) is the CENTAUR system [21]. It is a combination of different tools to define the syntax, transformations and an expression evaluation and reasoning framework using Prolog and Coq [15].

Semantic anchoring is a more recent approach for defining semantics of modeling languages [22]. The semantics is defined based on semantic units which are minimal languages with well-defined semantics for models of computations. The abstract syntax of domain-specific modeling languages is transformed to the abstract syntax of a semantic unit. In [22] an example of semantic anchoring with tool support for defining and transforming models is given. The work also covers similar topics and tool support addressed in this paper but is primarily about giving operational semantics through generated AsmL [23] sources. Other approaches, e.g, [24] are based on MOF [25] for which formal semantics exist [26]. In [27] the authors propose a composition of semantic units when modeling heterogeneous systems that do not match a single semantic unit. The composition is not supported by tools yet. Heterogeneous UML semantics approaches such as [28] also use a posteriori composition of semantics. In our approach we circumvented this problem by starting with a powerful enough system model.

A completely integrated approach to define a formal language and its semantics is shown in [29]. The abstract syntax and static semantics of modeling languages can both be expressed in one Alloy [30] model. A major advantage is the integrated development of all parts of the language using only one formalism. Alloy relies on the small scope hypothesis and uses only a bounded search space to find counterexamples.

7   Conclusion and Future Work

The main contribution of this work is the provision of a flexible tool support for system model-based semantics definitions. The predicative semantic mapping helps us to cope with underspecified models. We provide the system model as a predefined and rather general semantic domain that can be reused in various semantics definitions for structural, behavioral and interaction concepts. Furthermore, the form of semantics definition based on sets allows for an easy explanation of composition and refinement of models.

The syntax and semantics can fully be defined using the tools MontiCore and Isabelle/HOL. Using a theorem prover allows us to define semantics in a very flexible and modular, yet machine-readable way. A MontiCore generator is used to deeply embed the abstract syntax of a language defined in MontiCore into Isabelle/HOL. Based thereon, also concrete models can be translated into Isabelle theories that provide means to directly use the semantics for verification purposes. The whole approach was shown for a simple example.

Using a theorem prover gives us great power and flexibility to handle all kinds of verification problems. But clearly, automation is rather poor compared to, e.g., model checking, since proofs have to be conducted manually. Future work will therefore be concerned with the question how to improve automation, e.g., by generating a set of helpful auxiliary lemmas and definitions. The identification, management, and consistent configuration of variation points has not been discussed in detail, this will be a matter of future work, too. Finally, we plan to further investigate which conclusions we can draw from the integrated semantics of languages, hoping to find new insights of how different languages interact with each other.

References

1. Object Management Group: Unified Modeling Language: Superstructure Version 2.1.2 (07-11-02) (2007), http://www.omg.org/docs/formal/07-11-02.pdf
2. Harel, D., Rumpe, B.: Meaningful Modeling: What's the Semantics of "Semantics"? Computer 37(10), 64–72 (2004)
3. France, R., Evans, A., Lano, K., Rumpe, B.: The UML as a Formal Modeling Notation. Computer Standards & Interfaces 19, 325–334 (1998)
4. Breu, R., Grosu, R., Huber, F., Rumpe, B., Schwerin, W.: Towards a Precise Semantics for Object-Oriented Modeling Techniques. In: Kilov, H., Rumpe, B. (eds.) Proceedings ECOOP 1997 Workshop on Precise Semantics for Object-Oriented Modeling Techniques, Technische Universität München, TUM-I9725, pp. 53–59 (1997)
5. Nipkow, T., Paulson, L.C., Wenzel, M.: Isabelle/HOL - A Proof Assistant for Higher-Order Logic. Springer, Heidelberg (2002)
6. Krahn, H., Rumpe, B., Völkel, S.: Monticore: Modular development of textual domain specific languages. In: Proceedings of Tools Europe (2008)
7. Winskel, G.: The Formal Semantics of Programming Languages. Foundations of Computer Science Series. MIT Press, Cambridge (1993)
8. Rumpe, B.: Formale Methodik des Entwurfs verteilter objektorientierter Systeme. Doktorarbeit, Technische Universität München (1996)
9. Broy, M., Cengarle, M.V., Grönniger, H., Rumpe, B.: Modular Description of a Comprehensive Semantics Model for the UML (Version 2.0). Informatik-Bericht 2008-06, Technische Universität Braunschweig (2008)
10. Cengarle, M.V., Grönniger, H., Rumpe, B.: System Model Semantics of Class Diagrams. Informatik-Bericht 2008-05, Technische Universität Braunschweig (2008)
11. Cengarle, M.V., Grönniger, H., Rumpe, B.: System Model Semantics of Statecharts. Informatik-Bericht 2008-04, Technische Universität Braunschweig (2008)
12. Naraschewski, W., Wenzel, M.: Object-oriented verification based on record subtyping in higher-order logic. In: Grundy, J., Newey, M. (eds.) TPHOLs 1998. LNCS, vol. 1479, pp. 349–366. Springer, Heidelberg (1998)

13. Zhang, Y., Xu, B.: A survey of semantic description frameworks for programming languages. SIGPLAN Not. 39(3), 14–30 (2004)
14. Mosses, P.D.: Formal Semantics of Programming Languages: An Overview. Electronic Notes in Theoretical Computer Science 148(1), 41–73 (2006)
15. Terrasse, D.: Encoding natural semantics in coq. In: Alagar, V.S., Nivat, M. (eds.) AMAST 1995. LNCS, vol. 936, pp. 230–244. Springer, Heidelberg (1995)
16. Nipkow, T.: Winskel is (almost) right: Towards a mechanized semantics textbook. Formal Aspects of Computing 10, 171–186 (1998)
17. van Oheimb, D.: Analyzing Java in Isabelle/HOL: Formalization, Type Safety and Hoare Logic. Ph.D thesis, Technische Universität München (2001)
18. Bertot, Y.: Theorem proving support in programming language semantics (July 2007)
19. Berghofer, S., Strecker, M.: Extracting a formally verified, fully executable compiler from a proof assistant. Electronic Notes in Theoretical Computer Science 82(2), 377–394 (2004); COCV 2003, Compiler Optimization Meets Compiler Verification
20. Leroy, X.: Java bytecode verification: Algorithms and formalizations. Journal of Automated Reasoning 30(3), 235–269 (2003)
21. Borras, P., Clement, D., Despeyroux, T., Incerpi, J., Incerpi, J., Kahn, G., Lang, B., Pascual, V.: Centaur: the system. SIGPLAN Not. 24(2), 14–24 (1989)
22. Chen, K., Sztipanovits, J., Abdelwahed, S., Jackson, E.K.: Semantic anchoring with model transformations. In: Hartman, A., Kreische, D. (eds.) ECMDA-FA 2005. LNCS, vol. 3748, pp. 115–129. Springer, Heidelberg (2005)
23. AsmL Website, http://www.research.microsoft.com/fse/asml
24. Wachsmuth, G.: Modelling the Operational Semantics of Domain-Specific Modelling Languages. In: Lämmel, R., Visser, J., Saraiva, J. (eds.) GTTSE 2007. LNCS, vol. 5235, pp. 506–520. Springer, Heidelberg (2008)
25. Object Management Group: MOF Specification Version 2.0 (2006-01-01) (January 2006), http://www.omg.org/docs/ptc/06-05-04.pdf
26. Boronat, A., Meseguer, J.: An Algebraic Semantics for MOF. In: Fiadeiro, J.L., Inverardi, P. (eds.) FASE 2008. LNCS, vol. 4961, pp. 377–391. Springer, Heidelberg (2008)
27. Chen, K., Sztipanovits, J., Neema, S.: Compositional specification of behavioral semantics. In: DATE 2007: Proceedings of the conference on Design, automation and test in Europe, San Jose, CA, USA, EDA Consortium, pp. 906–911 (2007)
28. Cengarle, M.V., Knapp, A., Wirsing, A.T.M.: A Heterogeneous Approach to UML Semantics, pp. 383–402 (2008)
29. Kelsen, P., Ma, Q.: A Lightweight Approach for Defining the Formal Semantics of a Modeling Language. In: Czarnecki, K., Ober, I., Bruel, J.-M., Uhl, A., Völter, M. (eds.) MODELS 2008. LNCS, vol. 5301, pp. 690–704. Springer, Heidelberg (2008)
30. Jackson, D.: Alloy: a lightweight object modelling notation. Software Engineering and Methodology 11(2), 256–290 (2002)

Typing Component-Based Communication Systems

Michael Lienhardt, Claudio Antares Mezzina,
Alan Schmitt, and Jean-Bernard Stefani

INRIA, France

Abstract. Building complex component-based software systems, for instance communication systems based on the Click, Coyote, Appia, or Dream frameworks, can lead to subtle assemblage errors. We present a novel type system and type inference algorithm that prevent interconnection and message-handling errors when assembling component-based communication systems. These errors are typically not captured by classical type systems of host programming languages such as Java or ML. We have implemented our approach by extending the architecture description language (ADL) toolset used by the Dream framework, and used it to check Dream-based communication systems.

1 Introduction

Building software systems from components has many benefits [33], including easier maintenance and evolution. However, component-based systems are not exempt from subtle assemblage errors that are not captured by the type systems provided with the implementation languages. These errors are hard to catch because they may be purely an artifact of a faulty assemblage, and thus may arise even if individual components and their interconnections are correct. As noted in [24], this is for instance the case with data manipulation errors. These errors may occur when handling protocol data units in a communication stack built from components or micro-protocols with frameworks like Appia [27], Click [18], Coyote [5], Dream [20], or Ensemble [34].

Dealing with assemblage errors in system software and communication systems has already been approached in five main ways. The first one uses theorem proving to check the expected properties of an assemblage on a formal specification of the behavior of individual components and of the assemblage, as in Ensemble [24]. The second approach uses an architecture description language (ADL) to specify component behaviors and assemblage constraints, typically component dependencies, and to automatically verify the assemblage consistency, as in Aster [15], Knit [30], or Plastik [16]. The third approach relies on type systems for interaction contracts, as in the Singularity system [11] or in web service workflows [14]. The fourth approach uses model checking to verify the expected properties of a formally specified assemblage, as in the Vercors system [3]. A fifth approach relies on property-preserving composition, as described in [4], where it is applied to deadlock-free assemblages.

D. Lee et al. (Eds.): FMOODS/FORTE 2009, LNCS 5522, pp. 167–181, 2009.

The theorem-proving approach is comprehensive and can address arbitrary properties, but it requires theorem-proving expertise, which is not readily available for systems programmers. The ADL approach is more automatic, but it typically supports a limited set of architectural constraints, and a limited set of behavioral checks that fail to address subtler run-time errors such as data manipulation errors. The type-system approach can be made entirely automatic if type inference is decidable, but the type systems devised so far fail to deal with the data handling errors we consider in this paper. The model-checking approach is automatic, but may require considerable expertise in the property language used, again not necessarily available for systems programmers. The property-preserving composition approach also can be made entirely automatic, for instance using model checking techniques, but to this date does not readily apply to the data handling errors we consider.

We thus propose an extension of the ADL approach with a type analysis devised to deal with a class of data manipulation errors that occur in ill-formed communication systems assemblages. More specifically, our approach involves: (i) the definition of a simple process calculus that allows to specify an operational model of a component assemblage (where program execution is abstracted by a reduction relation); (ii) the definition of a type system, that operates on programs abstracted as terms of the process calculus, and that ensures that typable assemblages do not exhibit the targeted class of errors; (iii) an extension of the target ADL to allow architecture descriptions with process annotations characterizing the abstract behavior of selected components; (iv) the addition of a type analyzer in the ADL assembly toolchain to statically verify component assemblages. Technically, the paper makes two main contributions: (i) we define a novel type system, which combines rows [31] with process types [36,25], to track message flows in component assemblages; (ii) we define a total type inference algorithm for automatically checking annotated component assemblages.

Outline. The paper is organized as follows. Section 2 details the assemblage verification we target. Section 3 presents the calculus and Section 4 the type system that we use to abstract the behavior of communication components and to characterize them. Section 5 discusses type inference and its implementation in actual assemblage tool chains. Section 6 discusses related work and Section 7 concludes the paper.

2   Assemblages in Dream

To explain the assemblage verifications we target in this paper, we use the example of the Dream framework, which we now briefly present. Dream is a component-based framework, written in Java, designed for the construction of communication systems (protocol stacks, communication subsystems of middleware for distributed execution). It is built on top of the Java implementation of the Fractal component model [6].

The primary data structure in Dream is called a *message*. Messages are used to implement protocol data units (i.e. the data that communication protocols exchange during their execution). Messages are exchanged between Dream components through input and output *channels*. A message is a list of *labeled chunks*, which can be any Java objects including messages. Within a component, messages can be freely manipulated. Basic operations, like removing, adding, or accessing chunks are provided. The Dream framework comprises a library of components that encapsulate functions and behaviors commonly found in communication subsystems. These include: *message queues* that are used to store messages, *transformers* that transform a message received on their single input channel and deliver the result to their single output channel, *routers* that forward messages received on their single input channel to one or several output channels, *multiplexers* that forward messages received on their input channels to their single output channel, *aggregators* that aggregate messages received on one or several input channels and deliver the aggregated message on their single output channel, *deaggregators* that are dual to aggregators, and *conduits* that allow messages to be exchanged between different address spaces.

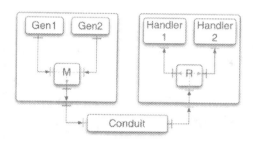

Fig. 1. A DREAM Assemblage

Figure 1 shows a simple assemblage of Dream components that corresponds to two communicating sites, Site A sending different kinds of messages to Site B. The assemblage comprises two generator components, Gen1 and Gen2, that emit different messages. These messages are then sent to a multiplexer, then handled by the Conduit component and transferred to Site B. On Site B, router R forwards messages to the Handler 1 or Handler 2 component, based on the structure of the incoming messages. Verifying the correctness of the assemblage implies verifying structural constraints to guarantee that input and output channels are properly matched, and ensuring that a component does not receive a message it is not able to handle (typically, a message with missing or unexpected chunks). In our simple example above, this could be the case if the component Conduit could not handle messages generated by the two components Gen1 and Gen2 (e.g. because of a missing chunk), or if one handler could not process the messages forwarded to it. In the presence of complex assemblages, such an analysis can quickly become difficult.

3   Calculus

Our process calculus aims to capture the abstract behavior of components appearing in communication frameworks. It is at the same level of abstraction than an architecture description language (ADL). Alternatively, it can be understood as a simple ADL. This allows us to apply our approach to different communication frameworks, written in different programming languages.

Syntax. The syntax of the calculus is given below. It is parameterized by the set of primitive components (noted p) which can be used in assemblages.

$D ::=$		Assemblage	$\delta ::=$		Tag list
	p	Primitive		$\emptyset$	Empty tag
	$\mid\ c[I\ /\ O][D]$	Composite		$\mid\ \downarrow r; \delta$	*down* tag
	$\mid\ \bar{e}\langle M \rangle$	Message		$\mid\ \uparrow r; \delta$	*up* tag
	$\mid\ D_1 \mid D_2$	Parallel			
			$v ::=$		Value
$M ::= v^\delta$		Routed value		c	Base value
				$\{a_1 = v_1; \ldots; a_n = v_n\}$	Record

An assemblage is a parallel composition of components and messages. Components can be primitive or composite. A composite takes the form $c[I\ /\ O][D]$, where c is a name, I is the set of input channels of the composite, O is the set of output channels of the composite, and D is its inner assemblage. The specification of input and output channels I and O in a composite may hide input or output channels of its inner assemblage, by not mentioning them. Messages take the form $\bar{e}\langle M \rangle$, where e is a channel name, and M is a routed value. In the following we write J for a parallel composition of messages. A routed value is a record or a base value decorated with a list of routing tags. We always assume that each tag occur at most once in a list. Intuitively, a list of routing tags δ encodes a particular message flow in a component assemblage. Primitive components can act on these flows, as illustrated by the router and multiplexer primitive components described below. Although each tag is unique in a tag list, component assemblages can contain loops (e.g., through a combination of routers and multiplexers), and record fields can contain records. These two features allow the modeling of complex communication stacks, including ones featuring protocol tunneling, such as IP over IP.

The set of primitive components is a parameter of the calculus, and can be extended as required. It is assumed to contain at least the following primitive components: components Add, Sub, and Select provide classical basic operations on extensible records; components Router and Mult provide elementary routing and multiplexing capabilities; component Conn corresponds to a simple unidirectional connector.

Operational semantics. The operational semantics of the calculus is defined classically by a reduction relation between terms that operates modulo a structural equivalence. The structural equivalence is not given here for lack of space (see [22] for details), but it essentially states that the parallel operator is associative, commutative, and that the order of fields in a record does not matter. The reduction relation is defined as a binary relation on assemblages that satisfies the rules given below. In the rules, a statement of the form "$D_1 \rhd D_2$" can be read "D_1 reduces to D_2".

$$\text{R:CTX} \quad \frac{D \rhd D'}{\mathbb{E}[D] \rhd \mathbb{E}[D']}$$

$$\text{R:IN} \quad \frac{e \in I}{\overline{e}\langle M\rangle \mid c[I \,/\, O][D] \rhd c[I \,/\, O][\overline{e}\langle M\rangle \mid D]}$$

$$\text{R:OUT} \quad \frac{s \in O}{c[I \,/\, O][\overline{s}\langle M\rangle \mid D] \rhd c[I \,/\, O][D] \mid \overline{s}\langle M\rangle}$$

$$\text{R:PRIM} \quad \frac{\texttt{match}(p, J)}{J \mid p \rhd p \mid \gamma(p, J)}$$

Rule R:CTX stipulates that reduction is possible inside an evaluation context $\mathbb{E}$ (composite environment or other assemblages in parallel, see [22] for details). Rules R:IN and R:OUT stipulate how messages flow in and out of composite components. Rule R:PRIM is actually a rule schema describing the evolution of primitive components. Informally, it states that if a set of messages J *matches* the input schema of primitive component p (premise $\texttt{match}(p, J)$), then p can consume input messages J and produce output messages described by $\gamma(p, J)$. The relation $\texttt{match}$ and the function γ must be defined for all primitive components of interest. For instance, they are defined as follows for $\texttt{Add}$, $\texttt{Select}$, $\texttt{Mult}$, and $\texttt{Router}$. Let $M = \{a_1 = v_1; \ldots; a_n = v_n\}^{\delta_1}$, $R = \{a = v; a_1 = v_1; \ldots; a_n = v_n\}^{\delta_1}$, and a, a_i all distinct. We set:

$$\texttt{match}(\texttt{Add}[e_1\, e_2/s](a), \overline{e_1}\langle M\rangle \mid \overline{e_2}\langle v^{\delta_2}\rangle) \qquad \gamma(\texttt{Add}[e_1\, e_2/s](a), \overline{e_1}\langle M\rangle \mid \overline{e_2}\langle v^{\delta_2}\rangle) = \overline{s}\langle R\rangle$$

$$\texttt{match}(\texttt{Select}[e/s](a), \overline{e}\langle R\rangle) \qquad \gamma(\texttt{Select}[e/s](a), \overline{e}\langle R\rangle) = \overline{s}\langle v^{\delta_1}\rangle$$

$$\texttt{match}(\texttt{Mult}[e_1\, e_2/s](r), \overline{e_1}\langle v^{\delta}\rangle) \qquad \texttt{match}(\texttt{Mult}[e_1\, e_2/s](r), \overline{e_2}\langle v^{\delta}\rangle) \qquad \text{if} \quad r \notin \delta$$

$$\gamma(\texttt{Mult}[e_1\, e_2/s](r), \overline{e_1}\langle v^{\delta}\rangle) = \overline{s}\langle v^{\uparrow r;\delta}\rangle \qquad \gamma(\texttt{Mult}[e_1\, e_2/s](r), \overline{e_2}\langle v^{\delta}\rangle) = \overline{s}\langle v^{\downarrow r;\delta}\rangle$$

$$\texttt{match}(\texttt{Router}[e/s_1\, s_2](r), \overline{e}\langle v^{\delta}\rangle) \qquad \text{if } r \in \delta$$
$$\gamma(\texttt{Router}[e/s_1\, s_2](r), \overline{e}\langle v^{\delta_1;\uparrow r;\delta_2}\rangle) = \overline{s_1}\langle v^{\delta_1;\delta_2}\rangle$$
$$\gamma(\texttt{Router}[e/s_1\, s_2](r), \overline{e}\langle v^{\delta_1;\downarrow r;\delta_2}\rangle) = \overline{s_2}\langle v^{\delta_1;\delta_2}\rangle$$

$\texttt{Add}$ and $\texttt{Select}$ provide usual record manipulation. $\texttt{Mult}$ adds a tag to a routed value to signal the input channel on which it received it. $\texttt{Router}$ checks the tags of the received routed values to send them on the appropriate channel.

Errors. We say that an assemblage D *cannot process* a message $\overline{e}\langle M\rangle$ if a primitive component p in D may accept a message on e but cannot process the message $\overline{e}\langle M\rangle$: there are some N and J such that $\texttt{match}(p, \overline{e}\langle N\rangle \mid J)$ but for every J' we don't have $\texttt{match}(p, \overline{e}\langle M\rangle \mid J')$. We then define an assemblage D to be *in error* if $D = \mathbb{E}[\overline{e}\langle M\rangle \mid D']$ and $\overline{e}\langle M\rangle$ cannot be processed by D'. Intuitively, an assemblage is correct if no message manipulation error may occur, i.e., every primitive component that may accept a message can process it.

4 Types

4.1 Type System

Syntax. Our type system is based on two main ideas: (i) the type of values exchanged on channels are *routed types*: rows (extensible record) or base types, decorated with routing information; (ii) the type of an assemblage is an *assemblage type*, presented as a function from its input channel types to its output channels types. The syntax of types is defined below.

$E ::=$		Value type	$T ::=$		Routed type
	η	Variable		$\xi[E]$	Value flow
	$\{W\}$	Row		$r(T_1, T_2)$	Tagged pair
	τ	Base type			
			$S ::=$		Channel type
$W ::=$		Row definition		$\emptyset$	Empty declaration
	ρ	Row variable		$e : (T)$	Channel declaration
	$a : \text{Pre}(E); W$	Used Field		$S \cup S$	Union
	$a : \text{Abs}; W$	Unused Field			
	Abs	Empty Row			

The type of an assemblage, written F in the following, takes the form of a type scheme $\forall \alpha_1 \ldots \alpha_n.S_I \to S_O$ where α_i are type variables (standing for arbitrary types), S_I collects the types of input channels in the assemblage, and S_O collects the types of output channels in the assemblage. We write $dc(S)$ for the channel names that appear in S. A channel type takes the form $e : (T)$, where e is a channel name, and T is a routed type. A routed type is either a value flow $\xi[E]$, where the value type E is carried by the data flow ξ, or a tagged pair of the form $r(T_1, T_2)$, where r is a tag, and T_1, T_2 are routed types. Rows are defined classically [31] with presence and absence information: $a : \text{Pre}(E)$ stands for a field named a that is present in a record, with type E; $a : \text{Abs}$ indicates that field a is not present. Base types, i.e., types associated with base values, are a parameter of the type system (base types typically include integers, strings, or concrete data types).

Informally, a routed type is a binary tree where each leaf corresponds to a value type carried by a data flow, and the branch leading to it defines the routing annotation carried by the value (a given routing tag appears at most once on each branch). For instance, the type $r_1(\xi_1[\text{int}], r_2(\xi_2[\text{string}], \xi_2[\eta]))$ consists of three branches corresponding to three different values. The second branch $r_1(\_, r_2(\xi_2[\text{string}], \_))$ corresponds to a flow accepting only strings tagged with at least the tags $\downarrow r_1$ and $\uparrow r_2$. This tree structure uses explicit references to data flows as they enable *type duplication*, which is a requirement to properly deal with routing and multiplexing. Type duplication allows two multiplexers in a row to type check correctly and is the main innovation of this type system (see the discussion in Section 4.2).

Typing. Types for primitive components are given by a function Υ that maps primitive components to assemblage types. Just as the set of primitive components is a parameter of our calculus, function Υ is a parameter of our type system and needs to be defined for every primitive component to be typed. To ensure that these assemblage types correspond to the operational semantics of the primitive components, the function Υ must obey two constraints: (i) for each primitive component p, the input channel type of $\Upsilon(p)$ should only allow valid patterns; (ii) the output type of the parallel composition of a primitive component p with one of its valid input pattern J must contain the type of $\gamma(p, J)$. Formally, for all primitive component p and all J with $\mathtt{match}(p, J)$, there exists an assemblage type $S_1 \rightarrow S_2$ such that $p \mid J : S_1 \rightarrow S_2$ holds, and there exists S_2' with $S_2' \subset S_2$ such that $p \mid \gamma(p, J) : S_1 \rightarrow S_2'$ holds. These constraints ensure that the type of a primitive component is consistent with its behavior (defined by relation $\mathtt{match}$ and function γ). For instance, the types associated with the primitive components introduced before, and of a simple connector $\mathtt{Conn}[e/s]$ (that forward any value received on its input channel e to its output channel s), can be defined as follows:

$$\Upsilon(\mathtt{Add}[e_1 e_2/s](a)) = \forall \alpha, \rho, \xi.\ e_1 : (\xi_1[\{a : \mathrm{Abs}; \rho\}]) \cup e_2 : (\xi_2[\alpha]) \rightarrow s : (\xi_1[\{a : \mathrm{Pre}(\alpha); \rho\}])$$
$$\Upsilon(\mathtt{Select}[c/s](a)) = \forall \alpha, \rho, \xi.\ e : (\xi[\{a : \mathrm{Pre}(\alpha); \rho\}]) \rightarrow s : (\xi[\alpha])$$
$$\Upsilon(\mathtt{Router}[e/s_1 s_2](r)) = \forall \alpha, \beta, \xi, \xi'.\ e : (r(\xi[\alpha], \xi'[\beta])) \rightarrow s_1 : (\xi[\alpha]) \cup s_2 : (\xi'[\beta])$$
$$\Upsilon(\mathtt{Mult}[e_1\, e_2/s](r)) = \forall \alpha, \beta, \xi, \xi'.\ e_1 : (\xi[\alpha]) \cup e_2 : (\xi'[\beta]) \rightarrow s : (r(\xi[\alpha], \xi'[\beta]))$$
$$\Upsilon(\mathtt{Conn}[e/s]) = \forall \alpha, \xi.\ e : (\xi[\alpha]) \rightarrow s : (\xi[\alpha])$$

The type system is equipped with a (classical) subtyping relation $\leq$, which we do not detail fully here, for lack of space. For instance, the subtyping rules for assemblage types T:FUNC and T:GEN, and tagged pairs T:TAGPAIR, are given below (note the contravariance in T:FUNC, which is as expected):

$$\frac{S_1 \leq S_1' \qquad S_2 \leq S_2'}{S_1' \rightarrow S_2 \leq S_1 \rightarrow S_2'} \text{T:FUNC}$$

$$\frac{F \leq F'}{\forall \alpha.F \leq \forall \alpha.F'} \text{T:GEN}$$

$$\frac{T_1 \leq T_1' \qquad T_2 \leq T_2'}{r(T_1, T_2) \leq r(T_1', T_2')} \text{T:TAGPAIR}$$

The typing rules in our type system comprise rules for assemblages and rules for routed values. Typing judgements take the form $D : F$ for assemblages, $v : E$ for simple values, and $\mathcal{R} \vdash R : T$ for routed values. The environment $\mathcal{R}$ is a set of routing tags. The typing rules make use of the $\precsim$ binary relation between channel types, which is defined as follows: given two channel types $S \triangleq \bigcup_{i \in I} e_i : (T_i)$ and $S' \triangleq \bigcup_{j \in J} e_j' : (T_j')$, we note $S \precsim S'$ iff for all $i \in I, j \in J, e_i = e_j'$ implies $T_i \leq T_j'$.

Typing rules for assemblages are given below:

$$\frac{\text{T:PRIM}}{\Upsilon(p) = F} \qquad \frac{\text{T:SUBST}}{D : F} \qquad \frac{\text{T:INST}}{D : \forall\alpha.F} \qquad \frac{\text{T:GEN}}{D : F} \qquad \frac{\text{T:CHANNEL}}{\emptyset \vdash M : T}$$
$$\frac{}{p : F} \qquad \frac{}{D : \sigma(F)} \qquad \frac{}{D : F} \qquad \frac{}{D : \forall\alpha.F} \qquad \frac{}{\overline{e}\langle M\rangle : \emptyset \rightarrow e : (T)}$$

$$\frac{\text{T:SUB}}{D : F \qquad F \leq F'} \qquad \frac{\text{T:PAR}}{D : S_1 \rightarrow S_2 \qquad D' : S_1' \rightarrow S_2'}{S_2 \precsim S_1' \qquad S_2' \precsim S_1 \qquad dc(S_1) \cap dc(S_1') = \emptyset}$$
$$\frac{}{D : F'} \qquad \frac{}{D \mid D' : (S_1 \cup S_1') \rightarrow (S_2 \cup S_2')}$$

$$\frac{\text{T:BOX}}{D : S_1 \rightarrow S_2 \qquad S_1' \precsim S_1 \qquad S_2 \precsim S_2' \qquad S_2' \precsim S_1' \qquad dc(S_1') = I \wedge dc(S_2') = O}{c[I \: / \: O][D] : S_1' \rightarrow S_2'}$$

Rule T:PRIM states that the type of a primitive component is given by function Υ. Rules T:SUBST, T:INST, and T:GEN are classical rules for substitution, instantiation, and generalization, respectively. Since type duplication is integrated into substitutions, because of the different forms of type variables and their associated constraints (e.g., unique occurrence of tags in routing annotations), our notion of substitution σ in rule T:SUBST is slightly more complex than usual. It mostly behaves as expected, replacing variables with terms (see discussion in Section 4.2; formal details can be found in [22]).

The parallel composition D_1 of two assemblages D and D' yields a function having the *capacity* of both assemblages, i.e. , that accepts as input any message either D or D' accepts, and that can generate any message either D or D' can generate. Rule T:PAR has three side conditions: the first two ($S_2 \precsim S_1'$ and $S_2' \precsim S_1$) ensure that all values (S_2 and S_2') sent on input channels for $D \mid D'$ are indeed valid inputs for this program; the third one ($dc(S_1) \cap dc(S_1') = \emptyset$) states that D and D' must have distinct input channels to avoid the possibility of *implicit routing*, i.e. , of distinct components listening on the same channel, thus doing a routing operation without an explicit router to support it. Rule T:BOX specifies the constraints that apply to obtain the type $S_1' \rightarrow S_2'$ of a composite. The sets S_1' and S_2' must give a type to every channel mentioned in I and O. If a channel is mentioned in both, then the output type must be a subtype of the input type ($S_2' \precsim S_1'$) as this corresponds to a loop We also impose that the valid inputs of the component must be valid ones for the component's inner process (stated by the constraint $S_1' \precsim S_1$), and that all outputs of this process must be valid output of the component (stated by the constraint $S_2 \precsim S_2'$).

Typing rules for routed values are given below (we have left out rules and conditions that apply to base values and base types):

T:RECORD

$$\frac{\forall 1 \leq i \leq n, v_i : E_i \qquad \forall 1 \leq i \neq j \leq n, a_i \neq a_j}{\{a_1 = v_1; \ldots; a_n = v_n\} : \{a_1 : \text{Pre}(E_1); \ldots; a_n : \text{Pre}(E_n); \text{Abs}\}}$$

T:EMPTY

$$\frac{v : E}{\mathcal{R} \vdash v^\emptyset : \xi[E]}$$

T:UP

$$\frac{\mathcal{R} \uplus \{r\} \vdash v^\delta : T \qquad \mathcal{R} \uplus \{r\} \vdash T_k}{\mathcal{R} \vdash v^{\uparrow r; \delta} : r(T, T_k)}$$

T:DOWN

$$\frac{\mathcal{R} \uplus \{r\} \vdash v^\delta : T \qquad \mathcal{R} \uplus \{r\} \vdash T_k}{\mathcal{R} \vdash v^{\downarrow r; \delta} : r(T_k, T)}$$

Rule T:RECORD is the standard typing rule for extensible record, using rows. The three typing rules T:EMPTY, T:UP and T:DOWN, construct a routed type by induction on the cardinality of the routing annotation. Rule T:EMPTY is used when the routing annotation is empty: the routing type is in such case just a leaf representing the value's type. Rules T:UP and T:DOWN define how we construct the routing type tree when one or more elements are present in the routing annotation. We write $\mathcal{R} \uplus \{r\}$ for the disjoint union of the tow sets. Generic flows that are built in a routing type derivation will then be instantiated during the exploration of the rest of the program with the typing rule T:INST. The use of routing tags environments $\mathcal{R}$ in these three rules ensures the validity of the constructed routed type.

Example assemblage. Assume that the generators, handlers, multiplexer, router and conduit components in Figure 1 are primitive components, and their types are as given in the following table. We can type the assemblages SiteA and SiteB as indicated in the last two lines of the same table.

Component	Types
Gen1	$\forall \xi. \emptyset \to s_1 : (\xi[E_1])$
Gen2	$\forall \xi. \emptyset \to s_2 : (\xi[E_2])$
Handler1	$\forall \xi. e_1 : (\xi[E_3]) \to \emptyset$
Handler2	$\forall \xi. e_2 : (\xi[E_4]) \to \emptyset$
M	same type as $\text{Mult}[s_1 \, s_2/t_A](r)$
R	same type as $\text{Router}[t_B/e_1 \, e_2](r)$
Conduit	same type as $\text{Conn}[t_A/t_B]$
SiteA	$\forall \xi. \emptyset \to t_A : (r(\xi[E_1], \xi'[E_2]))$
SiteB	$\forall \xi. t_B : (r(\xi[E_3], \xi'[E_4])) \to \emptyset$

If we assume further that E_3 can be transformed using sub-typing and substitution into E_1, and similarly for E_4 into E_2, then we can type the (closed) assemblage

$$c[\emptyset \, / \, \emptyset][\text{SiteA} \mid \text{Conduit} \mid \text{SiteB}]$$

with the type: $\emptyset \to \emptyset$.

Properties of the type system. The type system is sound with respect to reduction and guarantees correct execution, as shown by the subject reduction and correction theorems, and type inference is decidable (see proofs in [22]):

Theorem 1 (Subject Reduction). *Let D and D' be two assemblages such that $D \, \triangleright \, D'$, and F an assemblage type such that $D : F$ holds. Then there exists F' such that $D' : F'$.*

Theorem 2 (Correction). *Let D be an assemblage and F a process type such that $D : F$ holds. Then D has no error.*

Theorem 3 (Inference). *Type inference is decidable.*

4.2   Discussion

Type duplication. In our presentation of the type system, we have, for lack of space, glossed over several details (which can be found in [22]). In particular, our notion of substitution is more complex than the usual one because of type duplication. Let us explain this by way of an example. One of the objectives of this type system was to allow flexible data flows in programs, using a routing tree structure to type our channels. Let us consider a program where a component Rem that remove a a field follows a multiplexer. The output type of the multiplexer is of the form $r(\xi_1[\eta_1], \xi_2[\eta_2])$, whereas the input type of Rem is of the form $\xi_3[\{a : \mathrm{Pre}(\eta_3); \rho\}]$. The difficulty here is that we need to be able to unify these two types to get a valid type system. With our definition of substitution, this unification is made in two steps. We first *duplicate* the type $\xi_3[\{a : \mathrm{Pre}(\eta_3); \rho\}]$ into

$$T \triangleq r(\xi_4[\{a : \mathrm{Pre}(\eta_3); \rho\}], \xi_5[\{a : \mathrm{Pre}(\eta_3); \rho\}])$$

One can remark that the two branches of the resulting routing tree have the same row and type variables. But because they are declared in different flows (ξ_4 and ξ_5), they can be instantiated with different terms. We then have two tree structures with the same form that we can simply unify into T.

Duplication allows to instantiate a leaf in a routing tree into a whole subtree, while keeping the constraint of the leaf (here, the constraint being that the message must have the field 'a' defined) and allowing the variables on the fresh leaves to be instantiated independently. One can see duplication as a way to enable polymorphism without using type schemes.

Routing on tags. One may notice that routing in our calculus is based on routing tags, and not, as could be envisaged, on message values or on (the presence of) fields in record values. Likewise, the type system could depend only on rows for message types. In fact, an earlier version of our calculus and type system did exactly that, and is described in [23]. Both calculus and type system in this earlier version are more expressive than the ones presented here. For instance, the type system in [23] allows types associated with a single channel to be union types, in contrast to the type system in this paper. Unfortunately, for reasons explained in [23], type inference in our earlier type system is undecidable. Our calculus and type system in the present paper thus trade expressivity in favor of the decidability of inference, which is ultimately due to the fact that routing types are finite trees.

Limitations. Our type system has a few limitations. We already pointed out that there can only be a single type for channel and a set of tags (union types are not supported). Also, since a routing type is a binary tree, one has to encode router and multiplexer types with more than two output or input channels by a combination of binary routers and multiplexers. Another consequence is the complexity of encoding routers that route on fields into our calculus, as is the case in the Dream framework. Typically, we encode the presence of a field a in a message with a pair of tags $\uparrow a$ (when the field a is present) and $\downarrow a$ (when a is absent from the message). This simple encoding is difficult to apply in complex assemblages involving loops with multiple routers and multiplexers. An encoding can be found in most cases, but can be tricky to define and manipulate. However, based on our experience with the Dream and Click frameworks (see below), these limitations are not show-stoppers, and we have not in practice encountered the difficult cases mentioned above.

5   Type Inference and Its Implementation

A key property of our type system (in contrast to our previous work [23]) is that type inference is decidable. We have devised and proved correct a constraint-based algorithm, along the lines of [28,9]. We do not have the space to present the type inference algorithm: its definition and proof can be found in [22]. The algorithm comprises a constraint generator that computes from a given program a set of constraints a type must satisfy to type the input program, and a constraint solver that decides whether the generated constraint set has a solution (the program is typable) or not (the program is not typable). Technically, our type inference is based on the one defined in [9], extended to deal with routing types, channel types, and type duplication.

We have implemented the type inference algorithm in OCaml, and used it to extend the assemblage tool chains used by the Dream and Click frameworks. In the case of Dream, we have extended the Fractal ADL toolchain described in [19]. Figure 2 provides an overview of this toolchain. It is organized as a component-based framework, that comprises essentially a front-end, realized by the `Loader` component in Figure 2, and a back-end, that comprises the `ASTProcessingOrganizer` and the `Scheduler` components in Figure 2. The back-end is responsible for the generation and execution of tasks such as code generation, code installation, code deployment, etc. The `Loader` component reads a set of input files and produces an Abstract Syntax Tree (AST). This tree provides a unified representation of the system architecture that can be described through a combination of description languages, such as ADL, IDL, or DSL. The `Loader` is organized essentially as a pipeline comprising parsers for the various possible input languages, and semantic analyzers. We have integrated our type analyzer as a specific semantic analyzer component in this pipeline. We have also devised an extension to the XML-based Fractal ADL to take into account our type annotations for primitive components, and added its associated parser component in the `Loader` pipeline.

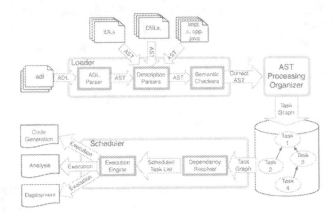

Fig. 2. Fractal ADL toolchain

In the case of Click, a C++ software framework dedicated to the component-based construction of configurable routers [18], assemblages are specified by configuration files written in a simple scripting language [17]. We found it simpler to just document type annotations for Click in a separate, additional configuration file. This way, our type analyzer remains an entirely separate and external analysis tool for Click, and its use does not require any change to the Click toolset.

We also conducted several experiments to check the correctness of non-trivial assemblages built using both frameworks. We have no space to report fully on these experiments but they demonstrate that our approach is practical, requiring minimal extensions to existing assemblage toolsets, and that it can indeed be applied to different component-based frameworks, implemented in different programming languages. The following table provides an indication of the time taken to check (correct) Dream and Click assemblages. The Dream assemblage originates from the Cosmos project, which develops protocols for roaming mobile devices. The Click assemblages are examples taken from the Click website. The performance of our type analyzer appears quite reasonable, bearing in mind that the complexity of type inference in our system is non-polynomial.

Assemblage	Components	Primitive	Channels	Time (sec)
COSMOS (Dream)	439	340	662	180.428
dnsproxy (Click)	9	8	7	0.025
fromhost-tunnet (Click)	24	22	24	0.166
mazu-nat (Click)	60	56	54	4.489

6   Related Work

Type systems checking architectural constraints or component assemblages have been the subject of several works in the past decade. For instance, the work done on the Wright language [2] supports the verification of behavioral compatibility constraints in a software architecture. Work on Plastik [16] deals mostly with structural constraints, although in a dynamical setting. Work on ArchJava [1] uses ownership types to enforce communication integrity between components. Another work develops behavioral types for component assembly [8], which is close to the notion of session types as developed in [38]. None of these type systems capture the errors we deal with in this paper, namely incorrect message manipulation operations. The type system we propose in this paper is more related to the ones defined for PICT [29], the π-calculus [25] or the $\lambda\pi_v$-calculus [37], although with provision for extensible record types that these systems do not have. We know of no type system that is capable of dealing with our notion of message errors along with the complex data flows that are allowed in our calculus. Indeed, type systems such as [7,13,29,32] are too restrictive concerning data flow manipulation, and cannot adequately deal with *routers* and *multiplexers*. On the other hand, type systems which provide some means to handle data flows by way of session types and process types [8,25,36,38] do not take in account structured mutable messages.

Type inference for distributed calculi has been studied in the setting of the Join-calculus [10], Mobile Ambients-like calculi [26], Dπ [21], which have an inference algorithm, and PICT, which has not. In our earlier work [23], type inference was undecidable. Undecidability was caused by channels being mapped to a finite set whose cardinality is not constrained, thus allowing a form of polymorphic recursion in loops [12]. In the present work, because of the use of tags, we only allow a kind of *finite* polymorphism in loops, thus obtaining decidable type inference. Finally, one can consider the *routing process* present in the calculus as a weak form of *type analysis* [35] on rows.

7   Conclusion

We have presented in this paper an approach and a novel type system to deal with data handling errors that may occur in communication systems built with component-based communication frameworks. Our approach, which can be characterized as a domain-specific type analysis, extends previous approaches based on architecture descriptions analysis, to deal with both structural and behavioral errors. It complements structural verifications that are the traditional remit of ADL-based approaches, and can as well be an interesting complement to behavior verification tools based on model-checking. We have implemented a type analyzer tool that comprises a total type inference algorithm for component assemblages, and applied it to the checking of several configurations built with two different communication frameworks. These experiments demonstrate, in our view, that our approach is indeed promising and practical.

We plan to extend this work in several directions. We are currently trying to generalize the notion of tagged types in order to apply to concurrent functional languages, and to extend our approach to deal with reconfiguration errors in dynamically evolving assemblages.

References

1. Aldrich, J., Chambers, C., Notkin, D.: Architectural Reasoning in ArchJava. In: Magnusson, B. (ed.) ECOOP 2002. LNCS, vol. 2374, p. 334. Springer, Heidelberg (2002)
2. Allen, R., Garlan, D.: A Formal Basis for Architectural Connection. ACM Transactions on Software Engineering and Methodology 6(3) (1997)
3. Barros, T., Cansado, A., Madelaine, E., Rivera, M.: Model-checking Distributed Components: The Vercors Platform. Electr. Notes Theor. Comput. Sci. 182 (2007)
4. Bensalem, S., Bozga, M., Sifakis, J., Nguyen, T.H.: Compositional Verification for Component-Based Systems and Application. In: Cha, S(S.), Choi, J.-Y., Kim, M., Lee, I., Viswanathan, M. (eds.) ATVA 2008. LNCS, vol. 5311. Springer, Heidelberg (2008)
5. Bhatti, N.T., Hiltunen, M.A., Schlichting, R.D., Chiu, W.: Coyote: A system for constructing fine-grain configurable communication services. ACM Trans. Comput. Syst. 16(4) (1998)
6. Bruneton, E., Coupaye, T., Leclercq, M., Quema, V., Stefani, J.B.: The Fractal Component Model and its Support in Java. Software - Practice and Experience 36(11-12) (2006)
7. Cardelli, L.: Types for mobile ambients. In: Proceedings 26th Annual ACM Symposium on Principles of Programming Languages, POPL (1999)
8. Carrez, C., Fantechi, A., Najm, E.: Behaviour contracts for a sound assembly of components. In: König, H., Heiner, M., Wolisz, A. (eds.) FORTE 2003. LNCS, vol. 2767. Springer, Heidelberg (2003)
9. Pottier, F.: A constraint-based presentation and generalization of rows. In: Symposium on Logic in Computer Science, LICS (2003)
10. Conchon, S., Pottier, F.: JOIN(X): Constraint-Based Type Inference for the Join-Calculus. In: Sands, D. (ed.) ESOP 2001. LNCS, vol. 2028, pp. 221–236. Springer, Heidelberg (2001)
11. Fahndrich, M., Aiken, M., Hawblitzel, C., Hodson, O., Hunt, G., Larus, J., Levi, S.: Language Support for Fast and Reliable Message-based Communication in Singularity OS. In: 1st EuroSys Conference. ACM, New York (2006)
12. Henglein, F.: Type inference with polymorphic recursion. ACM Trans. Program. Lang. Syst. 15(2), 253–289 (1993)
13. Roger Hindley, J.: Basic simple type theory. Cambridge University Press, New York (1997)
14. Honda, K., Yoshida, N., Carbone, M.: Multiparty asynchronous session types. In: 35th ACM Symposium on Principles of Programming Languages (POPL 2008). ACM, New York (2008)
15. Issarny, V., Bidan, C., Saridakis, T.: Achieving Middleware Customization in a Configuration-Based Development Environment : Experience with the Aster Prototype. In: 4th Int. Conf. on Configurable Distributed Systems (1998)
16. Joolia, A., Batista, T., Coulson, G., Gomes, A.: Mapping ADL Specifications to an Efficient and Reconfigurable Runtime Component Platform. In: WICSA 2005. IEEE Computer Society, Los Alamitos (2005)
17. Kohler, E., Morris, R., Chen, B.: Programming language optimizations for modular router configurations. In: ASPLOS (2002)
18. Kohler, E., Morris, R., Chen, B., Jannotti, J., Kaashoek, M.F.: The Click Modular Router. ACM Trans. Comput. Syst. 18(3) (2000)

19. Leclercq, M., Ozcan, A.E., Quema, V., Stefani, J.B.: Supporting heterogeneous architecture descriptions in an extensible toolset. In: 29th Int. Conf. on Soft. Eng. (ICSE). IEEE Computer Society, Los Alamitos (2007)
20. Leclercq, M., Quema, V., Stefani, J.B.: DREAM: A Component Framework for the Construction of Resource-Aware, Configurable MOMs. IEEE Distributed Systems Online 6(9) (2005)
21. Lhoussaine, C.: Type inference for a distributed π-calculus. Sci. Comput. Program. 50(1-3) (2004)
22. Lienhardt, M., Mezzina, C.A., Schmitt, A., Stefani, J.B.: Typing communicating component assemblages v2 (2008),
    http://sardes.inrialpes.fr/papers/dtv2.pdf
23. Lienhardt, M., Schmitt, A., Stefani, J.B.: Typing communicating component assemblages. In: GPCE 2008. ACM, New York (2008)
24. Liu, X., Kreitz, C., van Renesse, R., Hickey, J., Hayden, M., Birman, K., Constable, R.: Building Reliable, High-Performance Communication Systems from Components. In: ACM Symposium on Operating Systems Principles (1999)
25. Maffeis, S.: Sequence types for the pi-calculus. In: ITRS 2004. ENTCS, vol. 136, pp. 117–132. Elsevier, Amsterdam (2005)
26. Makholm, H., Wells, J.B.: Instant polymorphic type systems for mobile process calculi: Just add reduction rules and close. In: Sagiv, M. (ed.) ESOP 2005. LNCS, vol. 3444, pp. 389–407. Springer, Heidelberg (2005)
27. Miranda, H., Pinto, A.S., Rodrigues, L.: Appia: A flexible protocol kernel supporting multiple coordinated channels. In: ICDCS 2001. IEEE Computer Society, Los Alamitos (2001)
28. Palsberg, J., Wand, M., O'Keefe, P.: Type inference with non-structural subtyping. Formal Aspects of Computing 9, 49–67 (1997)
29. Pierce, B., Turner, D.: Pict: A programming language based on the pi-calculus. In: Plotkin, G., Stirling, C., Tofte, M. (eds.) Proof, Language and Interaction: Essays in Honour of Robin Milner, MIT Press, Cambridge (2000)
30. Reid, A., Flatt, M., Stoller, L., Lepreau, J., Eide, E.: Knit: Component Composition for Systems Software. In: OSDI 2000 (2000)
31. Rémy, D.: Type inference for records in a natural extension of ML. In: Theoretical Aspects Of Object-Oriented Programming. Types, Semantics and Language Design. MIT Press, Cambridge (1993)
32. Simonet, V., Pottier, F.: A constraint-based approach to guarded algebraic data types. ACM Trans. Program. Lang. Syst. 29(1), 1 (2007)
33. Szyperski, C.: Component Software., 2nd edn. Addison-Wesley, Reading (2002)
34. van Renesse, R., Birman, K., Hayden, M., Vaysburd, A., Karr, D.: Building Adaptive Systems Using Ensemble. Software – Practice and Experience 28(9) (1998)
35. Weirich, S.: Higher-order intensional type analysis. In: Le Métayer, D. (ed.) ESOP 2002. LNCS, vol. 2305, pp. 98–114. Springer, Heidelberg (2002)
36. Yoshida, N., Hennessy, M.: Assigning types to processes. In: 15th Annual IEEE Symposium on Logic in Computer Science, LICS (2000)
37. Yoshida, N., Hennessy, M.: Assigning types to processes. Inf. Comput. 174(2) (2002)
38. Yoshida, N., Vasconcelos, V.: Language primitives and type discipline for structured communication-based programming revisited: Two systems for higher-order session communication. Electr. Notes Theor. Comput. Sci. 171(4) (2007)

Epistemic Logic for the Applied Pi Calculus[*]

Rohit Chadha[1], Stéphanie Delaune[2], and Steve Kremer[2]

[1] University of Illinois at Urbana-Champaign, USA
[2] LSV, ENS Cachan & CNRS & INRIA Saclay, France

Abstract. We propose an epistemic logic for the applied pi calculus, which is a variant of the pi calculus with extensions for modeling cryptographic protocols. In such a calculus, the security guarantees are usually stated as *equivalences*. While process calculi provide a natural means to describe the protocols themselves, *epistemic logics* are often better suited for expressing certain security properties such as secrecy and anonymity.

We intend to bridge the gap between these two approaches: using the set of traces generated by a process as models, we define a logic which has constructs for reasoning about both intruder's epistemic knowledge and the set of messages in possession of the intruder. As an example we consider two formalizations of privacy in electronic voting and study the relationship between them.

1 Introduction

The applied pi calculus [2] is an extension of the pi calculus designed for specifying and verifying cryptographic protocols. The main difference from the pi calculus is that it allows one to manipulate complex data, instead of just names. The data is generated by an arbitrary abstract term algebra and interpreted modulo an equational theory. This allows one to abstractly specify cryptographic functions. For instance the equation $dec(enc(x, k), k) = x$ models that decryption cancels out encryption if the same key k is used. As the calculus is parametrized by an arbitrary equational theory, several complex cryptographic primitives have been conveniently modeled in literature. For example, blind signatures were modeled in [14] and non-interactive zero-knowledge proofs were modeled in [3]. This calculus has been successfully used to study a variety of security protocols, e.g. the direct anonymous attestation protocol [3], some electronic voting protocols [14]. Moreover, there exists tool support [5] for assisting the verification of protocols in the applied pi calculus.

As argued above the applied pi calculus is a convenient and flexible formalism for describing the processes which model the protocol. However, security properties are more difficult to specify. Some properties may directly be specified using observational equivalence, but this is generally not very natural and convenient. A more natural approach to verify protocols for correctness would be to define a suitable logic interpreted over the terms of the calculus and express the desired security goal in that logic.

Our main contribution is the definition of an epistemic logic for the applied pi calculus suitable for expressing important security goals. The logic itself is an LTL like

---

[*] This work has been partially supported by ANR SeSur AVOTÉ and NSF CCF 0448178.

D. Lee et al. (Eds.): FMOODS/FORTE 2009, LNCS 5522, pp. 182–197, 2009.

temporal logic with a special predicate Has that models deducibility of messages by an intruder and an epistemic knowledge operator K which allows us to reason about the intruder's *epistemic knowledge*. Other predicates of the logic are defined by *events* which annotate the protocol. Similar annotations have already been used for specifying authentication properties, initially by Woo and Lam [21] and more specifically in the applied pi calculus by Blanchet [6]. We emphasize here that our main motivation behind designing this logic is to express important security goals and *not* to study observational equivalence. In particular, a Hennessy-Milner theorem will not hold: observationally equivalent processes may satisfy different security goals.

Epistemic logics, going back to the BAN logic [8], are well-suited to express complex security properties. At that time, the logic was used to reason about authentication protocols. However, epistemic knowledge is particularly useful when reasoning about anonymity properties (*e.g.*, see [19]). Intuitively, an intruder (epistemically) knows that a property ϕ is true, if ϕ is true on every run which is indistinguishable for the intruder from the current one. In general epistemic logics this is modeled by an arbitrary equivalence relation on runs. In the context of security protocols, equivalence of runs is tightly related to the cryptographic functions used: an intruder which does not know k, should regard the runs outputting respectively $enc(0, k)$ and $enc(1, k)$ as equivalent. We formalize equivalence of runs by lifting the notion of *static equivalence* to protocol runs. We emphasize here that our logic contains the epistemic modality *only* for the intruder and not for other participants. This is primarily because the processes only keep track of messages in possession of the intruder.

We illustrate the expressiveness of our logic by expressing a range of security properties: secrecy, authentication as well as fairness in contract signing protocols. We then specify *privacy* in voting protocols, which relies on the epistemic knowledge of the intruder. We show that a definition of vote privacy in terms of process equivalence as defined in [14] implies vote privacy in terms of epistemic logic, as defined in [4]. Then we slightly weaken the equivalence based definition, replacing observational equivalence with trace equivalence. In that case, under reasonable assumptions, we show that the converse implication, i.e. epistemic privacy implies privacy as equivalence, also holds. This result is important in that it clarifies the relationship between two definitions of privacy employed in the literature. Furthermore, the result suggests that trace equivalence is more appropriate to model voter privacy even though observational equivalence is convenient to use because of the available tool support.

For the rest of the paper we reserve the phrase "intruder's knowledge" for his epistemic knowledge. We use the word "intruder's possession" for the set of messages that an intruder possesses (which is sometimes referred to as knowledge in security).

2 The Applied Pi Calculus

We present here the syntax and semantics of a slightly enriched applied pi calculus [2].

2.1 Syntax

The syntax of the applied pi-calculus assumes an order-sorted vocabulary consisting of a denumerable set of *names* of each sort, a denumerable set of *variables* of each sort and a *signature* Σ consisting of a finite set of *function symbols* with their arity. The details of the sort system are unimportant, as long as it differs *base types* and *channel types*. We always suppose that function symbols only operate on and return terms of base type. The grammar of the set of terms is defined as:

$$
\begin{array}{lll}
M, N, T := & & \text{terms} \\
\quad a, b, \ldots, \ldots k, m, n, \ldots & & \text{names} \\
\quad x, y, z, \ldots & & \text{variables} \\
\quad f(M_1, M_2, \ldots M_k) & & \text{function application}
\end{array}
$$

Of course function symbol application must respect sorts and arities. We shall use $u, v, \ldots$ to range over both names and variables. We write $vars(T)$ for the set of variables occurring in T. T is said to be a *ground* term if $vars(T) = \emptyset$.

Example 1. Let $\Sigma = \{\mathsf{enc}/2, \mathsf{dec}/2, \mathsf{pair}/2, \mathsf{proj}_1/1, \mathsf{proj}_2/1\}$ be a signature containing function symbols for encryption, decryption and pairing, each of arity 2, as well as left and right projection symbols of arity 1. The term $\mathsf{enc}(a, k)$ is ground.

There are two kinds of processes in the applied pi calculus– *plain* processes built up in a similar way to processes in the pi calculus except that messages can contain terms rather than just names, and *extended* processes which add *active substitutions* (explained below) and restriction on variables. Furthermore, we enrich plain processes with non-deterministic choice and a set of events $e, e_1, \ldots$ (parametrized by a sequence of terms of the correct sort). These events are "annotations" which are useful in formalizing security properties and (as we shall see later) play no part in observational equivalence. Extended processes are also enriched with *event stores*, which record the events that happen along an execution. We do not have replication in our calculus.

$$
\begin{array}{llll}
P, Q, R := & \text{plain processes} & A, B, C := & \text{extended processes} \\
\quad 0 & \text{null process} & \quad P & \text{plain process} \\
\quad P \mid Q & \text{parallel composition} & \quad A \mid B & \text{parallel composition} \\
\quad P + Q & \text{non-det. choice} & \quad \nu n.A & \text{name restriction} \\
\quad \nu n.P & \text{name restriction} & \quad \nu x.A & \text{variable restriction} \\
\quad \text{if } M = N \text{ then } P \text{ else } Q & \text{conditional} & \quad \{^M/_x\} & \text{active substitution} \\
\quad \mathsf{in}(u, x).P & \text{message input} & \quad [\mathsf{e}(\widetilde{M})] & \text{event store} \\
\quad \mathsf{out}(u, N).P & \text{message output} & & \\
\quad \mathsf{e}(\widetilde{M}).P & \text{event} & &
\end{array}
$$

$\{^M/_x\}$ is the active substitution that replaces the variable x with the term M. Active substitutions generalize the "let" construct: $\nu x.(\{^M/_x\} \mid P)$ corresponds exactly to "let $x = M$ in P". An event store $[\mathsf{e}(\widetilde{M})]$ memorizes that the event $\mathsf{e}(\widetilde{M})$ happened. As usual, names and variables have scopes, which are delimited by restrictions and by inputs. Please note that the "event" construct is not a binding construct. We write $fv(A)$, $bv(A)$, $fn(A)$ and $bn(A)$ for the sets of *free* and *bound variables* and *free* and *bound names* of A, respectively. We say that an extended process is *closed* if all its variables are either bound or defined by an active substitution. An *evaluation context* $C[\_]$ is an extended process with a hole instead of an extended process.

Active substitutions are useful because they allow us to map an extended process A to its *frame*, denoted $fr(A)$, by replacing every plain process and event store in A with 0.

A frame is an extended process built up from 0 and active substitutions by parallel composition and restriction. The frame $fr(A)$ accounts for the set of terms statically possessed by the intruder (but does not account for A's dynamic behavior). The *domain of a frame* φ, $\mathrm{dom}(\varphi)$, is the set of variables for which φ defines a substitution (i.e. variables x for which φ contains a substitution $\{M/x\}$ not under a restriction on x). In such a case, i.e. when $x \in \mathrm{dom}(\varphi)$, x allows the intruder to refer to the term M.

2.2 Semantics

The semantics is defined in terms of a LTS which records the interaction of an extended process with the intruder. We associate an equational theory E to the signature Σ. E is defined by a set of equations $M = N$ and induces an equivalence relation over terms: $=_E$ is the smallest equivalence relation on terms, which contain all equations in E and is closed under substitution of terms for variables and bijective renaming of names.

Example 2. Considering the signature Σ of Example 1 we define the equational theory E_{enc} by the equations $\mathrm{dec}(\mathrm{enc}(x, y), y) = x$ and $\mathrm{proj}_i(x_1, x_2) = x_i$ for $i \in \{1, 2\}$. We have that $\mathrm{dec}(\mathrm{enc}(a, k), k) =_{\mathsf{E}_{enc}} a$.

We define the relation $\cong$ to be the smallest equivalence relation on extended processes that is closed under application of evaluation contexts and such that

PAR-0	$A \mid 0 \cong A$	CHOICE-A	$P + (Q + R) \cong (P + Q) + R$
PAR-A	$A \mid (B \mid C) \cong (A \mid B) \mid C$	CHOICE-C	$P + Q \cong Q + P$
PAR-C	$A \mid B \cong B \mid A$	ALIAS	$\nu x.\{M/x\} \cong 0$
NEW-C	$\nu u.\nu v.A \cong \nu v.\nu u.A$	SUBST	$\{M/x\} \mid A \cong \{M/x\} \mid A\{M/x\}$
NEW-PAR	$A \mid \nu u.B \cong \nu u.(A \mid B)$	REWRITE	$\{M/x\} \cong \{N/x\}$
	if $u \notin fn(A) \cup fv(A)$		if $M =_\mathsf{E} N$

We define *structural equivalence*, $\equiv$, to be $\cong$ closed under α-conversion on names and variables. In comparison to the original applied pi calculus we dropped the structural equivalence $\nu n.0 \equiv 0$ which will be important for deduction.

Example 3. Consider the following process P:

$$\nu s, k.(\mathrm{out}(c_1, \mathrm{enc}(s, k)) \mid \mathrm{in}(c_1, y).\mathrm{out}(c_2, \mathrm{dec}(y, k))).$$

The first component publishes the message $\mathrm{enc}(s, k)$ by sending it on c_1. The second receives a message on c_1, uses the secret key k to decrypt it, and forwards the resulting plaintext on c_2. P is structurally equivalent to the following extended process A:

$$A = \nu s, k, x_1.(\mathrm{out}(c_1, x_1) \mid \mathrm{in}(c_1, y).\mathrm{out}(c_2, \mathrm{dec}(y, k)) \mid \{^{\mathrm{enc}(s,k)}/_{x_1}\})$$

We have $fr(A) = \nu s, k, x_1.\{^{\mathrm{enc}(s,k)}/_{x_1}\} \cong \nu s, k.0$ (since x_1 is under a restriction).

Internal reduction $\rightarrow$ is the smallest relation on extended processes closed under structural equivalence and application of evaluation contexts such that

COMM $\mathrm{out}(a, M).P \mid \mathrm{in}(a, x).Q \rightarrow P \mid Q\{M/x\}$ THEN if $M = N$ then P else $Q \rightarrow P$
where $M =_\mathsf{E} N$

EVENT $e(\widetilde{M}).P \rightarrow P \mid [e(\widetilde{M})]$
ELSE if $M = N$ then P else $Q \rightarrow Q$

CHOICE $P + Q \rightarrow P$ where M, N are ground and $M \neq_\mathsf{E} N$.

As usual $\rightarrow^*$ denotes the reflexive transitive closure of $\rightarrow$.

The operational semantics is extended by a *labeled* operational semantics enabling us to reason about processes that interact with their environment. Below, a and c are channel names, x is a variable of base type and y is a variable of any type.

IN $\qquad\qquad \text{in}(a,y).P \xrightarrow{in(a,M)} P\{^M/_y\}$

OUT-CH $\qquad\quad \text{out}(a,c).P \xrightarrow{out(a,c)} P$

OPEN-CH $\qquad \dfrac{A \xrightarrow{out(a,c)} A' \quad c \neq a}{\nu c.A \xrightarrow{\nu c.out(a,c)} A'}$

OUT-T $\quad \text{out}(a,M).P \xrightarrow{\nu x.out(a,x)} P \mid \{^M/_x\}$
$\qquad\qquad\qquad\qquad\qquad x \notin fv(P) \cup fv(M)$

SCOPE $\dfrac{A \xrightarrow{\ell} A' \quad u \text{ does not occur in } \ell}{\nu u.A \xrightarrow{\ell} \nu u.A'}$

PAR $\dfrac{A \xrightarrow{\ell} A' \quad bv(\ell) \cap fv(B) = \emptyset}{A \mid B \xrightarrow{\ell} A' \mid B}$
$\qquad\quad bn(\ell) \cap fn(B) = \emptyset$

STRUCT $\dfrac{A \equiv B \quad B \xrightarrow{\ell} B' \quad A' \equiv B'}{A \xrightarrow{\ell} A'}$

Example 4. Continuing Example 3, we have that
$$A \xrightarrow{\nu x_1.out(c_1,x_1)} \xrightarrow{in(c_1,x_1)} \nu s,k.(\text{out}(c_2,s) \mid \{^{enc(s,k)}/_{x_1}\}) \stackrel{\text{def}}{=} A'.$$
The frame associated to A' is $fr(A') = \nu s,k.\{^{enc(s,k)}/_{x_1}\}$.

2.3 Equivalences

In this section we introduce two notions of process equivalences: *trace equivalence* and *labeled bisimulation*. These definitions are based on *static equivalence*, an equivalence on frames, and *static equivalence of traces*, which lifts static equivalence from frames to traces. Static equivalence is a notion of intruder's possession that has been extensively studied (e.g. [1]). Another notion, namely deducibility will be discussed in Section 3. The notion of static equivalence is useful to define labeled bisimilarity.

Definition 1 (static equivalence). *We say that two terms M and N are equal in the frame ϕ, and write $(M =_E N)\phi$, if there exists $\tilde{n}$ and a substitution σ such that $\phi \equiv \nu\tilde{n}.\sigma$, $\tilde{n} \cap (fn(M) \cup fn(N)) = \emptyset$, and $M\sigma =_E N\sigma$. We say that two closed frames ϕ_1 and ϕ_2 are* statically equivalent, $\phi_1 \sim \phi_2$, *when:*

- $\text{dom}(\phi_1) = \text{dom}(\phi_2)$, *and*
- *for all terms M, N we have that $(M =_E N)\phi_1$ if and only if $(M =_E N)\phi_2$.*

Example 5. Let $\phi = \nu k, s.(\{^{enc(s,k)}/_{x_1}\} \mid \{^k/_{x_2}\})$, $\phi' = \nu k.(\{^{enc(s',k)}/_{x_1}\} \mid \{^k/_{x_2}\})$ where s, s', k are names. We have $(\text{dec}(x_1,x_2) =_{E_{enc}} s')\phi'$ but $(\text{dec}(x_1,x_2) \neq_{E_{enc}} s')\phi$, thus $\phi \not\sim \phi'$ (for E_{enc}). However, $\nu k, s.\{enc(s,k)/x_1\} \sim \nu k.\{enc(s',k)/x_1\}$.

We now define two notions of indistinguishability in the presence of an active intruder. The first one is *trace equivalence*, the second one *labeled bisimulation*. As we are interested in the interactions of a process with the intruder (and not just the internal actions), we use the labeled transition system to define the possible "runs" of a process:

Definition 2 (trace). *A trace tr is a finite derivation* $\text{tr} = A_0 \xrightarrow{\ell_1} A_1 \ldots \xrightarrow{\ell_n} A_n$ *such that each A_i is a closed extended process where each ℓ_i is either empty (and represents* *an internal action) or is a labeled action ℓ_i with $fv(\ell_{i+1}) \subseteq \mathrm{dom}(A_i)$. The trace* tr *is said to be maximal if $A_n \not\xrightarrow{\ell}$ for any ℓ.*

We write tr$[i]$ *for the process A_i and* tr$[i, j]$ *for the trace $A_i \xrightarrow{\ell_{i+1}} A_{i+1} \dots \xrightarrow{\ell_j} A_j$. We shall say that $|\mathrm{tr}| = n$.*

We say that the trace tr *is of the form $A_0 \to^* \xrightarrow{\ell_{i_1}} A_{i_1} \to^* \xrightarrow{\ell_{i_2}} A_{i_{j+1}} \dots \to^* \xrightarrow{\ell_{i_r}} A_r \to^* A_n$ if ℓ_k is a labeled action for all $k = i_j, 1 \leq j \leq r$ and the internal action otherwise.*

Given a process A we define tr(A) *to be the set of all traces* tr *such that* tr$[0] = A$ *and* tr$_{\max}(A)$ *to be the set of all the maximal traces* tr *such that* tr$[0] = A$.

In order to define trace equivalence we lift static equivalence from frames to traces. In order to ensure that bisimilar processes are also trace equivalent we need to define α-equivalence of traces. Intuitively, we say that a labeled action ℓ in a trace tr binds n in the subsequent trace if n occurs as a bound name in ℓ. A trace tr can be α-renamed to tr$'$ if tr$'$ can be obtained by an α-renaming of the bound name n. The formal definition is given in the long version of this paper [9] where its motivation is also discussed. We write tr $\to_\alpha$ tr$'$ if tr$'$ is obtained from tr by an α-renaming of a bound name. The relation $\sim_\alpha$ is defined to be the reflexive, symmetric and transitive closure of $\to_\alpha$.

Intuitively, we say that two traces are statically equivalent to the intruder if the intruder performed the same actions in the trace and the intruder could not "statically" distinguish the processes resulting from these actions. Formally,

Definition 3 (static equivalence of traces $(\sim_t)$**).** *Let* tr *be a trace of the form $A_0 \to^* \xrightarrow{\ell_1} A_1 \to^* \xrightarrow{\ell_2} A_{j+1} \dots \to^* \xrightarrow{\ell_r} A_r \to^* B$. Let* tr$'$ *be a trace of the form $A_0' \to^* \xrightarrow{\ell_1'} A_1' \to^* \xrightarrow{\ell_2'} A_{j+1}' \dots \to^* \xrightarrow{\ell_l'} A_l' \to^* B'$. Then* tr $\leftrightarrow_t$ tr$'$ *if $r = l$, and*

- *for all $1 \leq i \leq r$, $\ell_i = \ell_i'$.*
- *for all $0 \leq i \leq r$, $fr(A_i) \sim fr(A_i')$ (static equivalence).*

The relation $\sim_t$ is the transitive closure of $\sim_\alpha \cup \leftrightarrow_t$.

We can now define trace equivalence.

Definition 4 (trace equivalence $(\approx_t)$**).** *Let A and B be two closed extended processes. We say that A is trace included in B, written $A \sqsubseteq_t B$ if for each trace* tr$_A \in$ tr(A) *there exists* tr$_B \in$ tr(B) *such that* tr$_A \sim_t$ tr$_B$. *The processes A and B are trace equivalent, written $A \approx_t B$, if $A \sqsubseteq_t B$ and $B \sqsubseteq_t A$.*

Trace equivalence is an appealing notion for modeling indistinguishability in presence of an active intruder and can be used to formalize many security properties (e.g. strong secrecy, anonymity properties, ...). However, bisimulation is often considered as it has better proof techniques and is easier to manipulate.

Definition 5 (labeled bisimilarity $(\approx)$**).** *Labeled bisimilarity is the largest symmetric relation $\mathcal{R}$ on closed extended processes, such that $A \mathcal{R} B$ implies*

1. $fr(A) \sim fr(B)$;

2. *if $A \rightarrow A'$, then $B \rightarrow^* B'$ and $A' \, \mathcal{R} \, B'$ for some B';*
3. *if $A \xrightarrow{\ell} A'$ and $fv(\ell) \subseteq \mathrm{dom}(A)$ and $bn(\ell) \cap fn(B) = \emptyset$ then $B \rightarrow^* \xrightarrow{\ell} \rightarrow^* B'$ and $A' \, \mathcal{R} \, B'$ for some B'.*

As expected labeled bisimulation implies trace equivalence, i.e. $\approx \; \subset \; \approx_t$. Hence bisimulation can be used as a proof technique to show trace equivalence.

3 Epistemic Logic

We shall now present the epistemic logic which allows us to reason about intruder's epistemic knowledge and the set of facts in its possession.

3.1 Syntax

The formulas of our logic consist of two levels. *Static formulas* are used to reason about a "snapshot" of the process. They include predicates for events that may have occurred in the past and a predicate for a set of terms that the intruder statically possesses. *Epistemic formulas* allow us to reason about the dynamic behavior of the process and the epistemic knowledge that the intruder can deduce from its past interactions with the process. The formulas use a term language which denotes the set of messages. The syntax of the logic is given in BNF form in Table 1 and discussed below.

Table 1. Syntax of the Epistemic Logic

Terms.
$$\widehat{T} ::= \widehat{n} \; [\![\; z \; [\![\; \widehat{f}(\widehat{T}, \ldots, \widehat{T})$$

Static formulas.
$$\delta ::= \top \; [\![\; \mathsf{Has}(\widehat{T}) \; [\![\; \widehat{\mathsf{evt}}(\widehat{T}, \ldots, \widehat{T}) \; [\![\; \neg\delta \; [\![\; \delta \vee \delta \; [\![\; \exists z.\delta$$

Epistemic formulas (with the proviso δ is a closed formula and has no free names).
$$\phi ::= \delta \; [\![\; \neg\phi \; [\![\; \phi \vee \phi \; [\![\; \mathsf{K}\phi \; [\![\; \Box\phi \; [\![\; \boxminus\phi$$

Term language. For the term language of our logic we shall assume that for each name n in the vocabulary of the applied pi calculus, there is a unique name $\widehat{n}$ in the logic. Similarly for each function symbol f in the vocabulary of the applied pi calculus, we have a unique function symbol $\widehat{f}$ in the logic. However, there is no particular correspondence between the set of variables in the logic and the applied pi calculus. We use $z, z_1, \ldots$ to range over the variables of the logic. The set of terms of the logic now consist of names, variables and function application (the usual restriction on sorts and arity apply here).

Static formulas. Static formulas assume a unary predicate Has whose argument is of base sort. This predicate is used to reason about the set of terms that the intruder possesses. It also assumes that for each event evt in the set of events for the calculus there is predicate $\widehat{\mathsf{evt}}$ (of the correct sort and arity). These predicates are used to reason about events that may have occurred in the past. The static formulas are built from these predicates using the connectives $\top$, negation $\neg$, disjunction $\vee$ and existential quantification $\exists z$. The usual connectives $\wedge$ $\bot$ and $\Rightarrow$ and the universal quantification $\forall$ can be derived from these connectives. We also assume the standard definitions of free and bound variables and substitution. A static formula is *closed* if it does not contain any free variable.

Epistemic formulas. Epistemic formulas reason about dynamic behavior of a process and are constructed from *closed* static formulas with no free names using the connectives conjunction $\wedge$, negation $\neg$, disjunction $\vee$, existential quantification $\exists z$ and the modalities $\square, \boxminus, \mathsf{K}$. The reason for using only closed formulas will become clear in Section 3.2. Disallowing names is not restrictive, as events can be used to refer to names. The formulas are interpreted over the possible "runs" of the process. The formula $\square\phi$ is true at some point in a run if ϕ is true for all possible future points whereas the formula $\boxminus\phi$ is true if ϕ is true for all past points. The formula $\mathsf{K}\phi$ is true if the intruder knows (in the epistemic sense) ϕ to be true based upon its interaction with the process in the past. The connectives $\bot$ and $\Rightarrow$ and the modality $\lozenge$ can be derived.

3.2   Semantics

We now define the semantics of the logic. We start by the denotation of terms.

Denotation of Terms. The terms of the logic are interpreted as ground terms of the applied pi calculus and use the concept of an assignment. An *assignment* ρ is a map which maps each logic variable $z \in \mathcal{Z}$ to a ground term of the applied pi calculus. Using the assignment ρ, the denotation of terms is defined inductively as

$$[\![\widehat{n}]\!]_\rho = n \qquad [\![\widehat{z}]\!]_\rho = \rho(z) \qquad [\![\widehat{f}(\widehat{T_1}, \ldots, \widehat{T_r})]\!]_\rho = f([\![\widehat{T_1}]\!]_\rho, \ldots, ([\![\widehat{T_r}]\!]_\rho)$$

Satisfaction of static formulas. The models of static formulas are pairs- one part of which is a *name distinct* closed extended process A term, i.e. a process such that $bn(A) \cap fn(A) = \emptyset$ and no name is bound twice; and the other part an assignment.

We need another definition for our semantics which formalizes a second notion of intruder's possession (e.g. [1]).

Definition 6 (Deducibility). *Let $\phi \cong \nu\tilde{n}.\sigma$ be a closed name-distinct frame and M be a term. We say that M is deducible from ϕ, denoted by $\phi \vdash M$ if there exists a term N such that $fn(N) \cap \tilde{n} = \emptyset$ and $N\sigma =_E M$. Such a term N is a recipe of the term M.*

Note that when $\nu\tilde{n}.\sigma \vdash M$, any occurrence of names from $\tilde{n}$ in M is bound by $\nu\tilde{n}$. It is for this reason that we introduce the relation $\cong$ (*cf.* Example in Remark 1, item 3).

Example 6. Consider the two frames ϕ and ϕ' given in Example 5. We have that $\phi \vdash k$, $\phi \vdash s$ and $\phi \vdash s'$. Indeed x_2, $\mathrm{dec}(x_1, x_2)$ and s' are recipes of the terms k, s and s'.

The interpretation of the static formulas given a name-distinct process term A and an assignment ρ is defined in Table 2. The interesting cases are the satisfaction of the predicates Has and $\widehat{\mathrm{evt}}$. Intuitively, the formula $\mathrm{Has}(\widehat{T})$ is satisfied if the intruder can deduce the denotation of $\widehat{T}$. The formula $\widehat{\mathrm{evt}}(\widehat{T_1}, \ldots, \widehat{T_r})$ is satisfied if the corresponding event $\mathrm{evt}([\![\widehat{T_1}]\!]_\rho, \ldots, [\![\widehat{T_r}]\!]_\rho)$ has occurred. The other definitions are standard. Note that the

Table 2. Satisfaction of static formulas

$A, \rho \models \top$	always
$A, \rho \models \widehat{\mathsf{evt}}(\widehat{T}_1, \ldots, \widehat{T}_r)$	iff $A \cong \nu \tilde{n}.(A \mid [\mathsf{evt}(M_1, \ldots, M_r)]) \wedge M_i =_\mathsf{E} [\![\widehat{T}_i]\!]_\rho \ \ 1 \le i \le r$
$A, \rho \models \mathsf{Has}(\widehat{T})$	iff $fr(A) \vdash [\![\widehat{T}]\!]_\rho$
$A, \rho \models \neg \delta$	iff $A, \rho \not\models \delta$
$A, \rho \models \delta_1 \vee \delta_2$	iff $A, \rho \models \delta_1$ or $A, \rho \models \delta_2$
$A, \rho \models \exists z.\delta$	iff $\exists$ a ground term M such that $A, \rho[z \mapsto M] \models \delta[M/z]$

assignment $\rho[z \mapsto M]$ is the same as ρ except that on z it takes the value M and the formula $\delta[M/z]$ is the formula obtained from δ by substituting the free occurrences of z by M.

Remark 1

1. If the formula δ is closed, *i.e.*, does not contain any free variables, then the satisfaction of δ depends only on the process and is independent of the assignment. For such formulas we can drop the assignment in the satisfaction relation.
2. Note that name-distinctness is crucial for the definition of satisfaction of the static formulas. The name distinctness allows us to uniquely identify the bound names and interpret them. Otherwise, the process $A = (\nu n.[\mathsf{evt}_1(n)]) \mid (\nu n.[\mathsf{evt}_2(n)])$ will satisfy $\widehat{\mathsf{evt}}_1(\widehat{n}) \wedge \widehat{\mathsf{evt}}_2(\widehat{n})$ which is clearly wrong as the two bound names refer to different nonces.
3. For a similar reason, we need to forbid α-renaming when evaluating predicates evt. Otherwise, (if we replace $\cong$ with $\equiv$ in the above semantics) we have that
$$\nu n_1, n_2.([\mathsf{evt}_1(n_1)] \mid [\mathsf{evt}_2(n_2)]) \models \exists z. (\widehat{\mathsf{evt}}_1(z) \wedge \widehat{\mathsf{evt}}_2(z)).$$
4. It can be checked that for any name-distinct closed frame ϕ, if $\phi \cong \nu \tilde{n}.\sigma$ and $\phi \cong \nu \tilde{n}'.\sigma'$ then $\tilde{n}$ and $\tilde{n}'$ are the same (upto ordering) and for any N such that $fn(N) \cap \tilde{n} = \emptyset$, $N\sigma =_\mathsf{E} N\sigma'$. Hence, if $A_1 \cong A_2$, we get that A_1 and A_2 satisfy the same set of static formulas.
5. The previous observation would not have been true if we had allowed the equivalence $\nu n.0 \equiv 0$. In particular, the intruder can deduce all ground terms in the process 0 while it cannot deduce the term n in the process $\nu n.0$.

Please note that even name-distinct processes which are equal modulo α-conversion may satisfy different static formula. However, if we limit ourselves to closed formulas with no free names, α-renaming does not affect the satisfaction.

Lemma 1. *Let δ be a closed static formula with no free names and A_1 and A_2 be two name distinct extended processes such that $A_1 \equiv A_2$. Then $A_1 \models \delta$ iff $A_2 \models \delta$.*

The above Lemma allows us to define the semantics of the epistemic formulas.

Satisfaction of epistemic formulas. We shall now define the satisfaction relation for epistemic formulas. As in the case of epistemic logic for distributed systems [15,16], the epistemic formulas will be interpreted over the possible "runs" of a process, i.e. the set of maximal traces (Definition 2). Please note that since we do not have replication in our process terms, all traces of a process are finite and our definition of maximal traces does capture all possible "runs". The traces are enough to interpret the temporal modalities $\square$ and $\boxminus$. In order to interpret the modality K, we need to consider an equivalence relation on the set of traces which identifies traces that are indistinguishable to the intruder: static equivalence on traces (Definition 3). An epistemic formula ϕ is interpreted over a triple - a closed extended process A, a maximal trace $\mathsf{tr} \in \mathsf{tr}_{\max}(A)$ and a position $0 \leq j \leq |\mathsf{tr}|$ in tr as described in Table 3.

Table 3. Satisfaction of epistemic formulas

$A, \mathsf{tr}, i \models \delta$	iff there is a name-distinct extended process A'
	such that $\mathsf{tr}[i] \equiv A'$ and $A' \models \delta$
$A, \mathsf{tr}, i \models \square\phi$	iff $\forall i \leq j \leq \lvert\mathsf{tr}\rvert.\ A, \mathsf{tr}, j \models \phi$
$A, \mathsf{tr}, i \models \boxminus\phi$	iff $\forall 0 \leq j \leq i.\ A, \mathsf{tr}, j \models \phi$
$A, \mathsf{tr}, i \models \mathsf{K}\phi$	iff $\forall \mathsf{tr}' \in \mathsf{tr}_{\max}(A), \forall 0 \leq j \leq \lvert\mathsf{tr}'\rvert$
	such that $\mathsf{tr}[0, i] \sim_t \mathsf{tr}'[0, j] \Rightarrow A, \mathsf{tr}', j \models \phi$
$A, \mathsf{tr}, i \models \neg\phi$	iff $A, \mathsf{tr}, i \not\models \phi$
$A, \mathsf{tr}, i \models \phi_1 \vee \phi_2$	iff $A, \mathsf{tr}, i \models \phi_1$ or $A, \mathsf{tr}, i \models \phi_2$

Remark 2. Our use of static equivalent traces as indistinguishable traces is reminiscent of what is often called *perfect recall* in distributed systems- the intruder distinguishes traces based upon the complete history of its interaction with the process. We could have, of course, chosen to define coarser equivalence relations. For example, we could have declared two traces to be equivalent if the intruder cannot "statically" distinguish the last processes in the respective traces.[1] However, a coarser relation would result in intruder "knowing" a smaller set of formulas to be true which may lead to declaring a protocol secure which otherwise will be insecure. Besides, an all powerful intruder should be able to record its history of interaction with the protocol.

Definition 7. *We say that $A \models \phi$ if for all $\mathsf{tr} \in \mathsf{tr}_{\max}(A)$ we have $A, \mathsf{tr}, 0 \models \phi$.*

Not that Lemma 1 will not be true if we replace structural equivalence with static equivalence. One reason is the presence of the predicates $\widehat{\mathsf{evt}}$ as static equivalence does not depend on presence/absence of such formulas. However, even if we were to consider the fragment of the logic without these predicates, statically equivalent processes may satisfy different static formulas (and thus Hennessy-Milner Theorem does not hold).

Lemma 2. *There are closed extended processes A_1 and A_2 and an epistemic formula ϕ such that $A_1 \approx A_2$ and $A_1 \models \phi$ but $A_2 \not\models \phi$.*

Proof. Consider the two processes $A_1 = \nu n.\{^{\mathsf{hash}(n)}/_x\}$ and $A_2 = \nu n.\{^n/_x\}$ where hash is unary function symbol which models a cryptographic hash function and hence cannot be inverted. We assume that the set of equations E is empty. We have that $A_1 \approx A_2$. We have also that $A_1 \models \exists z.(\mathsf{Has}(\mathsf{hash}(z)) \wedge \neg\mathsf{Has}(z))$ (the intruder has the hash of the nonce n but cannot invert it) while $A_2 \not\models \exists z.(\mathsf{Has}(\mathsf{hash}(z)) \wedge \neg\mathsf{Has}(z))$ (the intruder has every free name and can create its hash). $\square$

---

[1] This is similar in spirit to what is commonly called "knowledge" in security.

3.3 Examples

We now give some simple examples of security protocols that can be modeled in our logic. These examples do not use the knowledge operator. We refer to Section 4 for such an example. We only consider closed formulas (no free variables) and formulas without names. The idea is to annotate the process and to use the parametric events to refer to bound names. Specifically, we will show how to specify secrecy, authentication and fairness in exchange protocols in our formalism.

Example 7. This is a way to express the secret (in the sense of deducibility) of the name s in $P = \nu s.\mathsf{evt}(s).\mathsf{out}(c, s)$. Let $\phi = \Box\forall z.(\mathsf{evt}(z) \Rightarrow \neg\mathsf{Has}(z))$. Obviously, we have $P \not\models \phi$ as $P \to A_1 \xrightarrow{\nu x.out(c,x)} A_2$ is a trace in $\mathsf{tr}_{\mathsf{max}}(P)$ where $A_1 = \nu s.(\mathsf{out}(c, s) \mid [\mathsf{evt}(s)])$, $A_2 = \nu s.(\{{}^s/_x\} \mid [\mathsf{evt}(s)])$ and $(P, \mathsf{tr}, 2) \models \mathsf{evt}(s) \wedge \mathsf{Has}(s)$.

Another classical example is authentication modeled as an agreement property.

Example 8. Consider the following simple handshake protocol where k is a shared key and f any free symbol:
$$A \to B : \mathsf{enc}(n, k)$$
$$B \to A : \mathsf{enc}(f(n), k)$$

The goal of this protocol is to authenticate B from A's point of view. In the applied pi calculus this protocol is modeled by $\nu k.(A \mid B)$ where
$$A = \nu n.\ \mathsf{out}(\mathsf{enc}(n, k)).\ \mathsf{in}(x).\ \mathsf{if}\ \mathsf{dec}(x, k) = f(n)\ \mathsf{then}\ \mathsf{end}(n)$$
$$B = \mathsf{in}(y).\ \mathsf{begin}(\mathsf{dec}(y, k)).\ \mathsf{out}(\mathsf{enc}(f(\mathsf{dec}(y, k)), k))$$

The events begin and end are used to annotate the protocol. The authentication of B to A is then modeled by $\phi = \Box\forall z.(\mathsf{end}(z) \Rightarrow \mathsf{begin}(z))$.

Yet another, less classical example of property is fairness in contract signing protocols.

Example 9. In a fair contract signing protocols two agents want to exchange their corresponding signatures on a given contract in such a way that at the end of the protocol either both participants obtain the signed contract or none of them does so. Describing a complete example of such a protocol would be out of the scope of this paper and we refer the reader to [10] for more details. These protocols either terminate in a final state where the exchange has been aborted or in a final state where the exchange did succeed. For the purpose of our example, we suppose that the process modeling the participant P (either A or B) is annotated as follows: the event $\mathsf{Pend}(c)$ indicates that P is in a final state for some contract c; the event $\mathsf{Pcontract}(c)$ indicates that P successfully received the signed contract. Then, *fairness for A* can be modeled as
$$\phi = \Box\forall c.(\mathsf{Aend}(c) \Rightarrow (\neg\mathsf{Bcontract}(c) \vee \mathsf{Acontract}(c))).$$

The formula says that for any contract whenever A is in a final state ($\mathsf{Aend}(c)$), either B did not obtain the contract signed by A ($\neg\mathsf{Bcontract}(c)$) or A did obtain the contract signed by B ($\mathsf{Acontract}(c)$). Fairness for B can be modeled in a similar way.

4 Privacy in Electronic Voting Protocols

Many electronic voting protocols have been proposed in the literature and their formal analysis has received considerable attention [14,4]. One important security goal is *privacy of votes*– an intruder should not be able to learn (by its interaction with the protocol) how an honest voter Alice voted. This property has been formulated both as an observational equivalence, e.g. in [14], and as an epistemic property, e.g. in [4], although never within the same formalism. Our formalism allows us to consider both the formalizations and compare them within the same framework. For the sake of simplicity, we only consider single protocol instances in which two voters Alice and Bob participate and we assume that there are only two voting options available to Alice and Bob and we represent these options by 0 and 1.

Electronic voting protocols in applied pi calculus. We refer the reader to [14] for a detailed formal definition of electronic voting protocols in applied pi calculus. Herein, we state the salient points of the definition. We assume that there is a sort voteoption in our signature which contains at least two constants (0-ary function symbols), denoted by 0 and 1, that do not occur in E. Furthermore, we assume that the protocol can be expressed as a parametric *plain* process $V(x_a, x_b)$ with two free variables x_a and x_b of the sort voteoption.[2] For $v_a, v_b \in \{0, 1\}$, the voter process $V(v_a, v_b)$ represents the process in which Alice and Bob vote for options v_a and v_b respectively. Although these assumptions are sufficient to model privacy as observational equivalence, the definition in terms of epistemic logic requires us to introduce events to annotate the individual voter preferences and consider all possible traces within a single process.

Towards this end we introduce a parametric event votes(_, _) with two arguments of the sort voteoption which is not present in the voting process $V(x_a, x_b)$. From now on, we consider the following voting process which considers all voting scenarios:

$$\mathcal{V} = \sum_{v_a, v_b \in \{0,1\}} \text{votes}(v_a, v_b).V(v_a, v_b).$$

The process $\mathcal{V}$ shall henceforth be called a *voting process*.

Privacy as observational equivalence. We are ready to state the formalization of privacy as proposed in [14], which we shall call *strong privacy* for the rest of this section. Intuitively, the voting protocol represented as V respects strong privacy if the intruder cannot distinguish the two protocol instances in which Alice and Bob's votes are swapped.

Definition 8. *The voting process $\mathcal{V}$ respects* strong privacy *if* $V(0, 1) \approx V(1, 0)$.

Privacy as epistemic formula. We need a few definitions to state privacy as an epistemic formula. An inspection of the construction of $\mathcal{V}$ shows that since the events votes do not occur in V, any maximal trace of $\mathcal{V}$ consists of only one event votes(v_a, v_b) in the store and corresponds to Alice and Bob voting for option v_a and v_b respectively. Also (from construction of the epistemic logic in Section 3), we assume that there is a binary predicate in our logic corresponding to the event votes which we shall (again in the interest of keeping the syntax simple) denote by votes. We also assume that there are two 0-ary function symbols corresponding to the two voting options which shall again denote by 0 and 1. Now, given $v \in \{0, 1\}$ consider the formula

$$\text{Avote}(v) = \text{votes}(v, \mathbf{0}) \vee \text{votes}(v, \mathbf{1}).$$

---

[2] V being a plain process is a simplification and we could have started with a non-empty frame.

Intuitively the formula is true in a state reachable from V if Alice votes for option v. Similarly we can define formula $\mathsf{Bvote}(v)$.

Now, according to [4], a protocol respects *privacy for Alice* if the intruder cannot (epistemically) know which voting option Alice exercised. A protocol respects privacy if it respects privacy for both Alice and Bob. Please note that this definition does not usually hold for voting protocols in which the final tally of the votes are announced– a unanimous election always reveals each individual's vote. Hence, a more appropriate formulation is that whenever Alice and Bob vote differently, the intruder cannot learn how each of them voted. This gives us the following definition which states that intruder can learn how a voter voted only if the other voter voted the same option.

Definition 9 (privacy). *The voting process V respects* privacy *if* $V \models$ Aprivacy $\wedge$ Bprivacy *where*

- Aprivacy $\overset{\text{def}}{=} \wedge_{v \in \{0,1\}} \square(\mathsf{K}(\mathsf{Avote}(v)) \rightarrow \mathsf{Bvote}(v))$, *and*
- Bprivacy $\overset{\text{def}}{=} \wedge_{v \in \{0,1\}} \square(\mathsf{K}(\mathsf{Bvote}(v)) \rightarrow \mathsf{Avote}(v))$.

Strong privacy implies privacy. We now show that privacy in terms of observational equivalence implies privacy in terms of epistemic formulas. In fact we show a stronger statement, namely, that if $V(0,1) \approx_t V(1,0)$ then the protocol will respect privacy. The proof of the statement is given in the long version of this paper [9].

Theorem 1. *If $V(0,1) \approx_t V(1,0)$ then the voting process V respects privacy. Hence, if V respects strong privacy then it respects privacy.*

Now, privacy in terms of epistemic formulas does not imply strong privacy. One can construct examples which respect privacy but not strong privacy, based on the fact that bisimulation is a finer relation than trace equivalence. However, a partial converse of Theorem 1 holds– under reasonable assumptions privacy implies $V(0,1) \approx_t V(1,0)$.

Privacy implies trace equivalence. In order to state these assumptions, we need a few definitions. First we need the definition of a publishing trace. Intuitively, we say that a maximal trace tr is a publishing trace if the intruder learns which votes were cast (but not the link between the voters and individual votes) and can distinguish it from any other trace when the set of votes cast are different. For example, a publishing trace in which Alice and Bob vote 0 and 1 is distinguishable from one in which they cast 0 and 0 but not necessarily from one in which they cast 1 and 0 respectively. A maximal trace that is not publishing is said to be an abort trace. Intuitively, this says that the protocol could not be completed and hence votes are not published.[3]

Definition 10 (publishing and abort traces). *Given $v_a, v_b \in \{0,1\}$, a maximal trace* tr $\in$ tr$_{\max}(V(v_a, v_b))$ *is said to be a* publishing *trace if for any $v_a', v_b' \in \{0,1\}$ such that $\{v_a, v_b\} \neq \{v_a', v_b'\}$, there is no* tr$'$ $\in$ tr$(V(v_a', v_b'))$ *such that* tr $\sim_t$ tr$'$. *Otherwise* tr *is an* abort *trace.*

---

[3] We believe that a good electronic voting protocol should not have abort traces. However, this property has not been studied in literature.

We say that a protocol is equivalent for aborts if an abort trace can be mimicked irrespective of how Alice and Bob decided to vote.

Definition 11 (equivalent for aborts). *Given* $v_a, v_b \in \{0, 1\}$ *and* tr $\in$ $\text{tr}_{\max}(V(v_a, v_b))$ *an abort trace. We say that* V *is* equivalent for aborts *if for any* $v'_a, v'_b \in \{0, 1\}$ *there is a* tr$'$ $\in \text{tr}_{\max}(V(v'_a, v'_b))$ *such that* tr $\sim_t$ tr$'$.

We have the partial converse of Theorem 1. The proof is given in [9].

Theorem 2. *Let* $V = \sum_{v_a, v_b \in \{0, 1\}} \text{votes}(v_a, v_b).V(v_a, v_b)$ *be a voting process such that* V *is equivalent for aborts and respects privacy. Then* $V(0, 1) \approx_t V(1, 0)$.

Theorem 1 and Theorem 2 suggest that trace-equivalence is the more appropriate notion for defining privacy of votes in electronic voting even though the bisimulation-based definition (which implies privacy) has better proof techniques.

5 Related and Future Work

Related work. Several authors (e.g. [17,13,20]) have recognized the complementary nature of the process algebraic and epistemic approaches and the benefit to combine them. Different approaches have been proposed to bridge this gap. In [17], *function views* are used to represent partial information and make the interface between protocol and properties. In order to get epistemic specifications closer to a behavioral specification, van Eijck and Orzan [20] propose a dynamic epistemic logic. However, it seems that no mediation is necessary [16,13] and it is possible to bridge this gap by proposing a combined framework as it is also suggested in this paper. However, in the works cited above, the authors study abstract versions of protocols which do not take into account cryptographic primitives (e.g. encryption, signature, . . .) and their specific properties.

Some recent works [18,11] have been devoted to designing a logic to characterize *static equivalence*. In [18], they build upon the logic for frames and extend it with Hennessy-Milner modalities, yielding a logic for applied pi processes which characterizes labeled bisimilarity. However, as we already pointed out in the Introduction, our goal is different and we want to define a logic that is expressive enough to state a variety of security properties in a natural way. The advantage of this approach is evident in our example of formalizing privacy in e-voting protocols in which we were able to establish the exact relationship between two formal definitions of privacy in e-voting protocols.

Another similarity between our work and the work in [11] is that they also have epistemic modalities. The work in [11] has another advantage in that they reason about multiple agents and hence their logic has epistemic modalities for multiple agents and not just the intruder. This is however achieved by interpreting the logic over an agent-indexed family of frames with a frame representing the set of messages in an agent's possessions. Since they are mostly interested in studying static equivalence, they do not mention how these frames are obtained. An applied pi-calculus process only keeps track of the messages in intruder's possession and thus we have only one epistemic modality.

The problem of having a suitable language which allows for an expressive property logic is a well-known problem in the context of cryptographic protocols verification.

In [7,12], such a language and logic is proposed and allows specification of a large class of security properties. However, none of the underlying protocol languages is as expressive as the applied pi calculus. We are able to model a large class of protocols which may use less classical cryptographic primitives, specified by an equational theory, in an intuitive way. Therefore, our framework can be used for protocols such as electronic voting protocols, contract signing protocols, ...

Future Work. The formalism presented in this paper is a starting point, and we intend to study stronger anonymity properties such as coercion-resistance that arise in security protocols. Another line of investigation is to extend the formalism to allow for reasoning about epistemic knowledge of multiple agents, and this would involve extension of both the calculus and the logic. We also intend to study model-checking algorithms to verify whether a process satisfies a given formula. Finally, we also intend to investigate an axiomatization of the logic presented in the paper.

References

1. Abadi, M., Cortier, V.: Deciding knowledge in security protocols under equational theories. Theoretical Computer Science 387(1-2), 2–32 (2006)
2. Abadi, M., Fournet, C.: Mobile values, new names, and secure communication. In: Proc. 28th Symposium on Principles of Programming Languages, pp. 104–115 (2001)
3. Backes, M., Maffei, M., Unruh, D.: Zero-knowledge in the applied pi-calculus and automated verification of the direct anonymous attestation protocol. In: Proc. 29th IEEE Symposium on Security and Privacy (2008)
4. Baskar, A., Ramanujam, R., Suresh, S.P.: Knowledge-based modelling of voting protocols. In: Proc. 11th Conference on Theoretical Aspects of Rationality and Knowledge, pp. 62–71 (2007)
5. Blanchet, B.: An Efficient Cryptographic Protocol Verifier Based on Prolog Rules. In: Proc. 14th Computer Security Foundations Workshop, pp. 82–96 (2001)
6. Blanchet, B.: From Secrecy to Authenticity in Security Protocols. In: 9th International Static Analysis Symposium, pp. 342–359 (2002)
7. Borgström, J., Kramer, S., Nestmann, U.: Calculus of Cryptographic Communication. In: Proc. Workshop on Foundations of Computer Security and Automated Reasoning for Security Protocol Analysis (2006)
8. Burrows, M., Abadi, M., Needham, R.M.: A logic of authentication. ACM Trans. Comput. Syst. 8(1), 18–36 (1990)
9. Chadha, R., Delaune, S., Kremer, S.: Epistemic logic for the applied pi-calculus. Research Report LSV-09-06, Laboratoire Spécification et Vérification, ENS Cachan, France (March 2009)
10. Chadha, R., Kremer, S., Scedrov, A.: Formal analysis of multi-party contract signing. Journal of Automated Reasoning 36(1-2), 39–83 (2006)
11. Cohen, M., Dam, M.: A complete axiomatization of knowledge and cryptography. In: Proc. 22nd IEEE Symposium on Logic in Computer Science, pp. 77–88 (2007)
12. Corin, R., Saptawijaya, A., Etalle, S.: PS-LTL for constraint-based security protocol analysis. In: Proc. 21st International Conference on Logic Programming, pp. 439–440 (2005)
13. Dechesne, F., Mousavi, M.R., Orzan, S.: Operational and epistemic approaches to protocol analysis: Bridging the gap. In: Proc. 14th International Conference on Logic for Programming, Artificial Intelligence, and Reasoning, pp. 226–241 (2007)

14. Delaune, S., Kremer, S., Ryan, M.D.: Verifying privacy-type properties of electronic voting protocols. Journal of Computer Security (2009) (to appear)
15. Fagin, R., Halpern, J.Y., Moses, Y., Vardi, M.Y.: Reasoning About Knowledge. MIT Press, Cambridge (1995)
16. Halpern, J.Y., O'Neill, K.R.: Anonymity and information hiding in multiagent systems. Journal of Computer Security 13(3), 483–512 (2005)
17. Hughes, D., Shmatikov, V.: Information hiding, anonymity and privacy: a modular approach. Journal of Computer Security 12(1), 3–36 (2004)
18. Hüttel, H., Pedersen, M.D.: A logical characterisation of static equivalence. Electr. Notes Theor. Comput. Sci. 173, 139–157 (2007)
19. Jonker, H., Pieters, W.: Receipt-freeness as a special case of anonymity in epistemic logic. In: Proc. IAVoSS Workshop On Trustworthy Elections (2006)
20. van Eijck, J., Orzan, S.: Epistemic verification of anonymity. Electr. Notes Theor. Comput. Sci. 168, 159–174 (2007)
21. Woo, T.Y.C., Lam, S.S.: A semantic model for authentication protocols. In: Proc. 14th IEEE Symposium on Security and Privacy (1993)

On Process-Algebraic Proof Methods for Fault Tolerant Distributed Systems

Morten Kühnrich and Uwe Nestmann

[1] Department of CS, Aalborg University, Denmark
[2] School of EECS, Berlin Institute of Technology, Germany

Abstract. Distributed Algorithms are hard to prove correct. In settings with process failures, things get worse. Among the proof methods proposed in this context, we focus on process calculi, which offer a tight connection of proof concepts to the actual code representing the algorithm. We use Distributed Consensus as a case study to evaluate recent developments in this field. Along the way, we find that the classical assertional style for proofs on distributed algorithms can be used to structure bisimulation relations. For this, we propose the definition of uniform syntactic descriptions of reachable states, on which state-based assertions can be conveniently formulated. As a result, we get the best of both worlds: on the one hand invariant-style representation of proof knowledge; on the other hand the bisimulation-based formal connection to the code.

1 Introduction

Proof Methods for Distributed Algorithms. The wide-spread technique to describe algorithms in this field is using pseudo code, which is supposed to be self-explanatory, although it usually lacks a precise semantics; this also holds for the underlying communication network that connects distributed participants of the algorithm. Specifications of desired properties are usually expressed in natural language that often refers to terminology and concepts that are well-understood in temporal logics. Proofs in this area usually are in semi-formal style, omitting many details and reasoning steps; often, the involved proof structures are only very loosely connected to the pseudo code that describes the algorithm. Another technique to describe distributed algorithms employs automata (especially *I/O-automata* [Lyn96]). Here, the setting is more formal, although the behavior of the involved automata is still often only described via pseudo code. Proofs are carried out by induction that preserve (global) invariants along system runs; structured and hierarchical proofs are then realized through composition and hierarchical simulation methods.

The loose connection of proofs to the algorithm's description was the starting point for us to try out more syntactic methods, in our case process algebras and process calculi[1]. These come with a large set of compositional proof techniques and a powerful coinductive proof method, known as bisimulation.

---

[1] We prefer to use the term *process calculus* instead of *process algebra*, when we do not use proper algebraic laws. However, many people use the terms as synonyms.

D. Lee et al. (Eds.): FMOODS/FORTE 2009, LNCS 5522, pp. 198–212, 2009.

Proof Methods in Process Algebra. In the context of *process calculi*, verification usually boils down to prove an equation of the form

$$System \approx Specification$$

where *System* represents a (much) more detailed description of what is prescribed by the *Specification*, but where both are described within the same conceptual and linguistic framework. The symbol $\approx$ denotes some kind of meaningful equivalence or, better, congruence relation; often, notions of bisimilarity are chosen due to their distinctive power and accompanying co-algebraic proof method.

Since *System* usually contains far too many observable details, one often hides those implementation details from the outside observer to make it directly comparable to the *Specification*. The standard restriction operator, usually denoted by $P\backslash a$, hides observations on channel a, which might occur within P, and keeps them internal. Sometimes, even this simple hiding method is not good enough. Then, it may come in handy to have an additional so-called *wrapper code* sit next to the *System* that filters the behavior of the latter more intelligently before it is rendered observable. Equations get the form

$$\underbrace{(\; System \; \| \; Wrapper \;)\backslash\{a_1, \ldots, a_n\}}_{WrappedSystem} \approx SimpleSpecification$$

where $\|$ means that *Wrapper* is run in parallel with *System*, communicating with it, translating its outcome, such that it becomes comparable to the *Specification*. In fact, the actual specification may often be fully encoded within the *Wrapper* such that the *SimpleSpecification* term may become trivial, e.g., just checking for a success signal emanating from the *Wrapper*. While the complexity of the specification seems to be only moved into the wrapper, without gain, one may actually profit from this transfer, because the resulting equation shows much less externally observable behavior; the remaining internal behavior of the *WrappedSystem* is often much easier to deal with. The verification method via wrappers is more or less standard [BH00] and proved helpful in the context of security [SV00] and studies on the expressive power of process calculi [Fou98], where wrappers are called *relays* and even *firewalls*.

A Proof Method for Fault Tolerance. Francalanza and Hennessy have recently proposed a method based on the above approach that, in addition, applies to the domain of fault-tolerant distributed algorithms [FH07]. Concretely, they work in a setting where processes may *fail-stop*, i.e., without recovery, augmented with so-called *perfect failure detectors*. The challenge in this setting is to verify the correctness of distributed algorithms in the context of crashes. Let $\Gamma_k \triangleright Sys$ represent a system configuration; the environment Γ_k allows for k different process crashes. Interesting instances of k are $n-1$ or $\lceil \frac{n-1}{2} \rceil$, where n is the given number of processes in the distributed system. Then, one contribution of [FH07] is that a typical equation to be verified would be of the form:

$$(\Gamma_k \triangleright WrappedSystem) \approx (\Gamma_0 \triangleright SimpleSpecification)$$

with the side-condition that the *WrappedSystem* is to be composed using a non-crashable wrapper code, while the *SimpleSpecification* is not subject to failures at all. Based on this representation, an essential contribution of [FH07] concerning proof methods is the discovery of a decomposition principle, which allows them to split the right-above equation into two more easily provable parts:

$$(\Gamma_k \triangleright WrappedSystem) \overset{(1)}{\approx} (\Gamma_0 \triangleright WrappedSystem) \overset{(2)}{\approx} (\Gamma_0 \triangleright SimpleSpecification)$$

Here, (1) proves the fault tolerance of the *WrappedSystem*, while (2) does the actual verification w.r.t. the *SimpleSpecification*. This approach is appealing since it allows to prove (2), called *basic correctness*, without having to consider process failures. The authors exhibited this method on an arguably simple case study of a round-based Distributed Consensus algorithm in the context of perfect failure detectors ($\mathcal{P}$, in the terminology of [CT96]).

A non-trivial case study in the context of imperfect failure detectors. Our own previous work [NFM03] has been in the context of much weaker imperfect (or: unreliable) failure detectors ($\Diamond\mathcal{S}$, as of [CT96]). Therefore we had to deal with a much more complicated round-based Distributed Consensus algorithm. For its verification, we used a tailor-made distributed process calculus, similar to the one in [FH07], but at that time lacking a bisimulation theory. Moreover, to remain close and comparable to the informal proofs of Chandra and Toueg in [CT96], we did not use the traditional proof method sketched above, but followed the track of reachability analysis, based on inductions as in [Lyn96].

Thus, inspired by Francalanza and Hennessy, we set out to see in how far their bisimulation-based decomposition method also carries over to less trivial algorithms in an imperfect setting. For this, we chose the setting with imperfect failure detector $\mathcal{S}$, whose imperfection lies just between[2] the above-mentioned $\mathcal{P}$ and $\Diamond\mathcal{S}$. As a result, also the required algorithm to solve Distributed Consensus has a complexity in between the ones mentioned above. To verify this algorithm, we had to adapt the calculus of [FH07], mainly to incorporate imperfect failure detection. Then, we tried the proof method of [FH07] on this case study. The results of this undertaking is what the current paper is about.

Contributions. The main insights gained through this work are: (i) with imperfect failure detectors, the decomposition into equations (1) and (2) of [FH07] does not seem to simplify proofs; (ii) to tame the complexity of non-trivial state spaces, syntactic standard forms help characterizing the shape of reachable states[3]; (iii) we observe that invariants, as they are commonly used in traditional proofs on distributed algorithms, can be succinctly defined on the basis of standard forms; (iv) those invariants can be used to conveniently define the bisimulation relations that are used as witnesses in the respective proof method.

---

[2] $\mathcal{S}$ requires the existence of some non-suspectable process from the beginning, while $\Diamond\mathcal{S}$ just needs to guarantee this eventually, after a phase of uncertainty.

[3] This idea is already more or less visible in the Scheduler example of [Mil89].

Other Proof Methods. Fokkink et.al. [FGR04] pointed out that process algebras need proof methodology, not just methods. Over the years, they developed such a methodology centered on the notions of *cones* and *foci*, whose main use is to tame complicated process behavior by the identification of states where the specification and the system more directly "coincide". This methodology also includes assertional techniques and invariant proofs. However, their methodology has not yet been carried over to contexts with process failure.

On the model-checking side, we just mention two closely related examples. Kühnrich [Küh08] applies model-checking in the context of a model-driven development of an extension of the algorithm studied in the current paper. Tsuchiya and Schiper [TS08] use the model checker Spin to verify asynchronous round-based consensus algorithms. By abstraction, they manage to reduce the state space (with infinite runs) to a finite one that can be model checked. However, they can still only check correctness for fixed network sizes.

2 Distributed Process Calculi for Fault Tolerance

In this section, we introduce a distributed process calculus with process crashes and failure detection, inspired by [NFM03, NF03, FH07, Hen07]. The process model is standard, equipped with the following properties: (i) channel-based synchronous passing of values, (ii) user defined functions, (iii) recursion through parameterized process constants. Since there is no name-passing, the calculus is more like CCS than the Pi Calculus. As a novelty, it incorporates both perfect ($\mathcal{P}$) and imperfect ($\mathcal{S}$) failure detectors, as defined by Chandra and Toueg [CT96].

2.1 Syntax

We use four layers of the syntax (cf. Table 1): data values, guarded processes, processes, and networks. We assume the existence of a countably infinite set of channel, variable, and function names $\mathbf{A} = \{a, b, c, ...\}$ and a finite set $\mathcal{Loc}$ of *location names* that contains the special name $\star$.

Data values and expressions. $\bot$ denotes unknown values; integers are standard. Values can be paired and grouped into sets. $\mathbf{V}$ is the set of values derivable from the non-terminal v in the grammar and $\mathbf{A}$ is disjoint with $\mathbf{V}$. As a consequence there is no name-passing within the calculus. The expression language is composed of data values, variable patterns, pairing, and function application. The meaning of function symbols $\mathbf{f} \in \mathbf{A}$ is defined via a total Turing computable function apply : $\mathbf{A} \times \mathbf{V} \to \mathbf{V}$ that assigns meaning to function symbols $\mathbf{f} \in \mathbf{A}$.

Guarded processes. A message e is sent via the synchronous channel c by $\bar{c}\langle e \rangle.P$ with continuation P. Message reception on channel c is written $c(X).P$. If a message v is sent on c then $c(X).P$ becomes P with all instances of variables in X instantiated with values from v. Pattern X must be linear. Process $\mathcal{P}(\!(k)\!).P$ contacts a *perfect failure detector* and may only proceed as P when location k is detected to be dead. Process $\mathcal{S}(\!(k)\!).P$ contacts an *imperfect failure detector* and

Table 1. Syntax

DATA VALUES **V**
  $v \quad ::= \bot, 0, 1, 2, 3, \ldots \mid (v, v) \mid \{v, \ldots, v\}$

VARIABLE PATTERN
  $X \quad ::= x \mid (X, X), \text{ with } x \in \mathbf{A}$

EXPRESSIONS
  $e \quad ::= v \mid X \mid (e, e) \mid \mathtt{f}(e), \text{ with } \mathtt{f} \in \mathbf{A}$

GUARDED PROCESSES **G**
  $G \quad ::= \mathbf{0} \mid \bar{c}\langle e \rangle.P \mid c(X).P \mid \mathcal{S}(\!|k|\!).P \mid \mathcal{P}(\!|k|\!).P$
  $\quad\quad \mid G + G \mid \text{if } e \text{ then } G \text{ else } G$

PROCESSES **P**
  $P, Q \quad ::= \tau.P \mid G \mid K(e) \mid P \parallel P \mid P \backslash a$

NETWORKS **N**
  $M, N ::= \mathbf{0} \mid \ell[P] \mid N \parallel N \mid N \backslash a$

PROCESS EQUATIONS
  $D \stackrel{\text{def}}{=} \{K_j(X) = P_j\}_{j \in J}$ a finite set of process definitions

---

may proceed as P when location k is suspected to have crashed. Since failure detection is unreliable in this case, the process might incorrectly suspect location k and proceed as P, even though k is actually live. Guarded choice $G + G'$ is the choice between guarded processes G or G'. Branching **if** e **then** G **else** G' evolves to G if e evaluates to an integer greater than zero, otherwise to G'.

Processes. The process $\mathbf{0}$ models inaction; process $\tau.P$ can perform a silent transition and become P. Parallel composition $P \parallel P'$ runs processes P and P' in parallel. Parameterized process constants have the form $K(X)$; are defined w.r.t. to a finite set of process equations D of the form $\{K_j(X) \stackrel{\text{def}}{=} P_j\}_{j \in J}$.

Networks. The network $\star[P]$ is a process running at a location $\star$; it has the property that it can never crash. The intention is to use this location for wrapper code. The location $\ell[P], \ell \neq \star$ may however fail. An action a may be restricted to N by $N \backslash a$. Networks can be put in parallel $N \parallel N$; we write $\prod_\phi N$ for the parallel composition of a finite set of networks satisfying the logical predicate ϕ.

  The substitution of value v for a variable pattern X in expression e or process P is written $e\{v/X\}$ and $P\{v/X\}$ respectively. The operator $\mathrm{fn}(\cdot)$ defined on processes and networks is defined as usual. Notice that only data values can be substituted for names and that all variables of the pattern X must be free in P. We write $\bar{c}\langle e \rangle$ for $\bar{c}\langle e \rangle.\mathbf{0}$ and $c.P$ for $c(x).P$, $x \notin \mathrm{fn}(P)$ and $\bar{c}$ for $\bar{c}\langle \bot \rangle$. Restriction is generalized to sets of names in the obvious way. Lists are defined via right-recursive pairing and we write **let** $X = e$ **in** P for the local binding of X to e in P, formally defined by a process constant $(K(X) \stackrel{\text{def}}{=} P) \in D$. Finally define $a@i(x).P$ to denote $a(x).P + \mathcal{S}(\!|i|\!).P\{\bot/x\}$, $x \in \mathrm{fn}(P)$ meaning: either receive a value on channel a or suspect location i.

Some notational conventions: $\mathcal{R}_1\mathcal{R}_2$ is the composition of relations $\mathcal{R}_1$ and $\mathcal{R}_2$; $\mathcal{R}^*$ is the transitive closure of a relation $\mathcal{R}$. $|M|$ is the cardinality of the finite multiset M. We occasionally omit binders e.g. if $(x,y) \in S$ where S is a set and y is unused we write $(x, \cdot) \in S$.

2.2   Semantics

The semantics (see Table 2) of our calculus is mostly standard. It is based on configurations consisting of a book-keeping environment and process networks. The terminology of *trusted immortals* was introduced in [NF03, NFM03] to support a simple and direct definition of the failure detector properties of [CT96]. The essence is that the process ti $\in \mathcal{L}oc$, ti $\neq \star$ can neither crash (*immortal*) nor be suspected by any other process (*trusted*).

Definition 1 (Configurations). *Configurations C have either of the two forms $(\mathcal{L},n) \triangleright M$ or $(\mathcal{L},n) \triangleright_{\mathsf{ti}} M$, where $\mathcal{L} \subseteq \mathcal{L}oc$ is a finite set of locations, $n \in \mathbb{N}$ and M is a network. We define $\mathbf{C}$ as the set of all configurations.*

We define the projection dead$(\cdot)$ by dead$((\mathcal{L},n)) = \mathcal{L}oc \setminus \mathcal{L}$ and a predicate live$(\cdot,\cdot)$ in the following way: live$(\star, \Gamma)$ is true for all Γ; live$(\ell, (\mathcal{L},n))$ is true if $\ell \in \mathcal{L}$. Let $[\![e]\!]$ denote the evaluation of expression e, defined in the standard way.

Definition 2 (Evaluation of networks). *Let $>$ be the evaluation relation defined on configurations (assuming live(ℓ, Γ) everywhere), closed under restriction, parallel composition, reflexivity, transitivity and the following rules:*

$$
\begin{aligned}
\Gamma \triangleright_{\mathsf{ti}} \ell \, [\overline{c}\langle e\rangle.P] &> \Gamma \triangleright_{\mathsf{ti}} \ell \, [\overline{c}\langle [\![e]\!]\rangle.P] \\
\Gamma \triangleright_{\mathsf{ti}} \ell \, [K(e)] &> \Gamma \triangleright_{\mathsf{ti}} \ell \, [P\{[\![e]\!]/X\}], \quad (K(X) \stackrel{\text{def}}{=} P) \in D \\
\Gamma \triangleright_{\mathsf{ti}} \ell \, [\text{if } e \text{ then } P \text{ else } Q] &> \Gamma \triangleright_{\mathsf{ti}} \ell \, [P], \quad [\![e]\!] > 0 \\
\Gamma \triangleright_{\mathsf{ti}} \ell \, [\text{if } e \text{ then } P \text{ else } Q] &> \Gamma \triangleright_{\mathsf{ti}} \ell \, [Q], \quad [\![e]\!] = 0.
\end{aligned}
$$

Definition 3. *Structural congruence $\equiv$ is the least equivalence relation defined on configurations, satisfying commutative monoid laws for $(\mathbf{N}, |, \mathbf{0})$, closed under restriction and parallel composition and the rules:*

(Nil) $\Gamma \triangleright_{\mathsf{ti}} \ell \, [\mathbf{0}] \equiv \Gamma \triangleright_{\mathsf{ti}} \mathbf{0}$ (New) $\Gamma \triangleright_{\mathsf{ti}} \ell \, [P \setminus a] \equiv \Gamma \triangleright_{\mathsf{ti}} \ell \, [P] \setminus a$

$(Location)$ $\Gamma \triangleright_{\mathsf{ti}} \ell \, [P \parallel Q] \equiv \Gamma \triangleright_{\mathsf{ti}} \ell \, [P] \parallel \ell \, [Q]$

$(Scope)$ $\Gamma \triangleright_{\mathsf{ti}} M \parallel (N \setminus a) \equiv \Gamma \triangleright_{\mathsf{ti}} (M \parallel N) \setminus a, \quad a \notin \text{fn}(M)$

Let $\Rightarrow$ denote the relation $> \equiv$.
We write $C \Rightarrow^{\mathsf{T}} C'$, if $C \Rightarrow^* C'$ and $\nexists C'' \not\equiv C' : C' > C''$.

Actions $\alpha \in \text{Act}$ are of the form $\alpha ::= \tau \mid \overline{c}v \mid cv$. The transition relation $\longrightarrow \subseteq \mathbf{C} \times \text{Act} \times \mathbf{C}$ is the smallest relation generated by the rules of Table 2. Rule (TI) non-deterministically selects a trusted immortal. It is the rule that must be applied initially; this is necessary in interplay with (Susp) (see below). Rule (Stop) stops a live process from running if the total number of allowed failures is not zero. Rule (PSusp) models perfect failure detection. Rule (Susp) models

Table 2. Structural Operational Semantics

$$\text{(TI)} \quad \frac{\text{ti} \in \mathcal{L} \setminus \{\star\}}{(\mathcal{L},n) \rhd M \xrightarrow{\tau} (\mathcal{L},n) \rhd_{\text{ti}} M} \qquad \text{(Stop)} \quad \frac{\ell \neq \text{ti} \wedge \ell \in \mathcal{L}}{(\mathcal{L},n+1) \rhd_{\text{ti}} M \xrightarrow{\tau} (\mathcal{L}\setminus\{\ell\},n) \rhd_{\text{ti}} M}$$

$$\text{(PSusp)} \frac{\text{live}(\ell,\Gamma) \wedge \neg\text{live}(k,\Gamma)}{\Gamma \rhd_{\text{ti}} \ell \, [\mathcal{P}(\!|k|\!).P] \xrightarrow{\tau} \Gamma \rhd_{\text{ti}} \ell \, [P]} \qquad \text{(Susp)} \frac{\text{live}(\ell,\Gamma) \wedge k \neq \text{ti} \wedge k \neq \ell}{\Gamma \rhd_{\text{ti}} \ell \, [\mathcal{S}(\!|k|\!).P] \xrightarrow{\tau} \Gamma \rhd_{\text{ti}} \ell \, [P]}$$

$$\text{(Tau)} \frac{\text{live}(\ell,\Gamma)}{\Gamma \rhd_{\text{ti}} \ell [\tau.P] \xrightarrow{\tau} \Gamma \rhd_{\text{ti}} \ell [P]} \qquad \text{(SumL)} \frac{\text{live}(l,\Gamma) \wedge \Gamma \rhd_{\text{ti}} \ell \, [G_1] \xrightarrow{\alpha} \Gamma' \rhd_{\text{ti}} \ell \, [P]}{\Gamma \rhd_{\text{ti}} \ell \, [G_1 + G_2] \xrightarrow{\alpha} \Gamma' \rhd_{\text{ti}} \ell \, [P]}$$

$$\text{(Par)} \frac{\Gamma \rhd_{\text{ti}} M \xrightarrow{\alpha} \Gamma' \rhd_{\text{ti}} M'}{\Gamma \rhd_{\text{ti}} M \parallel N \xrightarrow{\alpha} \Gamma' \rhd_{\text{ti}} M' \parallel N} \qquad \text{(SumR)} \frac{\text{live}(l,\Gamma) \wedge \Gamma \rhd_{\text{ti}} \ell \, [G_2] \xrightarrow{\alpha} \Gamma' \rhd_{\text{ti}} \ell \, [P]}{\Gamma \rhd_{\text{ti}} \ell \, [G_1 + G_2] \xrightarrow{\alpha} \Gamma' \rhd_{\text{ti}} \ell \, [P]}$$

$$\text{(Snd)} \frac{\text{live}(\ell,\Gamma)}{\Gamma \rhd_{\text{ti}} \ell \, [\overline{c}\langle v\rangle] \xrightarrow{\overline{c}v} \Gamma \rhd_{\text{ti}} \mathbf{0}} \qquad \text{(Rcv)} \frac{\text{live}(\ell,\Gamma)}{\Gamma \rhd_{\text{ti}} \ell \, [c(X).P] \xrightarrow{cv} \Gamma \rhd_{\text{ti}} \ell \, [P\{v/X\}]}$$

$$\text{(Com)} \frac{\Gamma \rhd_{\text{ti}} M \xrightarrow{\alpha} \Gamma \rhd_{\text{ti}} M' \quad \Gamma \rhd_{\text{ti}} N \xrightarrow{\overline{\alpha}} \Gamma \rhd_{\text{ti}} N'}{\Gamma \rhd_{\text{ti}} M \parallel N \xrightarrow{\tau} \Gamma \rhd_{\text{ti}} M' \parallel N'}, \quad \alpha,\overline{\alpha} \neq \tau$$

$$\text{(Red)} \frac{C \Rightarrow C_1 \xrightarrow{\alpha} C_2 \Rightarrow s'}{C \xrightarrow{\alpha} C'} \qquad \text{(Res)} \frac{\Gamma \rhd_{\text{ti}} M \xrightarrow{\alpha} \Gamma' \rhd_{\text{ti}} M'}{\Gamma \rhd_{\text{ti}} M \setminus a \xrightarrow{\alpha} \Gamma' \rhd_{\text{ti}} M' \setminus a}, \quad \alpha \neq \overline{a}v, av$$

imperfect failure detection: processes never suspect themselves, nor the trusted immortal; every other process may be suspected at any time (see [CT96, NF03]). Rules for communication, sum and parallel composition are all standard. Rule (Red) describes the one way reduction of terms using value evaluations.

On the set of configurations, we define weak bisimilarity "up to". For this, let $\Longrightarrow \overset{\text{def}}{=} \xrightarrow{\tau}{}^*$. Then, $C \overset{\hat{\alpha}}{\Longrightarrow} C'$ is $C \Longrightarrow C'$, if $\alpha = \tau$, otherwise $C \Longrightarrow \xrightarrow{\alpha} \Longrightarrow C'$.

Definition 4. *Let $\mathcal{U}$ and $\mathcal{R}$ be binary relations over $\mathbf{C}$. We call $\mathcal{R}$ a weak bisimulation up to $\mathcal{U}$ if, whenever $C_1 \, \mathcal{R} \, C_2$ then*

- *if $C_1 \xrightarrow{\alpha} C_1'$ then there is C_2' with $C_2 \overset{\hat{\alpha}}{\Longrightarrow} C_2'$ and $C_1' \, (\mathcal{U}\mathcal{R}\mathcal{U}) \, C_2'$.*
- *if $C_2 \xrightarrow{\alpha} C_2'$ then there is C_1' with $C_1 \overset{\hat{\alpha}}{\Longrightarrow} C_1'$ and $C_1' \, (\mathcal{U}\mathcal{R}\mathcal{U}) \, C_2'$.*

Two configurations C_1 and C_2 are said to be weakly bisimilar up to $\mathcal{U}$, written $C_1 \approx_{\mathcal{U}} C_2$, if there is a weak bisimulation (up to $\mathcal{U}$) $\mathcal{R}$ such that $C_1 \, \mathcal{R} \, C_2$.

If $\mathcal{U}$ is the identity, then we get the standard bisimilarity $\approx$. If $\mathcal{U} = \equiv$, then we get a well-known proof technique for the standard bisimilarity.

2.3   Proof Methods and Methodology

Referring to the Introduction, the environment Γ_k would be represented in our calculus as $(\mathcal{L},k)$ for some $\mathcal{L} \subseteq \mathcal{L}oc$; likewise $(\mathcal{L},0)$ represents a (from now on) failure-free environment. Francalanza and Hennessy [FH07] managed to set up wrapper codes (one for each property to prove) such that *SimpleSpecification* boiled down to the trivial process $\overline{ok}$ running at the immortal location $\star$, the location of the wrapper code. The two equations in their methodology are then:

$$(\mathcal{L}oc, 0) \rhd (Sys \parallel Wrapper) \setminus R \approx (\mathcal{L}oc, 0) \rhd \star\overline{[ok]} \tag{1}$$
$$(\mathcal{L}oc, 0) \rhd (Sys \parallel Wrapper) \setminus R \approx (\mathcal{L}oc, n-1) \rhd (Sys \parallel Wrapper) \setminus R \tag{2}$$

Using transitivity of weak bisimilarity, they may be composed into:

$$(\mathcal{L}oc, n-1) \rhd (Sys \parallel Wrapper) \setminus R \approx (\mathcal{L}oc, 0) \rhd \star\overline{[ok]} \tag{3}$$

In the context of the chosen case study of [FH07], proving Equation 1 and 2 was easier than proving Equation 3 directly. That context was mainly corresponding to our calculus—except that only perfect failure detection was around. The difference, though, is crucial. With perfect failure detectors ($\mathcal{P}$), there is a gain when the correctness proof is split, as showed above. The proof of basic correctness (i.e., of Equation 1) is much simpler, because all its sub-expressions of the form $\mathcal{P}(\!(k)\!).P + Q$ are then equivalent to Q: no crash failures may occur, which means that no suspicion can be carried out at all. The proof of basic correctness hence eliminates all code after $\mathcal{P}(\!(k)\!)$ prefixes for any $k \in \mathcal{L}$. With imperfect failure detectors ($\mathcal{S}$), this is no longer the case. Expressions of the form $\mathcal{S}(\!(i)\!).P + Q$ cannot simply be rewritten to Q since the failure detector can make mistakes, even if no process crashes may occur! This has the implication that basic correctness (i.e., Equation 1) is hard to prove. We claim that, in the context of imperfect failure detectors, proving Equation 1 is even just as hard as proving Equation 3. So, in the remainder of this paper, we thus tackle Equation 3 directly for our case study.

3 Applying the Methodology to the Case Study

Distributed consensus is the following well-known problem: a fixed number n of agents each initially propose a value v_i, $1 \leq i \leq n$; then, eventually, the agents must agree on a common value $v_i \in \{v_1, \ldots, v_n\}$. The precise specification of the problem comprises three properties with temporal logic flavor: *Termination:* Every live process eventually decides some value. *Agreement:* No two processes decide differently. *Validity:* If a process decides value v, then v was proposed by some process. Table 3 presents an algorithm by Chandra and Toueg [CT96] that is supposed to solve Distributed Consensus in the context of failure detector $\mathcal{S}$.

Definition 5 (Vectors). *A n-vector is a map from set $\{1, \ldots, n\}$ to set $\mathbf{V}$. Let $\widetilde{\perp}$ denote the n-vector $(\perp, \perp, \ldots, \perp)$. Define an order $\leq$ on n-vectors by $V \leq V'$ if for every $\forall 1 \leq i \leq n : V(i) = \perp \vee V(i) = V'(i)$. We read $V \leq V$ as: V' holds at least the knowledge of V.*

The algorithm proceeds in three phases, during which it manipulates two particular vectors of each process. The vector V_p holds the current knowledge of agent p (the *knowledge vector*). If $V_p(i) = v$ then agent p knows that agent i proposed value v. The vector Δ_p is used to relay knowledge from the previous round (the *relay vector*). Each agent has a round variable r which allows agents to order messages. Variable q is used to iterate through all agent $1 \ldots n$. Variable M_p is a

Table 3. Distributed Consensus [CT96]

1: **Pseudo code for agent** p	17: $V_p(q) \leftarrow \Delta'(q)$
2: $V_p \leftarrow \tilde{\perp},\ V_p(p) \leftarrow v_p$	18: $\Delta_p(q) \leftarrow \Delta'(q)$
3: $\Delta_p \leftarrow V_p,\ M_p \leftarrow \emptyset$	19:
4:	20: **Phase 2:**
5: **Phase 1:**	21: **send** P2(V_p) to all
6: **for all** $r_p \leftarrow 1$ to $n-1$ **do**	22: **block until**
7: **send** P1(p, r_p, Δ_p) to all	23: **for all** $1 \leq q \leq n$ **do**
8: $\Delta_p \leftarrow \tilde{\perp}$	24: **receive** $m = $ P2(V)
9: **block until**	25: $M_p \leftarrow M_p \cup \{m\}$
10: **for all** $1 \leq q \leq n$	26: **or** suspect $S(\!|q|\!)$
11: **receive** $m = $ P1(q, r_p, Δ)	27: **for all** $q \leftarrow 1$ to n **do**
12: $M_p \leftarrow M_p \cup \{m\}$	28: **if** $\exists V' \in M_p : V'(q) = \perp$
13: **or** suspect $S(\!|q|\!)$	29: **then** $V_p(q) \leftarrow \perp$
14: **for all** $q \leftarrow 1$ to n **do**	30:
15: **if** $V_p(q) = \perp$ **and** $\exists \Delta' \in M_p$	31: **Phase 3:**
16: **with** $\Delta'(q) \neq \perp$ **then**	32: decide $= \min \{q \mid V_p(q) \neq \perp\}$

multiset which serves as a store for all received messages. Initially, every agent p knows its own value, i.e. $V_p(p) = v_p$, Δ_p equals V_p and store M_p is empty.

Phase 1 — obtaining knowledge. The agents broadcast and update their knowledge during $n-1$ rounds. When a received message contains a previously unknown value then both knowledge and relay vector will be updated. Newly learned values are relayed once because of the boolean predicate in line 15 and the fact that the relay vector is reset in the start of each round. It can be proven that every agent p that completes Phase 1 at least has the same knowledge as ti (the trusted immortal, that is the live and never wrongly suspected agent).

Phase 2 — correcting knowledge. If $V_i(j) = \perp$ for some agent i and j then either agent i has suspected agent j to have crashed or j stopped before sending messages to i. Such "not-known" values are distributed among all the participants. An agent k that receives knowledge vector V_i corrects coordinate j to $\perp$, i.e. $V_k(j) = \perp$. Destruction of knowledge in this fashion happens in line 29. It can be proved that every agent p that reaches the end of Phase 2 has the same $\perp$'s as ti. As an effect it holds that $V_{ti} = V_p$ for any such p at the end of Phase 2.

Phase 3 — selecting the final value. The two phases above ensure that the knowledge vector of every live agent is equal to V_{ti}. The first non-zero value in the knowledge vector is chosen. Since process ti knows it's own value i.e. $V_{ti}(ti) = v_{ti}$ this value cannot be $\perp$. So, every agent will agree on some number in the end.

3.1 Encoding the Case Study

In Table 5, we formulate system Sys in our calculus with a formalization of (i) the behavior of each agent, (ii) the communication between agents and (iii) failure detection. We identify agents via numbers, i.e. $\mathcal{L}oc \stackrel{\text{def}}{=} \{\star, 1, \ldots, n\}$. Agents and each phase of the algorithm are modeled via parameterized process constants.

Table 4. Auxiliary function declarations

$$
\begin{aligned}
\text{apply}(\texttt{data}, (r, M)) &\stackrel{\text{def}}{=} \{\Delta \mid (\Delta, r', i) \in M \wedge r = r'\} \\
\text{apply}(\texttt{data}, M) &\stackrel{\text{def}}{=} \{V \mid (V, i) \in M\}. \\
\text{apply}(\texttt{senders}, (r, M)) &\stackrel{\text{def}}{=} \{i \mid (\Delta, r', i) \in M \wedge r = r'\} \\
\text{apply}(\texttt{senders}, M) &\stackrel{\text{def}}{=} \{i \mid (V, i) \in M\}. \\
\text{apply}(\texttt{update}, (r, M, V, W)) &\stackrel{\text{def}}{=} W'
\end{aligned}
$$

$$
\text{where } W'(j) = \begin{cases} \Delta^r & , \Delta \in \texttt{data}(r, M) \text{ and} \\ & V(j) = \bot^0 \neq \Delta(j), \\ W(j) & , \text{otherwise} \end{cases}
$$

$$
\text{apply}(\texttt{correct}, (M, V)) \stackrel{\text{def}}{=} W
$$

$$
\text{where } W(i) = \begin{cases} \bot & , V' \in \texttt{data}(M) \text{ and} \\ & V'(i) = \bot^0 \\ V(i) & , \text{otherwise} \end{cases}
$$

To ease the correctness proof we need a way of expressing that a value v_i was learned in round r_i. Without changing the algorithm we extend the knowledge vector with round numbers: $(v_1^{r_1}, \ldots, v_n^{r_n})$ where v^r is shorthand for (v, r). We still compare vectors $V \leq V'$ by comparing the unannotated versions of V and V'. The *initial knowledge vector* I_i^0 for agent i is a map defined by $I_i^0(i) = v_i^0$ and $I_i^0(j) = \bot^0$ for $j \neq i$. The *initial relay vector* $I_i(i)$ for agent i is a map defined by $I_i(i) = v_i$ and $I_i(j) = \bot$ for $j \neq i$.

We define functions for the internal computation at each agent. First there are simple functions supporting primitive operations such as multiset manipulation, manipulation of vectors, and operations related to integers such as comparison and addition. The maximum of a finite multiset M of numbers is written $\max(M)$. Function $\texttt{getfst}(V)$ returns first non-zero component of V. If no such entry exists the value $\bot$ is returned. In Table 4 we define more advanced functions. The functions $\texttt{data}$ and $\texttt{senders}$ are used to project information on sent data and sender identities from a given multiset of messages M. We may call the function with a round number r as filter. The function $\texttt{update}$ updates vector W with respect to current knowledge V, round number r and received messages M corresponding to Phase 1, lines 14–18 in Table 3. Function $\texttt{correct}$ corrects the knowledge vector V with respect to received messages M, corresponding to Phase 2 in lines 27–29 in Table 3. The process constant $\mathsf{P1}_p(r, V, \Delta, M)$ corresponds to an agent p in Phase 1 which broadcasts its current knowledge and waits for incoming messages by process constant $\mathsf{C1}_p(r, V, M)$ (that defines the gathering of answers and updates of knowledge in Phase 1). Symbol r is the current round number, V is the current knowledge vector and Δ is the current communication vector and M is the (possibly empty) multiset of received messages for round r. Phase 2 is modeled by $\mathsf{P2}_p(V)$ and $\mathsf{C2}_p(V, M)$ corresponds to the gathering of information in Phase 2 analogously. Phase 3 is modeled by the process constant $\mathsf{P3}_p(V)$.

Table 5. Encoding of the algorithm of Table 3

1: $Sys \overset{\text{def}}{=}$

2: $\quad (\prod_{i=1}^{n} i\, [\text{P1}_i(1, I_i^0, I_i, \emptyset)])$

3: $\text{P1}_p(r, V, \Delta, M) \overset{\text{def}}{=}$

4: $\quad \textbf{if } (r < n) \textbf{ then}$

5: $\quad\quad \prod_{1 \leq i \leq n} \overline{a_{p,i,r}}\langle \Delta \rangle \,\|\, \text{C1}_p(r, V, M)$

6: $\quad \textbf{else } \text{P2}_p(V, M)$

7: $\text{C1}_p(r, V, M) \overset{\text{def}}{=}$

8: $\quad \textbf{let } i = 1 + \max(\text{senders}(r, M))) \textbf{ in}$

9: $\quad \textbf{if } i \leq n \textbf{ then}$

10: $\quad\quad a_{i,p,r}@i(\Delta).$

11: $\quad\quad\quad \text{C1}_p\Big(r, \text{update}(r, M, V, V),$

12: $\quad\quad\quad\quad\quad\quad\quad\quad M + (\Delta, r, i)\Big)$

13: $\quad \textbf{else}$

14: $\quad\quad \text{P1}_p\Big(r + 1, V,$

15: $\quad\quad\quad\quad \text{update}(r, M, V, \widetilde{\bot}), M\Big)$

16: $\text{P2}_p(V, M) \overset{\text{def}}{=}$

17: $\quad \prod_{1 \leq i \leq n} \overline{b_{p,i}}\langle V \rangle \,\|\, \text{C2}_p(V, M)$

18: $\text{C2}_p(V, M) \overset{\text{def}}{=}$

19: $\quad \textbf{let } i = 1 + \max(\text{senders}(M)) \textbf{ then}$

20: $\quad\quad \textbf{if } i \leq n \textbf{ then}$

21: $\quad\quad\quad b_{i,p}@i(V').\text{C2}_p(V, M + (V', i))$

22: $\quad\quad \textbf{else}$

23: $\quad\quad\quad \text{P3}_p(\text{correct}(M, V), M)$

24: $\text{P3}_p(V, M) \overset{\text{def}}{=}$

25: $\quad \overline{c_p}\langle \text{getfst}(V), V, M \rangle$

26: $Wrap(i, v) \overset{\text{def}}{=}$

27: $\quad \textbf{if } (i \leq n) \textbf{ then}$

28: $\quad\quad \mathcal{P}(\!|i|\!). \, Wrap(i + 1, v) \,+$

29: $\quad\quad c_i(v', V, M).$

30: $\quad\quad\quad \textbf{if } (v{=}\bot \vee v{==}v') \textbf{ then}$

31: $\quad\quad\quad Wrap(i + 1, v') \textbf{ else } \mathbf{0}$

32: $\quad \textbf{else if } (i == n + 1) \textbf{ then } \overline{ok}$

Constant $Wrap(i, v)$ is the wrapper code that checks for agreement. It collects all the decision values agent by agent and checks that they agree. If they all agree, then $\overline{ok}$ is released. Otherwise the checker becomes $\mathbf{0}$. The wrap code has to use perfect failure detectors since unreliable failure detectors may cause incorrect answers. For convenience, let $R \overset{\text{def}}{=} \{a_{i,j,k}, b_{i,j}, c_i\}_{1 \leq i,j,k \leq n}$.

Trying to formalize some intuitions about the algorithm, we quickly get to the point where we need to formulate properties that refer to the respective states of the processes, not their actions. Process calculi do not directly support this, except when we refer to the process constants—and their parameters— that we used to write down the code. To enable this kind of reasoning, we define dedicated syntactic forms that also capture the complete message space.

Definition 6. *A standard form C_ξ is a configuration of the form:*

$$\boxed{\Gamma} \,\triangleright\, \boxed{\text{ti}} \Bigg(\prod_{(p,r,i) \in \boxed{\Pi_1^{\text{out}}}} p\,\Big[\overline{a_{p,i,r}}\langle \boxed{\Delta_{p,r}}\rangle\Big] \,\|\, \prod_{(p,i) \in \boxed{\Pi_2^{\text{out}}}} p\,\Big[\overline{b_{p,i}}\langle \boxed{V_p^{\text{P2}}}\rangle\Big] \,\|$$

$$\prod_{p \in \boxed{\Pi_3^{\text{out}}}} p\,\Big[\overline{c_p}\langle \boxed{v_p}, \boxed{V_p^{\text{P3}}}, \boxed{M_p^{\text{P3}}}\rangle\Big] \,\|$$

$$\prod_{(p,r) \in \boxed{\Pi_1^{\text{col}}}} p\,\Big[\text{C1}_p\Big(r, \boxed{V_p^{\text{P1}}}, \boxed{M_p^{\text{P1}}}\Big)\Big] \,\|\, \prod_{p \in \boxed{\Pi_2^{\text{col}}}} p\,\Big[\text{C2}_p\Big(\boxed{V_p^{\text{P2}}}, \boxed{M_p^{\text{P2}}}\Big)\Big]$$

$$\prod_{c \in \text{dead}(\Gamma)} c\,[Q_c] \quad \|\; Wrap\,\big[\,Wrap(\boxed{j}, \boxed{w})\,\big] \Bigg) \setminus R$$

where $\text{dead}(\Gamma)$ *is disjoint with* $\Pi_1^{\text{out}}, \Pi_2^{\text{out}}, \Pi_3^{\text{out}}, \Pi_1^{\text{col}}, \Pi_2^{\text{col}}$. *Parameter ξ is a data structure consisting of all the boxed values above. We refer to its entities "by name", i.e., using boxed symbols. We will often write ξ instead of C_ξ.*

Our standard form is defined w.r.t. process constants. By the semantics, they are not necessarily fully unfolded. Since unfoldings may take place independently in different parts of terms, different process constants may be unfolded at different degrees, some too far, some too little. It requires a subtle definition to precisely relate any reachable configuration to some standard form.

Definition 7. *A configuration C with $C \Rightarrow^{\tau} C'$ has standard form C_ξ if there exist a vector family ξ such that $C_\xi \Rightarrow C'$.*

The connection of configurations to standard forms cannot be lost in transition.

Lemma 1 (Preservation of Standard Forms)
If $C \to C'$ and C has a standard form, then C' also has a standard form.

3.2 Weak Bisimulation Relations via Invariants

Definition 6 suggests that the reachable state space of Chandra and Toueg algorithm is reasonably complex. Agents may be in different phases, have different knowledge and different sets of relay vectors. Learning from Chandra and Toueg's proof sketch [CT96], we capture this combinatorial space via invariants.

Definition 8. *An invariant I is a boolean predicate defined on configurations such that $I(C)$ and $C \xrightarrow{\alpha} C'$ imply $I(C')$ for $\alpha \in \{\tau, \overline{ok}\}$.*

Invariants provide an abstraction from actual states to classes of states. It is this characteristic that we use when we give witness relations for our weak bisimulation relations. With the convention that $Spec = Wrap[ok]$ we require that it accepts the initial configuration and that success eventually is reached:

$$I\Big((\mathcal{L}oc, n{-}1) \triangleright (Sys \parallel Wrap(1, \bot)) \setminus R \Big). \tag{4}$$

$$\text{If } I(\xi) \text{ then } \xi \xRightarrow{\overline{ok}} \mathbf{0} \tag{5}$$

That enables us to construct a witness relation $\mathcal{R} \subseteq \mathbf{C} \times \mathbf{C}$ for Equation 3 (closed under symmetry) of the form:

$$\mathcal{R} = \big\{ (\xi, (\mathcal{L}oc, 0) \triangleright Wrap[\overline{ok}]) \mid I(\xi) \big\} \tag{6}$$

Lemma 2. *$\mathcal{R}$ is a weak bisimulation up to $\Rightarrow$ if I satisfies Equation 4 and 5.*

Equation 6 and the requirements to invariant I prepare for a proof of Equation 3.

Definition 9. *Let predicate I be the conjunction of the predicates (all defined below): control, validity, relay, receive$_1$, learn, preknow, receive$_2$ and know.*

The predicate *control* defines control criteria to the algorithm, e.g. agent p cannot be in Phase 1 and Phase 2 at the same time or agent p cannot be in two different rounds at the same time in Phase 1 etc.

Definition 10 (Control flow). *Define the predicate* $control(\xi)$ *as the conjunction of the expressions below:*

1. *if* $(p_1, \cdot) \in \boxed{\Pi_1^{\text{col}}}$ *and* $p_2 \in \boxed{\Pi_2^{\text{col}}}$ *and* $p_3 \in \boxed{\Pi_3^{\text{out}}}$ *then* $p_1 \neq p_2$ *and* $p_1 \neq p_3$ *and* $p_2 \neq p_3$.
2. *if* $(p, r) \in \boxed{\Pi_1^{\text{col}}}$ *and* $(p', r') \in \boxed{\Pi_1^{\text{col}}}$ *and* $p = p'$ *then* $r = r'$.
3. $1 \leq \boxed{j} \leq n + 1$
4. $\forall r : |\text{senders}(r, \boxed{M_p^{\text{P1}}})| = \max \left(\text{senders} \left(r, \boxed{M_p^{\text{P1}}} \right) \right)$
5. $|\text{senders} \left(\boxed{M_p^{\text{P2}}} \right)| = \max \left(\text{senders} \left(\boxed{M_p^{\text{P2}}} \right) \right)$
6. *If* $\exists p : (p, \cdot) \notin \boxed{\Pi_1^{\text{col}}}$ *and* $p \notin \boxed{\Pi_2^{\text{col}}}$ *and* $p \notin \boxed{\Pi_3^{\text{out}}}$ *then* $p < \boxed{j}$.

The next predicate formally describes what we mean by validity: all values in knowledge and relay vectors have been proposed by someone.

Definition 11 (Validity). *Let* U *be a vector which holds the initially proposed value by participant* i, *i.e.* $U(i) = v_i$ *for* $1 \leq i \leq n$ *and define the predicate* $validity(\xi)$ *as the conjunction of the expressions below:*

1. $\forall p : \boxed{V_p^{\text{P1}}}(p) = v_p^0$,   2. $\forall (p, r, i) \in \boxed{\Pi_1^{\text{out}}} : \boxed{\Delta_{p,r}} \leq U$
3. *If* $(p, r) \in \boxed{\Pi_1^{\text{col}}}$ *or* $p \in \boxed{\Pi_2^{\text{col}}}$ *or* $(p, i) \in \boxed{\Pi_2^{\text{out}}}$ *or* $p \in \boxed{\Pi_3^{\text{out}}}$ *then*
    $\boxed{V_p^{\text{P}}} \leq U$ *for* $\text{P} \in \{\text{P1}, \text{P2}, \text{P3}\}$.
4. $\forall (\Delta, r, i) \in \boxed{M_p^{\text{P1}}} \cup \boxed{M_p^{\text{P2}}} \cup \boxed{M_p^{\text{P3}}} : \Delta \leq U$
5. $\forall (V, i) \in \boxed{M_p^{\text{P2}}} \cup \boxed{M_p^{\text{P3}}} : V \leq U$, *if* $V \neq \bot$
6. *If* $p \in \boxed{\Pi_3^{\text{out}}}$ *then* $\boxed{v_p} = \texttt{getfst} \left(\boxed{V_p^{\text{P3}}} \right)$
7. $1 \leq \boxed{j} \leq n + 1 \ \wedge \ \exists i : \boxed{w} = v_i \vee \boxed{w} = \bot$,   8. *If* $\boxed{j} = 1$ *then* $\boxed{w} = \bot$

The next predicate says that values learned in round r are relayed in round $r+1$.

Definition 12 (Relays of knowledge, Phase 1). *Define the predicate* $relay(\xi)$ *by the following: If* $(p, \cdot) \in \boxed{\Pi_1^{\text{col}}}$ *and* $\boxed{V_p^{\text{P1}}}(j) = v^{r'}$, $v \neq \bot$ *for some* j *and* $r' \leq n - 2$ *then it holds that*

1. *if* $(p, r, \cdot) \in \boxed{\Pi_1^{\text{out}}}$ *and* $r \neq r' + 1$ *then* $\boxed{\Delta_{p,r}}(j) = \bot$
2. *if* $(p, r, \cdot) \in \boxed{\Pi_1^{\text{out}}}$ *and* $r = r' + 1$ *then* $\boxed{\Delta_{p,r}}(j) = v$

Knowledge propagates from ti to all live agents of the protocol.

Definition 13 (Received messages, Phase 1). *Define the predicate* $receive_1(\xi)$ *by the following:*

If (a) $(\text{ti}, \cdot) \in \boxed{\Pi_1^{\text{col}}}$ and (b) $\boxed{V_{\text{ti}}^{\text{P1}}}(j) = v^r \neq \bot$ for some j
then $0 \leq r \leq n - 2$ and $r' = r + 1$ implies $(\Delta, r', \text{ti}) \in \boxed{M_p^{\text{P1}}}$ and $\Delta(j) = v$.

Maybe the most important property: all agents learn from the trusted immortal.

Definition 14. *Define the predicate learn(ξ) by the following:*

If (a) $(\text{ti}, \cdot) \in \boxed{\Pi_1^{\text{col}}}$, *(b)* $\boxed{V_{\text{ti}}^{\text{P1}}}(j) = v^r \neq \bot$ *for some* j, *and (c)* $(p, r') \in \boxed{\Pi_1^{\text{col}}}$

then   i. if $0 \leq r \leq n - 2$ *and* $r' \geq r + 1$ *then* $\boxed{V_p^{\text{P1}}}(j) = v^{r''}$ *for some* r''.

   ii. if $r = n - 1$ *then* $\boxed{V_p^{\text{P1}}}(j) = v^{r''}$ *for some* r''.

The property that all agents learn from the trusted immortal also holds at the beginning of Phase 2 where every agent at least has the same knowledge as ti.

Definition 15. *Define predicate preknow(ξ) by:* $\forall (p, \cdot) \in \boxed{\Pi_2^{\text{out}}} : \boxed{V_{\text{ti}}^{\text{P2}}} \leq \boxed{V_p^{\text{P2}}}$.

The predicate below states that all agents receive from ti in Phase 2.

Definition 16. *Define the predicate receive$_2$(ξ) as follows: if all of 1.* $p \in \boxed{\Pi_2^{\text{col}}}$, *2.* $i := \max(\text{senders}(\boxed{M_p^{\text{P2}}}))$, *and 3.* $\text{ti} < i$, *then* $\exists V : (V, \text{ti}) \in M_p^{\text{P2}}$.

The effect is that everyone has the same knowledge as ti at the end of Phase 2 (or beginning of Phase 3), which is stated in the following predicate:

Definition 17. *Define the predicate know(ξ) by 1.* $\forall p \in \boxed{\Pi_3^{\text{out}}} : \boxed{V_{\text{ti}}^{\text{P3}}} = \boxed{V_p^{\text{P3}}}$ *and 2. If* $p \in \boxed{\Pi_3^{\text{out}}}$ *and* $0 < \boxed{j} < n + 1$ *then* $\boxed{w} = \boxed{v_p}$.

The following important theorem tells that I is an invariant.

Theorem 1. I *is an invariant which satisfies Equation 4.*

The proof that "$I(\xi)$ implies that $\xi \overset{ok}{\Longrightarrow} \mathbf{0}$" uses a progress measure as temporal distance of any agent i to termination. Our main theorem follows directly.

Theorem 2. *The relation in Equation 6 is a weak bisimulation up to* $\Rightarrow$ *with invariant* I *defined as in Definition 9.*

In summary, we have proved the required Consensus properties: Validity holds since it is part of the global invariant; Termination follows from the above-mentioned progress analysis ending up in a state where the wrapper code comes to an end; from the argument that the wrapped system is weakly bisimilar to ok, we get Agreement, obviously due to the design of the wrapper code.

4   Conclusion and Future Work

Our case study may offer several insights. The strategy, or: methodology, that worked quite nicely in our case, may be summarized as follows. The usage of a process calculus helps to keep a tight connection to the algorithm's code, so our proofs are meaningful. The formulation of the proof goal by wrappers is, although not a new idea, very useful in the context of fault tolerance. A novelty in our approach was the combination of imperfect failure detectors (as necessarily assumed by the case study) and perfect failure detectors (as idealis-tically assumed to have the wrapper code function properly). The introduction of standard forms to manage the complexity of state spaces is not a new idea either; it has mostly been used implicitly and often only in toy examples, but it seems to scale quite well. The reason we propose to turn standard forms explicitly into a method is that they provide a well-suited means to express the typical assertional state-based proof knowledge as invariants. Again, the mere use of invariants is not at all a new idea. However, their systematic integration within the bisimulation method seems novel.

Future work on this case study may involve confluence-oriented proof methods, as employed in [FH07, PM06], and to investigate in what flavor they appear in our invariant-oriented method. Likewise, it might support our claims to also carry out our proof case study on a non-wrapped equation, that is, to contrast our approach of this paper with a bisimulation-based proof of an equation without hiding that much external behavior in wrapper code.

References

[BH00]   Berger, M., Honda, K.: The two-phase commitment protocol in an extended pi-calculus. Electr. Notes Theor. Comput. Sci. 39(1) (2000)

[CT96]   Chandra, T.D., Toueg, S.: Unreliable failure detectors for reliable distributed systems. J. ACM 43(2) (1996)

[FGR04]   Fokkink, W., Groote, J.F., Reniers, M.: Process algebra needs proof methodology. EATCS Bulletin 82, 109–125 (2004)

[FH07]   Francalanza, A., Hennessy, M.: A fault tolerance bisimulation proof for consensus. In: De Nicola, R. (ed.) ESOP 2007. LNCS, vol. 4421, pp. 395–410. Springer, Heidelberg (2007)

[Fou98]   Fournet, C.: The Join-Calculus: A Calculus for Distributed Mobile Programming. Ph.D thesis, École Polytechnique, Paris, France (1998)

[Hen07]   Hennessy, M.: A Distributed Pi-Calculus. Cambridge University Press, Cambridge (2007)

[Küh08]   Kühnrich, M.: Formal model-driven design of distributed algorithms. In: Annual Doctoral Workshop on Mathematical and Engineering Methods in Computer Science (November 2008)

[Lyn96]   Lynch, N.: Distributed Algorithms. Kaufmann Publishers, San Francisco (1996)

[Mil89]   Milner, R.: Communication and Concurrency. Prentice Hall, Englewood Cliffs (1989)

[NF03]   Nestmann, U., Fuzzati, R.: Unreliable failure detectors via operational semantics. In: Saraswat, V.A. (ed.) ASIAN 2003. LNCS, vol. 2896, pp. 54–71. Springer, Heidelberg (2003)

[NFM03]   Nestmann, U., Fuzzati, R., Merro, M.: Modeling consensus in a process calculus. In: Amadio, R., Lugiez, D. (eds.) CONCUR 2003. LNCS, vol. 2761, pp. 399–414. Springer, Heidelberg (2003)

[PM06]   Philippou, A., Michael, G.: Verification techniques for distributed algorithms. In: Shvartsman, M.M.A.A. (ed.) OPODIS 2006. LNCS, vol. 4305, pp. 172–186. Springer, Heidelberg (2006)

[SV00]   Sewell, P., Vitek, J.: Secure composition of untrusted code: Wrappers and causality types. In: CSFW, pp. 269–284 (2000)

[TS08]   Tsuchiya, T., Schiper, A.: Using bounded model checking to verify consensus algorithms. LNCS. Springer, Heidelberg (2008)

Using First-Order Logic to Reason about Submodule Construction*

Gregor v. Bochmann

School of Information Technology and Engineering (SITE), University of Ottawa, Canada
bochmann@site.uottawa.ca

Abstract. We consider the following problem: For a system consisting of two components, the behavior of one component is known as well as the desired global behavior. What should be the behavior of the second component such that the behavior of the composition of the two conforms to the desired behavior ? - This problem has been called "submodule construction" or "equation solving". Solutions to this problem have been described in the context of various specification formalisms and various conformance relations. This paper presents a new formulation of this problem and its solution in first-order logic. It is also shown how the solutions for submodule construction in various specification formalisms can be derived from the solution in logic. The simple proof of correctness for the logic solution is then used to justify the particular forms of solutions in the different specification formalisms, such as (a) synchronous rendezvous at several interfaces, and (b) interleaved rendezvous (labeled transition systems).

1 Introduction

In automata theory, the notion of constructing a product machine S from two given finite state machines M_A and M_B , written $M = M_A \times M_B$, is a well-known concept (see Figure 1(a)). This notion is very important in practice since complex systems are usually constructed as a composition of smaller subsystems, and the behavior of the overall system is in many cases equal to the composition obtained by calculating the product of the behaviors of the two subsystems. Here we consider the inverse operation, called "equation solving" or "submodule construction": Given the composed system M and one of the components M_A, what should be the behavior of the second component M_B such that the composition of these two components M_A and M_B will exhibit a behavior equal to M. That is, we are looking for the value of X which is the solution to the equation $M_A \times X = M$ (see Figure 1(b)). Actually, since equality often cannot be realized, we are looking for the most general machine X which composed with M_A satisfies some conformance relation in respect to M. In this paper we consider trace inclusion as conformance relation.

A first paper of 1980 [1] (see also [2]) gives a solution to this problem for the case where the machine behavior is described in terms of LTS (communicating by

---

* This work was partly supported by a research grant from the Natural Sciences and Engineering Research Council of Canada.

D. Lee et al. (Eds.): FMOODS/FORTE 2009, LNCS 5522, pp. 213–218, 2009.

interleaved rendezvous). This work was later extended to the cases where the behavior of the machines is described by CSP, FSMs with queues, IOAs and synchronous FSMs. The problem has also been formulated for databases using relational algebra (see [3] for pertinent references). The main applications of this work are in the design of communication protocols, the construction of protocol converters for communication gateways, the selection of test cases of testing a module in a context, and for finding a controller for discrete event control systems [4].

The purpose of this paper is to show that, in fact, the equation solving (or submodule construction) problem can be formulated in logic. It turns out that (a) a solution with a structure similar to the solutions mentioned above exists, and (b) a proof of the correctness of this solution is quite simple, apparently much simpler than the existing proofs of correctness for the solutions in the contexts mentioned above. We show in this paper how the solutions for submodule construction in different contexts can be derived from the general solution in the logic context. The proof of correctness from the logic context can therefore be used to justify the particular forms of solutions in the contexts of different specification formalisms. In this paper we give an overview of the cases of (a) synchronous rendezvous at several interfaces, and (b) interleaved rendezvous (that is, labeled transition systems). A more detailed discussion, including examples, can be found in [3]. Other contexts are considered in [5], such as synchronous (I/O) automata with complete or partial behavior specifications, interleaving IOA with complete or partial behavior specifications, and finite state machines with queued communication, as well as relational algebra for databases. These contexts include much of the previous work mentioned above and also some not so common modeling approaches.

2   Equation Solving in the Logic Context

We use in this section first-order logic with typed variables. We consider a universe with three variables X_A, X_B, and X_C that may take values from three domains D_A, D_B and D_C, respectively. These domains may be infinite. Therefore, the set of possible value assignments to the variables is $U = D_A \times D_B \times D_C$. We write x_A, x_B, and x_C for possible values of the variables X_A, X_B, and X_C, respectively.

We are interested in relationships between values of different variables. For instance, we may consider a relation $R \subset D_A \times D_B$ which is a subset of pairs $< x_A, x_B >$ of values of the variables X_A and X_B. We also use predicates to characterize sets. For instance, the relation R may be characterized by a predicate $C(x_A, x_B)$ which is true exactly for those pairs $< x_A, x_B >$ that are in R.

The equation solving problem

In the following, we are interested in three relations $R_A \subset D_B \times D_C$, $R_B \subset D_A \times D_C$ and $R_C \subset D_A \times D_B$. We write $C_A(x_B, x_C)$, $C_B(x_A, x_C)$, and $C_C(x_A, x_B)$ for their respective characterizing predicates. We now consider the following proposition:

$$\forall < x_A, x_B, x_C > \in U : <x_B, x_C> \in R_A \land <x_A, x_C> \in R_B \Rightarrow <x_A, x_B> \in R_C \quad (1^{Rel})$$

This proposition may be equivalently rewritten in terms of the predicates as follows:

$$\forall <x_A, x_B, x_C> \in U : \quad C_A(x_B, x_C) \wedge C_B(x_A, x_C) \Rightarrow C_C(x_A, x_B) \qquad (1^{Pred})$$

The problem of equation solving is the following: We assume that R_A and R_C are given. What are the properties of relation R_B that ensure that proposition (1) is satisfied? – We would like to find a maximal solution R_B^{max} to this problem, that is, R_B^{max} together with R_A and R_C would satisfy (1), but any larger $R_B' \supset R_B^{max}$ would not satisfy this proposition.

The maximal solution

Starting from (1^{Pred}), it is easy to see that the following predicate characterizes the maximal solution:

$$C_B^{max}(x_A, x_C) = \forall x_B \in D_B : \quad C_A(x_B, x_C) \Rightarrow C_C(x_A, x_B) \qquad (2)$$

The right side of this definition can be equivalently transformed in several steps as follows:

$$\forall x_B \in D_B : \quad \neg C_A(x_B, x_C) \vee C_C(x_A, x_B)$$
$$\forall x_B \in D_B : \quad \neg (C_A(x_B, x_C) \wedge \neg C_C(x_A, x_B))$$
$$\neg \exists x_B \in D_B : \quad C_A(x_B, x_C) \wedge \neg C_C(x_A, x_B)$$

which leads to the following equivalent expression for the maximal solution:

$$C_B^{max} (x_A, x_C) = \neg \exists x_B \in D_B : \quad C_A(x_B, x_C) \wedge \neg C_C(x_A, x_B) \qquad (3)$$

The realized subset of R_C

We note that in general not all pairs $<x_A, x_B> \in R_C$ could be "realized" by R_A and R_B^{max}.

Definition: We say that a pair $<x_A, x_B> \in R_C$ is **realizable** by R_A and R_B if there exist a value $x_C \in D_C$ such that $<x_B, x_C> \in R_A$ and $<x_A, x_C> \in R_B$.

We call the subset of R_C that is realisable by R_A and R_B^{max} the maximally realisable subset of R_C (or "product"), written R_C^{prod}. We therefore have

$$<x_A, x_B> \in R_C^{prod} \quad iff \quad \exists x_C \in D_C : \quad <x_B, x_C> \in R_A \wedge <x_A, x_C> \in R_B^{max} \qquad (4)$$

The reduced maximal solution

We consider the relation $R_B^{incompatible}$ characterized by the following predicate:

$$C_B^{incompatible}(x_A, x_C) = \neg \exists x_B \in D_B : \quad C_A(x_B, x_C) \wedge C_C(x_A, x_B)$$

Lemma: There is no $<x_A, x_B> \in R_C$ that is realizable by R_A and $R_B^{incompatible}$.

Proof: Let us assume that there is a pair $<x_A, x_B> \in R_C$ that is realizable by R_A and $R_B^{incompatible}$. According to the definition of "realizable", this implies that there is a $x_C \in D_C$ such that $<x_B, x_C> \in R_A$ and $<x_A, x_C> \in R_B^{incompatible}$. Now, the definition of $R_B^{incompatible}$ implies that there is no $x'_B \in D_B$ such that $C_A(x'_B, x_C) \wedge C_C(x_A, x'_B)$. However, this is a contradiction, since x_B satisfies this condition for x'_B.

We conclude from the lemma above that those pairs $<x_A, x_C>$ of R_B^{max} that are in $R_B^{incompatible}$ do not contribute to the realization of R_C^{prod}. We therefore may eliminate from the solution R_B^{max} all pairs in $R_B^{incompatible}$ and still obtain the same set R_C^{prod} of realizable pairs $<x_A, x_B>$. We call this the **reduced maximal solution** to the equation solving problem. It is characterized by the following predicate:

$$C_B^{red}(x_A, x_C) = (\exists x_B \in D_B : C_A(x_B, x_C) \wedge C_C(x_A, x_B)) \wedge$$
$$(\neg\exists x_B \in D_B : C_A(x_B, x_C) \wedge \neg C_C(x_A, x_B)) \tag{5}$$

3 Submodule Construction for Synchronous Systems and LTS

State machines are often used as models for reactive systems that interact with their environment. Often one considers a system model which is the composition of several state machines. Therefore a state machine is normally a component within a system, it interacts with other components of the system and possibly also with the environment of the system; or the state machine represents the interactions of the whole system with its environment. Because of space limitations, this sections is much condensed. More details can be found in [3].

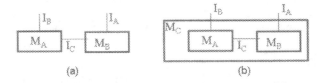

Fig. 1. (a) Two communicating components; (b) Submodule construction problem

A system component has one or more interfaces where interactions with the environment of the component take place. Each interface i is associated with a domain I_i; the elements of I_i are the possible interactions that may take place at that interface. We write $x_i^{(t)}$ for the interaction that takes place at interface i at time unit t. Clearly, $x_i^{(t)} \in I_i$ for all t. We write x_i for a sequence of interactions at interface i over a certain time period. We write I_i^* for the set of all sequences that can be formed by concatenating interactions from the domain I_i. We have $x_i \in I_i^*$.

We assume trace semantics for the specification of the dynamic behaviour of a system, that is, the dynamic behavior of a system M is defined in terms of the set of possible execution histories that could occur during the execution of the component. For a system with n interfaces i (i = 1, ..., n), an execution history consists of a tuplet $< x_1, x_2, ... x_n >$ where x_i (i = 1, ..., n) is the sequence of interactions that occurred at interface i during the execution history. We therefore assume that the specification S of the behavior of M is given in the form of a (normally infinite) set of such tuplets. As in Section 2, instead of talking about the set S of tuplets, one may also talk about the predicate C that characterizes this set.

3.1 Submodule Construction for Synchronous Systems

For synchronous systems, there is an interaction at each interface during each global time unit. Therefore, for a system as shown in Figure 1(b), the formula

$$\forall <x_A, x_B, x_C> \in U: \ C_A(x_B, x_C) \wedge C_B(x_A, x_C) \Rightarrow C_C(x_A, x_B) \qquad (1^{syn})$$

states that the traces of the composition of machines M_A and M_B are included in the traces of M_C. In order to compare this formula with what has been discussed previously in the literature, we have to introduce the hiding operator. When one of the interfaces (say i) is hidden, we obtain a visible behaviour which only involves the non-hidden interfaces. For a behavior C of a machine with n interfaces, we use the notation "$hide^{(syn)}_i (C(x_1, x_2, \dots x_n))$" to represent the predicate of the behaviour when interface i is hidden. As discussed by Abadi and Lamport, this predicate has the following form:

$$<x_1, \dots, x_{i-1}, x_{i+1}, \dots, x_n> \in hide^{(syn)}_i (C(x_1, x_2, \dots x_n))$$
$$iff \ \exists x_i \in I_i^*: \ <x_1, \dots, x_{i-1}, x_i, x_{i+1}, \dots, x_n> \in C(x_1, x_2, \dots x_n)$$

We note that (1^{syn}) has the form of (1^{Pred}) and we can follow the derivations of Sections 2.3 through 2.5. Using the above formula for hiding, we can rewrite Equation (5) of Section 2 for the reduced maximal solution as follows:

$$C_B^{red} (x_A, x_C) = hide^{(syn)}_B (C_A(x_B, x_C) \wedge C_C(x_A, x_B))$$
$$\setminus hide^{(syn)}_B ((C_A(x_B, x_C) \wedge (I_A^* \times I_B^* \setminus C_C(x_A, x_B)))) \qquad (5^{syn})$$

3.2 Submodule Construction for Interleaving Semantics

In this modeling framework, we also have rendezvous interactions at interfaces, but interleaving semantics is assumed, which means that at most one interaction (on a single interface) may occur during each time unit. We use in the following the same modelling framework as for synchronous machines, but introduce the following changes:

- We allow an interface to have the value *null* during a given time unit, which means that no interaction takes place at this interface during this time unit.
- In a system of several components with n interfaces, a possible execution history $<x_1, x_2, \dots x_n>$ must satisfy the following constraint, called **interleaving constraint:**

$$IC(x_1, x_2, \dots x_n) = \text{for all } t: x_i^{(t)} \in I_i \text{ implies } x_j^{(t)} = null \text{ for all } j \neq i.$$

We say that two execution histories are equivalent if they exhibit the same sequence of non-null interactions. This leads to the following formula of interface hiding:

$$<x_1, \dots, x_{i-1}, x_{i+1}, \dots, x_n> \in hide^{(LTS)}_i (C(x_1, x_2, \dots x_n))$$

$$iff \ IC(x_1, \dots, x_{i-1}, x_{i+1}, \dots, x_n)$$
$$\wedge \ \exists <x_1', \dots, x_{i-1}', x_i', x_{i+1}', \dots, x_n'>: (IC(x_1', \dots, x_{i-1}', x_i', x_{i+1}', \dots, x_n')$$
$$\wedge \ <x_1', \dots, x_{i-1}', x_{i+1}', \dots, x_n'> \cong <x_1, \dots, x_{i-1}, x_{i+1}, \dots, x_n>$$
$$\wedge \ <x_1', \dots, x_{i-1}', x_i', x_{i+1}', \dots, x_n'> \in C(x_1, x_2, \dots x_n))$$

Because of the interleaving constraint, the formulas (1^{syn}) and (2) become:

$$\forall < x_A, x_B, x_C > \in U : IC(x_A, x_B, x_C) \wedge C_A(x_B, x_C) \wedge C_B(x_A, x_C) \Rightarrow C_C(x_A, x_B) \quad (1^{LTS})$$

$$C_B^{max}(x_A, x_C) = IC(x_A, x_C) \wedge \forall < x_A', x_B', x_C' > \in U :$$
$$IC(x_A', x_B', x_C') \wedge <x_A', x_C'> \cong <x_A, x_C> \wedge C_A(x_B', x_C') \Rightarrow C_C(x_A', x_B') \quad (2^{LTS})$$

And the reduced maximal solution becomes

$$C_B^{red}(x_A, x_C) = hide^{(LTS)}{}_B (C_A(x_B, x_C) \wedge C_C(x_A, x_B)$$
$$\wedge \neg hide^{(LTS)}{}_B (C_A(x_B, x_C) \wedge \neg C_C(x_A, x_B)) \quad (5^{LTS})$$

This solution was presented (using a different notation) in [1], which was the first paper on submodule construction to our knowledge. We note that this formula is the same as (5^{syn}), except that a different hiding operator is used.

4 Conclusions

We have shown in this paper that the problem of submodule construction can be formulated in a general setting using first-order logic. It turns out that solutions to this problem in logic are quite simple, and they can be mapped (together with their proof of correctness) into the different specification formalisms considered in earlier work. Therefore this paper provides, in a sense, new proofs of correctness for the solutions of the submodule construction problem described earlier.

We consider in this paper trace semantics, that is, the behaviour of the system, or of a component, is characterized by the set of possible execution histories. This is adequate for safety properties, but ignores issues of liveness, progress, absence of deadlocks and fairness.

It is to be noted that the complexity of the algorithms for constructing the missing submodule depends on the specification formalism used. For state machines the complexity is polynomial if the interactions at the interface I_C in Figure 1(b) are visible by M_C, however, if they are hidden, as we assume in this paper, the algorithms become exponential, because the hiding introduces non-determinism and the algorithm to find a deterministic automaton equivalent to a non-deterministic one is exponential. The problem becomes undecidable for behavior specifications in CSP.

References

[1] Bochmann, G.V., Merlin, P.M.: On the construction of communication protocols. In: ICCC, pp. 371–378 (1980); reprinted in Communication Protocol Modeling, Sunshine, C.(ed.). Artech House Publ., (1981); russian translation: Problems of Intern. Center for Science and Techn. Information, vol. 2, Moscow, pp. 146-155 (1981)

[2] Merlin, P., Bochmann, G.V.: On the Construction of Submodule Specifications and Communication Protocols. ACM Trans. on Programming Languages and Systems 5(1), 1–25 (1983)

[3] Extended version of this paper,
http://www.site.uottawa.ca/~bochmann/dsrg/PublicDocuments/Publications/Boch09a.pdf

[4] Ramadge, P.J.G., Wonham, W.M.: The control of discrete event systems. Proceedings of the IEEE 77(1) (January 1989)

[5] Bochmann, G.V.: Submodule construction – the inverse of composition (submitted)

A Model-Checking Approach for Service Component Architectures[*]

João Abreu[1], Franco Mazzanti[2], José Luiz Fiadeiro[1], and Stefania Gnesi[2]

[1] Department of Computer Science, University of Leicester
University Road, Leicester LE1 7RH, UK
{jpad2,jose}@mcs.le.ac.uk
[2] Istituto di Scienza e Tecnologie dell'Informazione A. Faedo, CNR
Via G. Moruzzi 1, 56124, Pisa, Italy
{franco.mazzanti,stefania.gnesi}@isti.cnr.it

Abstract. We present a strategy for model-checking the correctness of service composition. We do so in the context of SRML, a formal modelling framework for service-oriented computing being defined within the SENSORIA project. We introduce a methodology for encoding patterns of typical service interaction with UML state machines and present a strategy for checking SRML specifications of service composition based on such patterns. For that purpose, we use the action-state branching time temporal logic UCTL and the model-checker UMC.

1 Specifying Service Composition with SRML

The SENSORIA Reference Modelling Language (SRML) [3,5] is a domain specific language for service-oriented architectures, inspired by the Service Component Architecture [8]. SRML provides primitives for modelling composite services whose business logic involves the orchestration of interactions among elementary components and the invocation of services provided by external parties.

Fig.1 is an example of a *service module* – the primitive that SRML offers for modelling service composition. A service module defines a distributed orchestration of a set of external services through a configuration of components and wires. Each of these components, wires and external services is typed by a specification of the interactions it can engage in or coordinate (in the case of wires). Components are typed by stateful models of the behaviour of the actual components that will execute during service delivery. Requires-interfaces, which represent the interfaces of the external services, are typed by what we call *business protocols* — behavioural constraints defined with patterns of the UCTL temporal logic [4] that need to be matched by the behaviour offered by the external services. Every service module has a *provides-interface* that is also typed by a business protocol advertizing the properties offered by the service at its interface level — in the example, the provides-interface CR is typed by the

---

[*] This work was partially sponsored through the IST-2005-16004 Integrated Project SENSORIA: Software Engineering for Service-Oriented Overlay Computers.

D. Lee et al. (Eds.): FMOODS/FORTE 2009, LNCS 5522, pp. 219–224, 2009.

business protocol *Customer* shown in Fig. 2. Finally, wires are typed by connectors that coordinate the interactions between components and external services [2]. A service module is said to be correct if the composition of components, wires and external-services that it specifies entails the properties advertized by its provides-interface.

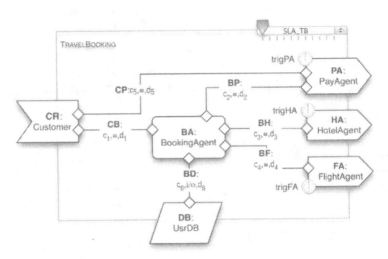

Fig. 1. The service module *TravelBooking*. *TravelBooking* uses the components *BA* and *DB* plus a set of wires to orchestrate three existing independent services — for booking a flight, booking a hotel and processing the payment.

Interactions, which have a conversational nature, consist of an asynchronous exchange of typed events between the parties that compose the service, where each type of event has a particular meaning from the business point of view (like requesting, replying, commiting, revoking, etc.). Service modules are interpreted over a particular type of Doubly Labelled Transition Systems (L^2TS) in which transitions are labelled by the publication, execution and discard of events [3] — UCTL logic is used to reason about such L^2TSs.

2   Specifying Service Interfaces with SRML

In SRML, the properties that are required from the external services that form the module, and also the properties that the module provides, are expressed through a business protocol in two ways: by declaring a set of typed interactions and by declaring a set of constraints that correlate the events of those interactions. The type that is associated with each interaction defines not only the set of events the service can engage in as part of that interaction, but also the conversational protocol that the service follows to engage in those events. The additional constraints that are specified in the business protocol – the behaviour – are used to impose further restrictions on that conversation or to correlate different interactions.

BUSINESS PROTOCOL Customer **is**

> **INTERACTIONS**
>> **r&s** login
>>> ⌂ usr:username, pwd:password
>> **r&s** bookTrip
>>> ⌂ from,to:airport,
>>> out,in:date
>>> ⊠ fconf:fcode,
>>> hconf:hcode,
>>> amount:moneyvalue
>> **snd** payNotify
>>> ⌂ status:boolean
>> **snd** refund
>>> ⌂ amount:moneyvalue
>
> **BEHAVIOUR**
>> **initiallyEnabled** login⌂?
>> login⊠! ∧ login⊠.Reply **enables** bookTrip⌂?
>> bookTrip✓? **ensures** payNotify⌂!
>> payNotify⌂! ∧ payNotify.status **enables** bookTrip⟰?
>> bookTrip⟰? **ensures** refund⌂!

Fig. 2. The business protocol *Customer*, which types the provides-interface *CR*

In order to specify behaviour constraints, SRML relies on a set of pre-defined patterns of behaviour that are encoded by abbreviations of UCTL formulas. The following table presents the abbreviations that encode three of the most commonly used patterns, which have been identified in a number of case studies:

initiallyEnabled e	$A\left(true_{\{\neg e_{\dot{c}}\}}W_{\{e?\}}true\right)$
a enables e	$\left(AG[a]\neg EF < e_{\dot{c}} > true\right) \wedge \left(A[true_{\{\neg e?\}}W_{\{a\}}true\right)$
a ensures e	$\left(AG[a]AF[e!]true\right) \wedge \left(A[true_{\{\neg e!\}}W_{\{a\}}true]\right)$

The abbreviation *"initiallyEnabled e"* states that the event *e* will never be discarded (until it is actually executed) — this abbreviation is typically used to define the first interaction to take place during a session with a service. For instance *Customer* (shown in Fig. 2), which specifies the provides-interface of *TravelBooking*, declares that the request-event *login* is ready to be executed as soon as a session is created. The abbreviation *"a enables e"* states that after *a* happens the event *e* will not be discarded and that before *a* it will never be executed. In *Customer* this pattern is used to declared that, after the login is accepted (but not before), the service will be ready to execute a request to book a trip. Finally the abbreviation *"a ensures e"* states that after *a* happens the event *e* will for certain be published, but not before. This abbreviation is used in *Customer* to declare that after a request to revoke a booking is executed (but not before), a refund will be sent.

In the interaction declaration of a business protocol, two-way interactions can be typed by *s&r* (send and receive) or *r&s* (receive and send) to define that the service being specified engages in the interaction as the requester or as the supplier, respectively. Each of these two roles, requester and supplier, has a set of properties associated with it. The following table presents the UCTL encoding of two of the properties associated with an interaction i of type $r\&s$.

A reply will be published after and only after the request-event was executed.	i♠? ensures i✉!
A revoke cannot be enabled before the execution of the commit-event.	$A[true_{\{\neg i\text{♉?}\}} W_{\{i\checkmark?\}} true]$

3 Encoding Service Composition with State Machines

In order to be able to model-check properties of service behaviour in the context of SRML in general, and the correctness of service modules in particular, we need to restrict ourselves to those modules in which state machines are used for modelling the components, the wires and the behaviour required from external services. This is because the UMC model-checker [7] takes as input a system of UML communicating state machines, with which it associates a L^2TS that represents the possible computations of that system — model-checking is then performed over this L^2TS using UCTL logic. Using UML state machines for defining workflows is quite standard. However, the case of wires and requires-interfaces is not as simple. In the case of wires, we need to ensure that the SRML computational model [3] is adhered to in what concerns event propagation and related phenomena and in the case of requires-interfaces, we need to be able to represent the patterns discussed in the previous section with state machines.

Encoding requires interfaces. A business protocol, which specifies the interface behaviour of a service, defines not one particular service, but a family of services that can be discovered, ranked and selected [6]. By associating a specific state machine with a requires-interface we are choosing a canonical model of the required behaviour.

As discussed in the previous section the specification of a requires-interface consists of a typed declaration of the interactions that the selected service should be ready to engage in and a set of behaviour constraints that correlate the events of those interactions. Our strategy for encoding a requires-interface as a state machine entails creating a concurrent region for each of the interactions that the external service is required to be involved in – the interaction-regions – and a concurrent region for all of the behaviour constraints – the constraint-regions – except for the constraints defined with the pattern "*initiallyEnabled e*": these are modelled by the instantiation of a state attribute.

The role of each of the interaction regions is to guarantee that the conversational protocol that is associated with the type of the interaction is respected. Events of a given interaction are published, executed and discarded exclusively by the interaction-region that models it. The role of the constraint-regions is to flag, through the use of special state attributes, when events become enabled and when events should be published – the evolution of the interaction-regions, and thus the actual execution, discard and publication of events, is guarded by the value of those flags. Constraint-regions cooperate with interaction-regions to guarantee the correlation of events expressed by the behaviour constraints.

Following this methodology, each interaction declaration and each behaviour constraint encodes part of the final state machine in a compositional way. Associated with each interaction type and each constraint pattern, there is a particular statechart structure that encodes it. A complete mapping from interactions types and behaviour patterns to their associated statechart structure can be found in [1]. Naturally, the encoding we propose for specifications of requires-interfaces is defined so that the transition system that is generated for a service module satisfies the UCTL formulas associated the requires-interfaces of that module.

Encoding wires. In SRML, the coordination of interactions, which are declared locally for each party of the module, is done by the wires. For each wire, there is a connector that defines an interaction protocol with two roles and binds the interactions declared in the roles with those of the parties at the two ends of the wire [2]. With our methodology for encoding wires with UML state machines, every connector defines a state machine for each interaction. This state machine is responsible for transmitting the events of that interaction from the sending party to the receiving co-party. Parties publish events by signalling them in the state machine that corresponds to the appropriate connector; this state machine in turn guarantees that these events are delivered by signalling them in the state machine that is associated with the co-party. The relation between parameter values that is specified by the interaction protocol of the connector is ensured operationally by the state machine that encodes that connector – data can be transformed before being forwarded. The statechart contains a single state and as many loops as the number of events that the connector has to forward.

4   Model-Checking Service Modules: The *TravelBooking* Example

In order to model-check that the composition specified by the module *Travel-Booking* provides the properties specified in *Customer*, we have encoded each of its external-required interfaces and each of its connectors using the methodology described in the previous section. Adding the two components that orchestrate the system, we ended up with a set of fifteen communicating UML state machines. Because every input source of a UMC model must also be modelled via an active object, we had to define a machine that initiates the interactions advertised in the provides-interface *Customer*, thus modelling a generic client of the service. Using this system as input to the UMC model-checker, we can verify if the doubly labelled transition system that is generated — we will refer to it as T — does satisfy the formulas associated with the provides-interface *Customer*, shown in Fig. 2. If T does not satisfy some of these formulas, than there is something in the module *TravelBooking* that needs to be corrected.

Having used UMC to model-check *TravelBooking*, we found out that all the constraints were satisfied by T except one: "*payNotify*! ∧ *payNotify.status en-*

ables bookTrip⇑?". This is because there is a path in T on which the event *book-Trip⇑* is discarded after the event *payNotify*▲ is published with a positive value for the *payNotify.status* parameter. This means that the publication of event *payNotify*▲ with a positive *payNotify.status* by the service does not guarantee that the revoke event of interaction *payNotify* becomes enabled for execution. If the composition was implemented as it is, it would be possible for a client to ask for a booking to be revoked and have this request ignored by the service.

After analysing the path of T that leads to the failure of the property, we understood that the problem is that, because *PA* interacts directly with the client through the wire *CP*, it is possible for the payment notification (represented by *payNotify*▲) to be received by the client before *BA* receives the confirmation for the payment (which is sent via another wire, *BP*). If the client tries to revoke the booking immediately, *BA* will not accept it because it does not yet know that the payment of the booking has been accepted by *PA*.

In order to fix this problem we have redesigned the architecture of the module *TravelBooking* by removing the wire *CP*. In the new architecture, *PA* does not interact directly with the client anymore. When the payment is executed by *PA*, the component *BA* is notified and is in turn responsible for notifying the client. Only then can the client choose to revoke the booking.

Acknowledgements

We would like to thank Antónia Lopes and Laura Bocchi for helping us stay on the right path (and states).

References

1. Abreu, J.: A Formal Framework for Modelling Service Component Architectures. Ph.D thesis (forthcoming)
2. Abreu, J., Bocchi, L., Fiadeiro, J.L., Lopes, A.: Specifying and Composing Interaction Protocols for Service-Oriented System Modelling. In: Derrick, J., Vain, J. (eds.) FORTE 2007. LNCS, vol. 4574, pp. 358–373. Springer, Heidelberg (2007)
3. Abreu, J., Fiadeiro, J.L.: A Coordination Model for Service-Oriented Interactions. In: Lea, D., Zavattaro, G. (eds.) COORDINATION 2008. LNCS, vol. 5052, pp. 1–16. Springer, Heidelberg (2008)
4. Beek, M.H.t., Fantechi, A., Gnesi, S., Mazzanti, F.: An action/state-based model-checking approach for the analysis of communication protocols for Service-Oriented Applications. In: Leue, S., Merino, P. (eds.) FMICS 2007. LNCS, vol. 4916, pp. 133–148. Springer, Heidelberg (2008)
5. Fiadeiro, J.L., Lopes, A., Bocchi, L.: A Formal Approach to Service Component Architecture. In: Bravetti, M., Núñez, M., Zavattaro, G. (eds.) WS-FM 2006. LNCS, vol. 4184, pp. 193–213. Springer, Heidelberg (2006)
6. Fiadeiro, J.L., Lopes, A., Bocchi, L.: An abstract model of service discovery and binding (2008) (submitted), www.cs.le.ac.uk/people/jfiadeiro
7. Mazzanti, F.: UMC User Guide v3.3. Technical Report 2006-TR-33, Istituto di Scienza e Tecnologie dell'Informazione A. Faedo, CNR, http://fmt.isti.cnr.it/WEBPAPER/UMC-UG33.pdf (2006)
8. SCA Consortium. Service component architecture specifications (2007)

Dynamic Symbolic Execution
of Distributed Concurrent Objects*

Andreas Griesmayer[1], Bernhard Aichernig[1,2],
Einar Broch Johnsen[3], and Rudolf Schlatte[1,2]

[1] International Institute for Software Technology, United Nations University
(UNU-IIST), Macao S.A.R., China
{agriesma,bka,rschlatte}@iist.unu.edu
[2] Institute for Software Technology, Graz University of Technology, Austria
{aichernig,rschlatte}@ist.tugraz.at
[3] Department of Informatics, University of Oslo, Norway
einarj@ifi.uio.no

Abstract. This paper extends dynamic symbolic execution to distributed and concurrent systems. Dynamic symbolic execution is used to systematically identify equivalence classes of input values and has been shown to scale well to large systems. Although mainly applied to sequential programs, this scalability makes it interesting to consider the technique in the distributed and concurrent setting as well. In order to extend the technique to concurrent systems, it is necessary to obtain sufficient control over the scheduling of concurrent activities to avoid race conditions. Creol, a modeling language for distributed concurrent objects, solves this problem by abstracting from a particular scheduling policy but explicitly defining scheduling points. This provides sufficient control to apply the technique of dynamic symbolic of interleaved processes. The technique has been formalized in rewriting logic and executes in Maude.

1 Introduction

Distributed and concurrent systems, e.g. web services, are becoming increasingly important for long-running infrastructure and applications. They typically consist of loosely coupled components which communicate asynchronously, potentially running on different hardware systems. For critical distributed systems, the use of formal methods, both for design and verification, remains a challenge. In the general case, the complexity of such systems makes full verification seem impossible, even for medium sized examples.

The challenge is to find a verification technique that scales to the combinatorial explosion in the number of possible runs in such models. A promising technique that seems to scale well to large systems is *dynamic symbolic execution* [1,4,9]. The idea is to calculate a symbolic execution in parallel with the

---

* This research was carried out as part of the EU FP6 project *Credo*: Modeling and analysis of evolutionary structures for distributed services (IST-33826).

concrete test run of a given formal model. The result is a set of conditions over symbolic input values representing the path of the last run.

The problem is that dynamic symbolic execution is of limited use with the concurrency models of today's programming languages. The reason is that dynamic symbolic execution does not work in settings where the execution of expressions is not atomic. Hence, its main application so far has been limited to single-threaded programs and to client-server applications with simple serialized communication flows. In this work we overcome this limitation by choosing a modeling language that provides the appropriate level of concurrency control: Creol [6], an executable object oriented modeling language whose execution model was designed to assist in the development of distributed systems.

We have implemented the dynamic symbolic execution technique in Maude [2], which is the execution platform of Creol, allowing us to perform the symbolic run dynamically while the concrete run is executed. The tool, and an application to testing, is covered in more detail in [5].

1.1 Related Work

Symbolic execution is a widely used program analysis technique that represents the values of variables as symbolic expressions instead of concrete data. An execution of a program is performed by manipulating those expressions instead of computing concrete values.

Application of symbolic execution to verification was already proposed in 1976 by King [7], who shows symbolic execution for a simple sequential language and presents an interactive tool EFFIGY to traverse the execution tree. However, there are limits to the feasibility of this technique, due to the sheer number of possible execution paths induced by non-determinism. To make the process feasible for large systems one can either reduce the amount of information that is tracked, or the number of paths to search. An example for the first kind are static analysis tools like ARCHER from Engler et al. [10], which concentrate on certain properties of interest for the analysis. In this paper, we reduce the number of paths that are searched at a time by *dynamic symbolic execution*. In [1], Boyer et al. show the interactive tool SELECT that computes input values for a run selected by the user. One of the first automated tools was DART from Godefroid et al. [4], which automatically extracts a program's interface and generates a test driver to perform random testing. Several extensions to these approaches exist, among the most notable the PEX tool from Tillmann et al. [9] for creating *parameterized unit tests* for single-threaded .NET programs. We extend dynamic symbolic execution to Creol's concurrency model, including the treatment of local scheduling points in the distributed objects.

2   The Modeling Language Creol

Creol is a high-level executable modeling language targeting distributed systems in which concurrent objects communicate asynchronously [6]. The language decouples communication from synchronization. Furthermore, it allows local scheduling to be left underspecified but controlled through explicitly declared process release points. The language has a formal semantics defined in rewriting logic [8] and executes on the Maude platform [2]. In the remainder of this section, we present Creol and point out its essential features for DSE.

A concurrent object in Creol executes a number of processes that have access to its local state. Each process corresponds to the activation of one of the object's methods; a special method run is automatically activated at object creation time, if present, and captures the object's active behavior. Objects execute concurrently: each object has a processor dedicated to executing the processes of that object, so processes in different objects execute in parallel. In contrast to, e.g., Java, each Creol object strictly encapsulates its state; i.e., external manipulation of the object state happens via calls to the object's methods only. Only one process can be active in an object at a time; the other processes in the object are *suspended*. A process can be *released* using Creol's **await** statement, in which case another proces may be activated.

Communication in Creol is based on method calls. These are a priori asynchronous; method replies are assigned to labels (also called *future variables*, see [3]). There is no synchronization associated with *calling* a method. *Reading a reply* from a label, however, is a blocking operation and allows the calling object to synchronize with the callee. A method call that is directly followed by a read operation models a synchronous call. Thus, the calling process may decide at runtime whether to call a method synchronously or asynchronously.

The language syntax of the subset of Creol used in this paper is presented in a Java-like style. We omit some features of Creol, including interfaces, inheritance, non-deterministic choice and many built-in data types and their operations. For a full overview of Creol, see for example [6].

2.1 Representation of a Run

A run of a Creol system captures the parallel execution of processes in different concurrent objects. Such a run may be perceived as a sequence of execution steps where each step contains a set of local transitions on a subset of the system's objects. However, only one process may be active at a time in each object and different objects operate on disjoint data. Therefore, the transitions in each execution step may be performed in a truly concurrent manner or in any sequential order, as long as all transitions in one step are completed before the next execution step commences. For the purposes of dynamic symbolic execution the run is represented as a sequence of statements which manipulate the state variables, together with the conditions which determine the control flow. Due to space restrictions, we concentrate on statements for the concurrency model, namely asymchronous method calls and await statements. The representation of the other statements is straight forward and can be studied in more detail in [5].

An asynchronous method call in the run is reflected in four execution steps (the label value l uniquely identifies the steps that belong to the same method call): $o_1 \xrightarrow{l} o_2.m(\bar{e})$ represents the *call* of method m in object o_2 from object

o_1 with arguments $\overline{e}$; $o_1 \xrightarrow{l} o_2.m(\overline{v})$ represents when the called objects starts execution, where $\overline{v}$ are the local names of the parameters for m; $o_1 \xleftarrow{l} o_2.m(\overline{e})$ represents the emission of the return values from the method execution; and $o_1 \xleftarrow{l} o_2.m(\overline{v})$ represents the corresponding reception of the values. These four events fully describe method calling in Creol. In this execution model the events reflecting a specific method call always appear in the same order, but they can be interleaved with other statements.

Conditional statements in Creol are side effect free and therefore only represented in form of the statements of the branch that was actually executed. For the sake of computing the input values, however, the condition of the taken branch is recorded as $\langle g \rangle$. Remark that statements **await** g requires careful treatment: if it evaluates to *false*, no code is executed. To reflect the information that the interpreter failed to execute a process because the condition g of the **await** statement evaluated to *false*, the negated condition $\langle \neg g \rangle$ is recorded.

3   Dynamic Symbolic Execution of Distributed Objects

Conventional symbolic execution uses symbols to represent arbitrary values during execution. When encountering a conditional branch statement, the run is forked. This results in a tree covering all paths in the program. In contrast, dynamic symbolic execution calculates the symbolic execution *in parallel* with a concrete run that is actually taken, avoiding the usual problem of eliminating infeasible paths. Decisions on branch statements are recorded, resulting in a set of conditions over the symbolic values that have to evaluate to *true* for the path to be taken. We call the conjunction of these conditions the *path condition*; it represents an equivalence class of concrete input values that could have taken the same path. Note, in the case of non-determinism, there is no guarantee that all inputs will take this path.

We extend this method to the concurrency model of Creol and define the rules to actually compute the symbolic values for a given run. The formulas given in this section very closely resemble the rewrite rules of Creol's simulation environment [6], defined in rewriting logic [8] and implemented in Maude [2]. The rules are presented here in a slightly simplified manner to improve readability.

Denote by $\overline{s}$ the representation of program statements. Let $\sigma = \langle v_1 \triangleright e_1, v_2 \triangleright e_2, \ldots v_n \triangleright e_n \rangle = \langle \overline{v} \triangleright \overline{e} \rangle$ be a map which records *key–value* entries $v \triangleright e$, where a variable v is bound to a symbolic value e. The value assigned to key v is accessed by $v\sigma$. For an expression e and a map σ, define a parallel substitution operator $e\sigma$ which replaces all occurrences of every variable v in e with the expression $v\sigma$ (if v is in the domain of σ). For simplicity, let $\overline{e}\sigma$ denote the application of the parallel substitution to every expression in the list $\overline{e}$. Furthermore, let the operator $\sigma_1 \uplus \sigma_2$ combine two maps σ_1 and σ_2 such that, when entries with the same key exist in both maps, the entry in σ_2 is taken. These operators are defined as equations in rewriting logic and are evaluated in between the rewrite steps. In the symbolic state σ, all expanded variable names are bound to symbolic expressions. However, operations for method calls do not change the value of the symbolic state, but generate or receive *messages* that are used to communicate actual parameter values between the calling and receiving objects. Similar to the expressions bound to variables in the symbolic state σ, the symbolic representations of these actual parameters are bound in a map Θ to the actual and unique label value l provided for each method call by Creol's operational semantics. Finally, the conditions of control statements along an execution path are collected in a list $\mathcal{C}$; the concatenation of a condition c to $\mathcal{C}$ is denoted by $\mathcal{C}\hat{}\,c$.

The *configurations* of the rewrite system for dynamic symbolic execution are given by $\bar{s}[\Theta, \sigma, \mathcal{C}]$, where $\bar{s}$ is a run represented as a sequence of statements, Θ and σ are the maps for messages and symbolic variable assignments as described above, and $\mathcal{C}$ is the list of conditions. The run $\bar{s}$ (as described in Section 2.1) is generated on the fly by the concrete rewrite system for Creol. Again, we concentrate on the statements for method calls and process release. A method `call` emits a message with the expressions for the method:

$$o_1 \xrightarrow{l} o_2.m(\bar{e}); \bar{s}[\Theta, \sigma, \mathcal{C}] \implies \bar{s}[\Theta \uplus \langle l \rhd \bar{e}\sigma \rangle, \sigma, \mathcal{C}]$$

Because of the asynchronous behavior of Creol, the call might be received at a later point in the run (or not at all if the execution terminates before the method was selected for execution) by another rule, that handles the binding of a call to a new process and assigns the symbolic representation of the actual parameter values to the local variables in the new process ($\sigma \uplus \langle \bar{v} \rhd l\Theta \rangle$). The emission and reception of return values are handled similarly to call statements and call reception.

For conditionals, the local variables in the condition are replaced by their symbolic values ($\langle g \rangle; \bar{s}[\Theta, \sigma, \mathcal{C}] \implies \bar{s}[\Theta, \sigma, \mathcal{C}\hat{}\,\langle g\sigma \rangle]$). This process is identical for the different kinds of conditional statements (**if**, **while**, **await**). The statement itself acts as a **skip** statement; it changes no variables and does not produce or consume messages. The resulting expression $g\sigma$ directly characterizes the equivalence class of input values that reach and fulfill the condition.

3.1   Application to Testing

Approaches to test case generation for structural coverage intend to find test sets that perform runs in the system for a specific coverage criterion. Two runs that cover the same parts of a system can be considered equivalent. A good test set should maximize the coverage, while minimizing the number of equivalent runs in order to avoid superfluous efforts in executing the tests.

Dynamic symbolic execution on a run gives the set of conditions that are combined to the path condition $\mathcal{C} = \bigwedge_{1 \leq i \leq n} c_i$ (for n conditions), characterizing exactly the equivalence class of t_S that can repeat the same execution path. Only one test case that fulfills $\mathcal{C}$ is required. A new test case is then chosen to specifically avoid that a particular branch is taken by violating the respective c_i. To maximize decision coverage (DC), for instance, test cases have to be created such that for each of the conditions c_i, there is also a test case that violates this condition. The process of generating new test cases ends after all combinations required for the coverage criteria are explored.

More details and examples on how to use DSE to generate test cases in distributed systems can be found in the technical report to this paper [5].

4   Conclusions

The main contribution of this work is the novel extension of dynamic symbolic execution to non-trivial distributed and concurrent object models. This has been achieved by exploiting the properties of the Creol modeling language; in particular local scheduling control of the processes and strict encapsulation of the object state. This paper demonstrates how dynamic symbolic execution, combined with the executable architectural models of Creol, can be used to systematically derive equivalent input values, while avoiding the combinatorial explosion inherent in distributed concurrent systems. Our approach has been formalized in rewriting logic and implemented in Maude.

References

1. Boyer, R.S., Elspas, B., Levitt, K.N.: Select-A formal system for testing and debugging programs by symbolic execution. SIGPLAN Not. 10(6), 234–245 (1975)
2. Clavel, M., Durán, F., Eker, S., Lincoln, P., Martí-Oliet, N., Meseguer, J., Quesada, J.F.: Maude: Specification and programming in rewriting logic. Theoretical Computer Science 285, 187–243 (2002)
3. de Boer, F.S., Clarke, D., Johnsen, E.B.: A complete guide to the future. In: de Nicola, R. (ed.) ESOP 2007. LNCS, vol. 4421, pp. 316–330. Springer, Heidelberg (2007)
4. Godefroid, P., Klarlund, N., Sen, K.: DART: directed automated random testing. In: PLDI 2005: Proceedings of the 2005 ACM SIGPLAN conference on Programming language design and implementation, pp. 213–223. ACM, New York (2005)
5. Griesmayer, A., Aichernig, B., Johnsen, E.B., Schlatte, R.: Dynamic symbolic execution of distributed concurrent objects. Technical Report No. 408, UNU-IIST (March 2009)
6. Johnsen, E.B., Owe, O.: An asynchronous communication model for distributed concurrent objects. Software and Systems Modeling 6(1), 35–58 (2007)
7. King, J.: Symbolic execution and program testing. Communications of the ACM 19(7), 385–394 (1976)
8. Meseguer, J.: Conditional rewriting logic as a unified model of concurrency. Theoretical Computer Science 96, 73–155 (1992)
9. Tillmann, N., de Halleux, J.: Pex - white box test generation for.NET. In: Beckert, B., Hähnle, R. (eds.) TAP 2008. LNCS, vol. 4966, pp. 134–153. Springer, Heidelberg (2008)
10. Xie, Y., Chou, A., Engler, D.: Archer: using symbolic, path-sensitive analysis to detect memory access errors. In: ESEC/FSE-11: Proceedings of the 9th European software engineering conference held jointly with 11th ACM SIGSOFT international symposium on Foundations of software engineering, pp. 327–336. ACM, New York (2003)

Checking the Conformance of Orchestrations with Respect to Choreographies in Web Services: A Formal Approach[*]

Gregorio Díaz[1] and Ismael Rodríguez[2]

[1] Universidad de Castilla-La Mancha
Gregorio.Diaz@uclm.es
[2] Universidad Complutense de Madrid
isrodrig@sip.ucm.es

Abstract. In this paper we present a formal model to represent orchestrations and choreographies, and we provide some semantic relations to detect their *conformance*, i.e., whether a set of orchestrations representing some web services leads to the overall communications described in a choreography.

1 Introduction

We present a formal framework to define *models* of asynchronous web services as well as to study them. Our main goal is allowing to define orchestrations and choreographies as well as to *compare* them. That is, given the orchestration of some web services and a choreography defining how these web services should interact, we provide a diagnostic method to decide whether the interaction of these web services necessarily leads to the required observable behavior, i.e. whether the orchestration *conforms to* the choreography. Models of orchestrations and choreographies are constructed by means of two different languages, and some formal semantic relations define how the terms defined in both languages are compared. Our modeling languages focus on accurately defining asynchronous communication aspects. In particular, languages explicitly consider service identifiers, specific senders/addressees, message buffers, etc.

There are few related works that deal with the asynchronous communication in contracts for web service context. In fact, we are only aware of three works from van der Alst et al. [7], Kohei Honda et al. [4] and, Bravetti and Zavattaro [2]. In particular, van der Alst et al. [7] present an approach for formalizing compliance and refinement notions, which are applied to service systems specified using open Workflow Nets (a type of Petri Nets) where the communication is asynchronous. The authors show how the contract refinement can be done independently, and they check whether contracts do not contain cycles. Kohei Honda et al. [4] present a generalization of binary session types to multiparty sessions for π-calculus.

---

[*] Research partially supported by projects TIN2006-15578-C02, PEII09-0232-7745, and CCG08-UCM/TIC-4124.

D. Lee et al. (Eds.): FMOODS/FORTE 2009, LNCS 5522, pp. 231–236, 2009.

They provide a new notion of types which can directly abstract the intended conversation structure among n-parties as *global scenarios*, retaining an intuitive type syntax. They also provide a consistency criteria for a conversation structure with respect to the protocol specification (contract), and a type discipline for individual processes by using a *projection*. Bravetti and Zavattaro [2] allow to compare systems of orchestrations and choreographies by means of the *testing* relation given by [1,3]. Systems are represented by using a process algebraic notation, and operational semantics for this language are defined in terms of labeled transitions systems. On the contrary, our framework uses an extension of *finite state machines* to define orchestrations and choreographies, and a semantic relation based on the *conformance* relation [5,6] is used to compare both models. In addition, let us note that [2] considers the suitability of a service for a given choreography *regardless* of the actual definition of the rest of services it will interact with, i.e. the service must be valid for the considered role *by its own*. This eases the task of finding a suitable service fitting into a choreography role: Since the rest of services do not have to be considered, we can search for suitable services for each role *in parallel*. However, let us note that sometimes this is not realistic. In some situations, the suitability of a service actually depends on the activities provided by the rest of services. For instance, let us consider that a *travel agency* service requires that either the *air company* service or the *hotel* service (or both) provide a transfer to take the client from the airport to the hotel. A hotel providing a transfer is *good* regardless of whether the air company provides a transfer as well or not. However, a hotel not providing a transfer is valid for the travel agency *only if* the air company does provide the transfer. This kind of subtle requirements and conditional dependencies is explicitly considered in our framework. Thus, contrarily to [2], our framework considers that the suitability of a service depends on what the rest of services actually do.

2   Formal Model

In this section we present our languages to define models of orchestrations and choreographies. Some preliminary notation is presented next.

Definition 1. Given a type A and $a_1, \ldots, a_n \in A$ with $n \geq 0$, we denote by $[a_1, \ldots, a_n]$ the *list of* elements $a_1, \ldots, a_n$ of A. We denote the empty list by $[\,]$.

Given two lists $\sigma = [a_1, \ldots, a_n]$ and $\sigma' = [b_1, \ldots, b_m]$ of elements of type A and some $a \in A$, we have $\sigma \cdot a = [a_1, \ldots, a_n, a]$ and $\sigma \cdot \sigma' = [a_1, \ldots, a_n, b_1, \ldots, b_m]$.

Given a set of lists L, a *path-closure* of L is any subset $V \subseteq L$ such that for all $\sigma \in V$ we have

- either $\sigma = [\,]$ or $\sigma = \sigma' \cdot a$ for some σ' with $\sigma' \in V$.
- there do not exist $\sigma', \sigma'' \in V$ such that $\sigma \cdot a = \sigma'$ and $\sigma \cdot b = \sigma''$ with $a \neq b$.

We say that a path-closure V of L is *complete* in L if it is *maximal* in L, that is, if there does not exist a path-closure $V' \subseteq L$ such that $V \subset V'$. The set of all complete path-closures of L is denoted by $\texttt{Complete}(L)$.   □

We present our model of web service *orchestration*. The internal behavior of a web service in terms of its interaction with other web services is represented by a *finite state machine* where, at each state s, the machine can receive an input i and produce an output o as response before moving to a new state s'. Moreover, each transition explicitly defines which service must send i: A sender identifier snd is attached to the transition denoting that, if i is sent by service snd, then the transition can be triggered. We assume that all web services are identified by a given identifier belonging to a set ID. Moreover, transitions also denote the *addressee* of the output o, which is denoted by an identifier adr. Let us note that web services receive messages asynchronously. This is represented in the model by considering an *input buffer* where all inputs received and not processed yet are cumulated.

Definition 2. Given a set of service identifiers ID, a *service* for ID is a tuple (id, S, I, O, s_{in}, T) where $id \in ID$ is the identifier of the service, S is the set of states, I is the set of inputs, O is the set of outputs, $s_{in} \in S$ is the initial state, and T is the set of transitions. Each transition $t \in T$ is a tuple (s, i, snd, o, adr, s') where $s, s' \in S$ are the initial and final states respectively, $i \in I$ is an input, $snd \in ID$ is the required sender of i, $o \in O$ is an output, and $adr \in ID$ is the addressee of o. A transition (s, i, snd, o, adr, s') is also denoted by $s \xrightarrow{(snd,i)/(adr,o)} s'$.

Given a service $M = (id, S, I, O, s_{in}, T)$, a *configuration* of M is a pair $c = (s, b)$ where $s \in S$ is a state of M and b is an *input buffer* for M. An input buffer for M is a list $[(id_1, i_1), \ldots, (id_k, i_k)]$ where $id_1, \ldots, id_k \in ID$ and $i_1, \ldots, i_k \in I$. The *initial configuration* of M is $(s_{in}, [\,])$. The set of all input buffers is denoted by $\mathcal{B}$.

Let $b = [(id_1, i_1), \ldots, (id_k, i_k)] \in \mathcal{B}$ with $k \geq 0$ be an input buffer. We define the following functions: $\texttt{exists}(b, id, i)$ holds iff $(id, i) \in \{(id_1, i_1), \ldots, (id_k, i_k)\}$; $\texttt{insert}(b, id, i) = b \cdot (id, i)$; $\texttt{remove}(b, id, i) = [(id_1, i_1), \ldots, (id_{j-1}, i_{j-1}), (id_{j+1}, i_{j+1}), \ldots, (id_k, i_k)]$ provided that $j \in \mathbb{N}$ is the minimum value such that $j \in [1..k]$, $id = id_j$, and $i = i_j$. $\qquad\qquad\square$

Once we have presented our model of web service orchestration, we provide a way to compose services into systems. In formal terms, a system is a tuple of services. The configuration of a system is given by the tuple of configurations of each service in the system.

Definition 3. Let $ID = \{id_1, \ldots, id_p\}$. In addition, for all $1 \leq j \leq p$, let $M_j = (id_j, S_j, I_j, O_j, s_{j,in}, T_j)$ be a service for ID. We say that $\mathcal{S} = (M_1, \ldots, M_p)$ is a *system of services* for ID.

For all $1 \leq j \leq p$, let c_j be a configuration of M_j. We say that $c = (c_1, \ldots, c_p)$ is a *configuration* of $\mathcal{S}$. Let $c'_1, \ldots, c'_p$ be the initial configurations of $M_1, \ldots, M_p$, respectively. We say that $(c'_1, \ldots, c'_p)$ is the *initial configuration* of $\mathcal{S}$. $\qquad\square$

Next we formally define how systems *evolve*, i.e. how a service of the system triggers a transition and how this affects other services in the system. In fact, the next definition presents the *operational semantics* of systems. In general, outputs of services will be considered as inputs of the services these outputs are sent to. Besides, we consider a special case of input/output that will be used to denote a *null* communication. In particular, if the input of a transition is *null* then we are denoting that the service can take this transition without waiting for any previous message from any other service, that is, we denote a *proactive* action of the service. Similarly, a *null* output denotes that no message is sent to other service after taking the corresponding transition. In both cases, the sender and the addressee of the transition are irrelevant, respectively, so in these cases they will also by denoted by a *null* symbol.

Definition 4. Let $ID = \{id_1, \ldots, id_p\}$ be a set of service identifiers and $S = (M_1, \ldots, M_p)$ be a *system of services* for ID where for all $1 \leq j \leq p$ we have that $M_j = (id_j, S_j, I_j, O_j, s_{j,in}, T_j)$. Let $c = (c_1, \ldots, c_p)$ be a configuration of S where for all $1 \leq j \leq p$ we have $c_j = (s_j, b_j)$.

An *evolution* of S from the configuration c is a tuple $(c, snd, i, proc, o, adr, c')$ where $i \in I_1 \cup \ldots \cup I_p$ is the input of the evolution, $o \in O_1 \cup \ldots \cup O_p$ is the output of the evolution, $c' = ((s'_1, b'_1), \ldots, (s'_p, b'_p))$ is the new configuration of S, and $snd, proc, adr \in ID$ are the sender, the processer, and the addressee of the evolution, respectively. All these elements must be defined according to one of the following choices:

(a) *(evolution activated by some service by itself)* For some $1 \leq j \leq p$, let us suppose $s_j \xrightarrow{(null,null)/(adr',o)} s' \in T_j$. Then, $s'_j = s'$ and $b'_j = b_j$. Besides, $snd = null$, $proc = id_j$, $adr = adr'$;

(b) *(evolution activated by processing a message from the input buffer of some service)* For some $1 \leq j \leq p$, let $s_j \xrightarrow{(snd',i)/(adr',o)} s' \in T_j$ and let us suppose $\texttt{exists}(b_j, snd', i)$ holds. Then, $s'_j = s'$ and $b'_j = \texttt{remove}(b_j, snd', i)$. Besides, $snd = snd'$, $proc = id_j$, and $adr = adr'$;

where, both in (a) and (b), the new configurations of the rest of services are defined according to one of the following choices:

(1) *(no message is sent to other service)* If $adr' = null$ or $o = null$ then for all $1 \leq q \leq k$ with $q \neq j$ we have $s'_q = s_q$ and $b'_q = b_q$.

(2) *(a message is sent to other service)* Otherwise, let $id_g = adr'$ for some $1 \leq g \leq k$. Then, we have $s'_g = s_g$ and $b'_g = \texttt{insert}(b_g, id_j, o)$. Besides, for all $1 \leq q \leq k$ with $q \neq j$ and $q \neq g$ we have $s'_q = s_q$ and $b'_q = b_q$. $\qquad\square$

We distinguish two kinds of traces. A *sending trace* is a sequence of outputs ordered as they are *sent* by their corresponding senders. A *processing trace* is a sequence of inputs ordered as they are *processed* by the services which receive them, that is, they are ordered as they are taken from the input buffer of each addressee service to trigger some of its transitions. Both traces attach some information to explicitly denote the services involved in each operation.

Definition 5. Let S be a system and let c_1 be the initial configuration of S. In addition, let $(c_1, snd_1, i_1, proc_1, o_1, adr_1, c_2)$, $(c_2, snd_2, i_2, proc_2, o_2, adr_2, c_3), \ldots,$ $(c_k, snd_k, i_k, proc_k, o_k, adr_k, c_{k+1})$ be k consecutive evolutions of S.

Let $a_1 \leq \ldots \leq a_r$ denote all indexes of non-null outputs in the previous sequence, i.e. we have $j \in \{a_1, \ldots, a_r\}$ iff $o_j \neq null$. Then, $[(proc_{a_1}, o_{a_1}, adr_{a_1}), \ldots,$

$(proc_{a_r}, o_{a_r}, adr_{a_r})]$ is a *sending trace* of S. In addition, if there do not exist $snd', i', proc', o', adr', c'$ such that $(c_{k+1}, snd', i', proc', o', adr', c')$ is an evolution of S then we also say that $[(proc_{a_1}, o_{a_1}, adr_{a_1}), \ldots, (proc_{a_r}, o_{a_r}, adr_{a_r}), \texttt{stop}]$ is a sending trace of S. The set of sending traces of S is denoted by $\texttt{sendTraces}(S)$.

Let $a_1 \leq \ldots \leq a_r$ denote all indexes of non-null inputs in the previous sequence, i.e. we have $j \in \{a_1, \ldots, a_r\}$ iff $i_j \neq null$. Then, $[(snd_{a_1}, i_{a_1}, proc_{a_1}), \ldots, (snd_{a_r}, i_{a_r}, proc_{a_r})]$ is a *processing trace* of S. In addition, if there do not exist $snd', i', proc', o', adr', c'$ such that $(c_{k+1}, snd', i', proc', o', adr', c')$ is an evolution of S then we also say that $[(snd_{a_1}, i_{a_1}, proc_{a_1}), \ldots, (snd_{a_r}, i_{a_r}, proc_{a_r}), \texttt{stop}]$ is a processing trace of S. The set of all processing traces of S is denoted by $\texttt{processTraces}(S)$.   □

Next we introduce our formalism to represent choreographies. Contrarily to systems of orchestrations, this formalism focuses on representing the interaction of services as a whole. Thus a single machine, instead of the composition of several machines, is considered.

Definition 6. A *choreography machine* C is a tuple $C = (S, M, ID, s_{in}, T)$ where S denotes the set of states, M is the set of messages, ID is the set of service identifiers, $s_{in} \in S$ is the initial state, and T is the set of transitions. A transition $t \in T$ is a tuple (s, m, snd, adr, s') where $s, s' \in S$ are the initial and final states, respectively, $m \in M$ is the message, and $snd, adr \in ID$ are the sender and the addressee of the message, respectively. A transition (s, m, snd, adr, s') is also denoted by $s \xrightarrow{m/(snd \to adr)} s'$. A *configuration* of C is any state $s \in S$.   □

The next definition presents the operational semantics of choreography machines. Contrarily to systems of services, *null* inputs/outputs are not available, i.e, all communications are effective. Evolutions are activated simply by taking any transition from the current state.

Definition 7. Let $C = (S, M, ID, s_{in}, T)$ be a choreography machine and $s \in S$ be a configuration of C.

An *evolution* of C from s is any transition $(s, m, snd, adr, s') \in T$ from state s. The *initial configuration* of C is s_{in}.   □

As we did before for systems of services, next we identify the sequences of messages that can be produced by a choreography machine.

Definition 8. Let c_1 be the initial configuration of a choreography machine C. Let $(c_1, m_1, snd_1, adr_1, c_2), \ldots, (c_k, m_k, snd_k, adr_k, c_{k+1})$ be $k \geq 0$ consecutive evolutions of C. We say that $\sigma = [(snd_1, m_1, adr_1), \ldots, (snd_k, m_k, adr_k)]$ is a *trace* of C. In addition, if there do not exist m', snd', adr', c' such that $(c_{k+1}, m', snd', adr', c')$ is an evolution of C then we also say that $[(snd_1, m_1, adr_1), \ldots, (snd_k, m_k, adr_k), \texttt{stop}]$ is a trace of C. The set of all traces of C is denoted by $\texttt{traces}(C)$.   □

Now we are provided with all the required formal machinery to define our *conformance relations* between systems of orchestrations and choreographies.

Definition 9. Let S be a system of services and C be a chorography machine.

We say that S *conforms to* C *with respect to sending actions*, denoted by $S \ \mathtt{conf}_s \ C$, if either $\emptyset \subset \mathtt{Complete}(\mathtt{sendTraces}(S)) \subseteq \mathtt{Complete}(\mathtt{traces}(C))$ or we have $\emptyset = \mathtt{Complete}(\mathtt{sendTraces}(S)) = \mathtt{Complete}(\mathtt{traces}(C))$.

We say that S *fully conforms to* C *with respect to sending actions*, denoted by $S \ \mathtt{conf}_s^f \ C$, if $\mathtt{Complete}(\mathtt{sendTraces}(S)) = \mathtt{Complete}(\mathtt{traces}(C))$.

We say that S *conforms to* C *with respect to processing actions*, denoted by $S \ \mathtt{conf}_p \ C$, if $\emptyset \subset \mathtt{Complete}(\mathtt{processTraces}(S)) \subseteq \mathtt{Complete}(\mathtt{traces}(C))$ or $\emptyset = \mathtt{Complete}(\mathtt{processTraces}(S)) = \mathtt{Complete}(\mathtt{traces}(C))$.

We say that S *fully conforms to* C *with respect to sending actions*, denoted by $S \ \mathtt{conf}_p^f \ C$, if $\mathtt{Complete}(\mathtt{processTraces}(S)) = \mathtt{Complete}(\mathtt{traces}(C))$.

We say that S *conforms to* C, denoted by $S \ \mathtt{conf} \ C$, if $S \ \mathtt{conf}_s \ C$ and $S \ \mathtt{conf}_p \ C$.

We say that S *fully conforms to* C ($S \ \mathtt{conf}^f \ C$) if $S \ \mathtt{conf}_s^f \ C$ and $S \ \mathtt{conf}_p^f \ C$. $\square$

3 Conclusions and Future Work

In this paper we have presented a formal framework for defining models of orchestrations and choreographies. We have defined some formal semantic relations allowing to detect whether the behavior described by the orchestration of each involved web service correctly leads to the behavior described by a choreography. The suitability of a service for a given choreography may depend on the activities of the rest of services it will be connected with, which contrasts with previous works [2]. In order to take into account the effect of asynchrony, we have separately considered the moments where messages are sent and the moments where they are actually processed.

References

1. Boreale, M., Nicola, R.D., Pugliese, R.: Trace and testing equivalence on asynchronous processes. Inf. Comput. 172(2), 139–164 (2002)
2. Bravetti, M., Zavattaro, G.: Contract compliance and choreography conformance in the presence of message queues. In: Bruni, R., Wolf, K. (eds.) WS-FM 2008. LNCS, vol. 5387. Springer, Heidelberg (2009)
3. Castellani, I., Hennessy, M.: Testing theories for asynchronous languages. In: Arvind, V., Ramanujam, R. (eds.) FSTTCS 1998. LNCS, vol. 1530, pp. 90–102. Springer, Heidelberg (1998)
4. Honda, K., Yoshida, N., Carbone, M.: Multiparty asynchronous session types. In: POPL, pp. 273–284 (2008)
5. Tretmans, J.: Conformance testing with labelled transition systems: Implementation relations and test generation. Computer Networks and ISDN Systems 29, 49–79 (1996)
6. Tretmans, J.: Testing concurrent systems: A formal approach. In: Baeten, J.C.M., Mauw, S. (eds.) CONCUR 1999. LNCS, vol. 1664, pp. 46–65. Springer, Heidelberg (1999)
7. van der Aalst, W.M.P., Lohmann, N., Massuthe, P., Stahl, C., Wolf, K.: From public views to private views - correctness-by-design for services. In: Dumas, M., Heckel, R. (eds.) WS-FM 2007. LNCS, vol. 4937, pp. 139–153. Springer, Heidelberg (2008)

A Type Graph Model for Java Programs[*]

Arend Rensink and Eduardo Zambon

Formal Methods and Tools Group, EWI-INF, University of Twente
P.O. Box 217, 7500 AE, Enschede, The Netherlands
{rensink,zambon}@cs.utwente.nl

Abstract. In this work we present a type graph that models all executable constructs of the Java programming language. Such a model is
useful for any graph-based technique that relies on a representation of
Java programs as graphs. The model can be regarded as a common representation to which all Java syntax graphs must adhere. We also present
the systematic approach that is being taken to generate syntax graphs
from Java code. Since the type graph model is comprehensive, i.e., covers
the whole language specification, the technique is guaranteed to generate a corresponding graph for any valid Java program. In particular, we
want to extract such syntax graphs in order to perform static analysis and model checking of programs written in Java. Although we focus
on Java, this same approach could be adapted for other programming
languages.

1 Introduction

A graph is a flexible structure that is used to represent several different artifacts
in computer science. However, the mathematical definition of a graph alone does
not allow us to restrict a representation to a certain pattern or form. Such
restrictions can be enforced by means of a *type graph*, a model that describes
constraints over the sets of nodes and edges of a graph.

A program written in a certain language can be transformed into a syntax
tree by a parser. When additional information such as bindings are included in
the representation, the syntax tree is extended into a *syntax graph*. One main
contribution of our work is to define a type graph model for syntax graphs that
represent programs written in Java. The type graph model is complete, i.e., it
covers the entire language specification up to version 1.6 [10]. We believe that
this model can be of interest to any graph-based technique that relies on a
representation of Java programs as graphs. As one example, suppose a visual
programming/modeling tool that generates Java code from a graph; this could
for instance, be used in the context of graph transformation-based model transformation [1] or code refactoring [3]. By enforcing the graph to be an instance
of this type graph model, the tool can generate syntactically correct code.

---

[*] The research reported herein was carried out as part of the GRAIL project, funded
by NWO (Grant 612.000.632).

D. Lee et al. (Eds.): FMOODS/FORTE 2009, LNCS 5522, pp. 237–242, 2009.

In our current research we aim to perform static analysis [7] and model checking [2] of Java programs using GROOVE [8], a tool for state space exploration where states are represented as graphs, and the transitions from one state to another are given by graph transformation rules. A syntax graph is the static representation of a program as a graph, and it is the required initial structure for the subsequent elaboration of the states that constitute the dynamic behavior of the program. Thus, the work here presented is the first, necessary step in our planned method for the verification of code.

In this document we focus on the approach taken for the construction of the type graph model. Due to space limitations, it is not possible to actually present the model, and we refer the interested reader to the accompanying technical report [9], where all the details are given.

2 Description of Approach Taken

The task of constructing syntax graphs from given source code consists of two major steps, (i) the building of a type graph model to represent the syntactical elements of the chosen programming language, and (ii) the development of a tool that constructs a valid syntax graph from syntactically correct code. A syntax graph is considered to be valid when it is an instance of the type graph model developed in step (i). Essentially, the work to be done in (ii) boils down to writing a compiler that produces a syntax graph as its target language, instead of machine code.

We decided to adapt an open-source Java compiler for our purposes. In doing so, the implementation effort is kept to a minimum, since we have only to modify the code generation phase of the compiler to construct the syntax graphs. Also, by analysing the source code of the compiler we are able to elaborate the type graph model in a very straightforward way. Thus, with this solution, the definition of the type graph and the construction of the syntax graph generator go hand in hand, and we have the guarantee that a syntax graph generated from code is compliant with the type graph model.

2.1 Creating the Type Graph

In order to develop our chosen approach we decided to use the Eclipse Java Compiler [4]. This compiler is also written in Java, and its source code is available for use under the Eclipse Public License. The compiler source is divided in several packages, among which the package `org.eclipse.jdt.internal.compiler.ast`[1] is of particular interest, since it is where the classes that compose the Abstract Syntax Tree (AST) built by the compiler are grouped. By analysing the package contents we are able to construct the type graph model, which is presented in [9].

---

[1] Through the rest of the paper we adhere to the following convention: elements of Java code are shown in `typewriter` font, while elements of the type graph or instance graphs are shown in sans serif font.

```
class IfStmt extends Stmt {
  // fields
  Expr condition;
  Stmt thenStmt;
  Stmt elseStmt;
  ...
  // AST traversal method
  void traverse(ASTVisitor v){
    condition.traverse(v);
    thenStmt.traverse(v);
    if (elseStmt != null)
      elseStmt.traverse(v);
    ...
  }
  ...
}
```

Fig. 1. Example of the type graph elaboration from the compiler source code

The **ast** package contains, for example, classes like **Expr** and **Stmt** to represent expressions and statements of the Java language. In fact, every syntactical element of the language has a corresponding class in the **ast** package and those classes are grouped in a certain hierarchy. The top most class is **ASTNode**, which defines a common super type for all elements of the AST. The **ast** package also provides an AST visitor pattern interface [5], which has methods to navigate over the nodes of the AST in a depth-first-like manner.

The way the type graph is elaborated from the elements of the **ast** package can be best explained with an example. Figure 1 shows the relevant code of the class that represents an "if" statement and the corresponding part of the type graph constructed from this code. We start with the class name, **IfStmt**, that gives rise to an homonymous node type in the type graph. Also, since **IfStmt** is a subclass of **Stmt** we create another node type for the super class and we insert an inheritance relation in the type graph, between the corresponding node types. The class fields that are references to other classes of the AST become compositions (in some cases, ordered ones) in the type graph, with labels matching the field names. In this example, the fields named **condition**, **thenStmt**, and **elseStmt** give rise to three compositions in the type graph, with corresponding labels. Additionally, the way the visitor pattern is implemented in the class provides some guidance over the cardinalities of the compositions just created. From the implementation of the **traverse** method we see that fields **condition** and **thenStmt** are always visited. Therefore we can conclude that the IfStmt node type must have mandatory condition and thenStmt compositions, a fact that is illustrated by the cardinality 1 of those compositions in the type graph.

On the other hand, the check for non-nullness of the `elseStmt` field indicates that it may not always exists. Therefore we mark the cardinality of its composition in the type graph as 0..1.

By analysing the classes of interest of the `ast` package in the same way as described in the example above we can construct a large part of the type graph model. However, there are some elements of the type graph that still need to be manually created. As an example we can cite the associations that resolve name and type references, which correspond to the binding edges on syntax graphs. The intuition for identifying where these associations must be created is simple: any reference should have an association with a corresponding declaration. However, the information needed to create these associations is not present in the compiler source code in a uniform way, and therefore manual intervention is necessary. The rationale behind our decisions over what does or does not have to be manually inserted into the type graph comes from our intended purpose for the syntax graphs. Thus, we insert only the elements that we deem necessary for static analysis and simulation.

The resulting type graph obtained from the analysis described in this section is formed by 75 node types, mapped directly from the compiler classes. The complete type graph is presented and explained in our technical report [9].

2.2   Constructing Syntax Graphs from Code

To construct syntax graphs from Java code we must change the back end of the Eclipse Java Compiler. By stopping the compiler after parsing and code analysis but before machine code generation we are able to profit from the work done by the compiler until this stage. Specifically, name and type references are already resolved, simplifying the construction of the syntax graph. We developed a syntax graph generator that implements the AST visitor interface provided by the compiler and we plugged it in the compiler back end. To build the syntax graph, our generator visits the AST, performing the following steps.

- For each node in the AST the generator creates a corresponding node in the syntax graph. The types of a syntax graph node are obtained through reflection. By using reflection in Java, one is able to query the virtual machine for run-time information of objects. In our case we obtain the class hierarchy of an AST node via reflection and store this information as a label of the syntax graph node.
- For the construction of edges in the syntax graph we keep an auxiliary mapping of AST nodes into syntax graph nodes. This mapping, along with the bindings produced by the compiler, is sufficient for creating the edges, including the ones that resolve references.

For each node type of the type graph we created a test case input program. With these test cases we can inspect the syntax graphs produced by our tool and check for implementation errors. An example of such test case is given in Fig. 2, along with the syntax graph generated. The complete set of input test cases can be found in the corresponding technical report [9]. The syntax graph

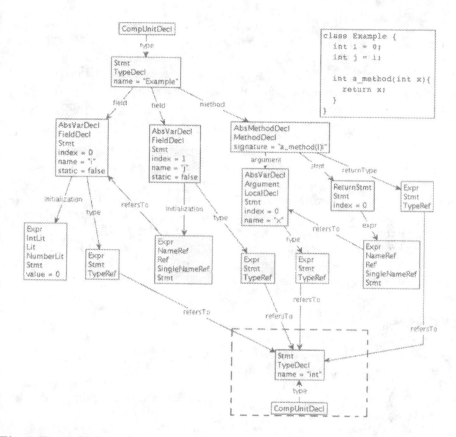

Fig. 2. Example of a syntax graph built from code. The dashed box represents a system wide compilation unit where primitive types of the language are declared.

in Fig. 2 has a node labeled TypeDecl, which represents a class. The name of the declared class is stored as an attribute of the node, which also has three outgoing edges that correspond to the field and **method** compositions. It is important to note that name and type reference nodes have an outgoing edge that binds the reference to its corresponding declaration. We consider the existence of a "system" compilation unit, where the primitive types of the language, and also the classes of `java.lang.*`, are declared. Part of this "system" compilation unit is shown in the bottom of Fig. 2 (within the dashed box), with the declaration of the primitive type `int`.

3   Conclusion and Future Work

To sum up, the contributions of our work are threefold.

- We have created a comprehensive type graph that covers all executable elements of the Java programming language. Such type graph can be of interest as a model for tools that represent Java programs as graphs.

- We have shown a straightforward and systematic approach for the construction of the type graph model by analysing a compiler source code. Although our described method focused on Java, we believe that it can be adapted (with varying degrees of difficulty) to other programming languages as well.
- We explained how the back end of a compiler can be adapted in order to automatically construct a syntax graph representation from source code.

The work described in this paper is the first step in our planned approach for the verification of Java programs. Now that we are able to generate syntax graphs from code the next step is the construction of *flow graphs*, structures that model the sequential execution relation between elements of the syntax graph. We plan to define graph transformations rules over syntax graphs for flow graph construction, as described in [6]. Together, a syntax graph and a flow graph form a *program graph*. The subsequent step is then use the GROOVE tool to simulate the execution of program graphs. Another important aspect of this step is that we want to apply abstract interpretation techniques to simplify the program graphs and thus improve the performance of the simulation.

References

1. Alanen, M., Lundkvist, T., Porres, I.: Creating and reconciling diagrams after executing model transformations. Sci. Comput. Program. 68(3), 155–178 (2007)
2. Baier, C., Katoen, J.P.: Principles of Model Checking. MIT Press, New York (2008)
3. Baumer, D., Gamma, E., Kiezun, A.: Integrating refactoring support into a Java development tool. In: OOPSLA 2001 Companion (2001)
4. Eclipse Foundation: JDT core component development resources, http://www.eclipse.org/jdt/core/dev.php
5. Gamma, E., Helm, R., Johnson, R., Vlissides, J.: Design Patterns: Elements of Reusable Object-Oriented Software. Addison-Wesley Professional Computing Series. Addison-Wesley Publishing Company, New York (1995)
6. Kastenberg, H., Kleppe, A., Rensink, A.: Defining object-oriented execution semantics using graph transformations. In: Gorrieri, R., Wehrheim, H. (eds.) FMOODS 2006. LNCS, vol. 4037, pp. 186–201. Springer, Heidelberg (2006)
7. Nielson, F., Nielson, H.R., Hankin, C.: Principles of Program Analysis. Springer, New York (1999)
8. Rensink, A.: The GROOVE simulator: A tool for state space generation. In: Pfaltz, J.L., Nagl, M., Böhlen, B. (eds.) AGTIVE 2003. LNCS, vol. 3062, pp. 479–485. Springer, Heidelberg (2004)
9. Rensink, A., Zambon, E.: A type graph model for Java programs. Technical Report TR-CTIT-09-01, University of Twente, Enschede (February 2009)
10. Sun Microsystems: The Java language specification, http://java.sun.com/docs/books/jls/

Conformance Testing of Network Simulators Based on Metamorphic Testing Technique

Tsong Yueh Chen, Fei-Ching Kuo, Huai Liu*, and Shengqiong Wang

Centre for Software Analysis and Testing, Swinburne University of Technology
{tychen,dkuo,hliu,shengqiongwang}@swin.edu.au

Abstract. Network simulators, which implement network protocols under some simulated conditions, have been widely used to analyze the feasibility of network protocols. Conformance testing of the simulator against the protocol is a very important task in the community of telecommunications. However, many current conformance testing methods face a problem of finding a systematic mechanism to verify the test outputs. This paper proposes to use an innovative testing approach, metamorphic testing (MT), to alleviate such a problem. We select one ad-hoc on-demand distance vector (AODV) simulator for study and test its conformance against the AODV protocol by the MT technique. Through our experiments, we illustrate the applicability of MT in the protocol conformance testing, confirm the reliability of the selected AODV simulator, and demonstrate the cost-effectiveness of MT using the mutation analysis technique.

1 Introduction

A network protocol specifies a set of mechanisms for exchanging messages among communication entities in a network system. A protocol must be feasible and its implementation must also conform to the protocol in order to deliver expected services in the network system [2]. Simulation is an important method for analyzing the feasibility of a protocol [7]. The network simulator, a protocol implementation under simulated network environments, is particularly useful to identify potential problems of the implemented protocol. It is important to ensure conformance between the simulator and the protocol.

Protocol conformance testing tests a protocol entity against the protocol specification. It aims to gain confidence in the correctness of the implementation with respect to a given specification [7]. International Organization for Standardization (ISO) has defined a framework and common terminologies for conformance testing of Open Systems Interconnection (OSI) systems [6]. Many approaches have been proposed to conduct conformance testing under various circumstances, such as unique input/output sequences generation method [7] and model-based approaches [13].

Many current conformance testing methods only work well when the network protocol can be modeled as a fully specified finite state machine (FSM). For such

---

* Corresponding author.

D. Lee et al. (Eds.): FMOODS/FORTE 2009, LNCS 5522, pp. 243–248, 2009.

protocols, we can always expect the correct output given any testing input [7]. For many other network protocols, which are not completely modeled by FSM, it is normally difficult to find a systematic verification mechanism for test results [8]. Such a verification mechanism is normally called the testing oracle [4] in the context of software testing. If there does not exist an testing oracle (known as the oracle problem in software testing), it is then very difficult to verify the correctness of the simulator's output.

Metamorphic testing (MT) [4] is an innovative testing method to alleviate the oracle problem. MT first identifies some properties from the specification of the software under test. These properties, which are known as metamorphic relations (MRs), are then used to generate some test cases. MT verifies the outputs of test cases based on MRs. Besides the alternative verification mechanism, MT has many other advantages. For example, it can be effectively applied by end users without too much knowledge of software testing. MT can also automatically generate a large number of test cases at a low cost, and MT test outputs can be verified by some simple script. MT have been successfully applied to detecting bugs in various programs [3,9].

MT is basically a general technique used in the testing of software with any form of specification. In other words, no matter whether the software specification can be modeled by FSM or not, MT can always provide a mechanism to verify the test results. MT can identify some key properties from the specification, and generate test cases based on these properties. When a network protocol specification or a network simulator is updated, regression testing [12,15] is always conducted to re-run the testing to ensure the correctness of the updates. Provided that the key properties identified by MT remain unchanged during the updates, all associated MT test cases can be re-used in the regression testing. In the paper, we attempt to apply MT into the conformance testing of a network simulator against its network protocol. A case study is conducted on an ad-hoc on-demand distance vector (AODV) simulator to illustrate the applicability and effectiveness of MT in conformance testing.

2   AODV Protocol and Its Simulator

Ad-hoc on-demand distance vector (AODV) routing protocol [14] is a reactive protocol, that is, it establishes a route from a source node to a destination node only "on demand". AODV avoids the counting-to-infinity problem by using "sequence numbers" mechanism on route updates. It also uses a so-called "blacklist" mechanism to avoid invalid connection attempt. Concer [5] has developed an AODV simulator based on OMNeT++ [11], a discrete event simulation environment. One of us has worked on this simulator and has extensive domain knowledge of it, so we selected this specific simulator as the target program of our case study. The simulator depicts the AODV protocol with a number of nodes in a simulated field without obstacles. Each node in the field is comprised of five layers, namely, the application, network, date link, physical, and mobility layers. Inside a node, a higher layer (such as the application layer) consumes certain services offered by the lower layer (such as the network layer), but all layers is designed to be invisible to the implementation details of other layers.

Network simulators usually return some outputs relating to network protocol attributes, which are generally presented as the forms of network performance, such as, latency and throughput. Latency in a packet switched network is measured by the time from the source node sending a packet to the destination node receiving it, and throughput is the amount of digital data per time unit that pass through a certain node in the network. However, it is difficult to verify the correctness of these outputs, because the values of these outputs depend on various simulation environments, such as CPU and memory.

3 Metamorphic Testing

Most software testing techniques (such as random testing and branch testing [10]) assume that the oracle exists. However, the oracle may not exist in some practical situations. For example, given a program for finding the shortest path in an undirected graph, when the graph is nontrivial, there is no oracle to effectively verify whether the returned outcome is really the shortest path between two nodes.

Metamorphic testing (MT) was proposed to test programs when oracle problem occurs [4]. MT requires domain knowledge to identify some important properties from the specification. These properties are called metamorphic relations (MRs). Some traditional testing techniques are first used to generate some *source test cases*. MRs are then applied to construct some *follow-up test cases* from source test cases. Both source and follow-up test cases are executed on the program under test. The test results are checked against MRs. If a relation is violated, a fault is said to be detected. For example, in the shortest path program, there is a permutation property: the program can produce the same outcome for a graph and the graph's permutation. Let a graph G be the source test case. We can generate G′, a permutation of G, as the follow-up test case. The MR is that the program should produce the same output for G and G′.

4 Metamorphic Testing on AODV Simulator

As mentioned in Section 2, it is very difficult to verify the correctness of the test outputs of the AODV simulator. In this study, we attempt to use MT to test the conformance between the simulator and the AODV protocol. Our testing is mainly focused on two main outputs, latency and throughput, and two key mechanisms, the "sequence numbers" and "black-list" mechanisms. In the case study, in order to simplify the testing environment, we have modified the source codes in the application and mobility layers of the AODV simulator. Since the AODV protocol is implemented in the network layer, the modifications will not affect the conformance testing. The simplified testing environment we use in this study is a simulated network which contains a fixed number of nodes. Our testing is conducted mainly on a pair of randomly selected nodes (denoted by A and

B), which are randomly moving inside the network. We identify the following 11 MRs. Among them, MRs 1 to 7 have an additional prerequisite that there is always a connection between A and B; while MRs 1 to 5 and 8 to 10 further requires that the network's topology remains unchanged.

MR1: The source test case is that A sends a data packet P to B. The resultant latency and throughput are l_1 and r_1, respectively. The follow-up test case is that the locations of A and B are changed, and then A sends the same packet P to B. The resultant latency and throughput are l_2 and r_2, respectively. We should have the relations $l_2 \approx l_1$ and $r_2 \approx r_1$.

MR2: The source test case is that A sends a data packet P to B. The resultant latency and throughput are l_1 and r_1, respectively. The follow-up test case is that B sends the same data packet P to A. The resultant latency and throughput are l_2 and r_2, respectively. We should have the relations $l_2 \approx l_1$ and $r_2 \approx r_1$.

MR3: The source test case is that A sends a data packet P to B with channel delay c_1. The resultant latency is l_1. The follow-up test case is that A sends the same data packet P to B with a different channel delay c_2. The resultant latency is l_2. We should have the relation $\frac{l_1}{c_1} \approx \frac{l_2}{c_2}$.

MR4: The source test case is that A sends a data packet P_1 with packet size s_1 to B. The resultant throughput is r_1. The follow-up test case is that A sends a different data packet P_2 with packet size s_2 to B. The resultant throughput is r_2. We should have the relation $\frac{r_1}{s_1} \approx \frac{r_2}{s_2}$.

MR5: The source test case is that the routing table of A contains the route p_1 to B. The follow-up test case is that all route entries in A's routing table are deleted, and then A requests to identify a new route p_2 to B. We should have the relation $p_1 = p_2$.

MR6: The source test case is that A sends a data packet P to B via a route with h_1 hops. The resultant latency is l_1. The follow-up test case is that the route from A to B is changed to a new one with h_2 hops, and then A sends the same data packet P to B. The resultant latency is l_2. We should have the relation that if $h_1 > h_2$, then $l_1 > l_2$.

MR7: The source test case is that A sends a data packet P to B via a route with h_1 hops. The resultant sequence number is q_1. The follow-up test case is that the route from A to B is changed to a new one with h_2 hops, and then A sends the same data packet P to B. The resultant sequence number is q_2. We should have the relation that if $h_1 > h_2$, then $q_1 > q_2$.

MR8: The source test case is that A requests to transmit a data packet P to B (first transmission). The follow-up test case is that after a while, A requests to transmit the same packet P to B again (second transmission). We should have the relation (1) if the first transmission is successful, the second transmission should also be successful, or (2) if A only broadcasts a Route Request (RREQ) packet for searching a route to B but does not forward the packet at the first transmission, A should buffer the data packet at the second transmission.

MR9: The source test case is that A requests to transmit a data packet P to B (first transmission). The follow-up test case is that A's neighbor node C requests to transmit the same packet P to B (second transmission). We should have the relation (1) if the first transmission is successful, A should reply to C a Route Reply (RREP) packet at the second transmission, or (2) if A only broadcasts RREQ for searching a route to B but does not forward P at the first transmission, it should broadcast RREQ again for searching a route to B at the second transmission.

MR10: The source test case is that A's neighbor node C requests to transmit a data packet P to B (first transmission). The follow-up test case is that A requests to transmit the same packet P to B (second transmission). We should have the relation (1) if A replies to C an RREP packet at the first transmission, the second transmission should be successful, or (2) if A only broadcasts RREQ for searching a route to B and C does not forward the packet at the first transmission, A should broadcast RREQ again for searching a route to B at the second transmission.

MR11: The source test case is that A is put into the black list of B, and then A requests to transmit a data packet P to B. B will reply with a certain number (n_1) of RREP packets to A. The follow-up test case is that A is deleted from the black list of B, and then A requests to transmit the same packet P to B. B will reply with a certain number (n_2) of RREP packets to A. We should have the relation $n_1 < n_2$.

For each MR, we generated a certain number of source test cases by random testing technique [10], and at least one follow-up test case is generated based on the source test case and according to MR. In our experiment, we applied all these *MT test cases* to test the original version of the AODV simulator. In order to further investigate the effectiveness of MT in protocol conformance testing, we also used mutation analysis technique [1] to randomly seed some faults into the target program. We generated six mutants whose faults are related to key attributes of the simulator. All MT test cases were also applied to test these mutants. The experimental results showed that MT did not detect any fault in the original simulator, but the fault in each mutant has been revealed by at least one MR. With respect to the effectiveness of MT technique, we found that the success rates in detecting faults of our MRs and MT test cases are about 26% and 17%, respectively. Such results are very impressive in terms of the cost-effectiveness of a testing method.

5   Conclusion

Network simulator is an important tool for analyzing the network protocol. It is critical to ensure the conformance between the simulator and the protocol. However, protocol conformance testing is sometimes faced with an oracle problem, that is, there does not exist a systematic mechanism to verify the correctness of the test output given any possible program input. We are not aware of any systematic work dealing with the oracle problem in protocol conformance testing. In this paper, we proposed to apply metamorphic testing (MT), an innovative approach to alleviating the oracle problem, into the protocol conformance testing of network simulators. We selected ad-hoc on-demand distance vector (AODV) protocol and one of its simulators as our case study. Some key attributes are identified from the AODV protocol, and 11 metamorphic relations (MRs) are defined based on these attributes. We generated a large number of MT test cases based on these MRs, and checked the test results against these MRs. Our experimental results showed that the selected simulator conforms to the AODV protocol with respect to the chosen MRs and the used MT test cases. We also used MT to test some fault-seeded mutants of the simulator. The results of the mutation analysis showed that MT is very effective in detecting faults.

In this pilot study, we only conducted MT under a simplified testing environment. Some of our MRs may not be valid when the testing environment becomes more complicated. It is of great importance to identify more MRs that can be used in more general scenarios. It is also worthwhile to apply MT to test various applications of different network protocols.

Acknowledgment

This project is supported by an Australia Research Council grant (DP0771733). We are grateful to Chi Zhang for conducting some preliminary experiments.

References

1. Andrews, J.H., Briand, L.C., Labiche, Y.: Is mutation an appropriate tool for testing experiments? In: Proc. of ICSE 2005, pp. 402–411 (2005)
2. Blumer, T.P., Sidhu, D., Chung, A.: Experience with formal methods in protocol development. ACM Comput. Commun. Rev. 21(2), 81–101 (1991)
3. Chen, T.Y., Ho, J.W.H., Liu, H., Xie, X.: An innovative approach for testing bioinformatics programs using metamorphic testing. BMC Bioinform. 10, 24 (2009)
4. Chen, T.Y., Tse, T.H., Zhou, Z.Q.: Fault-based testing without the need of oracles. Inform. Softw. Tech. 45(1), 1–9 (2003)
5. Concer, N.: Ad-hoc network simulator (2005),
   http://www.omnetpp.org/filemgmt/singlefile.php?lid=87
6. ISO. Information technology - open systems interconnection - conformance testing methodology and framework. ISO/IEC 9646
7. Lai, R.: A survey of communication protocol testing. Journ. Syst. Softw. 62(1), 21–46 (2002)
8. Machado, P.D.L., Andrade, W.L.: The oracle problem for testing against quantified properties. In: Proc. of QSIC 2007, pp. 415–418 (2007)
9. Murphy, C., Kaiser, G., Hu, L., Wu, L.: Properties of machine learning applications for use in metamorphic testing. In: Proc. of SEKE 2008, pp. 867–872 (2008)
10. Myers, G.J.: The Art of Software Testing. John Wiley and Sons, Chichester (2004)
11. OMNeT Community. OMNeT++ system, http://www.omnetpp.org
12. Onoma, A.K., Tsai, W.-T., Poonawala, M.H., Suganuma, H.: Regression testing in an industrial environment. Commun. ACM 41(5), 81–86 (1998)
13. Paradkar, A.M.: Towards model-based generation of self-priming and self-checking conformance tests for interactive systems. In: Matsui, M., Zuccherato, R.J. (eds.) SAC 2003. LNCS, vol. 3006, pp. 1110–1117. Springer, Heidelberg (2004)
14. Perkins, C., Belding-Royer, E., Das, S.: Ad hoc on-demand distance vector routing. RFC3561 (2008)
15. Rothermel, G., Untch, R.H., Chu, C., Harrold, M.J.: Prioritizing test cases for regression testing. IEEE Trans. Softw. Eng. 27(10), 929–948 (2001)

Author Index